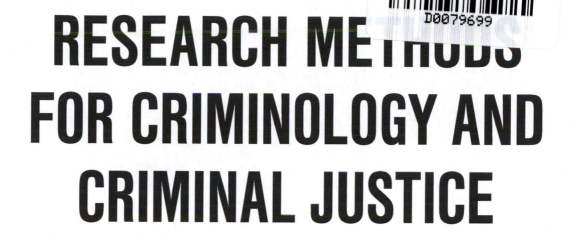

RESEARCH METHODS FOR CRIMINOLOGY AND CRIMINAL JUSTICE

RICHARD D. HARTLEY
University of Texas at San Antonio

LEE ELLIS
Minot State University

ANTHONY WALSH
Boise State University

ROWMAN & LITTLEFIELD
Lanham • Boulder • New York • London

Executive Editor: Kathryn Knigge
Assistant Editor: Charlotte Gosnell
Higher Education Channel Manager: Jonathan Raeder
Interior Designer: Integra Software Services Pvt. Ltd.

Credits and acknowledgments for material borrowed from other sources, and reproduced with permission, appear on credits page 352.

Published by Rowman & Littlefield
An imprint of The Rowman & Littlefield Publishing Group, Inc.
4501 Forbes Boulevard, Suite 200, Lanham, Maryland 20706
www.rowman.com

6 Tinworth Street, London SE11 5AL, United Kingdom

Copyright © 2021 by The Rowman & Littlefield Publishing Group, Inc.

British Library Cataloguing in Publication Information Available

Library of Congress Cataloging-in-Publication Data

Names: Hartley, Richard D., author. | Ellis, Lee, author. | Walsh, Anthony, author.
Title: Research methods for criminology and criminal justice / Richard D. Hartley, University of Texas at San Antonio, Lee Ellis, Minot State University, Anthony Walsh, Boise State University.
Description: Lanham : Rowman & Littlefield, 2020. | Includes bibliographical references and index.
Identifiers: LCCN 2020007286 (print) | LCCN 2020007287 (ebook) | ISBN 9781538144107 (cloth) | ISBN 9781538129517 (paperback) | ISBN 9781538129524 (epub)
Subjects: LCSH: Criminology—Research—Methodology. | Criminal justice, Administration of—Research—Methodology.
Classification: LCC HV6024.5 .H37 2020 (print) | LCC HV6024.5 (ebook) | DDC 364.072—dc23
LC record available at https://lccn.loc.gov/2020007286
LC ebook record available at https://lccn.loc.gov/2020007287

∞™ The paper used in this publication meets the minimum requirements of American National Standard for Information Sciences—Permanence of Paper for Printed Library Materials, ANSI/NISO Z39.48–1992.

We dedicate this book to all of the students whose class participation has forced us to better articulate our own understanding of research methodology in social and behavioral science. In this way, we have been able to continue learning through teaching.

Brief Contents

Contents

Preface

Why learn research methods? Unlike most other courses of study, research methods will not acquaint you with a specific topic or subject area. Rather, it focuses on how scientists—in this case those in criminology and criminal justice—go about finding answers to their field's important questions. A course in research methods provides the tools that make it possible for students to better understand how research is conducted thereby also making them better consumers of research studies in criminology and criminal justice. This text will acquaint you with the most fundamental research tools and concepts, and assist you in understanding how we advance knowledge in the field of criminal justice.

This text is also unusually broad in two respects. First, even though it has been written primarily for criminology and criminal justice majors, there is an underlying recognition that the social and behavioral sciences share essentially all of the same research methods in attempting to better understand social phenomena. Consequently, the text begins by introducing students to each of the social and behavioral sciences, as well as to related disciplines, such as psychiatry, history, and education.

The second way the text is broad has to do with the geographic dispersion of the examples that are discussed; a concerted effort was made not to limit examples to studies only conducted in the United States. One more fairly unique feature of this text is that it closely integrates research methods with statistics. This integration is made possible in part by devoting two chapters (13 and 14) to acquainting students with the most fundamental statistical concepts that underlie much of the research in the discipline. In no way do these two chapters substitute for a course in statistics. Instead, they ensure that whether students have taken statistics or not, they understand the essential role of statistics in designing and interpreting nearly all criminal justice research.

Finally, a fair number of criminal justice students look forward to their first course in research methods with the enthusiasm of a dental patient in need of a root canal. Not only does the subject sound dry and technical but the thought of statistical concepts being interwoven with research methods makes research methods intimidating, especially for those who may not have had a course in statistics. Although learning research methods takes effort, this text has been designed to be user-friendly, even when dealing with some fairly complex theoretical and methodological concepts. The most critical points are clearly stated and illustrated with examples from real research chosen to be interesting in their own right.

Specific Comments for Students Interested in Conducting Research

This book was mainly written to give students a tour of how the scientific method is used for studying social and behavioral phenomena. Before you begin this journey, however, we want to give some pointers on how to engage the subject of research methods to be able to get the most out this text. This will be especially helpful to those of you who one day want to be conducting research at a professional level. Much of what is needed to go beyond the basics presented in this book must be acquired not by further classroom instruction, although taking advance research methods classes can help, but by actually "getting your feet wet." Therefore, as soon as possible, begin exercising your research and writing skills and then look for help from researchers at your university or in the field.

Your department or university may even have opportunities for you to volunteer to assist on research projects. If so, expect to learn new things and gradually improve your research skills every time you get involved in a research project. As you gain experience, however, your learning will become increasingly subtle and specific to a particular area of study. In brief, the best advice that can be given for how to become a competent researcher is similar to what the New Yorker said to a tourist who asked how to get Carnegie Hall. The New Yorker replied, "Practice, man, practice." There is no substitute for practice once the basics of research methods are understood. In the beginning, however, do not bite off more than you can chew, and do not become frustrated if you are not understanding all of the processes involved in conducting research. Some research concepts can be complicated to understand and conducting research can be a time-consuming endeavor, but the more you learn and "do" under the supervision of those more experienced, the more you will begin to understand the various methods, their purposes, and application.

Four additional suggestions can be offered to help you if you are really interested in perfecting your research skills. First, seek out the advice and criticisms of researchers in your department. Take their comments, not as divinely revealed truth, but as suggestions from those who are older and wiser and who nearly always want to be helpful. If you have a "thin skin" when others criticize your ideas, your career as a researcher will be filled with frustration. On the other hand, if you can accept criticism as evidence that improvement is always possible, criticism can be extremely useful to you. This does not mean you should automatically follow all advice that others give you; it simply means that, as much as your intellectual integrity will allow, you should accommodate as many negative reactions to your work as you possibly can. The more you write, the more you will realize that no one's research efforts are beyond improvement, but the more people you have critique your work, the closer your writing will get to perfection (within human limits).

Second, become proficient in statistics. This text was planned and organized specifically to emphasize the importance of statistics in social science research.

Nevertheless, it omits details that researchers need to be familiar with in order to carry out empirical research. Besides taking courses in statistics, you can gain valuable insights by reading research reports with an eye toward knowing which statistical methods were used and why. Becoming acquainted with at least one of the statistical software programs currently available for use with computers is also important for all contemporary researchers.

Third, become familiar with the essential linkage between scientific theory and empirical research. Learn to shuttle between these two complementary realms of scientific thought. As you do so, you will sharpen your intellectual abilities to formulate empirically testable hypotheses.

Fourth, maintain a sensitivity to the ethical issues that surround research. Whether you are drawn more to pure research, or that solely seeking to advance knowledge, or applied research, that which is conducted to seek practical solutions, never lose sight of the social fabric of which you and the entire scientific enterprise are a part. The threads of this fabric can be frayed by those who disregard the impact of their work on the lives of others. Rest assured that knowledge engenders social change, albeit ever so slowly. As a social scientist, you must not be irresponsible in promoting that change.

If you plan to pursue a career in which research methods are important, it may also be wise to keep this text as a reference. From time to time, you will want to refresh your memory about various research concepts, and those of you who want to become more extensively involved in scientific research will always need material to reference for determining the best course of action when undertaking various types of projects.

In closing, we hope you will get more from this text than an understanding of the process of conducting social scientific research. Our ultimate goal has been to share some of the wonder and enjoyment that social and behavioral scientists experience when they peer beneath some tiny portion of the thick shroud that continues to cover the secrets of our existence as thinking social creatures.

Richard D. Hartley
Lee Ellis
Anthony Walsh

About the Authors

Richard D. Hartley received his PhD from the School of Criminology and Criminal Justice at the University of Nebraska at Omaha. He is currently a professor in the Department of Criminology & Criminal Justice at the University of Texas at San Antonio where he teaches courses on research design, quantitative analysis, and criminal courts. His research interests include decision-making practices for criminal court outcomes and evaluation research. Books that Hartley has coauthored include *Criminal Courts: Structure, Process and Issues* (2018) and *Statistics for the Social and Behavioral Sciences* (forthcoming, 2020).

Lee Ellis holds a PhD in criminology from Florida State University. For more than thirty years, he taught anthropology, sociology, and criminology courses at Minot State University in North Dakota. From 2009 through 2011, Ellis was a visiting professor in the Department of Anthropology and Sociology at the University of Malaya in Kuala Lumpur, Malaysia. Books that he has coauthored include *Criminology: An Interdisciplinary Approach* (2007), *Handbook of Social Status Correlates* (2018), and *Handbook of Crime Correlates* (2019).

Anthony Walsh received his PhD in criminology from Bowling Green State University in Ohio. He worked in law enforcement and corrections before drifting into what he considers semi-retirement in academia at Boise State University, Idaho, where he teaches criminology, statistics, law, and criminal justice assessment. His primary interests are biosocial criminology, the philosophy of law, and amateur cosmology. He is the author, coauthor, or editor of forty-two books and about 150 articles. His latest book is *God, Science, and Society: The Origin of the Universe, Intelligent Life, and Free Societies.*

Chapter 1

The Scientific Method and Criminology and Criminal Justice as Social Sciences

Are children from smaller families more or less likely to become delinquent/ criminal when compared to children from larger families? Do criminals commit suicide at higher or lower rates than the general population? Jot down what you think the answers to these questions might be and then compare your answers to the results from actual scientific research.

All over the world, answers to thousands of questions are being sought by researchers in the fields of criminology and criminal justice. Findings from these research studies are often published in scholarly journals. This book is designed to teach you the concepts and techniques used by researchers to write these reports. You will learn how to critically read, interpret, and eventually contribute to the ever-growing body of knowledge in criminology, criminal justice, and related disciplines. Note that to avoid being unnecessarily wordy, most references to **criminal justice/criminology** throughout this text will simply identify criminal justice. On the other hand, when referring to those in the profession of criminal justice, we will use the term **criminologists**. The few exceptions will be when specific distinctions need to be made.

The two questions at the beginning of this chapter are among those for which there are now numerous research findings; nearly all of these findings have led to the same conclusions. Before learning what those conclusions might be, take a moment to imagine how you might conduct a research project designed to answer either of these questions.

For the first question, how would you measure family size along with people's varying degrees of involvement in delinquent/criminal behavior? Concerning the second question, how could you obtain information on the prevalence of suicide in a criminal population and then compare it to suicide rates in a general population? To objectively address these questions, where would you locate people willing to provide the necessary information, and how many individuals should be studied? What would one do with whatever data were collected? Are there ethical issues that should be considered when pursuing these types of investigations?

While reading this text, you will gradually become acquainted with the logic and terminology underlying both criminological and criminal justice research and research in all of the other social (and behavioral) sciences. Although a text such as this one can teach most of the basics, a high level of proficiency in social science research comes only through years of practice. In fact, it is safe to say that those who conduct such research on a regular basis learn new things to help refine their research skills every time they undertake a new study.

Let's turn to the two questions posed at the beginning of this chapter, both of which have been investigated by dozens of scientific studies. In brief, here is what the scientific evidence indicates:

Regarding the relationship between the number of brothers and sisters (i.e., siblings) and an individual's likelihood of being delinquent and criminal, more than 70 studies have examined this topic. About 90% of these studies found that persons with the fewest number of siblings (including those with no siblings at all) had significantly lower probabilities of delinquency and crime than did persons who came from larger families (Ellis, Farrington, & Hoskin, 2019:170). The remaining 10% of studies simply failed to find a significant relationship between number of siblings and offending behavior. In other words, not a single study reported higher offending rates among individuals with the fewest number of siblings.

Turning to suicide and criminality, more than 50 studies have been published (Ellis et al., 2019:290). These studies have not only examined actual completed suicides but also suicide attempts; a few have even measured what is known as suicide ideation (serious thoughts of suicide). Each of these studies has concluded that offenders are more likely to contemplate, attempt, and even commit suicide than is true for persons with little or no criminal history.

Documenting these relationships is worthwhile, but criminologists are also interested in explaining why these and many other relationships exist. Typically, scientific explanations come in the form of what are known as theories. The important role of theories in scientific research is discussed later in this text.

⬗ Learning to Become a Researcher

This book has been written to help readers become part of the worldwide community of scientists who are contributing to the ever-growing knowledge base of criminal justice and all of its related disciplines such as sociology, psychology, and political science.

Although some may have difficulty with the terminology that scientists use to describe their research designs and findings, the terms can be mastered with serious effort. The research methods used by social scientists have a major element of common sense, even though what they discover using these methods can sometimes defy common sense!

Because this text emphasizes the interdisciplinary nature of criminal justice research, we will start by describing each of the social (and behavioral) sciences within which criminal justice is embedded. We will also present examples of how these disciplines are interrelated with the criminal justice community in specific research projects.

⬗ Circumscribing Criminology and Criminal Justice

Scientific attempts to understand criminal behavior (and the legal systems that societies have instituted to control such behavior) go back to the early 1800s in Europe. Various intellectuals suggested that instead of demons and other supernatural forces being responsible for crime, the causes might be found within each individual offender and/or within the societies where they live (Masters & Roberson, 1990:54). A variety of theories of criminal behavior have emerged from these ideas, nearly all of which can be subsumed under two main criminological traditions: an environmentalist tradition and a biosocial tradition. (Some have identified a third strictly biological tradition, but no criminologist has ever argued that social environmental factors have no role to play in crime causation.)

The environmentalist tradition asserts that human behavior, including that which is socially defined as criminal, is largely the result of social environmental circumstances, including such factors as poverty, poor upbringing, and associating with the "wrong" peers. In other words, all people have essentially equal probabilities of running afoul of the law; what alters those probabilities are the social conditions to which each person is exposed. Numerous environmental theories have been proposed over the roughly two centuries that criminology has been recognized as a discipline (Walsh & Ellis, 2007).

Biosocial theorizing in criminology can be traced to the late Cesare Lombroso, a military physician who is often considered criminology's founder. Although Lombroso recognized that environmental factors had an important role to play in crime causation, he also felt that not all individuals were equally likely to engage in crime. Instead, Lombroso (1911) contended that some individuals had certain biological predispositions toward unlawful activities, and that it might be possible to identify these individuals as possessing "primitive physical traits" that were better adapted to living in times before industrialization than in modern societies. He called these traits, **atavistic**, basically meaning "evolutionary throw-back traits." Though this proposal has been largely dismissed by today's criminologists, Lombroso is still recognized as having led the way toward the emergence of criminology.

Prior to the 1970s, the study of crime and delinquency was almost exclusively taught under the disciplinary umbrella of sociology. Since that time, colleges and universities have come to offer specialized courses and even entire majors in criminology and criminal justice (Adams, 1976). Today, although most sociology departments still teach courses in criminology, the field of criminal justice has emerged as a social science in its own right. Programs that specialize in criminology emphasize attempts to understand the causes of criminal behavior, whereas criminal justice programs focus more on studying the criminal justice system and on crime prevention, crime treatment, and crime investigation techniques (criminalistics). Many departments include both terms in their names because they house faculty who research the causes of crime, the criminal justice system, and crime prevention strategies. For example, the lead author of this book is a faculty member in a Department of Criminology & Criminal Justice.

⊖ Circumscribing the Social Sciences

The term **social** (including **behavioral**) **science** is used to refer to the disciplines whose primary objective is to understand behavioral and sociocultural phenomena. Criminal justice is obviously part of the social sciences and often shares knowledge with other social scientists. For this reason, criminal justice students need to be acquainted with the social sciences in general and how they all seek a better understanding of all aspects of behavior.

BOX 1.1 CURRENT ISSUES

When and Where Did the Social Sciences Begin?

The answer depends somewhat on which social science one is considering, but historians generally agree that during the first half of the 1700s (i.e., the 18th century), the disciplines of anthropology, economics, psychology, political science, and sociology all began to emerge in European universities (Brittain, 1990:105). Then, about 50 years later Lombroso began to speculate about what he saw as the evolutionary roots of criminal behavior.

It wasn't until the end of the 1800s, however, that these disciplines began to professionalize. This professionalization primarily took the form of establishing university departments with full-time faculty in each of the disciplines, along with the publication of specialized journals in each of these disciplines. In other words, rather than simply offering a special course or occasionally writing a book about some new discipline, professionalization involved having actual departments and periodic journals widely available in an academic discipline.

Although the social sciences are quite diverse, they all focus on some aspect of behavior or other social phenomena, including culture, technology, ideas, and aesthetics. Some social scientists even come full circle by reflecting upon the complex sociocultural processes that have given rise to science itself (e.g., the sociology of science). Other social scientists extend their interests in behavior and social living to nonhuman animals, either for the purpose of gaining insights into human behavior or as areas of study in their own right.

As one reads through the descriptions of the following major social science disciplines, notice how each makes a valuable contribution to the understanding of the richness and wonder of the human species and of the extraordinary social and cultural fabrics that we all help to weave. The social science disciplines are listed in alphabetical order; none is more important than another. Some disciplines are simply easier to characterize than others. Following our description of each discipline is a brief account of how it has contributed to research in the fields of criminology and criminal justice.

Anthropology

Anthropology is the study of man (or humankind). The discipline began to form in the mid-1800s as the academic/intellectual community of Europe became increasingly interested in human origins and in studying the ethnic and cultural diversity of the human species. Two major branches of anthropology are recognized: physical and cultural (Lieberman, 1989:680). **Physical (or biological) anthropology** primarily attempts to piece together fossil evidence of the physical evolution of humans. It also tries to link the emergence of the human species from several extinct ancestral forms of humanlike creatures based on fossil evidence. Most of these fossils were unearthed throughout the 20th century, although a few extend back to the mid-1800s. Using various scientific dating techniques, these fossils have been found to be as much as 6 million years old, which is roughly when modern-day humans and modern-day chimpanzees last shared a common ancestor (Cormier et al., 2017; Varki & Gagneux, 2017).

Cultural anthropologists specialize in studying the vast array of human cultures and social customs exhibited by people throughout the world (Haviland, 2000:11). Cultural anthropologists often work closely with sociologists in studying contemporary industrialized societies.

In recent decades, a number of anthropologists have studied social behavior in nonhuman primates, especially apes (Kummer, 2071). Jane Goodall (1990), whose observations of wild chimpanzees since the 1960s have provided tremendous insights into the behavior of humankind's closest living relative, has been a researcher at the forefront of this work. Pertinent to criminology, Goodall (1977) and others (Mitani et al., 2002; Watts, 2004) have documented infanticide and other types of "murders" among chimpanzees as well as other nonhuman primates, suggesting that humans are not alone in sometimes exhibiting a darker side (Wrangham, 1999).

Other anthropological research has also addressed some interesting criminological questions, such as whether "crime" exists in preliterate societies just as it does in societies where most people are able to read and write. Because crime is a legal concept and all laws must be in written form, preliterate societies have no crime! Nevertheless, one can still ask whether they have behaviors that would otherwise be criminal. Several anthropologists have asked people living in preliterate societies to state the cause of death for each of their deceased friends and relatives, paying special attention to deaths due to the intentional actions of others. Based on these studies, anthropologists have concluded that "virtual homicides" do indeed occur in preliterate societies, sometimes at high rates. A recent review concluded that these intentional killings in preliterate societies appear to range from 4/100,000 per year to more than 300/100,000 per year (Ellis et al., 2019:5–7).

These estimates need to include the finding that many homicides are assaults in which victims die. One study estimated that the homicide rates in urban America might be as much as five times greater without the availability of well-trained first responders providing emergency medical services to assault victims (Harris et al., 2002). Of course, there are no such services in preliterate societies, a fact that could at least partially account for why many preliterate societies appear to have high rates of what are termed **homicide** in societies with written laws.

Yet another example of how anthropology has contributed to the field of criminal justice comes from a discipline known as **forensic anthropology**. Basically, this is an applied branch of physical anthropology that is used in many crime investigations, particularly homicides in which long-deceased victims need to be identified, sometimes based on just a few teeth or bone fragments (Byers, 2005).

Economics

Economics began taking shape as a social science near the end of the 19th century. Those affiliated with the discipline try to understand all aspects of human financial affairs, ranging from individual and family finances (microeconomics) to the financial activities of states, nations, and the world (macroeconomics). Economics is closely related to the fields of business and finance. It also has major ties with the fields of political science in studying how political policies affect economic affairs. Many links can also be found between economics and sociology, inasmuch as both disciplines are interested in understanding how people form social hierarchies based on political power and wealth (social stratification).

Many research projects have involved work between economists and criminologists. For example, an English study was reported in which injuries due to violence were found to be statistically linked to the price of beer. As prices rose, admissions to hospital emergency rooms for violence-related injuries declined (Matthews et al., 2006). More recently, two economists reported that female crime appears to be significantly diminished by education. They reported that "a one-year increase in average schooling levels reduces female arrest rates for both violent and property crime by more than 50%" (Cano-Urbina & Lochner, 2019:224).

Economists have also contributed to several studies designed to detect the deterrent effects of increasing arrest rates, conviction rates, and average lengths of sentences (e.g., Witte, 1980; Cornwell & Trumbull, 1994). Studies involving both economists and criminologists have estimated that allowing private citizens to carry weapons may have a deterrent effect on violent crime (e.g., Lott & Mustard, 1997), although other studies cast doubt on this conclusion (reviewed by Ellis et al., 2019:149).

Geography

Geography literally means "earth measurement." However, as the discipline developed, it usually focused on how politically drawn boundaries impact, and are affected by, features of the earth's surface. Although geography is considered a social science, it has close ties with geology, a physical science dealing with physical features of the earth and the formation of those features, along with meteorology, which studies the earth's weather patterns.

Probably the most unique feature of geography relative to the other social sciences is its heavy reliance on maps. In fact, mapping marks the beginnings of criminology that actually predate the work of Lombroso. Interestingly, it involved an 18th-century French astronomer named Adolpe Quetelet. Instead of studying the heavens, Quetelet devoted much of his career to mapping the prevalence of crime in several European countries, leading to what is sometimes known as **cartographic criminology**.

Today, cartographic criminology has experienced a major resurgence with the emergence of global positioning system (GPS) technology combined with modern computer graphics. Basically, GPS utilizes multiple satellites to obtain and keep track of objects and events anywhere on earth. As a result of this technology, numerous studies of how crime is geographically concentrated are currently revolutionizing crime prevention efforts (e.g., Althausen & Mieczkowski, 2001; Padgett, Bales, & Blomberg, 2006; Vasiliauskas & Beconytė, 2016). Cartography is even being used to help track the whereabouts of offenders on probation or parole (Nellis, 2005; Stacey, 2006).

Political Science

The Greek philosopher Aristotle (along with his book, *Politics*) is usually considered the first political scientist. As a recognized discipline apart from philosophy itself, however, political science did not begin to appear until the late 1700s. Coincidentally, this is around the time that Europe began replacing their monarchies with constitutional democracies.

Today, political scientists study all kinds of governments and the political forces that drive them. In addition, political scientists analyze voting patterns and shifts in public opinion, and the dynamics of international relationships. Political science issues are often interwoven with issues of economics, geography, sociology, and history. Further, because political processes are responsible for the laws under which the criminal justice system operates, there are strong connections between political science and criminal justice. In this regard, political scientists have an abiding interest in criminal justice research for guidance in future legislative decision making. For example, studies indicate that some offenders may be much more prone toward career criminality (called **life-course persistent offenders**) than others (called **adolescent-limited offenders**) (Moffitt, 1993; Moffitt & Walsh, 2003). This evidence has led to legislative proposals for improving sentencing guidelines designed to distinguish between these two types of offenders (e.g., Sampson & Laub, 2005; Tyler, 2004).

Psychology

Psychology began to form as a discipline apart from its roots in philosophy in the early 18th century. The word **psychology** literally means study of the mind (or study of the psyche or spirit). Early in the discipline's development, many psychologists expressed discomfort with the view that "the mind" could ever be studied in an objective way (Brozek, 1990). Therefore, more recent definitions of psychology usually emphasize that it is primarily the study of behavior and of the cognitive processes, such as thoughts and emotions, underlying behavior (Dewsbury, 1984:244; Cooper, Heron, & Herward, 1987:7).

A survey of psychological literature revealed that over the past century, the discipline has increasingly turned its attention toward studying the brain as holding the key to understanding behavior, thoughts, and emotions. This trend has increasingly linked psychology with biology, especially neurology and neurochemistry (Davis et al., 1988). Nevertheless, psychologists still retain close ties with other social scientists, particularly in terms of research methodology (Bunge, 1990).

Connections between psychology and criminal justice have mushroomed in recent decades. Several criminal justice/criminology journals now mainly publish articles of a psychological nature. These articles address such topics as how criminal and delinquent behavior are related to a variety of personality traits, alcoholism and drug addiction, intelligence and learning disabilities, and mental disorders and illnesses (Ellis et al., 2019).

Social Work

Social work is a specialized discipline for helping the poor, disabled, and otherwise disadvantaged maintain a quality life. Social workers attempt to restore and enable their clients to be as physically and mentally healthy and self-sufficient as possible. Personnel in social work and criminal justice have collaborated on many mutual research interests. For example, both have undertaken to better understand and how best to reduce the incidence of spouse abuse (e.g., Carney & Buttell, 2006; Echeburua et al., 2006). Similarly, social workers have helped to devise neighborhood programs for delinquency prevention that can be objectively assessed in terms of effectiveness (e.g., Hawkins & Weis, 1985; Jacoby, 2018).

Overall, social work has much in common with criminal justice, partly because social work clients often experience legal difficulties. Another similarity is that practitioners in both disciplines often envision the same basic approaches to crime prevention and treatment. Furthermore, both social work and criminal justice have roots in sociology, a discipline now to be briefly explored.

Sociology

Sociology began to establish itself as a major social science in the mid-1800s after a French philosopher/scientist by the name of **Auguste Comte** argued that a special science was needed to study human societies and social relationships. Comte championed the idea that all matter evolves through major stages, beginning with inorganic matter, proceeding through simple life-forms, and advancing further to multicellular organisms. Eventually, some multicellular organisms form social collectives that Conte called "super organisms" or societies. He coined the term *sociology* to describe the discipline that would study societies and social relationships upon which societies are based.

As sociology began to take root in North America in the late 19th century, many of its adherents developed an interest in understanding criminal behavior. Thus, what Lombroso had called **criminal anthropology** became increasingly associated with sociology. Today, of course, the fields of criminal justice and criminology are so large and diverse that they have become increasingly independent of sociology. Nevertheless, the intellectual links between criminal justice/criminology and sociology remain strong. This is reflected in the fact that most departments of sociology still offer courses in criminology, and many universities still have their sociology and criminal justice departments combined. Also, much of the criminal justice research in contemporary times is conducted by persons trained mainly in sociology.

⊖ The Near Social Sciences

To get a complete picture of the breadth and scope of the social sciences, three more disciplines should be mentioned: education, psychiatry, and public health. Many examples can be cited of researchers in each discipline who have contributed to the field of criminal justice (and vice versa).

Education

As a discipline, **education** involves studying the process of acquiring and transmitting knowledge and facilitating learning, usually in an academic setting. Many educators engage in research to improve teaching techniques and to determine why students vary in learning abilities and interests. The research methods they use are the same as those used in criminal justice and social science generally.

Psychiatry

Psychiatry literally means "correcting the mind." As practiced, psychiatry usually works toward providing treatment to persons with some form of mental illness or disability. Psychiatrists have background both in medicine and in psychology. Thus, the treatment they provide can range from psychological counseling to prescribing drugs and sometimes even brain surgery. Despite the variety of treatment options, most psychiatric research relies on methods used in the social and behavioral sciences. Many psychiatrists have become extremely interested in a clinical condition known as psychopathy. This psychiatric condition has been found to be highly associated with persistent criminality.

Public Health

Public health is a discipline that, like psychiatry, is closely allied to medicine. Researchers in this discipline study the health of large populations, rather than individual patients. Public health officials work closely with social scientists and generally utilize the same research methods.

Several efforts have been made in recent years to deal with neighborhood concentrations of crime using what is known as the "public health model." This model confronts crime much as one would deal with a communicable disease outbreak and seems to have at least significant short-term beneficial effects (Garcia & Herrero, 2007; Sampson et al., 1997).

⊖ Other Disciplines That Utilize Social Science Research Methods

Practitioners of two disciplines have come to employ social science research methodology: journalism and business. Their use of social research methodology is as follows: People in the fields of journalism, communications, and public relations collect social science data in the form of public opinion surveys (Cameron et al., 1992). Interestingly, the amount of coverage that a social science study receives in the popular press appears to actually influence the subsequent likelihood of the study being cited by the scientific community (Phillips et al., 1991). This suggests that journalists not only conduct social science research, but they also impact the social science community.

Regarding business, those in marketing and advertising are increasingly utilizing survey research methodology. Like their journalism counterparts, business students should know how to select samples that are representative of a target population, how to phrase questions in ways that elicit the most meaningful responses, and how to analyze and interpret the responses obtained. In short, the number of people who use social science methods is vast and growing. As a result, the knowledge being accumulated is also expanding and impacting everyday life. Those in the field of criminal justice are among those utilizing a vast array of social science research methods. This text will help you orient and sharpen your skills in this regard.

⊖ Two Special Disciplines Linked to Social Science

Having described the main social sciences and other disciplines that employ many of the same methods, two disciplines have a special role to play in social science even though they rarely use the scientific method themselves. These two disciplines are philosophy and history (Carr, 1962:70; Brittain, 1990).

Philosophy

The prefix *philo* means "to love" and the suffix *sophia* denotes wisdom or knowledge. Philosophy has roots going back at least to ancient Greece. As the term has developed, it now refers to intellectual efforts to understand the meaning of life, the nature of good and evil, and the breadth and limit of human knowledge. **Philosophy** is usually classified as a humanity rather than a social science because it rarely employs the scientific method. Instead, certain philosophical assumptions are recognized as making the scientific method possible. Even today, most doctoral degrees awarded in science—from the physical sciences to the biological sciences to the social sciences—are PhDs, meaning doctorates of philosophy.

Though philosophers rarely conduct scientific research, they continue to provide key assumptions that make science itself possible. These assumptions will be discussed later in this chapter. As noted earlier, philosophy lies at the heart of all science in that certain unprovable philosophical assumptions must be made (or at least implied) for science to function. For example, empiricism—the idea that our senses provide us with more or less accurate information—is ultimately a philosophical assumption that cannot be proven. Likewise, determinism—the view that only natural (including social) events cause other natural events (without free will and supernatural intervention)—is beyond scientific proof. Thus, science is built on certain philosophical assumptions. As a result, philosophy is "above" science in the sense that it offers assumptions that make science possible.

The influence of philosophy on the fields of criminology and criminal justice is substantial. Philosophers provide the rational framework for identifying the proper role of the criminal justice system in people's lives—the nature and extent to which humans should be allowed to freely choose their actions and be held responsible for the choices they make. Another contribution of philosophy to the field of criminal justice comes in the way of the rationale that people give for exacting punishment on others for their misbehavior. Is it the need for revenge, for deterrence, or simply to incapacitate the offender that should motivate us?

History

History builds on the word *story*. Accordingly, historians attempt to provide written accounts of past events, especially events that were consequential in human affairs. Even though historians conduct research, their methods normally differ from those used in the social sciences. Specifically, historians usually seek to answer questions about the nature of unique past events, whereas social scientists usually attempt to generalize about entire categories of events. For example, historians might try to chronicle the events leading up to a particular war, while social scientists would more often try to identify events leading up to wars in general (Vasquez, 1996:161).

Another difference between research conducted by historians and research conducted by social scientists involves the use of statistics. Because most of the questions that historians attempt to answer deal with unique events, historians use statistics far less often than do social scientists. Nevertheless, noteworthy exceptions exist to this rule. For instance, one historian analyzed old jail records to determine the characteristics of persons incarcerated for crimes in England during the 18th century (Beattie, 1975). Among other things, the study revealed that the sex ratio was similar to that typical of the sex ratio in prisoners today, i.e., mostly males. Another historian used registration records to assess the characteristics of German citizens who join the Nazi Party around the time of the World War II (Kater, 1983). Therefore, although some historians do statistical analyses of their data similar to what is typical of social scientists, their methods rarely involve statistical analyses. Links between the fields of history and criminal justice are considerable. For example, historical accounts of the early beginnings of the criminal justice system provide valuable insight into this institution's current functioning (Neubauer & Fradella, 2018).

⊜ Features of the Scientific Method

Now that the scope of social sciences and their allied disciplines has been identified, consider this question: What is it that makes a discipline "scientific"? The answer boils down to a unique set of methods. Thus, the degree to which a social science is truly scientific depends upon the extent to which its practitioners use a set of methodological rules and assumptions to answer their questions.

These rules are collectively known as the **scientific method**. The characteristics of this method can be identified as follows.

Empiricism

Ultimately, science can deal with all things that are **empirical** phenomena. Such phenomena are those that can be sensed (i.e., seen, heard, felt, tasted, or smelled). In other words, all scientific knowledge rests on what can be perceived through the senses, with sight and sound being the most frequently used. We can qualify the previous paragraph by stating that there are instances in which scientists hypothesize the existence of things that have not yet been sensed, at least not directly. These would include phenomena that are too small (like various subatomic particles), too remote (such as black holes), or ones that may exist even though our current methods are inadequate for measurement (life on other planets). Nevertheless, all phenomena with which scientists can deal are at least conceivably empirical.

You might question the relevance of empiricism to the study of humans, particularly in the case of our thoughts and attitudes. However, in these cases, social scientists usually infer the existence and measurability of thoughts and attitudes through interviews and responses to questionnaires. Before leaving the issue of empiricism, note that there is no way of proving with absolute certainty that our sensory experiences accurately represent what exists. Thus, all sciences rest on an unprovable philosophical assumption. As we will see, there are other essentially unprovable assumptions that must be made for the scientific enterprise to function.

Verifiability

The characteristic of **verifiability** assumes that we can use our own empirical observations to confirm or refute the empirical observations of others, and that they, in turn, can cross-check ours. For various reasons, mistaken (or even fabricated) observations are occasionally reported. Gradually, such observations will be followed by repeated attempts to replicate. Repeated failures to replicate means that the earlier reported finding was in all likelihood an error. Verifying the findings of other researchers is achieved through **replication**, which involves essentially repeating their original study. It is hard to exaggerate the importance of replication in scientific research. In the words of one English psychologist, "replication is the life-blood of science" (Eysenck, 1994:44).

Cumulativeness

The famous physicist Isaac Newton was once asked by a friend how he came up with his ideas about the nature of gravity. He replied, "If I have seen further [than others], it is by standing on the shoulders of giants." Newton's response reflects the cumulative nature of scientific knowledge. One of the most exciting features of the scientific method is that scientists do not start from scratch when attempting to understand something. Instead, they find out what others have already learned and then attempt to add just a little more to this ever-growing "knowledge base." In doing so, they know that eventually other scientists will follow them and add a bit more to the unending effort for better understanding.

As scientists become increasingly familiar with the subject areas they are pursuing, they will see that the questions gradually shift and become more refined. This is because it is not necessary to scientifically answer most questions more than a half-dozen times or so unless, of course, researchers keep getting different answers. Although the scientific process tends to be painstakingly slow, over the long term it brings our collective empirical experiences into ever-increasing clear focus. This **cumulative** feature of the scientific method means that published research findings are, in a real sense, timeless. Readers will find research reports being published today in which findings from decades earlier are still being cited. Thus, unlike most publications, scientific reports tend to be read years, decades, and even centuries after they first appeared in print.

Self-Correcting

Science is considered **self-correcting** because, when errors in observations are made, sooner or later the mistakes will be identified (Stokes, 1974; Silberner, 1982:41). Ultimately, no statement about scientific observations is ever considered beyond further investigation, although from a practical standpoint many statements can be considered "virtually certain." For example, a recent review of criminological literature revealed that all 62 studies of sex differences in the commission of murder concluded without exception that males were more likely than females to be the perpetrators (Ellis et al., 2019:420). This review leaves little doubt that there are sex differences in the commission of murder. Despite the unanimity of studies conducted so far, scientists must always be open to the possibility that, in some country at some time in the future, exceptions to this sex difference will be found. So, it would be contrary to the spirit of science to assert that "It is now an irrefutable fact that males are more likely than females to commit murder." The more accurate statement would be "All of the evidence reported so far indicates that more males commit murders than do females." Notice that this latter statement leaves open the possibility of exceptions eventually being found.

Determinism

Determinism is another unproven (and unprovable) philosophical assumption that scientists make when they attempt to explain why things happen. Basically, this assumption is that any explanation given for a phenomenon must entail only empirical (or natural), as opposed to supernatural, factors. Although there is no way to prove that supernatural entities (God, the devil, etc.) are not actually causing whatever is being observed, by removing the supernatural from consideration, scientists can at least hope to identify and comprehend the natural cause(s). For example, say that supernatural forces are actually responsible for sex differences in the commission of murder. If this is the case, criminologists are unlikely to identify any natural factors responsible for the differences. Consequently, scientists normally assume that the cause(s) for whatever they are studying are all natural in origin rather than being supernatural. This assumption is captured by the concept of determinism.

Little controversy exists about the utility of the determinist assumption for studying physical or even biological phenomena. When it comes to studying human behavior, however, the determinist assumption also implies that, in the strictest sense, there is no "free will." Consider the following: Say that someone theorizes that the reason people commit crime is that they freely choose to do so. Although this proposed theory would be able to immediately explain every crime that ever occurs, it would not be a good scientific theory. Can you see the problem with such a theory? The main problem is that it can be tested only after the fact: You wait for someone to commit a crime, and then you explain his/her doing so in terms of his/her free will. It would be impossible to test the theory in any predictive sense.

The issue of free will has been debated by theologians and other philosophers for centuries and, obviously, it will not be settled here. Nevertheless, you should know that when scientists try to understand something, even human behavior, they assume that the determining forces are neither supernatural nor "free-will" in nature (Ruse, 1987; Russell, 1945; Viney, 1986). Students of research methods must understand that determinism is ultimately an unprovable assumption that is useful in science so as to maintain the focus of scientific inquiry on factors that can be empirically verified. Also, determinism does not deny that humans (or other animals) make choices. It simply assumes that all choices individuals make can be ultimately explained in terms of natural (including social) factors.

Ethical/Ideological Neutrality (Value Free)

The **ethical/ideological neutrality** of the scientific method does not mean that scientists must divest themselves of all moral principles and political beliefs in order to conduct research. In fact, an entire chapter of this text is devoted to discussing many important ethical issues that social scientists need to keep in mind regarding research projects. Ethical/ideological neutrality simply means that scientists should not allow ethics and ideology to influence what they observe and report. Is it possible for scientists to be totally neutral from an ethical and ideological standpoint, especially when studying human behavior? There is a long-standing controversy surrounding this question, especially when studying people with cultural backgrounds unfamiliar to the observer (Brittain, 1990:108; Mahoney, 1987).

The best insurance against observational bias is to never take the results of just one or even two studies as proof. Scientists should conduct numerous replications (or near-replications), using a variety of methodologies and samples before asserting that a particular finding is well established (Bornstein, 1990). Another way to avoid bias is to make social science a multicultural and multi-ideological endeavor. Fortunately, people in nearly all countries and political persuasions have an interest in objectively studying most phenomena (Brittain, 1990:108). This fact gives reason for optimism about the social sciences

BOX 1.2 WHAT DO YOU THINK?

What Comprises the Scientific Spirit?

Anyone acquainted with people who work in the social sciences knows that they are a diverse group of individuals. One would be hard pressed to find any point of view upon which they all agree. So, what drives social scientists (including those in criminal justice) to do what they do? With rare exceptions, social scientists (along with their colleagues in the physical and biological sciences) share what is called the scientific spirit. What comprises the scientific spirit? This spirit can be distinguished from the scientific method in that it reflects more about attitudes than about a set of agreed-upon rules.

Probably the strongest components of the scientific spirit are (a) curiosity, (b) persistence, and (c) skepticism. Let us briefly examine each of these three traits: Like children who cannot resist taking a watch apart to see how it works, social scientists have a burning desire to understand what they have chosen to study. Sometimes their curiosity is driven by a desire to make changes, such as those who study the conditions responsible for poverty. Other times, understanding itself is their primary motivation.

The desire to understand is sometimes so intense that researchers sacrifice jobs, friendships, and even family responsibilities to shed light on some scientific mystery. Although most would agree that sacrifices such as these are going too far, persistence is still a central ingredient of the scientific spirit.

Perhaps the most distinctive aspect of the scientific spirit is that of skepticism, which refers to a stubborn resistance to believing something without compelling evidence. This feature of the scientific spirit has given scientists a reputation for being cantankerous oddballs. Skepticism has also often pitted science against many religious teachings; skepticism is the antithesis of faith. In science, there are no authorities to go to for truth. The weight of the evidence, whatever it may be, holds sway on the conclusions that scientists reach. And, because evidence is never complete, the spirit of science is one that never closes the door on the possibility that current conclusions may be wrong.

What do you think? Can you think of any other traits that might characterize the scientific spirit? Do you have to exhibit all of these traits to be a good scientist? Do others who are not scientists also share these same traits?

gradually becoming a universal human enterprise focused on identifying truth, no matter how comfortable or uncomfortable it may be from an ethical or ideological perspective.

Statistical Generalizability

Statistics are important in science, including social science. Sometimes the statistics involved in a study are very simple, such as finding averages and calculating percentages; at other times, the statistics are exceedingly complex. The view underlying this text is that it is impossible to grasp social science research methods without at least a rudimentary knowledge of statistics. For this reason, two chapters in this book are devoted to presenting a basic explanation of the types of statistics most often used in social science research.

Table 1.1 summarizes the characteristics of the scientific method as herein identified. They are all important and interrelated to one another.

TABLE 1.1   Defining the Components of the Scientific Method

Component	Description	Comment/Qualification
Empirical	Ultimately, scientific evidence is assessed in terms of what can be sensed.	Sometimes scientific concepts must be inferred from what can be sensed.
Verifiable	What one scientist observes should also be observable by others.	The uniqueness of some empirical observations makes their verification by others impossible.
Cumulative	Scientific knowledge gradually accumulates, so that the questions become more and more refined over time.	The rate of knowledge accumulation is often imperceptible from year to year.
Self-correcting	Replications of research eventually cause mistaken reports of findings to be dismissed as erroneous.	Although errors occur, their ill effects on the accumulation of scientific knowledge are only temporary.
Deterministic	Neither supernatural nor free-will explanations are typically considered as causes; only "natural" (including social) causes are specifically considered.	The scientific method is ill-equipped to know if either of these factors is in fact responsible for whatever scientists are studying.
Ethical/ Ideological Neutrality	Scientific knowledge should not be selectively reported based on beliefs about what "should be."	Such neutrality can best be assured by making sure that science is open to people with all types of belief systems.
Statistical Generalizability	Even though "chance events" play a role in affecting empirical events, studying large numbers of such events allows important systematic patterns to emerge.	Science cannot explain everything, so it focuses on patterns that exceed the acceptable limits of statistical probabilities.

⬤ Types of Issues Addressed by Social Scientists

Nearly every issue that scientists attempt to address can be subsumed under one of four categories. These categories are (a) measurement, (b) relationships, (c) causal relationships, and (d) evaluations. Brief descriptions of each of these follow.

Measurement

When a researcher conducts a scientific study, he or she must decide how to measure the variables that are involved. In other words, what is the best way to operationalize each variable that is going to be studied? The sorts of details that must be addressed can be found in efforts to measure criminal behavior. Should relatively trivial thefts (even from one's parents) and acts of vandalism be included, and, if so, should they be given the same weight as serious criminality, such as robbery and rape? Should speeding or drunk driving be included? What about drug offenses, even if laws vary from one state or country to another regarding what drugs are and are not illegal. Also, what sort of response options should be provided to participants in the study? Should they be allowed to report how many times they recalled engaging in each illegal act or simply report that they have or have not engaged in crime?

Obviously, these are important questions that are likely to affect a study's ultimate findings. Although researchers are free to define and measure variables as they wish, they need to disclose how they defined and measured each crucial variable in any research report of the findings. Without such information, readers will be unable to confidently replicate the study that was conducted.

Relationships

After addressing measurement questions, researchers will usually seek to answer questions about how two or more variables are related. To give an example, studies have been undertaken to assess racial/ethnic variations in self-reported "problem drinking." Two studies conducted in the United States reported that blacks exhibited more problem drinking (including alcoholism) than do whites (Flaskerud & Hu, 1992; Pope, Smith, Wayne, & Kelleher, 1994). However, a study conducted in England came to the opposite conclusion (Cochrane & Howell, 1995). Of course, even if all three of these studies used the same methodology, they could all be correct if there are cultural factors involved in causing problem drinking.

Causal Relationships

Social scientists are very interested in causal relationships. In other words, although it is interesting to know that two or more variables are related in some statistical sense, it is also informative to discover whether one of those variables is causing one or more of the others. Unfortunately, it is difficult to answer causal questions without conducting what is known as controlled experimentation. Controlled experiments are often impossible to conduct in the social sciences, especially in criminal justice, because they raise serious ethical considerations. Nevertheless, quite a few experiments have been conducted, and their findings are often quite revealing. Fortunately, there are ways to address most causal questions in the social sciences without conducting actual experiments. The nature of these methods will be given some attention in a chapter dealing with multivariate statistics.

Evaluation

After one or more causes of a phenomenon have been at least tentatively identified, scientists sometimes seek to alter the prevalence of that phenomenon. When this is done, studies are often conducted to assess how well the intervention actually worked. In these evaluation studies, researchers seek to determine whether or not the intervention undertaken had any effects in the intended direction. Numerous studies in criminal justice attempt to evaluate crime reduction programs, for example. Other programs have been undertaken to treat individuals with criminal histories so as to reduce future criminal episodes. The success or failure of these programs is often subjected to scientific scrutiny.

⊖ Summary

The overarching theme of this text is that criminal justice is part of the social sciences. Much of the research in these fields uses methodologies also used in the social sciences in general. Accordingly, this introductory chapter provides basic descriptions of the social sciences and examples of where these disciplines have helped those in criminal justice to better understand criminal and related behavior.

The social sciences covered were anthropology, economics, geography, political science, psychology, social work, and sociology. Also mentioned were the so-called near social sciences, consisting of education, psychiatry, and public health. The field of criminal justice shares with these disciplines the goal of better understanding some important aspect of human behavior. Findings by researchers in one discipline, no matter how specialized it might be, will almost certainly contribute to the understanding of the whole. As a result, students of criminal justice should always look for opportunities to draw whatever knowledge they can from other disciplines and to contribute to that pool of knowledge in any way they can.

Seven characteristics of the scientific method were identified to help distinguish it from all other ways of acquiring human knowledge. We noted that the scientific method is (1) empirical, (2) verifiable, (3) cumulative, (4) self-correcting, (5) deterministic, (6) ethically/ideologically neutral, and

(7) statistically generalizable. The scientific method is distinguishable from the scientific spirit, the latter referring to a set of attitudes that help to make scientists a rather distinctive group of people. The three main attitudes associated with the scientific spirit are intense curiosity, an unrelenting focus on understanding, and a willingness to question everything.

Empirical refers to those things that can be seen, felt, heard, tasted, and smelled. Verifiable means that others are assumed to have the same abilities to make empirical observations as oneself has and that scientists can therefore cross-check one another's observations. Cumulative refers to the tendency to pursue new questions after several studies have verified the answers to old ones. The self-correcting nature of science means that errors made in empirical observations are eventually identified as such. Determinism is the essentially unprovable assumption that natural forces, rather than supernatural forces or free will, are responsible for whatever it is that scientists set out to understand. Ethical/ideological neutrality means that scientists strive to prevent their moral/religious/ideological beliefs to bias any empirical observations they make. Statistical generalizability refers to the tendency by scientists to describe what they have observed using standard statistical rules as much as possible.

The four main types of issues (or questions) addressed by social science research were identified as those having to do with measurement, relationships, causal relationships, and evaluation. Measurement issues have to do with how best to objectively measure a phenomenon of interest. Relationship questions deal with identifying the degree to which one variable is associated with one or more additional variables. In the case of causal relationships, researchers seek to determine the order in which each variable appears to lead to other variables. Finally, evaluation issues have to do with assessing how well various attempts to change outcomes are actually able to do so.

⊕ Discussion Questions

1. Discuss the ways in which criminology and criminal justice are interdisciplinary.

2. Which three characteristics of the scientific method do you think are the most compelling toward achieving the goal of advancing knowledge in criminology and criminal justice?

3. Scientific attempts to understand criminal behavior can be traced back to the early 1800s in Europe. Since then a variety of theories of criminal behavior have emerged, nearly all of which can be subsumed under two main criminological traditions: an environmentalist tradition and a biosocial tradition. Discuss the main arguments of these two traditions.

● Exercises

1. Use the internet to identify at least two websites containing scholarly information about one of the social sciences other than criminal justice. Perhaps you can choose a social science that interests you the most. Write a 1-page single-spaced summary of what you learned from these two websites. (Be sure to list which two websites you used in case your instructor wants to consult them to verify your interpretation.)

2. Using the internet, locate two websites with information about how social scientists have dealt with the "free will" issue. Write a 1-page single-spaced report summarizing what you learned from these two websites. (Be sure to list which two websites you used in case your instructor wants to consult them to verify your interpretation.)

Chapter 2

Formulating Scientific Questions and Locating Background Research

How do criminologists come up with the scientific questions they investigate? Once they have formulated one or more questions, how do they find what other criminologists have already discovered regarding these same questions or others on similar topics? How do they locate previous research findings that are pertinent for them to discuss to provide a background for their study? How do they know they can trust the sources of the previous findings as accurate? This chapter will assist in answering these questions and provide an overview of the format and basic parts of most published research studies, such as an introduction, a literature review, a methodology section, findings and results, and conclusions.

This chapter will focus on the basics of how to construct research questions and the general ways that one can locate previously published research by criminologists and others who have also sought to find answers to similar questions. The first thing to understand is that social scientists, including criminologists, begin with a very fundamental and important concept in science, a **variable**. Criminologists spend a great deal of time exploring which variables are important in explaining crime and criminality, how best to measure these variables, and what types of analyses to use when examining whether or not relationships exist between important variables and crime.

The Nature of Scientific Variables

As stated in the introduction to the chapter, most of the questions criminologists attempt to answer can be boiled down to finding relationships between variables. Variables are empirical phenomena that take on different values or intensities. Crime itself is a variable that we need to conceptualize, define, and measure so that we can examine what types of crime exist and whether crime is increasing or decreasing. Any phenomenon that always takes on the same value or intensity is called a **constant**; constants are neither prevalent nor interesting to study. For example, one could argue that if there were no laws there would be no crimes. Although this is true, and it is a constant that for a crime to exist there has to be a law prohibiting the behavior, the law is a constant in examining crime.

Criminological researchers, however, rarely examine these types of relationships unless they are exploring how the passing of new or different laws might change human behavior. Obviously passing laws doesn't deter everyone from engaging in the prohibited behavior, and most persons do not commit serious criminal offenses. Criminologists are more interested in finding out what types of variables might be related to more or less crime. Examples of the types of variables that are of major interest to criminologists are attitudes, parenting activities, mental health, personality traits, religiosity, and social and financial statuses. These variables are important in examining **criminality**, which will be discussed more in depth in Chapter 7. For now, keep in mind that criminality is the propensity for an individual to engage in criminal behavior that is a micro-level variable whereas crime is more of an aggregate measure or macro-level variable. These variables, therefore, would help us to determine whether relationships exist between these things and delinquency or criminal activity. All of these variables take on widely different values both between people and within individuals over time. The role of criminologists and criminal justice researchers is to attempt to predict why some persons are delinquent or criminal and others abstain from engaging in unlawful behavior. For example, by any measure one chooses, some people are more criminal than others, and a given individual will usually be more criminal at some times in his or her life than during others. This is most often referred to as the age crime curve. By using a variety of measures of criminality and studying different criminal behaviors, research has shown that, on average, people in their teens and early twenties are significantly more criminal, and even the most criminal persons begin to desist offending in their late twenties and early thirties.

Categorizing Social Science Variables

Anyone interested in understanding and conducting research should become familiar with the five main categories of variables studied in the social and behavioral sciences. These variable types are also widely used in criminal justice research and are perhaps more aptly called dimensions because some variables could be placed under more than one category. For our purposes, we'll label them as categories. Recall our discussion of the relationships between the different social science disciplines in Chapter 1. Most of the social and behavioral sciences use these classifications and variables in their discipline's research studies. As summarized in Table 2.1, these categories are as follows: demographic variables, social institutional variables, cultural variables, behavioral/personality variables, and cognitive variables.

TABLE 2.1   Categories of Social Science Variables

Types of Variables	Description	Examples
Demographic	Basic variables used to describe human populations	Sex, Age, Race/Ethnicity
Social Institutional	Variables used to describe institutional functioning and people's activities within institutional settings	Employment status, Homicide rate, Incarceration rate
Cultural	Variables having to do with the physical or social practices in a particular sociocultural setting	Technological development, Language spoken, Clothing fashions
Behavioral/ Personality	Variables pertaining to traits that can be overtly observed (although they are often self-reported)	Degree of hyperactivity, Criminality, Extroversion/ introversion
Cognitive	Variables having to do with traits that can only be indirectly or personally observed	Attitudes toward the death penalty, Feelings of depression, Intelligence

Demographic variables are those pertaining to basic human characteristics such as age, sex, race, ethnicity, marital status, years of education, and income and are widely used to describe human populations. Such variables are often used by governmental agencies such as the US Census Bureau to anticipate fluctuations in the utilization of public services. These are also used in criminal justice research to gauge any disparities that might be occurring in the system. Research conducted or funded by the National Institute of Justice, the Bureau of Justice Statistics, and the Federal Bureau of Prisons often uses demographic variables to describe criminal justice populations. Researchers use these demographic variables to ascertain whether so-called extra-legal factors (i.e., race, ethnicity, and sex) influence criminal justice outcomes while controlling for other legally relevant variables. Justice, it is said, is blind; however, numerous studies have shown that race, ethnicity, sex, and socioeconomic status are related to decision-making practices at various criminal justice stages.

The boundaries delineating demographic variables are not precisely drawn. Religious affiliation and even political party affiliation are generally recognized as demographic variables, although many governmental agencies do not follow uniform methods in collecting data of this nature. The reason for this is not just the personal nature of such variables but also the fact that such information has been misused by politicians and other government officials for policy implementation.

Social institutional variables include the functioning of social institutions and the tangible manifestations of culture. Economic variables, such as a nation's unemployment rate or its inflation rate, would be examples of social institutional variables. Criminal justice examples would include homicide rates, suicide rates, indices of dissimilarity, and level of social disorganization in a neighborhood, to name a few.

Cultural variables are numerous and can be subsumed under two subcategories: artifactual and customary. **Artifactual cultural variables** have to do with the wide variety of material things characterizing most human societies, such as the types of houses we live in, the neighborhoods in which they are located, and the types of media we consume, such as the television programs and movies we watch. **Customary cultural variables**, on the other hand, are values and practices that most members of a particular society share. Examples of customary cultural variables include the languages we speak, the day-to-day social customs we perform and expect others to perform, and the rules we (usually) follow in our day-to-day lives. Criminologists might be interested in the different types of customary cultural variables across populations in the country, how they affect behaviors or adherence to the law, and how the formal law might be invoked differently depending on these variables' presence or absence in individuals.

Behavioral/personality variables are those dealing with how we act as individuals. Making a sharp distinction between a behavioral variable and a personality variable is impossible; the former pertains to more specific acts, such as smoking and drinking or use of recreational drugs, while the latter has to do with acts that are more consistent and characteristic of a specific person-like agreeableness, such as attention seeking and introverted versus extroverted behaviors. Criminological research has attempted to find relationships between these behavioral and personality traits and the propensity to engage in criminal behaviors. Many students are interested in rare crimes, such as serial murder, and are infatuated with determining whether serial killers have psychopathic personality traits. Many psychologically based criminological theories point to personality traits as causes for criminal behaviors. Numerous studies, therefore, have been aimed toward understanding whether certain personality traits might be associated with a greater likelihood of criminality. Many of these researchers are also attempting to refine and better measure these personality variables in humans in order to have more valid tests of their relationship with criminality.

Cognitive variables encompass the emotions we feel, the individual attitudes we hold, the thoughts and intellectual abilities we possess, and the mental health/illness with which we are either blessed or cursed. Because cognitive variables cannot be directly observed by anyone except ourselves, they present special problems to those attempting to scientifically study them. Nevertheless, major efforts continue to be made in this regard, and self-report studies, which will be discussed in Chapter 10, are integral to measuring these variables in the persons we wish to study.

Qualifying Remarks about Social Science Variables

Four additional points are worth making in regard to the nature of social science variables. First, as stated earlier, some variables can be put into more than one of the five categories just presented. For example, most attitudes can be considered cognitive variables, but they can also be investigated as cultural phenomena to the extent that they may be widespread in one culture and rare in others. Another example of a variable that can be variously categorized is criminal behavior. It can be considered a behavior variable, but it can also be thought of as reflecting the actions of legislative bodies, because the behavior that is *criminal* varies somewhat from one society to another (Conklin, 1986). Despite these nuances, the five categories of variables are usually distinguishable and cover nearly all the variables at the heart of all of the social science disciplines.

Second, many criminal justice and other behavioral researchers are interested in variables outside the social sciences. For instance, in recent decades, psychologists in particular have focused increasing proportions of their research attention on brain functioning. Among the reasons for this is growing information on the relevance of brain functioning to our thoughts and emotions, which in turn impact our behavior (Leger, 1992). Many social scientists have also become keenly interested in health, in the physical environment, and even in the food we eat in light of growing evidence that all these variables can affect specific behavior, including criminality. In the final analysis, it would be difficult to identify any variable that social scientists have *not* studied in relationship to law-violating behavior. Numerous variables are related to crime; as such, criminologists have used many of them in attempts to explain or predict criminality and delinquency (for a comprehensive review of the many correlates of crime uncovered by social science research, see Ellis et al., 2019).

Third, most criminologists study just one species: humans. Because most criminologists are affiliated with universities, they often administer questionnaires to their students, asking them about various aspects of their lives and their past engagement in various types of delinquent or criminal behavior. Obviously, research in criminal justice also involves offenders, defendants, and prisoners. Nevertheless, in the "real world," as researchers refer to it, the environment is not as controlled as it is in the classroom or a lab; therefore, experiments or questionnaires with students in an artificially controlled environment tend not to be highly generalizable to the outside world.

Fourth, later in this text, a distinction will be made between independent (causal) variables and dependent (effect) variables. Social scientists refer to the *caused* variable as the dependent variable and the *causing* variables as the independent variables. For example, if you wanted to study the causes for varying burglary rates in different neighborhoods, the burglary rate would be the dependent variable; the factors about the neighborhood that affect burglary, say, the number of vacant houses, average housing value, average age of persons in the neighborhood, and number of streetlights, would be independent variables that may be causing the level of burglary in a particular neighborhood. Because the identification of these two types of variables is not always simple, extensive coverage will be given to them in Chapter 8, where the focus is on conducting experiments.

Conceptual versus Operational Definitions of Variables

Scientists must take care in defining the variables they choose to study. To understand why, consider the following hypothetical problem: Two researchers conduct separate studies of juvenile delinquency. One researcher finds that juveniles from lower socioeconomic families are more likely to be delinquent than those from middle socioeconomic status families, while the second researcher comes to the opposite conclusion. Hoping to settle the issue, both researchers conduct new studies, and both confirm their own original findings. What could account for their continued failure to agree with one another? Although there are several possibilities, one of the most basic revolves around how each is defining delinquency. Essentially, if they are including different behaviors under the definition of delinquency, they are studying different variables.

Scientists recognize two distinct types of definitions for variables: conceptual definitions and operational definitions. A **conceptual definition** is typical of what one finds in a dictionary. Such a definition uses familiar terms to describe a word (or phrase) that is unfamiliar. The other type of definition used in science,

BOX 2.1 CURRENT ISSUES

Should Jurisdictions Use a Standard Definition and Measure of Recidivism?

Consider the definition and measurement of a very important and often used variable, recidivism. Recidivism is basically the measure we use to account for an individual who has been sent to jail or prison or placed on probation and, upon release, reoffends. Indeed, many jurisdictions across the country are very interested in lowering their recidivism rates by implementing various types of programs.

Depending on how a researcher or jurisdiction defines and measures recidivism, however, the recidivism rate might be very low or very high. Consider all the decisions necessary in defining what constitutes recidivism. Is it any new arrest for any offense? The same offense? Is a violation of probation, say failing to meet with your probation officer or failing a random drug test, considered an offense for recidivism purposes? Should jurisdictions only include new arrests in their county? What about a probationer who is rearrested in another county? Does the county in which the individual is on probation have to count that as an instance of recidivism? Hopefully, you can see that if a jurisdiction conceptualized and operationalized recidivism very narrowly, say, as only a new arrest for the same offense within the same county, the county's recidivism rate would be much lower compared to a jurisdiction that had a much broader definition that included a new arrest for any offense in any county in the state. Unfortunately, some jurisdictions use the very narrow definition to make it seem like they are doing a better job at lowering recidivism rates than would be true if they adopted a broader, more accurate measure. Should the criminal justice system mandate that a standard definition of recidivism be used to measure this phenomenon across the country? Do you think it should be very narrow to include new arrests within the same county because ultimately county officials are responsible for public safety within the county's geographic boundaries, and only citizens who live within the county pay taxes for the operation of the county's jails and criminal justice system? Or do you think a more accurate measure of how the county's criminal justice system is doing should include a broader definition that attempts to include all arrests in any county or state? Should taxpayers demand that county officials use a more all-encompassing definition to assess the success of the system and programs at preventing or reducing recidivism?

an **operational definition**, specifies in empirical terms precisely what should be done to observe variations in some variable or exactly how that variable should be measured. As can be seen in the previous example, conceptualization and operationalization are very important tasks in the research process. How a researcher conceptualizes and measures particular variables will affect what the outcome of the study will be.

If the measurement of recidivism sounds complicated, imagine the multiple other variables representing human traits and behaviors that criminologists want to study. As examples, think about how you might measure social status or social class. What about homelessness? Maybe an operational definition of homelessness would include not having a permanent address for more than 6 months. Some students who move home in the summer or change residence every semester might be considered homeless. You can see that conceptualizing and accurately measuring some phenomena are not easy. Nonetheless, both types of definitions are important in science, as are researchers' continued attempts to improve the accuracy of definitions and measurement of what are very complex phenomena (i.e., human behavior) but that are important subjects in our discipline. In this same vein, no scientific definition is fixed in stone. If a researcher has a good reason for either conceptually or operationally defining a term in a new way, no rule or authority in science exists to prevent it. The criteria used to judge the merit of new definitions for variables (especially operational definitions) have to do with how "useful" they happen to be in collecting data in the real world.

⬤ Levels of Measurement

Any operational definition of a variable must specify how its variability is measured. The level at which a variable is measured will be important to the types of analyses that can be utilized in studying it. This requires that crucial decisions be made about **levels of measurement** (or **levels of calibration**). According to work pioneered by S. S. Stevens (1946), there are generally four levels of measurement. A basic understanding of these levels is important for choosing statistics that are most appropriate for the data being collected. As these four levels are presented, notice that their order begins with the least complex and ends with the most complex. Also notice that the more complex levels also include the characteristics of the lesser levels.

The first level of measurement is referred to as **nominal**. Measuring a variable at this level simply involves naming the calibrating units. These are names given to variables for distinction purposes. Examples of variables that are most often measured at this level would be sex, race, religious preference, political affiliation, and college major. These variables are used for naming purposes because there is no ordered meaning to the categories. For example, political affiliation could be divided into democrats, republicans, and independents. These categories are for distinction only; democrats do not have more or less political affiliation than republicans or independents. These are simply names to distinguish among people according to their political affiliation.

The second level of measurement is **ordinal**. Measurement at this level involves arranging the calibrating units into a logical order or rank. Not many variables are measured at this level, but one example involves ranking people according to criteria such as rank in the military or occupational prestige. The key feature of ordinal measurement is that there is an order in the calibrations without any assumption that the distances between each calibrating unit are equal. For example, we could measure a person's fear of crime on a scale ranging from not fearful to somewhat fearful to fearful and, finally, very fearful. These levels are ordered from least fearful to most fearful, yet we cannot say that someone who is very fearful is twice as fearful as someone who is not fearful. The levels are ranked but there is no equal distance between ranks.

Interval measurement is the third level. It involves not only having an order to the calibrating units (as in ordinal measurement), but the intervals are equidistant; that is, the distance between each successive unit is equal. Many social science variables are measured, or assumed to be measured, at this level. Examples include scores on academic achievement tests, self-rated aggressiveness measured on a scale from 1 to 10, and sentence length in months for those sent to prison: A 13-month sentence is one more month than a 12-month sentence, and a 19-month sentence is one more month than an 18-month sentence.

The fourth and most complex level of measurement is **ratio** measurement. It not only specifies a specific distance between each successive calibration unit, but it also assumes that there is a point at which the variable literally does not exist. This point is designated as zero (Ward, 1995). Examples of variables usually measured at a ratio level are height and weight, income in dollars, and number of prior arrests. Such variables can describe true ratios: At six feet, Bill is twice as tall as his little sister Sally, who is three feet tall; Jack earns $75,000 per year, which is three times Frank's annual income of $25,000.

As shown in Table 2.2, nominal and ordinal measurement can be consolidated into **categorical measurement**; interval and ratio levels are collectively known as **scale measurement**. Scale measurement has definite advantages, although there are certainly variables that should not be measured at the interval or ratio level (Wang & Mahoney, 1991). One advantage to scale measurement is that precise averages can be calculated and compared. To illustrate, try to answer this question: What was the average sex of the students in your high school graduating class? Such a question is rather nonsensical because the variable of *sex* is measured at a nominal level with no mathematical properties. In other words, there is no more or less of the variable between males and females; it is simply a measure to distinguish between categories of a variable. Also, in order to take advantage of most advanced statistical analyses, variables must be scale measures or measured at the interval or ratio level. This is because many of these advanced analytic tests are based on the mean and variance of variables that cannot be calculated for nominal or ordinal-level variables. The typical way we conceive of *average* does not really apply to variables measured nominally. (In Chapter 13, more will be said about the concept of average and its relationship to levels of measurement.)

It is useful to distinguish levels of measurement from the closely related concepts of **discrete** and **continuous variables**. A discrete variable is one that exists in two or more segments (regardless of how researchers decide to measure it). For example, the variable of sex exists in two segments, and the variable of religious preference exists in terms of the number of religious denominations that there happens to be in a population under study. Normally, discrete variables are measured at either the nominal or the ordinal level.

A continuous variable is one that does not exist in segments but instead varies gradually from low to high or weak to strong. Examples of continuous variables are age, academic ability, and the degree to which one is fearful of crime. Researchers can measure continuous variables at any of the four levels.

TABLE 2.2   The Four Levels at Which Scientific Variables Are Measured

Levels of Measurement		Description	Examples
Basic	**Consolidated**		
Nominal	Categorical	Naming each calibrating unit in order to classify and distinguish	Race/Ethnicity, Religious denomination
Ordinal		Naming and ordering each calibrating unit	Occupational prestige, Rank in high school graduating class
Interval	Scale	Specifying distances between calibrating units	Preference for sour tastes (on a scale of 1 to 10); Academic ability
Ratio		Specifying the distances between calibrating units and designating a real zero	Height, Distance someone is from where he/she was born

For example, age could be measured in terms of the categories *infant, child, adolescent,* and *adult* (an ordinal level of measurement). This would obviously be more crude than measuring age at the interval level (e.g., years of age). Measuring continuous variables at the interval or ratio level is more exact and allows researchers to apply more precise statistics than measuring continuous variables at the ordinal or nominal level.

More will be said later about these measurement options. For now, bear in mind that the notion of discrete versus continuous variables refers to how variables actually exist in the real world; the four levels of measurement (or calibration) refer to how variables may be measured. Later, readers will see that decisions made by scientists regarding the measurement of variables are substantially influenced by the level at which variables exist in the real world and by whether the variables exist in discrete or continuous form.

Formulating and Refining Scientific Questions

Where do criminologists come up with research questions that are worthy of study? The short answer is anywhere; that is, the number of questions that can be topics of study is almost limitless. A more precise answer, however, is that questions usually have their genesis in one of three places. First, they might come from personal experiences. For example, a researcher might have an alcoholic relative and, as a result, may wonder about the prevalence or causes of alcohol addiction. Or, a researcher may observe statistics about racial, ethnic, and sex differences in the composition of the prison population, leading him or her to want to study the discretionary practices of police officers, prosecutors, and judges.

Second, scientific questions arise from reading something interesting in the popular press or seeing it on television. For instance, a researcher might be spurred to explore the causes of crime after reading a story about a recent spike in domestic violence arrests or hearing lawmakers discuss passing new laws to increase punishment because they believe it will deter future crime. Third, scientific research is often inspired by learning of the findings from a research study conducted by someone else or by learning about a new theoretical advancement. Even the findings of a study may raise new questions about the relationships between variables and motivate the researcher to conduct additional research to study the phenomenon further. These internally generated sources for scientific research topics are particularly important, and they will be discussed more extensively in a chapter devoted to theory and hypothesis testing (Chapter 4). In fact, most social science research feeds off other, earlier social scientific research. Researchers find out about results of other research studies and decide to attempt to further advance knowledge by conducting their one research and building further knowledge of the topic.

⬤ Locating Information on Topics of Interest

Given a basic understanding of the concept of a variable and of how variables are operationalized to formulate scientific questions, what does a researcher do to find information on what others may have already discovered regarding a particular issue? Most research involves looking at previous research or literature that has been conducted on the topic of interest. Most research studies in social sciences are attempts to fill voids (areas where there is little research or where there are conflicting outcomes) or add something new to what is currently known about the topic. Crime has been studied for more than 200 years, so we know quite a bit about the correlates of offending from previous research studies. Where would a researcher go to begin compiling such information? The best single answer requires that one become familiar with electronic databases of journal article publications.

Publications in the Social/Behavioral Sciences

One should be prepared to be amazed the first time one delves into electronic databases of published journal articles. These massive databases contain thousands of published research articles on a variety of research topics published every year in scientific journals. What is particularly astonishing is how voluminous and diverse they are in the subjects covered. Just about any variable one can think of in terms of the five categories identified in Table 2.1 will produce hundreds of journal articles published on or related to it. Note that each publication will have a short paragraph at the beginning of the article, called an **abstract**, that the persons searching can read to ascertain if the published research is related to what they are interested in studying.

Today, students pay fees as part of their university tuition to subscribe to massive databases, most of which will allow full-text copies of the articles to be downloaded and printed in either PDF or html format. Criminology and criminal justice students should talk to their professors or visit the university library to find out which databases their university subscribes to and which are the most helpful for their topic of interest. The procedures are similar to those used for locating books on specific topics, with the following exception: Electronic searches tend to be much more specific than book searches. The most common social science and criminal justice electronic databases available at most universities include the following:

Academic Search Premier

Ebsco Databases

ICPSR (Inter-university Consortium for Political and Social Research)

National Criminal Justice Resources Services (NCJRS)

JSTOR

ProQuest Social Sciences

PsychINFO (the electronic version of *Psychological Abstracts*)

Sociological Abstracts

These databases are especially useful because they allow one to press a few buttons and obtain a copy of the entire published article. The article can be read online or printed out. No one really knows exactly how many articles are published every year in criminal justice, partly because what constitutes criminal justice research is ever increasing and expanding (remember, criminal justice is a very interdisciplinary field). Nevertheless, hundreds of journals are currently published worldwide in the criminal justice field; these journals publish several dozen articles each year. Most of these articles can be found via these large databases.

Google Scholar (http://scholar.google.com) is another search engine. Google Scholar allows one to search for articles on specific topics without charge and will even identify the names and referencing information for those articles, along with allowing one to access abstracts. If you are conducting a Google Scholar search from a university computer and it is a journal to which they subscribe, you can usually obtain a full-text (PDF) version of the article from Google for free.

⊖ Distinctiveness of Scientific Communication

How can a scientific report be distinguished from other types of written reports? The answers to this question are highlighted in Table 2.3 with some additional comments on each point made in the following paragraphs.

Most of the databases discussed earlier in the chapter have methods for narrowing a search to include only scholarly articles or government documents

BOX 2.2 WHAT DO YOU THINK?

Should Peer-Reviewed Research Articles Be More Accessible to the General Public?

Very few people in the general public are familiar with scientific journal publications, but it is vital for social scientists to be familiar with them. Because the major journal publications all cost hundreds of dollars per year, which probably amounts to hundreds of thousands of dollars in subscription fees, nearly all subscribers are university libraries and other institutions rather than individual scientists. This means that faculty members and students have access, but those not enrolled in university classes would not be able to search for and read published research articles. What do you think, should the scientific community make this information more available to the public? Would the public take the time to look for and read these research results and findings? There have been some calls for scientists to also construct shortened, perhaps two-page, versions of their research studies that highlight the research questions, methodology, and important findings so that politicians and lawmakers, as well as the general public, can have easy access and more readable information on scientific research discoveries. Some university community relations departments will also summarize faculty research projects or interview the researchers about their discoveries for the purpose of writing short stories and findings for publication on their public information pages. These shortened versions are efforts to make scientific research and findings more accessible to those not familiar with scientific research publications. Criminologists hope that law and policy makers will use these short reports to assist them in making informed decisions about criminal justice system policies and practices.

TABLE 2.3   Features of Most Scientific Reports That Distinguish Them from Popular Articles

Features	Scientific Articles	Popular Articles
Appears in Eye-Catching Periodicals	Rare	Common
References and Citations to Previous Research	Almost always	Almost never
Multiple Authors	Common	Rare
Title of Article Exceeds Five Words	Common	Uncommon
Carefully Describes How Data Were Obtained	Almost always	Almost never
Inclusion of Detailed Statistical Information	Almost always	Almost never

or to only search other types of publications like magazine and newspaper articles. In order to differentiate between scholarly research articles and others, some rules can be followed. First, scientific articles will not lure you to read them by flashy packaging. Unlike popular magazines, scientific articles usually appear in journals with relatively plain-appearing covers, and often the same covers are used issue after issue. Even though journals that publish scientific articles typically pay nothing to the authors for their work, publishing in most scientific journals is still very competitive. Rejection rates in some of the top journals are as high as 95%, meaning that only 5% of researchers who send their manuscripts in for review will actually get their research published. The main purpose of scientific articles is to convey new knowledge to the field.

Second, few popular articles cite references to other articles and/or books, although nearly all scientific articles do. References are essential for making both the verifiability and cumulative features of the scientific method possible. Most research builds on previous research; therefore, citing this previous research as a framework for study is essential. Third, many scientific articles are written by several authors; few popular articles are. The main reason for multiple authorship in science is that research is often a team effort. Fourth, the titles of scientific articles are usually longer than the titles of popular articles. Whereas titles of popular articles are largely intended to capture the reader's attention, the main purpose of scientific article titles is to give the reader a good idea of what the article covers. Nearly all scientific articles focus on at least two variables, and many deal with multiple variables.

Fifth, popular articles do not spell out in detail how all the information covered was collected. In scientific articles, authors are obligated to tell readers how the data were collected, usually in the methodology section, so that anyone wishing to replicate or extend the study can do so. Sixth, popular articles rarely include much statistical information. Scientific articles, on the other hand, almost always do. One needs to be acquainted with the main types of statistics used in the social sciences and criminal justice before beginning to read published research reports.

⊖ How Scientific Research Gets Reviewed and Sometimes Published

Most decisions about the publication of scientific research reports are made by way of a process known as **peer review**. This means that when a journal editor receives a manuscript submitted by its author(s), he or she sends the manuscript to two, three, or four individuals who the editor believes would be qualified to pass judgment on the merit of the report. Each peer reviewer (also called a *referee*) is expected to read and comment on the manuscript. Based on the comments received, and often the editor's own reading of the manuscript, one of three decisions is made: rejection, acceptance, or varying degrees of revise-and-resubmit.

In the peer review process, the author's name does not usually appear on the manuscript; this is so the author's identity is not known to the reviewers. Also, the reviewers' identities are not known to the author, a process known as **blind peer review**. From this gauntlet review process, far more scientific articles are rejected than accepted, especially the first time they are submitted. Such a review process differs considerably from the way decisions are made regarding the publication of popular articles; these are usually assigned to an author by a magazine editor. The acceptance of popular articles is usually based on readability and potential appeal to readers.

⊜ Summary

This chapter introduced several of the most basic concepts of social science and criminal justice research. It began by subsuming social science variables into five categories. These were demographic variables, social institutional variables, cultural variables, behavioral/personality variables, and cognitive variables. Two types of definitions for variables were distinguished: conceptual definitions and operational definitions. The former refers to "dictionary" definitions, or how we will describe the variable, while the latter refers to "empirically verifiable" definitions, or how we will go about measuring a variable. Together, these two types of definitions help to ensure that the same variables are under scrutiny in different studies. When two studies ostensibly fail to agree on a finding, one of the first possibilities to consider is that the studies were not working with the same variable in operational terms.

There are four levels of measurement or levels at which variables may be calibrated. The simplest (or lowest level) is nominal. All that is required at this level is to name the measurement units without making any assumptions about how they should be arranged relative to one another. In the ordinal measurement of a variable, the levels are arranged in an order relative to one another but without concern for the varying distances that may exist between each unit. Interval measurement requires that an equal distance exist between each of the units of measurement. Ratio measurement meets the requirement of interval measurement in addition to the assumption that zero represents the complete absence of the variable. In other words, variables measured at this level have a fixed, meaningful, zero point.

Closely related to the concept of levels of measurement is the issue of how variables actually exist in the real world. In particular, continuous variables were distinguished from discrete variables. Continuous variables, such as social status and number of months sentenced to prison, exist in infinitely fine gradations. Discrete variables, such as citizenship status or ethnicity, exist as clearly distinguishable units.

The formulation of questions in criminal justice research will be discussed in greater detail in Chapter 4, which is devoted to theory construction and hypothesis testing, but for now three main sources for scientific questions can be identified. Many questions arise from personal experiences, while others come from ideas that are presented to us through the mass media. Another source for scientific questions is from science itself, where findings from one investigation lead to new questions.

This chapter also dealt with how to locate scientific information on specific variables, including how variables are related to one another. Electronic databases of peer-reviewed journal publications were discussed. These databases provide researchers with a wealth of information on what their colleagues have found so far. After discussing how these publications can be accessed, the most common of these databases were listed. Also, electronic search engines such as *Google Scholar*, which is popular and a widely used method today, have the capability of retrieving copies of entire articles online, usually in PDF format, which the interested party can then peruse to determine any relevance to their topic of interest.

The final focus of this chapter was on the differences between articles presenting scientific research reports and popular articles found in newspapers and magazines. Six features were listed, most of which will be elaborated on in later chapters.

⊖ Discussion Questions

1. Think of a variable that could be used to measure some aspect of your family for each of the categories of social science variables listed in the chapter.

2. Describe the difference between a conceptual and operational definition of a variable. Now come up with both a conceptual and operational definition for crime.

3. Think of one or two variables that you believe are related in some way to criminality. Now determine ways to measure these variables in accordance with the four different levels of measurement (nominal, ordinal, interval, or ratio). *Note:* Some variables may not be able to be measured at an interval or ratio level.

⊖ Exercises

1. Go to the search page for a journal database that is available to you through your enrollment at your current institution (you may want to ask your instructor which databases they use) and then search for scientific peer-reviewed articles on a criminology or criminal justice topic that interests you. Click on 5–10 articles and read the abstracts. Do these articles use similar variables to operationalize the topic under study? If not, how do they differ? Are the main findings similar across the studies?

2. Download the full text of one of the articles you found for exercise 1, go to the research methods section, and list the variables utilized in the study. Try to determine at what level of measurement each of them is measured (nominal, ordinal, interval, or ratio).

3. Go to the website for the National Archives of Criminal Justice Data (https://www.icpsr.umich.edu/icpsrweb/content/NACJD/index.html), click on the discover data icon, and type a keyword to search one of the criminal justice topics. Click on one of the research projects and read the summary. List any research questions that guided the study as well as how the researcher(s) collected the data. You may have to click on the methodology link to get some of this information.

Chapter 3

Ethical Issues in Social and Behavioral Science Research

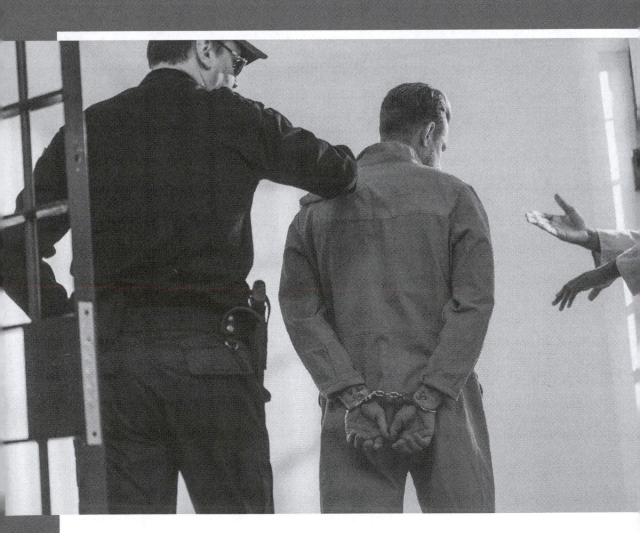

Suppose that someone asked you to participate in a research study where they will pay you $80 a day for two weeks to pretend you are either a prison guard or prisoner and interact with other participants in their roles in the aforementioned positions. Further, suppose that you are chosen to take the role of a prisoner and throughout the day are subjected to threatening and dehumanizing behavior? What rights do you have as a participant who accepted money to stop participating in the study? What obligations does the researcher who is conducting the study have to ensure your safety and well-being? Further, does the researcher have to tell you up front what may happen to you or how the results from the research study will be used? When conducting research, many ethical issues can arise that a researcher must be prepared to handle. As you will see in this chapter, many different protocols must be followed, such as getting informed consent from participants before their participation so they have a general idea of what they are volunteering to do. Sometimes social scientists can justify deceiving research participants or cause them some discomfort or even emotional stress to study human behavior. Who decides, however, what the risks of certain studies might be to participants and whether they are justified to gain scientific knowledge?

E thical questions in social and behavioral science research are always present and must be carefully considered and planned for, especially for studies that involve human subjects. Months before planning to conduct human subjects research, researchers must weigh the potential risks to the participants against the potential benefits in the form of improved understanding for the field. In addition to the Stanford Prison Experiment, several other examples of unethical research have garnered widespread scrutiny and attention. Even though not all risks can be known a priori, and some potential risks may be difficult to precisely measure, reasonable guidelines are in place and protocols that must be followed to ensure that researchers minimize harm to persons as they attempt to make new research discoveries. Criminologists and those who conduct research on the criminal justice system and its actors have to be especially concerned about ethical issues: The substance of their projects tends to involve offenders and victims, some of whom may not have been caught by, or reported their victimization to, authorities. Participants of research in the criminal justice field are also often inmates or probationers, or prison guards or police officers, and the subject of the research itself may be related to ethical decision-making practices in the administration of justice.

The opening scenario is taken from a very famous, or infamous, depending on your view, research study undertaken in the early 1970s by psychologist Phillip Zimbardo; the study was dubbed the Stanford Prison Experiment. Dr. Zimbardo was interested in studying whether brutality by guards in actual prisons might be a product of their individual personalities or the social environment in which they worked. Zimbardo had to stop the experiment after a few days due to the dehumanizing treatment that "mock" guards were imposing on "mock" prisoners. This results of this study generally revealed that social environment could play a role in a person's behavior; seemingly normal college students (guards) acted very brutally toward other students (prisoners) in a matter of a few days in a structure that was set up with rigid role expectations (McLeod, 2018). Indeed, partly because of this experiment, as well as the numerous issues in studying those on both sides of the law, many guidelines have been put in place to provide ethical oversight of criminological research studies and to assure safe treatment of the participants involved in this research.

This chapter focuses on the guidelines and regulations that have been established to guide researchers and to protect participants. The topics discussed in this chapter generally fall under three major headings. First, we explore the general rules for treatment of research participants. We will examine issues related to revealing the purposes of a research study to the participants who will be involved. We will also discuss whether and under what circumstances it might be acceptable to explicitly deceive or even frighten subjects in order to gain new knowledge as well as the safeguards that would need to be in place in order to do this. The second part of the chapter looks at the professional ethics that researchers expect of one another. For example, what does the field expect from researchers in the way of giving credit to other researchers from whom they have taken ideas? Third, we will turn our attention to the responsibilities that social science researchers have to humanity as a whole. Some questions about human behavior need to be very carefully explored. We also need to ensure that treatment of humans is taken very seriously to the point that research not be undertaken when the risks outweigh the benefits to science.

◒ Responsibilities to Participants of Research

There are certain long-standing ethical principles to which social scientists have always been bound regarding how they should treat human subjects. Other ethical and even legal responsibilities are mandated by the federal government and institutions that oversee research. Research in criminology and criminal justice is no exception. Many of the behaviors we are interested in studying are against the law and as such could be dangerous to study or at least put researchers in situations that lead to ethical dilemmas. Likewise, even asking victims of crime about their experiences may lead to emotional stress via sensitive questions that cause them to relive traumatic situations. In this section, we will discuss issues related to the following topics: (a) the confidentiality of data, (b) obtaining informed consent, (c) deception and harm to human participants of research, (d) getting approval to conduct research with human participants, and (e) responsibilities to fellow researchers and humanity.

Confidentiality of Participant Data

Confidentiality refers to the assurance given by a researcher not to reveal the identity of those who provide information as participants of research. Such assurances are generally considered morally equivalent to the assurances that newspaper and television reporters make not to disclose the identity of their sources without permission. It is also similar to the confidentiality to which physicians, ministers, and professional counselors are bound in their relationships with their clients. A special type of confidentiality, called **anonymity**, refers to the practice of insuring that no identifying information of participants will be obtained in the course of collecting data. Anonymity is most easily assured with questionnaires completed by the participants themselves as opposed to information obtained by direct observation or an interview. Guarantees of both confidentiality and anonymity should not be made by a researcher unless he or she intends to abide by those commitments.

Even though researchers have a moral obligation to honor promises of confidentiality, the legality of such assurances is somewhat less certain. Therefore, if a researcher asks subjects to report information that could be used against them in a court of law (such as their involvement in criminal acts), it is best to either make sure that their identities can never be traced (collect anonymous data) or the researcher should be prepared to risk prosecution for keeping participant identities confidential should some governmental agency want access to them (Frankfort-Nachmias & Nachmias, 1992). Most funded research requires that researchers have a protocol in place for maintaining confidentiality of subjects by using code numbers and storing data in files, electronic or hard copy, that are secure (no one else has access to, password protected, or encrypted). If a researcher is uncertain about their ability to maintain the confidentiality of information provided by participants or the identity of the participants themselves, they should probably collect identifying information.

Researchers are protected from the government requesting information related to the identity of research study participants or the information that they have given to researchers. Several funding agencies will issue **certificates of confidentiality**, which protect researchers from having to disclose participant identities or information in criminal proceedings; the government would have to convince a grand jury or judge to compel them to provide this information. To date, there have only been a few instances where a researcher faced arrest and incarceration for refusing to disclose the identity of subjects in a research project (Monaghan, 1993). One case involved a sociologist who had collected data from several people (animal-rights activists) who had broken into university laboratories and destroyed equipment. Law-enforcement agencies were interested in apprehending those responsible for these break-ins and subpoenaed the researcher's records, which the researcher refused to provide. If researchers are going to be collecting information from persons related to criminal, and especially serious or violent, behavior, they will need to seriously consider issues of confidentiality and disclosure.

To maintain the confidentiality of data, the following procedures should be followed. First, keep all data under lock and key or, in the case of electronic data, password protected or encrypted, restricting access to original data to only research colleagues working on the project. Second, although it is sometimes necessary to know the names of subjects while data are being collected, coded, and verified, it is often no longer necessary afterward. Therefore, the names of subjects should be permanently detached from the data records and destroyed (Riecken & Boruch, 1979:258) after data collection is complete.

Informed Consent

Most often, institutions where researchers are employed will require that researchers obtain **informed consent** from study participants. Providing informed consent entails informing prospective subjects of the basic purpose of a study and then obtaining their permission to be a participant (with the understanding that their participation is voluntary and they are free to withdraw at any time). There are three main exceptions. One involves subjects who are being directly observed while in public (e.g., observing protesters marching in a public space). Another exception involves subjects in ethnographic studies, where researchers have not traditionally sought informed consent, although suggestions have been made that this should not be an exception (Fluehr-Lobban, 2000). Third, in some experimental studies, subjects cannot be made aware of a study until after the data have been collected. Thus, informed consent cannot be granted. In the latter case, approval from a special oversight committee called an IRB (institutional review board) must be granted. Informed consent is either explicit (i.e., in written form), or implicit.

Explicit informed consent involves having each subject sign a statement that spells out in detail the nature of the study. Implicit informed consent occurs when a person is asked to complete and return an anonymous questionnaire, and he or she does so. Informed consent does not mean that subjects must be told everything about the nature of a study, because detailed information could often jeopardize the validity of any findings. Rather, prospective subjects must be given sufficient information about the study so as to make an informed decision about whether to become involved as a participant. The concept of informed consent clearly implies that participation in a study is not coerced. However, such an implication is difficult to avoid in some cases, especially with captive populations such as those in prison. Imagine that a researcher needed a pool of subjects in order to test the effectiveness of a prison rehabilitation program. Prisoners would be implicitly coerced into being subjects if there was the possibility of early release being made even partially contingent upon participating in the study (Greenland, 1988). Confidentiality of which inmates are participating might also be difficult in a closed prison environment.

Deceiving or Causing Harm to Human Participants

The concepts of **deception** and causing harm to participants of research are often closely related. Many studies conducted by social scientists can cause people to be embarrassed or emotionally traumatized. If some deception is necessary for the nature of the study, participants are denied the opportunity to make an informed decision as to whether or not to become involved in a potentially embarrassing or traumatizing experience. Typically, deception in the context of social science research involves providing misleading information to prospective participants. Deception comes in two distinguishable forms: deception by omission and orchestrated deception. If a researcher deceives subjects simply by not giving them complete information about a study, this is considered **deception by omission**. For instance, in an experiment undertaken by researchers at Georgia State University, male participants were told that the study was designed to assess how conversations were associated with "chemical changes in saliva." This statement was true but not very specific. What the subjects were not told was that the researchers had a specific interest in learning whether the act of conversing with an attractive, flirtatious female (a confederate of the experiment or someone who was a part of the study) caused male testosterone levels in saliva to rise (Dabbs et al., 1987). Although the researchers obviously could have been more precise about the purpose of the study, doing so could have altered the findings because subjects would have been aware that the flirtatious behavior was artificial and the body might not have the natural reaction. Usually, if subjects are given only general, but still accurate, information about the purpose of a study and there is no significant risk of emotional or physical harm, the study would be considered ethical, especially if subjects are debriefed or told the true nature of what the researchers were attempting to study at the end of their participation.

Orchestrated deception, on the other hand, involves concocting instructions or circumstances so as to lead subjects to believe something that is not true. One example is the bogus pipeline experiment, which uses a technique to try to maximize honesty and frankness by subjects. In these experiments, subjects were specifically deceived into believing that any lie or even half-truth they provided in an interview would be detected by a super-sophisticated polygraph machine. Those who were inclined to lie in order to be "politically correct" or to avoid hurting other people's feelings were likely to experience considerable emotional distress. Consequently, some researchers have questioned whether this type of research is ethically justified. We will discuss how decisions about whether these types of studies are ethical are made later in the section on obtaining institutional approval for research, but the fact that many bogus pipeline studies have been conducted recently suggests that researchers have put sufficient safeguards in place to minimize any emotional harms so that they meet ethical standards of research.

Nonetheless, two extreme positions exist as to whether researchers should be allowed to deceive (and, in the process, sometimes emotionally harm) subjects. One position is that deceptive research should be banned (Baumrind, 1971; Warwick, 1975). Those who advocate this view defend it by noting that persons who agree to participate in social science research have a fundamental right to assume that they will not be tricked, humiliated, or emotionally traumatized. The second position is that deception and small risks of emotional harm to subjects can be justified if the knowledge to be gained is sufficient, and there is no other way to obtain the knowledge (Milgram, 1964; Forsyth, 1991). For example, if by causing some emotional discomfort to people one can discover ways to prevent crime, victimization, or other social problems, most would probably regard the trade-off as justified. This position has been adopted by most committees that have drafted guidelines for social science research (e.g., the American Psychological Association, the American Sociological Association, and the American Society of Criminology).

Deception is most common in experimental research because researchers are usually trying to study reactions and behaviors to certain types of stimuli or situations. Survey research studies or research that utilizes interviews or focus groups rarely involve deception or risk of emotional harm to subjects because they are trying to collect accurate information on people's behaviors, personality traits, or opinions and beliefs. The only exceptions that might cause participants some discomfort would be surveys asking participants to reveal information about their sexual and/or illegal behavior. These surveys would have to explicitly disclose the nature of the survey questions and of the participants' right not to answer any questions they are uncomfortable answering.

Today, any deception used in social science research lasts only as long as the duration of participation in the study. At the end of the study, participants are usually **debriefed** (i.e., informed of the true nature of the study). Debriefing sessions following the involvement in a research project are considered important in order to reduce the risk of any long-term adverse effects that might result from participation. For example, a number of experiments were carried out in the 1980s to search for evidence of males becoming more sexually aggressive after viewing various types of pornographic films (e.g., Malamuth & Check, 1981, 1983, 1985; Donnerstein et al., 1987; Zillman & Bryant, 1984). Consequently, most researchers who conduct experiments in which sexually explicit films are shown make sure that all subjects are carefully debriefed afterward. Follow-up evaluations of the debriefings indicate that they are effective in eliminating the risk of subsequent aggression (reviewed by Malamuth & Check, 1984; Ellis, 1989:34).

Consider a study conducted by Rojas and Kinder (2007) that sought to determine whether completing questionnaires about sexual behavior and abuse causes harm to those participants who have a history of being sexually abused as children. Participants completed a questionnaire that measured the occurrence of sexual abuse as a child. They also completed a questionnaire measuring anxiety, depression, anger, and curiosity. In the latter questionnaire, they were instructed to fill it out with regard to how they felt while completing the sexual abuse questionnaire. The results showed that roughly 31% of the

250 survey participants indicated sexual abuse history. The authors then sought to examine whether there were significant differences regarding the anxiety, depression, and anger questionnaire between those who did and did not have a history of sexual abuse as a child. The findings revealed that there were no significant differences. The authors concluded that these results suggest that participating in research on sexual behavior or childhood sexual abuse does not result in increases in anxiety, depression, or anger for those participants who have been abused. This is significant for researchers who want to study topics that may be embarrassing or emotional to subjects. Obtaining approval for this type of research from an institutional review board can sometimes be difficult

Most social science codes of ethics do not ban the use of deception and harm to research participants per se, but more restrictions are placed on researchers now than was true in the early half of the 20th century. The main reason for this is that researchers no longer make independent decisions about whether their studies are ethical. Most countries have established committees that oversee scientific research, especially that which involves human participants.

⊖ Obtaining Institutional Approval for Conducting Research

Until the middle of the 20th century, all decisions regarding the appropriateness of social science research were made by the researchers directly involved in designing the research. This began to change during the 1960s in the wake of evidence that some scientists were making poor ethical judgments. By the 1970s, public attention in several Western countries was drawn to various ethically questionable research practices, and pressure mounted for governmental intervention, especially in the United States. A study now known as the Tuskegee Syphilis Study, funded by the US Public Health Service, used roughly 600 low-income (200 or so were a control group) African American males with syphilis to study the effects of untreated syphilis on the body (Brandt, 1978). This study went on for decades; most participants were not even aware that they had syphilis. They were denied treatments until the early 1970s even though penicillin had been widely used as the preferred treatment for the disease beginning in the early 1950s.

This type of egregious treatment in the name of science prompted the government and many professional social science organizations to formalize ethical guidelines and to establish enforcement procedures (Green, 1971). The federal government specifically passed the National Research Act of 1974, which established a National Commission for the Protection of Human Subjects of Biomedical and Behavioral Research that was tasked with identification of basic ethical principles for use of human subjects in research (US Department of Health and Human Services, 2019). The commission issued a report in 1979 referred to as the **Belmont Report**, which outlined three main principles for ethics in research involving human participants. These were respect for persons, beneficence, and justice.

Respect for persons encompasses the idea that "individuals should be treated as autonomous agents, and … persons with diminished autonomy are entitled to protection." The principle of *beneficence* has to do with protecting participants from harm and states that researchers should "maximize possible benefits and minimize possible harms" in any study. Finally, *justice* refers to the notion that the benefits and burdens of a research study should be distributed fairly across all participants. Many professional organizations use the Belmont Report to undergird their policies and guidelines for oversight of research. Professional organizations in criminology and criminal justice also followed suit. Both the **American Society of Criminology** (ASC) and the **Academy of Criminal Justice Sciences** (ACJS) have put forth guidelines for the treatment of human participants of research. We would encourage you to explore and familiarize yourself with these associations' codes of ethics. The ASC's code of ethics is available online at https://www.asc41.com/ASC_Official_Docs/ASC_Code_of_Ethics.pdf. The ACJS code of ethics is available online at: https://www.acjs.org/page/Code_Of_Ethics.

Regarding academic research generally, probably the most far-reaching federal regulations were those requiring all institutions receiving federal research funds (primarily universities and hospitals) to maintain a committee to oversee all research involving human subjects. These committees are called **Institutional Review Boards for the Protection of Human Subjects,** or **Institutional Review Boards** (**IRBs**). In Britain and its commonwealths (including Canada and Australia), the equivalents of the IRBs are called *Research Ethics Committees* (*RECs*) (McNeil et al., 1992:317). Inasmuch as IRB and REC requirements are very similar, references to both henceforth will be simply *IRB*.

The regulations surrounding the functioning of IRBs are too complex to describe in detail here and beyond the scope of this chapter. However, students should be familiar with some of the most basic procedures. Before a researcher is permitted to conduct a study other than simply performing a secondary analysis on data already collected, a written proposal of the research study must be submitted to the IRB at the institution where the researcher works. IRBs have members from various disciplines, and they meet periodically to consider these research applications. Their focus is not on the technical or theoretical merits of the proposed study but on the ethical and legal issues surrounding it (Bersoff & Bersoff, 2000). Ordinarily, IRBs include an attorney and medical professional to weigh in on any medical or legal liabilities.

Under the guidelines put forth by the federal government, an IRB can handle applications in one of three ways. First, its members can declare a project exempt, such as when a researcher is simply seeking to observe subjects in public locations or conduct a content analysis of printed material such as a public newspaper. Second, an IRB can carry out an expedited review, which would merely seek to clarify a few minor procedural points about a proposed research project that might involve little more than asking subjects to complete an anonymous questionnaire. Third, the board can conduct a full-board review, which often entails scrutinizing the entire proposed project, including the research questionnaire or instruments to be used, and may even involve interviewing the principal investigator for details surrounding the project, especially as they relate to potential risks and safeguards put in place to minimize harms. IRBs seek assurance that any deception or risk of physical or even emotional harm to participants can be explicitly justified by the knowledge gained from the results of the study. They also try to make sure that the same information could not be obtained in less deceptive ways.

To illustrate the type of study that today would have difficulty being approved by an IRB, consider experiments undertaken by Stanley Milgram (1963) in the late 1960s, before IRBs were mandated. In Milgram studies, participants were led to believe that they controlled an apparatus for inflicting electrical shock onto other "subjects" (actually confederates of the study). The participants were then instructed to inflict increasing levels of shock, ostensibly to punish the subjects for inaccurate recall of a list of nonsense words. Because these experiments were actually undertaken to determine the conditions under which people would follow orders to the point of harming others, the research was very deceptive. Most of the participants of these studies experienced considerable emotional distress, especially when they were instructed to inflict shock at levels that were in the "danger" zone of the gauges they controlled; in other words, they were told the shocks could be lethal (Milgram, 1963:375).

Many other examples of deception and/or the induction of emotional harm to participants appear in past research. These include studies that have exposed subjects to gruesome photographs, pressured them to lie or cheat, or falsely informed them that they possessed undesirable personality traits or that they failed a basic competency test (Neuman, 1991:442). For example, a cutting-edge study conducted jointly by Brazilian and US researchers in the early 2000s raised some ethical concerns. Ironically, the study was designed to better understand how humans process information of a moral nature (Moll et al., 2002). Using magnetic resonance imaging (MRI) to measure brain circuitry, the researchers presented subjects with various photographs, including ones likely to evoke moral indignation, such as actual physical assaults, poor children abandoned in the streets, and war casualties. Along with emotionally neutral photographs, subjects were also shown unpleasant pictures without moral overtones (e.g., bodily injuries, feces). This allowed researchers to isolate certain brain circuits that were more or less unique to emotionally ladened moral disgust. This study is an example of the sort of research that continually challenges researchers and members who serve on IRBs in the United States and comparable committees in other countries.

⊜ Responsibilities to Fellow Social and Behavioral Scientists

This section pertains to how social and behavioral scientists relate to one another rather than to the research participants they work with. Students should also pay particular attention to parts of this discussion because some of these rules also pertain to writing academic papers for your university courses (I am sure that most of your professors have warned you about the consequences of plagiarism). The following topics will be addressed: types of scientific fraud, ways of keeping scientific fraud at a minimum, and obtaining data collected by others for the purpose of verification.

Types of Scientific Fraud

In science, fraud refers to intentional misrepresentation of scientific ideas or findings. Scientific fraud can be subsumed under two categories: (a) plagiarism and (b) intentional misrepresentation of one's research findings. **Plagiarism** is the intentional representation of someone else's writings or ideas as your own. It comes in three main forms. Most common is copying sentences or entire passages from an article or book without crediting the original author. This type of plagiarism has been the reason for many Fs being handed out to students on assignments, has been identified in scholarly journals (e.g., Hudson, 1998), and has damaged the careers of otherwise reputable researchers (D'Antonio, 1989; Blum, 1989). Even public figures and music artists have had their reputations and accomplishments tarnished because of accusations, founded and otherwise, of stealing portions of others' speeches or songs. To avoid plagiarizing, never use the exact phrase of another writer without doing the following. In the case of a phrase or sentence or two, place quotation marks around the quoted passage and cite the author's or authors' names and year the study was published, along with the page number where the passage can be found. If several sentences are being quoted, the passage should be indented. Even sentences where someone else's words are being paraphrased should be avoided unless that person is explicitly given credit.

The other two forms of plagiarism are ghostwriting, and unwarranted coauthorship. Ghostwriting occurs often in popular books (such as autobiographies by celebrities) but is considered unethical in professional writing (including students' papers, theses, and dissertations). Attempts have been made in the United States to shut down companies that sell their services as ghostwriters, especially those catering to academic markets. Unwarranted coauthorship refers to the inclusion as a coauthor of someone who made no significant contribution to the manuscript. This sometimes happens when a subordinate is pressured by someone in authority to undeservedly include his or her name as an author of manuscript (Goodyear et al., 1992). Guidelines have been proposed regarding who should be listed as authors of a scientific publication and in what order (Culliton, 1988a). Although there are ways of contributing to a scientific publication that warrant being listed as an author besides actually writing the manuscript, usually there should be some active participation in formulating the methodology, in analyzing the results, and in writing some of those parts of the paper to make coauthorship justified.

Falsifying data involves fabricating or misrepresenting data or findings from analyses of data. Why would researchers falsify their research findings? There appear to be both internal and external motivating forces (Wilson, 1991). Internally, researchers tend to be hardworking and ambitious. As such, they wish to be recognized for making valuable contributions to their field. One way to make a contribution is to discover something new, but such discoveries nearly always take considerable time to plan and execute. It is tempting to cut corners and simply *report* made-up or slightly altered findings rather than do all of the necessary work, especially if one is confident in theoretical terms as to what should be found according to previous research.

Externally, scientists who conduct and publish research are financially rewarded for doing so by the universities or hospitals that employ them because the reputations of these institutions depend heavily on research excellence. Basically, the higher the quantity and quality of research, the more grants and other types of funding an institution is likely to receive. In addition, many large universities and hospitals use their researchers to compete for grants that can be used to help fund many other aspects of institutional functioning. This need for grant funds from scientific research has led some universities and hospitals to adopt "publish or perish" policies toward their faculty (Sapp, 1990). The pressure to publish is nearly always more intense for new researchers than for those who have already established a substantial track record and have earned tenure and garnered grants. It is believed this helps to explain why most persons who are convicted of scientific fraud are relatively young researchers (Smith, 1985).

Because the probability of being caught for engaging in scientific fraud is probably low, it is reasonable to assume that it may be considerably more prevalent than any statistics will ever indicate, especially in the case of "minor fraud" (Broad & Wade, 1982). Minor fraud would include researchers changing a few numbers in a data set to push a "not quite significant" finding over the .05 level or "conveniently omitting" findings that were inconsistent with one's theory (or political ideology).

Examples of Fraud, or Possible Fraud, in the Social Sciences

Some caveats about scientific fraud should be noted before providing examples. First, charges of fraud can easily be made. However, they are not only not always true, but sometimes not even warranted by evidence. Consider the assertion that Gregor Mendel, the 19th-century founder of modern genetics, faked some of his findings (Bauer, 1992:105). The basis for this charge was the almost perfect correspondence between what he predicted theoretically and what he observed. Some considered the fit "just too good—a 10,000 to 1 shot" (Silberner, 1982:40). Because Mendel's basic theory has been upheld by others, and because there is no way for Mendel to ever respond to the charge, it is unfair to take seriously the suggestion that he fabricated his data.

Second, fraud does not seem to be as much of a problem in social science as in other fields such as biology and medicine. Perhaps due to greater pressures to uncover new scientific discoveries, or because funding and the potential to earn money through patents is much greater in these fields, many cases of scientific fraud have been documented (e.g., Elmer-DeWitt, 1991; Roberts, 1991). Although it could be that fraud is relatively uncommon in the social sciences, another possibility is that detection of fraudulent social science research is more difficult than in many areas of biology and medicine. Today, most journals make author(s) adhere to strict regulations related to their data and findings and mandate that if requested the author(s) would make their data and analytic techniques available so that results and findings could be reproduced for accuracy.

Third, although the serious nature of scientific fraud is hard to exaggerate, the fact that all observations are open to verification by others means that fraudulent findings that are published will not permanently derail efforts to arrive at the truth (Silberner, 1982). Recall from Chapter 1 the discussion of verifiability as a key feature of the scientific method. Erroneous information (whether intended or accidental) may slow the accumulation of scientific knowledge, but it does not stop it.

Methods for Minimizing Scientific Fraud

Because most documented instances of scientific fraud (i.e., those in the fields of biology and medicine) involved young researchers, three suggestions have been offered for minimizing such fraud (Norman, 1984). First, as part of their college training, student researchers need to be closely supervised by those who have more-established careers, in which the importance of complete disclosure of findings is emphasized. Even results that are contrary to expectations should not be simply swept under the rug. Second, young researchers should be encouraged to present preliminary findings at review sessions and seminars to obtain feedback and encouragement. Through these presentations, researchers

BOX 3.1 CURRENT ISSUES

Who Should Be Held Responsible for Scientific Fraud?

One problem with disclosing cases of possible fraud is that the individuals who bring charges and the journals that publish their charges risk being sued for libel if the charges cannot be proven (Culliton, 1988b). One lingering issue surrounding scientific fraud pertains to the responsibility for instituting, enforcing, and investigating fraud charges. Should colleges, universities, and hospitals where research is being conducted take responsibility or should federal (or other) agencies that provide funding for the research? Under current guidelines, the institution at which the research took place holds the primary responsibility for investigating charges of fraud (Dong, 1991). What should be done with the author(s) who committed the fraud? Should they have to publish an apology? Be banned from conducting and publishing research for a period of time? Most journals today require authors to agree to releasing data for verification if requested. Sometimes, after a data set has been collected and the results published, interested researchers who had nothing to do with data collection may ask for access to the data for the purpose of verifying results. How should the original researcher respond to such a request? Often researchers do not want to give others the data they have spent so much time and effort in collecting. In the 1990s, the US congress passed a law mandating data sets that federal funding helped researchers collect to be shared with other researchers for the purpose of verifying the analysis. The law allows the researcher who collected the data exclusive access for 5 years, but beyond that time, the data should be considered public domain. Again, this applies only to data collected using federal funds. Obviously, fraud can be very destructive to the scientific process. Therefore, it is important to do all that is reasonable to prevent it. Thus far, the involvement of social scientists in fraud appears to be minimal.

learn that not all scientific findings are spectacular or easy to comprehend. Nonetheless, they can still be very important in the long term. Third, young researchers need to understand the importance of keeping accurate records of all observations and maintaining these records beyond the time the final report was written. By following this policy, researchers will need to rely less on memory and will be able to document findings whenever questions arise.

Ethics in Criminology and Criminal Justice Research

Ethical issues in research on criminal justice topics abound. Crime and criminals are very interesting topics of study; however, you can imagine the confidentiality issues that may arise when studying individuals who engage in criminal or delinquent behavior. Many of the subjects of self-report surveys discussed in Chapter 6 ask individuals to report on their delinquent or criminal behavior. Researchers conducting these surveys have to be sure that confidentiality or anonymity is afforded these individuals in order for them to fill out the questionnaire truthfully but also to protect their identities. Many researchers who study "subcultural" groups like gangs must also maintain the confidentiality of the group. Some research conducted in criminal justice could even be dangerous. Researchers again must balance the need for scientific knowledge with their ethical principles and safety.

Responsibilities to Humanity

Another ethical responsibility that researchers need to consider regarding their research is toward humanity in general. Judging the proper course to take in this regard is driven to a substantial degree by sociopolitical ideology, and, like people in general, researchers are not of one mind when it comes to ideology. Some of the most heated controversies with sociopolitical implications have had to do with nature–nurture issues. These issues have focused particularly on gender differences in interests and behavior along with racial/ethnic differences in academic performance and ability. Some researchers have proposed that the differences that have been documented have substantial biological and genetic causes, while others attribute all of the group variations in these traits to sociocultural factors. Raising these issues here is not for the purpose of offering proposals for their resolution but to acknowledge that they have profound ethical implications. For example, if it should be established that biological factors are partly responsible for males being more inclined to sexually assault women than vice versa (Thornhill & Palmer, 2000), different attitudes toward rapists would be more likely than if the causes are due to living in patriarchal societies. Similarly, if evidence should indicate that the only reasons for racial variations in average academic performance have to do with family

BOX 3.2 WHAT DO YOU THINK?

Should Knowledge Gained from Research on Crime and Criminality Be Used to Promote Responses Focused on Equality, or Should Research Be Conducted Regardless of Its Implications?

There is some debate among criminologists about the causes for differences in behavior. Some who do research in this area believe their knowledge should be used to help promote human equality and consider any research that suggests that groups of people are inherently different an anathema to such goal. Researchers with such an egalitarian philosophy would be unlikely to conduct research designed to identify any biological underpinnings of behavior. They might even choose to suppress supportive findings inadvertently obtained. On the other hand, researchers who believe most strongly in "knowledge for its own sake" regardless of any ideological implications would be more likely to conduct research that could suggest a role for biology in explaining group differences in behavior (Gordon, 1993). Some of these researchers may even relish the idea that sex and racial/ethnic groups differ as a result of biological factors and thus go out of their way to conduct research supporting their ideology. What does this comingling of scientific and sociopolitical agendas mean with respect to research ethics? Ultimately, part of the answer will depend upon one's own ideology. Nevertheless, in considering the ethical issues, students of research methods need to be aware of the sociopolitical undercurrent that pervades many important topics addressed by social and behavioral scientists.

and cultural traditions, or neighborhood and school environments, public policy would not be the same as if genetic and neurological factors are partly to blame (Gottfredson, 1994).

⊜ Summary

Since the formation of the social sciences in the 1800s, researchers have had to confront many ethical issues. These issues include drawing the line between acceptable and unacceptable methods of treating research participants and of storing data that have been collected. Other ethical issues have involved many aspects of conduct within the research community itself. Regarding participant treatment, they should be assured that personal information will not go beyond the researchers directly involved in the research (except in aggregated form). Confidentiality can be best assured when subjects are allowed to provide information anonymously. Other methods of keeping information confidential were also discussed. Informed consent means that persons are aware of the basic nature of the study and have agreed to participate in the research study in light of that knowledge. Such consent is especially important for experimental research and should be obtained in writing. If participants are completing anonymous questionnaires, informed consent is normally inferred by the fact that they completed the questionnaire, provided they are explicitly told that they are free to not answer any questions they choose.

Most of the potential harm to subjects of social science research is of an emotional nature, rather than of a physical or health nature. Guidelines for minimizing such harm were presented. Regarding deception, two forms are recognized: deception by omission and orchestrated deception. In many instances, subjects cannot be given complete information about the nature of a study until after the data have been collected. This is deception by omission and is considered a permissible component in studies where valid data could not be collected otherwise. In the case of orchestrated deception, where researchers specifically seek to mislead subjects, some ethicists have declared all forms to be unacceptable. Others, however, prefer to consider the purpose of the research and weigh the nature of the deception against the potential benefits in terms of the knowledge gained.

Since the 1970s, most universities and hospitals have established committees that oversee the research being conducted. In the United States, these committees are known as Institutional Review Boards (IRBs) and in Great Britain and its commonwealths, they are called Research Ethics Committees (RECs). Criminologists and those studying the criminal justice system confront many ethical issues because the persons they are interested in studying have usually either committed, or been victim of, some type of criminal offense. Researchers in our field thus have to think carefully about issues related to confidentiality of participant identities and information collected and be aware of the sensitivity and emotional strain that might be attached to the types of information we solicit from persons.

The ethical responsibilities that researchers have toward one another involve honestly representing the nature of whatever is found. Intentional misrepresentation of findings constitutes scientific fraud, and presenting someone else's writings as one's own is considered plagiarism. Studies indicate that young researchers are more likely to engage in fraud and plagiarism than older researchers. Intentional faking of a research finding is difficult to prove, and for this reason it may be far more prevalent than will ever be known. As to why scientists fake their findings, the motives have to do with the desire for recognition for making significant discoveries and competition for grants. For whatever reasons, there are more well-established examples of scientific fraud in the fields of biology and medicine than in the social sciences.

A few methods were identified for helping to minimize scientific fraud. These include providing greater supervision of young researchers. Also discussed was the need for more cooperation among scientists to allow for the examination and reanalysis of each other's data.

The final topic addressed in this chapter concerned ethical responsibilities that scientists have toward humanity in general. Such responsibilities are obviously important, but their fulfillment depends to a considerable degree on what individuals believe to be the best outcome for the future of humankind. Those whose primary goal is for greater human equality often choose not to address questions that could imply that humans are not biologically equal. This has been especially true in research on sex and racial/ethnic differences in behavior. Those whose goals for humanity include accepting inequality as inevitable are more likely to feel comfortable conducting research that focuses on the biological foundations for sex and racial/ethnic differences in behavior. In the middle are social scientists with a commitment to a "knowledge for its own sake" approach. In the final analysis, there is no easy solution to the ethical issues surrounding how humanity as a whole should be served by social science research.

Discussion Questions

1. What components of Milgram's mock prison study do you think were the most unethical? Do you think researchers should be able to replicate this today by conducting similar studies? If you could get IRB approval to conduct a study like Milgram's, what would be two of your most compelling arguments as to why this research is still important today?

2. What do you believe are the most pressing ethical issues in criminal justice research involving offender and incarcerated populations? What would you propose to best minimize these issues if you were to create some guidelines for researchers who want to study these populations?

3. Discuss the difference between confidentiality and anonymity and the ways in which assurances of these can be met for participants of research.

4. What are certificates of confidentiality, and how to they protect researchers? Further, who is authorized to issue them?

5. Do you think that some deception in research studies is okay in order to gain knowledge about certain types of human attitudes and behaviors? If yes, what in your mind are the best ways to minimize potential risks to participants where deception is part of a study?

Exercises

1. Go to the office of research home page for your university and discover the steps needed to apply for a research study approved by the Institutional Review Board (IRB). Do the steps seem reasonable or arduous? Ask one of your instructors about their experiences with the IRB and whether or not they had to change a project considerably due to ethical considerations raised by the IRB.

2. Go to the Department of Health and Human Services web page at https://www.hhs.gov/ohrp/regulations-and-policy/belmont-report/index.html and read the Belmont Report. Also watch the video related to the Belmont Report. Based on your reading and viewing, which parts of the report do you think are especially critical for researchers who want to study offender or incarcerated populations?

Chapter 4

Theories, Models, Hypotheses, and Empirical Reality

Criminologists use many different kinds of research tools to study crime and criminality. At the heart of most of their research endeavors are conceptual tools known as criminological theories. These theories put forth plausible explanations for understanding the causes of criminal offending. Accompanying theories are other conceptual tools, known as hypotheses and models, that assist in helping researchers to test these plausible explanations with empirical data from the real world. This chapter explores the nature of these conceptual tools and the important roles they play in assisting researchers to better understand human behavior.

Conducting scientific research can be an end in itself, but often scientists would like to add what they have learned from a study into the existing knowledge in their particular discipline. Being able to do so can assist in moving the field forward, advancing understanding of specific topics, and spurring other researchers to undertake further studies in the area or formulate new questions to be answered. The integration of knowledge from dozens, and sometimes even hundreds, of individual studies and then using such knowledge to predict future events involves constructing and testing theories, which are the cornerstone of scientific research (Schofield & Coleman, 1986). This chapter will discuss how theories (and related concepts) help to integrate and guide scientific research.

⊜ The Concept of Causation

Causation is central to scientific theorizing; this is especially true in criminology. The concept of **causation** is difficult to precisely define, in part, because it covers a wide range of phenomena. Nevertheless, if we say that variable A is a cause of variable B, we mean that variable A precedes variable B in time and that variable A is nearly always present wherever variable B is present. Complicating this picture is the fact that most variables are not simply present or absent but present to widely varying degrees. Furthermore, effects often result not from just one causal variable but from two or more variables that need to be accounted for or are possibly interacting to effect the dependent variable.

About the only thing that is true of all causal variables is that they must precede an event or behavior to be considered as having an effect on it. In other words, the way the universe is conceptualized means that it is impossible for an effect to precede a cause; the cause must precede the effect. This time order may be difficult to establish, especially when you are studying something such as criminal behavior. Consider Edwin Sutherland's (1939) Differential Association theory, which at a very rudimentary level proposed that all behavior, including criminal behavior, is learned and that it is learned through interaction with others. In other words, if you have delinquent or criminal friends, you will have a higher likelihood of engaging in delinquent or criminal behavior yourself. The theory that Sutherland, who is considered by some to be the father of positivistic criminology (which is the idea that in order to explain crime, one needs to collect data in the real world via measuring both cause and effect variables),

proposed is obviously much more complex than this, but how would a researcher establish that a particular individual began chumming around with some bad apples and this is what led to their engagement in criminal activity? Could it also be that something else led the individual to engage in the criminal activity, and throughout the course of offending he or she met some other offenders? Which came first, the criminal friends or the criminal behavior? Which is the cause and which is the effect? As you can see, establishing cause is not as easy as it might seem; however, criminologists follow some fairly strict rules for ascertaining cause-effect relationships and determining that the cause indeed preceded the effect and not vice versa. Being able to study a group of individuals over long periods of time assists with this, but the concept of *causation* is fraught with many complexities, and much effort has been expended in attempting to understand cause-effect relationships in predicting criminal behavior. As such, we cannot stress enough the importance of this concept in science. At the heart of most scientific theories are proposals about how variables are connected in causal sequences.

⊜ The Nature of Scientific Theorizing

The word *theory* often denotes something that might be a possible explanation for a phenomenon. Theories are therefore not facts. Statements such as "Oh, that's just a theory" imply that theories may not be based in truth. As this chapter will show, however, theories and empirical reality can be interrelated in ways that make it possible to understand why or how someone got involved in criminal offending. To begin to understand the importance of the role theory plays in criminological research, consider the following question: If a theory is not a fact (which it is not), why have criminologists expended great time and effort to propose theories of crime? To answer this question, a few basic scientific definitions are needed. A **theory** is a set of logically related statements from which a number of hypotheses may be derived (Taylor & Frideres, 1972). A **hypothesis** is a statement about empirical reality that may or may not be true. Unfortunately, the words *theory* and *hypothesis* are sometimes used interchangeably (McBroom, 1980; Laughlin, 1991). But they are not the same: A theory would offer an explanation for why such a hypothesis might or might not be true and would lead to additional testable hypotheses. Theories themselves cannot be tested, but the hypotheses derived from them can be.

Levels of Abstraction

Theories can also be thought of in terms of their levels of abstraction (Short, 1997). A theory as to why an increase in a particular crime happened in a certain city over a couple of years would be at a much lower level of abstraction than a theory intended to explain all crime in all places at all times. Criminologists are continually striving to understand the empirical reality of crime at higher and higher levels of abstraction. Indeed, Sutherland's (1939) Differential Association theory, as well as others (see Gottfredson and Hirschi's (1990), *A General Theory of Crime*) were proposed as general theories that could explain crime in different places and at different times. Because of this, both of these theories have been the subject of much research and have garnered considerable empirical support as well. In the last three decades, criminologists have made several attempts to test these theories in many different countries across the globe via a cross-national self-report survey called the International Self-Report Delinquency Survey, or ISRD (Junger-Tas, Marshall, & Ribeaud, 2003; Junger-Tas & Marshall, 2012). These surveys have found support for some of the so-called general theories in many countries having widely different types of societies according to values, cultures, and economic structures (Junger-Tas, 2012).

BOX 4.1 CURRENT ISSUES

What Is Truth?

In science, and in criminology, the concept of *truth* can be slippery. Despite the fact that research projects are partly a quest for the truth about the causes of criminal behavior, there is also a saying that findings from one study alone does not constitute truth. As a result, many scientists avoid using the term except in casual discourse. To the degree *truth* has meaning in science, it applies to hypotheses, not to theories. This is because, by definition, a theory cannot be directly tested and found to be true. A theory's truth can only be inferred if it leads to many hypotheses that are found to be true or supported.

Many studies have been found to support Sutherland's Differential Association theory; in other words, some of the hypotheses stemming from the theory have been found to be true in reality using empirical data. This is also the case for several other theories such as Strain theory (Merton, 1938), Social Control theory (Hirschi, 1969), and Self-Control theory (Gottfredson & Hirschi, 1990). So, which of these theories is correct in its assumptions about the true nature of crime causation? To some degree, they all are, and criminologists are always adding pieces to the puzzle of what we know about the causes of crime. As such, you will not likely hear a criminologist declare the hypothesis of *having delinquent friends being related to engaging in delinquency* to be true. Instead, he or she would (and should) state something to the effect that "a great deal of evidence supports such a hypothesis." Why so much caution? Because criminologists have not yet seen the findings from a future study, and a prudent scientist is always open to future contrary (or at least qualifying) evidence. Once a person states that "such-and-such is true," in principle, he or she is no longer open to additional evidence unless it supports his or her conclusion.

To be clear, the truth is our knowledge plus our ignorance. In other words, the truth is what we know plus some things we do not know, and criminologists slowly add bits and pieces of what they find to this knowledge base. To some degree, we may never fully get to the complete truth about crime causation, but we can lessen our ignorance, or the part we don't know, by continuing to study and conduct research on the causes of crime. Human behaviors are very complex, and so completely understanding them is a difficult endeavor. There are probably many reasons why different persons commit crime, so it might be difficult to pinpoint one or more things that are responsible in every individual case. The reasons might also vary depending on the type of crime being studied. More recently, criminologists have combined, or integrated, different theories in tests of crime causation and have made some interesting discoveries related to ideas that two different theories could both be influential in predicting criminal behavior.

Assessing the Merit of a Theory

Because the concept of "truth" cannot be applied to theories (although it may be applied in casual scientific discussions), "good" theories are said to have merit. The merit of a theory can be judged on the basis of six criteria: predictive accuracy, predictive scope, simplicity, falsifiability, compatibility, and aesthetic appeal.

Predictive accuracy, the most important basis for assessing a theory's merit, involves how accurately it predicts what researchers observe. If a theory does a poor job of predicting empirical reality, hypotheses are not supported; the theory is said to have little merit. In general, the assessment of a theory's predictive accuracy comes slowly. This may be because it takes time for tests of new theories to occur and because empirical observations may be difficult to make. Also, if erroneous results are obtained by any of the earlier studies (due to invalid measurements of one of the key variables, for example), the theory may be assumed to lack merit, thus discouraging other researchers from bothering to test hypotheses derived from it.

Predictive scope refers to the number of hypotheses that can be accurately predicted by a theory. Thus, if two competing theories accurately predict the same number of hypotheses, their predictive scope would be equivalent. Suppose that two imaginary criminological theories (theory A and theory B) have 4 hypotheses each, and that both theories accurately predict hypotheses 1, 2, and 3. However, unlike theory A, theory B also accurately predicts hypothesis 4. Thus, theory B would be considered to have more merit than theory A. We have used imaginary theories in this example because in the "real world," criminological theories are much more complicated. For instance, one theory may be able to generate many more hypotheses or emphasize certain of its postulations (for which hypotheses can be constructed) than another. Another possibility is that some hypotheses may be confirmed by one study but refuted by others. The bottom line is that the more hypotheses that a theory can generate that are found to be true, the greater its predictive scope will be.

Notwithstanding the discussion of predictive scope, sometimes simplicity is a beneficial attribute. Suppose for example that two theories are essentially equal in predictive accuracy and scope, but one is much easier to understand than the other. In this case, the theory that is easier to understand would be considered to have more merit. This criterion of simplicity in scientific terms has also been referred to as **parsimony** and **Occam's razor**. This latter term credits an 18th-century philosopher named William of Occam, who devoted much of his professional career to trying to distill scientific theories proposed by others down to their core principles (Dewsbury, 1984). Occam's razor, therefore, is a principle that encompasses the idea that the simplest explanation is the best one.

Theories can never be proved true in a strict empirical sense. If a theory could be proved, it would no longer be a theory! Nevertheless, theories vary in how easily they can be *dis*proved or falsifiable. **Falsifiability** or an absence of ambiguity is important because it demonstrates that a theory can be tested and shown to be false, or not supported with empirical data. In other words, the best one can say about a scientific theory is that it has not yet been disproved. Obviously, a theory can be so ambiguous that is impossible to disprove (Shearing, 1973). An ambiguous theory, however, is not considered to have merit because it is not *vulnerable* to disproof (Lakatos, 1970). Theories that are very precise in terms of leading to many testable hypotheses are said to have the greatest degree of *falsifiability*, and falsifiability is a very important element in a well-formulated scientific theory (Ember & Ember, 1988:197).

Assume that you have two competing theories of the same phenomenon, neither one of which has been well tested yet. However, one theory is compatible with other theories of related phenomena that have been found to generate accurate hypotheses, and the other theory is not compatible with these other theories. In this case, all else being equal, the first theory would be considered better than the second due to its greater **compatibility**.

Many of the world's most theoretically oriented scientists have reported that one criterion they use to develop confidence in their theories involves a sense of beauty, or **aesthetic appeal** (Forward, 1980; Chandrasekhar, 1987). An aesthetic sense alone is not very helpful for scientifically explaining the empirical world, but when combined with the other components of merit, an aesthetic sense can be valuable in theory construction. Ultimately, theory construction provides an arena in which science and artistic creativity often embrace (Judson, 1980).

⬯ The Role of Theory in the Research Process

Because scientific theories exist at levels of abstraction beyond what can be empirically verified, the only way theories can be tested is by deriving hypotheses from them and then testing these hypotheses. Figure 4.1 provides a rough sketch of how theories and hypotheses fit into the scientific research process. Beginning at the top and proceeding clockwise, we assume that a theory has been proposed. Then, one or more hypotheses are derived from a particular theory. The hypotheses are then empirically tested, and on the basis of those tests, generalizations are made about the nature of reality. From these generalizations, scientists sometimes fine-tune the original theory; at other times, they may replace it with another theory. Thereby, new rounds of hypotheses testing can be set into motion. In reality, things are much more complex and chaotic than Figure 4.1 implies, as the process of testing several different theories often proceeds over the course of several decades.

A useful way to think about scientific theories is that they are like fruit trees. In the case of trees, those that bear eatable fruit are better than those that are barren or produce fruit that is rotten or unpalatable. For scientific theories, those that lead to the greatest number of hypotheses are better (have more merit) than theories that make few if any testable predictions. Of course, if most of the hypotheses generated by a theory fail to be confirmed empirically, that is not good news for the theory either. So, for a scientific theory to be deemed to have merit, it should generate many empirically testable hypotheses, all (or nearly all) of which should be confirmed.

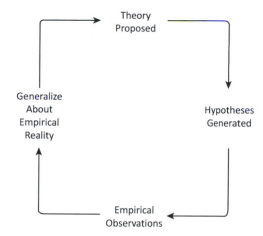

FIGURE 4.1   A Simplified Diagram Illustrating the Idealized Interrelationship between Scientific Theories, Hypotheses, Empirical Observations, and Generalizations

● Scientific Models, Laws, and Paradigms

In scientific theorizing, the term **model** is usually used to refer to some type of simplified representation of some aspect of a theory, although some have used the terms *model* and *theory* interchangeably (Hall & Hirschman, 1991). Even the concepts of *model* and *hypothesis* have been used as if there were no difference between them (Ekman, 1990). Here, distinctions among these three concepts—theories, models, and hypotheses—will be maintained. The distinction between a model and a theory is as follows: Whereas a theory puts forth an explanation in linguistic form, a model puts forth an explanation in a more tangible/physical form. In addition, a model is often used to illustrate and clarify one or more special aspects of a theory, rather than representing a theory in its entirety (Sienko & Plane, 1976). Three types of models are used in the social sciences: diagrammatic (or structural) models, equational models, and animal models.

A **diagrammatic** (or **structural**) **model** is one in which a geometric sketch (or sometimes an actual physical object) is used to help illustrate a theory. An **equational** (or **mathematical**) **model** is most commonly found in the physical sciences such as physics and astronomy, but a few examples from the social sciences can be given. Probably the most far-reaching equation used by social scientists was one first proposed in the 1960s by an American biologist named William Hamilton (1963, 1964). He proposed an equation to help explain altruism, which refers to self-sacrificing behavior by one individual on behalf of another. Careful observations have revealed that altruistic behavior is found not only in humans, but in many other social animals as well (Hebb & Thompson, 1954; Krebs, 1971). The most frequently documented cases of altruism involve the committed care and protection by parents on behalf of their offspring (Wittenberger, 1981:75).

Hamilton's formula for altruism was initially inspired by the observation that worker honeybees (who are sterile females) will selflessly die in defense of the hive. The theory on which the formula rests is an updated version of Darwin's theory of evolution (i.e., one incorporating genetic concepts). This neo-Darwinian theory implies that worker bees are genetically so similar to the queen (who is their sister) that workers have evolved the propensity to sacrifice themselves on behalf of the queen, and thereby ensure the perpetuation of their own genes. In other words, even though the worker bees are sterile, they are able to transmit their genes to future generations by assisting the queen in her very prolific reproduction. According to Hamilton's model, reproducing indirectly by helping close relatives reproduce has given rise to altruism in many species. He termed this phenomena **kin selection** as an extension of what Darwin termed **natural selection** (Brown, 1991).

Hamilton expressed his theory with the following equation:

$$P(\text{altruism}) = b_t\,(r) > c$$

where

$P(altruism)$ represents the probability of altruism

b_t is the potential reproductive benefit for an altruistic act

r is the degree of genetic relatedness between an altruist and a potential recipient

c is the probable reproductive cost (or risk) to the prospective altruist

This equation suggests that the probability of an altruistic act being exhibited by one animal toward another depends in part on the number of genes they share in common and the potential of the recipient of the altruistic act to subsequently transmit these genes to future generations (Peck & Feldman, 1988). Another factor is the risk to the altruist, with the highest risk being reserved for recipients with the closest genetic relatedness.

Most other equational models in the social sciences are found in the fields of economics and demography. Equational models have been developed for predicting upswings and downturns in national economies (Bradley et al., 1993), and shifts in societal birth and death rates (Hapke, 1972; Ahlburg, 1986; de Beer, 1991). Most of these models are derived from empirical information that certain variables tend to rise and fall in a specific pattern and/or that they tend to follow increases and decreases in other variables.

An **animal model** results from locating behavior in various nonhuman animal species that appears to resemble some aspect of human behavior. The methods are used to demonstrate that some type of behavior is at least roughly equivalent across various species. They usually involve combining science with intuition, similar to the processes surrounding the assessment of a measure's validity and reliability. Whether the causes of offending in humans are in any way similar to the causes of the modeled behavior in other species is an empirical question requiring research attention.

BOX 4.2 WHAT DO YOU THINK?

Can Criminologists Learn about the Nature or Causes of Crime from Nonhuman Species?

Go to https://digg.com/video/chimpanzee-war-cannibalism and watch the video. This video shows examples of "virtual criminal offenses" in nonhuman species. Videos like these of the animal kingdom have on many occasions captured behavior that in humans would be considered assault and homicide. Capturing these occurrences in other species reinforces the idea that a nonlegal equivalent of crime may exist outside the human species (Ellis, 1998). Whether the causes of offending in humans are in any way similar to the causes of the modeled behavior in other species is an empirical question requiring research attention. Could studying seemingly criminal behavior in animals help us understand the causes of offending in humans? Thinking back to Chapter 3, what ethical issues may or may not arise from studying subjects that are nonhuman? Although animal models might assist criminologists in understanding human behavior, the uniqueness of each species should always be recognized. For example, we probably share more likeness to primates and other animals than say rodents such as mice or rats. Overall, researchers should recognize and guard against overgeneralizing across species and should certainly never equate humans and other animals (Abelson, 1992). Also, simply because animal models appear to exist for many aspects of human behavior, models for many other aspects of human behavior may never be found. Finally, keep in mind that not all social scientists who study other animals do so to better understand humans. The study of behavior of nonhuman animals can be fascinating and informative in its own right.

Three factors are responsible for the use of animal models in the social sciences and criminology. First, researchers are under fewer ethical restraints when performing experiments on nonhumans than on humans, although there are bodies equivalent to IRBs for overseeing research involving animals. Second, it has become increasingly apparent that humans and other animals share a common biological heritage with one another (including similarly configured brains). This suggests that science can learn a great deal about human behavior by studying the behavior of other species (Relethford, 1990; Alcock, 1993). Third, because the causes of human behavior are usually more complex, it is often easier to identify some of the most basic causes of a behavior pattern in nonhumans before giving full attention to humans (Alonso et al., 1991). Nevertheless, cross-species parallels can always be overdrawn and must always be tempered with the realization that all species are at least somewhat unique.

Scientific Laws

A concept that can be distinguished from a scientific theory is that of a **scientific law**. A scientific law is a statement about what should always occur under a precise set of conditions. The best known scientific laws come from the physical sciences, such as Newton's law of gravity. This law states that the speed of an object in free fall (possible only in a complete vacuum) will accelerate at a very specific rate. There are no commonly recognized laws in the social sciences. Why? The main reason is that under current understanding, both individual and collective behavior are so complex as to defy prediction with the degree of precision expected of scientific laws (Coleman, 1964).

The difference between a scientific law and a scientific theory is that a law offers no specific explanation for what it is intended to predict. Scientific laws are merely statements about what will be observed under a specific set of conditions. Hypotheses are like laws except that hypotheses are usually tested within much broader limits of probability than is the case for scientific laws.

Scientific Paradigms

In the early 1960s, Thomas Kuhn (1962) published a widely read philosophy of science book in which he argued that scientists in each major discipline usually work for decades without agreeing on a common paradigm. A **paradigm** refers to a set of assumptions about the nature of the phenomenon to be explained and the approach that will be taken to obtain those explanations (Simberloff, 1976). Paradigms are best thought of as being more general and encompassing than theories; in fact, they are the broadest perspective within which all theories are thought to emanate.

Kuhn contended that at some point during its preparadigm stage, a discipline will have accumulated enough basic knowledge that someone within the discipline will propose a new perspective that will spark a paradigmatic revolution. This revolution may last for decades but will sooner or later transform the discipline into what Kuhn called normal science. By this, Kuhn meant that nearly all the scientists working in a particular discipline will settle on a common approach to the understanding of the phenomena they study.

Scientists in most of the physical sciences seem to have had their paradigmatic revolution and have now settled into normal science (McCann, 1978). This means that the main disputes among physicists, chemists, and the like are no longer about how to approach their disciplines but about detailed substantive issues. What about the social sciences and criminology? Most students only need to take courses from more than one instructor to know that the social sciences are all still in the preparadigm stage of development (Bauer, 1992).

⊖ Hypothesis Testing and Attempts to Generalize

Having made distinctions among scientific hypotheses, theories, and models, we can return to a discussion of hypothesis testing. In every study, two opposing hypotheses can be tested: a **research** (or **alternative**) **hypothesis** and a **null hypothesis**. Even though scientists are nearly always more interested in testing a research hypothesis than an opposing null hypothesis, the latter is always being tested by implication. Let us now extend the concept of hypothesis testing by illustrating how researchers go beyond testing specific hypotheses and attempt to make sweeping theoretical generalizations.

Universes as a Whole, Local Universes, and Samples

Suppose a particular theory leads a researcher to expect that females will have some characteristic (trait X) to a greater average degree than males. Furthermore, assume that the theory implies that trait X should be higher for females than for males not only in a few contemporary societies but for *all* times and in *all* societies. The implication then is that the universe (or population) referenced by this particular theory includes all humans throughout the world who have ever lived and will ever live.

Such a theory would be desirable from the standpoint of its theoretical merit because its predictive scope would be very broad. However, consider the difficulties one would have in testing this theory. Obviously, it would be impossible to draw a random sample from the entire universe. The best a researcher can do will be to draw samples from a few societies during the three or four decades of his or her career. Such sampling limitations confine a researcher to what is called the local universe, as opposed to the universe as a whole. In other words, even though the theory is stated very broadly in terms of the universe as a whole, all efforts to test it will be based on samples drawn from local universes. The distinction between a universe as a whole and samples drawn from a local universe is illustrated in Figure 4.2. Notice that other researchers working at other periods of time or in other areas of the world can assist in testing the generality of the theory by sampling other local universes. Through this process, the full extent to which the theory does or does not reflect empirical reality can be gradually assessed. Nevertheless, because of

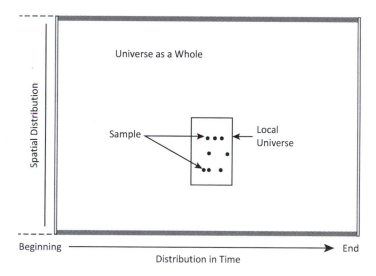

FIGURE 4.2 A Diagrammatic Representation of the Concepts of a Universe as a Whole, a Local Universe, and a Sample

the haphazard and opportunistic nature of sampling, a broad-ranging scientific theory can never be fully tested, even if all the samples happen to have been representative of the local universes from which they were selected.

To reiterate an important point about hypothesis testing, many scientific theories relate to universes that are much broader in time and space than any one researcher can ever hope to sample. Nonetheless, each sample drawn from a local universe to test one of the theory's hypotheses is valuable. After dozens of studies of several hypotheses derived from a theory, scientists are usually in a fairly good position to pass judgment upon the merit of a particular theory.

The Null Hypothesis and Type I and Type II Errors

Building on the concept of hypothesis testing, two types of error with reference to the null hypothesis need to be recognized. Recall that the null hypothesis is a standard benchmark hypothesis that asserts that there is no difference or no relationship with respect to whatever is being studied. The two possible errors are known as *type I error* and *type II error*, and they are illustrated in Figure 4.3. A **type I error** involves rejecting the null hypothesis when it is in fact true, and a **type II error** is defined as accepting the null hypothesis when it is actually false. (To keep them straight, students may want to memorize the nonsense rhyme *Type I reject null, type II accept null.*)

These two concepts underscore the inherent fallibility of the scientific process as individual hypotheses are tested. As you will learn in Chapter 13, when scientists test hypotheses, they normally risk up to a 5% chance of

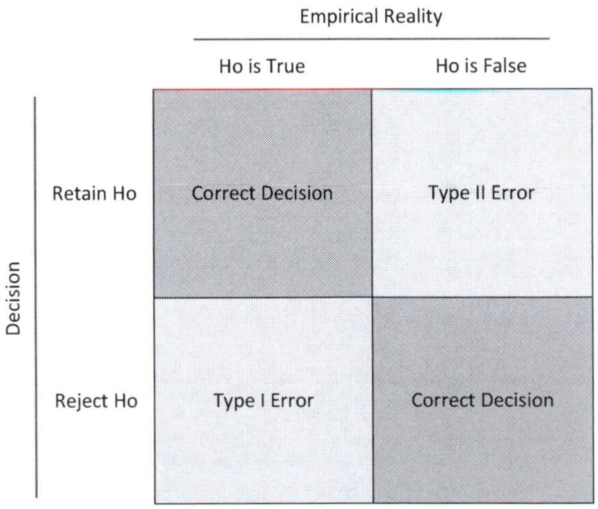

	Empirical Reality	
	Ho is True	Ho is False
Retain Ho	Correct Decision	Type II Error
Reject Ho	Type I Error	Correct Decision

Decision

FIGURE 4.3   A Diagrammatic Representation of a Researcher's Options concerning the Null Hypothesis (H_o) and the Possible Outcome of Each Decision

Source: Adapted by authors from Arney (1990).

making an erroneous decision about the acceptance/rejection of a hypothesis. (In other words, we are willing to risk that 5 times out of 100, we may have made an error in accepting or rejecting the null.) It is this degree of risk that is denoted by type I and type II errors. Despite the ever-looming risk that if one of these errors occurs every time a hypothesis is tested using a sample, scientists must bear in mind that no hypothesis stands or falls on the basis of a single study.

The bottom line of hypothesis testing is whether the hypothesis is derived from a theory as well as whether we have collected data (representative samples) in a systematic way. If not, such testing always has risks of leading to an erroneous inference. If one decides to reject the null hypothesis and accept some alternative, a type I error is being risked; if one decides to accept the null hypothesis, a type II error is being risked. The only way to avoid making these errors is to study the entire universe. For most phenomena of theoretical interest, the universe is much too large, both in time and space, to be studied in its entirety.

Closing Remarks Regarding Scientific Theorizing

It would be difficult to exaggerate the importance of theorizing and hypothesis testing in the social sciences generally and for criminology specifically. These concepts are at the heart of the scientific method. Theories help scientists integrate information that has already been learned, and they suggest new possibilities worth considering. Because most theories are highly abstract, hypotheses are used to connect theories to the "real world."

When compared to some of the physical sciences in which clear paradigms have formed, most social science theories currently pale. Recognition of the primitiveness of social or behavioral theories has led some to a feeling of what has been termed "physics envy," given that physics seems to represent the epitome of scientific sophistication and theoretical maturity. Nevertheless, progress is continually being made in criminal justice research with the results of thousands of hypotheses being reported every year. As these findings mount, theories are bound to become more elegant.

⬣ Summary

Scientific research can be conducted without any theoretical guidance, but the results of such research are often difficult to organize and interpret. Ultimately, theories make it easier for scientists to integrate and to comprehend findings from massive amounts of scientific research.

This chapter focused on illuminating the nature of scientific theorizing and hypothesis testing. It was noted that scientific theories are formulated to cover such a massive number of events that it is unrealistic to ever attempt to completely test these theories. Nevertheless, if several studies of several different hypotheses derived from a particular theory are confirmed, this can be considered substantial evidence in favor of a theory.

This chapter pointed out distinctions between such terms as empirical observations, hypotheses, and theories. If there are such things as "facts" in science, they are the empirical findings documented in research reports. But, unlike facts in ordinary discourse, *scientific* facts are tentative, always awaiting additional confirmation (or refutation) by those who conduct other studies.

Hypotheses are statements about empirical reality, which may or may not be true. Sometimes hypotheses come to a researcher "out of the blue," but generally they are derived from some theory. As suggested by Figure 4.1, a theory exists "above" empirical reality. Theories become connected to empirical reality when numerous hypotheses derived from them are confirmed by empirical observation.

Scientific theories are judged most importantly on their predictive accuracy and predictive scope. Other criteria are simplicity, falsifiability, and aesthetic appeal.

Scientific models include a host of special "tools" used by scientists to conceptualize reality. Although the terms *theories* and *models* are sometimes used interchangeably, a distinction is warranted. The most common difference is that theories are usually presented in linguistic form, whereas models are presented in some nonlinguistic form. Three categories of scientific models were identified: diagrammatic models, equational models, and animal models. Diagrammatic (or structural) models are presented in physical figures, including computer-generated models, such as in path analysis. Equational models use a mathematical equation to express a way of understanding some phenomenon or forecasting future events. Animal models have been used increasingly in the social sciences and criminology in recent years, partly because of growing evidence of the close genetic and neurological similarities between humans and other species (especially other mammals).

Scientific laws are statements that specify the conditions under which some outcome will occur. It was noted that scientific laws are rare in the social sciences relative to the physical sciences.

In hypothesis testing, two types of errors are possible, both of which are normally stated in terms of the benchmark null hypothesis. The type I error involves incorrectly rejecting the null hypothesis; the type II error involves incorrectly accepting the null hypothesis. Scientists typically risk no more than a 5% probability of making either of these errors when testing hypotheses.

⬤ Discussion Questions

1. What do you believe are the three most important criteria for assessing the merit of a theory? Explain why.

2. What are some differences between scientific models, scientific laws, and scientific paradigms?

3. Describe how the three categories of scientific models assist researchers to explain or express understanding of some phenomenon or forecasting future events.

4. Differentiate between type I and type II errors in research.

Exercises

1. Pick a contemporary criminological theory that has been the subject of a great deal of empirical research and use at least three of the criteria from the chapter to assess its merit.

2. Search for an article in one of your institution's journal databases using the terms "drug addiction" and "animal model" and read the article. In what ways do the researchers use animal models to explain drug use and addiction in human beings? Do you think this is a helpful method for understanding human behaviors?

Chapter 5

The Concepts of Reliability, Validity, and Precision in Measurement

Do you know any left-handers? Maybe, like one of the authors of this text, you're a lefty yourself. Here is a troubling bit of news: Most studies have indicated that left-handers are more likely to have been involved in criminal behavior than right-handers (Ellis et al., 2019:250). Is this true? In order to find out, one must be able to measure handedness and criminality in some objective and reasonably accurate ways. This chapter will explore issues related to the measurement of social science variables.

In Chapter 2, a distinction was made between **conceptually defining** and **operationally defining** variables. Recall that a conceptual definition simply uses other words to convey the meaning of a term, while an operational definition describes a set of empirical procedures that one goes through in order to measure a concept. Of course, one can have several different operational definitions (or operational measures) for the same variable. For example, criminal behavior might be measured using self-reports in one study while using official arrest data in another study. Both of these operational measures have come to be used because both have advantages and disadvantages in scientific research.

If there is more than one operational definition for a variable, it is reasonable and appropriate to ask which one is more accurate. How scientists go about answering such a question is the focus of this chapter. Criminal justice majors may wonder why they need to be concerned with measuring variables other than those directly related to criminal behavior or the functioning of the criminal justice system. There are three reasons. First, the better you understand behavior in general, the more you are likely to understand criminal behavior and the institutions that have been designed to deal with crime. Second, many of the variables that criminal justice researchers attempt to study in connection with criminal behavior are not crimes per se. For example, traits such as bullying, gang membership, and physical aggression during childhood and early adolescence are not crimes, but studies have shown that they are strongly correlated with criminality later in life (reviewed by Ellis et al., 2019:24). Third, as a part of the social science community, it is good for those in criminal justice to have a broad, rather than a narrow, focus. In this way, they can study criminality not as an isolated aspect of humanity, but as a condition that is intimately linked with many, if not most, other aspects of the human condition.

Using the Concept of Correlation to Discuss Measurement Accuracy

Many social science research methods are difficult to describe without invoking at least a few statistical concepts. Accuracy in the measurement of variables is one example. Therefore, before delving deeply into measurement accuracy, students should be aware of the concept of **correlation**. More will be said about this concept in Chapter 14, but a brief description is in order here. Correlation refers to how variables are related to one another, especially if those variables are measured on a continuous scale (e.g., from 1 to 10). To illustrate the concept of correlation, many studies have shown that having grown up in families with a lot of discord is positively correlated with involvement in delinquency and criminality (Ellis et al., 2019:181). In other words, individuals who grow up in discordant families (i.e., with lots of arguing, yelling, and overall failure to get along) appear to engage in more delinquency and crime than do persons growing up in families with little discordancy.

Research findings from studies of how these two variables—family discordancy and criminality—are related typically use some statistical terms. Let us consider these terms in very simple form: If the correlation (or relationship) between family discord and criminality were "perfect" (which it is not), one could simply measure the nature of someone's family discord and know *exactly* how many crimes he or she has committed. Thus, a "perfect" correlation is mathematically represented with the number 1.00. On the other hand, if there was absolutely no correlation between family and criminality, the number used to mathematically represent such a correlation would be 0.00. (Incidentally, scientists often represent correlations with the letter r, short for relationship.)

So, what is the *actual* correlation between risk-taking and criminality? In other words, what do empirical studies report the r to be? A recent statistical summary of the many relevant studies that have been published over the years concluded that the average correlation between family discord and involvement in crime (including delinquency) was $r = .27$ (Derzon, 2010:273). Such an "r" (also called a **correlation coefficient**) indicates that the relationship between family discord and engaging in crime is certainly greater than zero, although it is far from being "perfect." In more precise terms, one might describe an $r = .27$ as indicating that the correlation between family discord and criminality is "modest."

Overall, social scientists use correlations to describe and compare research findings more precisely than they could without the use of numbers. This chapter will include several references to correlation coefficients to help explain concepts having to do with accurately measuring variables.

⊖ Three Elements of Accurate Measurement

Measuring variables as accurately as is feasible is an important part of conducting research. Notice that we used the word "feasible" instead of "possible" because there are nearly always trade-offs that need to be considered. In other words, researchers must take the amount of time and effort that must be invested in order to obtain the information they are trying to get.

To give an example of compromises researchers must make in deciding how to measure variables, consider the variable of weight. What if a researcher were to simply ask each participant in a study their weight rather than asking them to stand on a scale? Even though weighing each participant would probably be more accurate, would it be worth the extra time and effort? An answer comes from a study of more than 16,000 Hispanic adults living in the United States. They were asked to self-report their weight and then were each individually weighed by the research team responsible for the study. The results from correlating these two measures of body weight was a correlation coefficient of $r = .97$ (Fernández-Rhodes et al., 2017). An earlier study likewise obtained a correlation of $r = .95$ between its self-report measure and its physical scale measure of body weight (Goodman et al., 2000). Similarly, a study in Japan obtained an $r = .98$ when self-reported weight was compared to weight determined by a physical scale (Yoshitake et al., 2012).

Nearly perfect correlations such as those between self-reported weight and objectively measured weight suggest that one gets essentially the same scores. So, if you were conducting research into which body weight is one of the variables that interests you, would you take the time to actually weigh each research participant or would you simply rely on self-reported weight? As you might suspect, most research that studies variables related to body weight will rely on self-reports unless having extremely accurate measurement is crucial for a particular study (or the study involves young children who may not know how much they weigh.)

Now consider research in the field of criminal justice. Say that a researcher wants to measure criminal behavior. Would self-report measures be just as accurate as self-report measures of body weight? Not only is this question harder to answer, but doing so requires delving into several issues having to do with measurement accuracy. Basically, one can think about measurement accuracy in science as consisting of three interrelated elements. These are referred to as reliability, validity, and precision. Each of these three concepts will be considered individually. However, as a prelude to doing so, students should keep in mind that terminology has never been fully standardized regarding these concepts, so one should not be surprised to find other sources identifying somewhat different definitions for reliability and validity measures and even giving them different names (Drost, 2011). Unless your instructor tells you otherwise, the terminology used here is what you should know for exam purposes.

⊖ Reliability

Reliability refers to the tendency for a variable to yield stable and consistent scores when it is being measured. Consider a silly example that again involves body weight. Say you stepped on a bathroom scale this morning, did it again this evening, and your reading in the evening was 20 pounds heavier than the reading you obtained in the morning. Obviously, you would suspect that it's time to buy a new scale, because no one gains 20 pounds in a single day. The same principle can be applied to measuring variables in the social sciences. Say, for example, that you are interested in studying traits associated with shoplifting, and you decide to use self-reports. To help ensure that people answer honestly, you would probably want to assure them that they can answer anonymously. However, for the sake of this illustration, assume that we are able to obtain responses from the same research participants on two different occasions, separated by a month. Of course, no researcher would expect perfect agreement between responses given by each individual due partly to faulty memory and maybe even to the possibility that another incidence of shoplifting occurred during the month-long interval between the two times data were collected. Nevertheless, one would still expect to find a reasonably high correlation between the responses given by the same individuals on the two occasions. If the correlation was low (e.g., say $r = .18$), one would have to suspect that there is something wrong with how you were asking your question. On the other hand, if you got a correlation of $r = .89$, this would give you considerable confidence that your information on shoplifting was fairly reliable. Now, let's focus on the issue of assessing reliability.

Ways of Assessing Reliability

There are four methods for making judgments about measurement reliability. These methods are known as test-retest reliability, cross-test reliability, intra-test reliability, and inter-rater reliability.

Test-retest reliability assesses how consistently similar scores are obtained with a specific testing procedure. The hypothetical example presented earlier regarding shoplifting would be an example of test-retest reliability. Another example of test-retest reliability involves a variable that has been frequently studied in connection with criminal behavior: the variable of boredom (Ellis et al., 2019:206). Back in the 1970s, a questionnaire was designed in part to measure people's variations in boredom susceptibility (Zuckerman, 1979). The researcher found that when a group of individuals were given the questions about their tendencies to be bored on two different occasions, separated by a 3-week interval, their scores were highly correlated (i.e., $r = .70$). A couple of decades later, a research team conducted a similar study on a different measure of boredom-proneness separated by a 1-week interval. This study obtained a correlation of $r = .83$ (Kass & Vodanovich, 1990). Both of these studies support the view that people's tendencies to be bored are fairly stable over time, at least over the course of a few weeks, and can be measured with reasonable confidence.

Another variable that has been repeatedly found associated with criminality and has been studied with regard to test-retest reliability is intelligence (Ellis et al., 2019:275-282). The test-retest reliability of most tests of intelligence has been shown to be quite high (Anastasi, 1976; Hunt, 1983). More precisely, researchers have typically obtained coefficients exceeding $r = .85$ when correlating standardized IQ test scores by subjects who take a test at 8 years of age and then repeat it at age 18 (reviewed by Sattler, 1982). Note that although these findings bode well for the reliability of standardized IQ tests, they leave open questions about the tests' validity.

Cross-test reliability correlates the results of two different operational measures of the same variable. If subjects who score high on one measure also score high on the other measure, and those who score low on one also score low on the other, researchers are encouraged to believe that both tests are reliable. Again, the higher the correlation coefficient, the greater the confidence from the standpoint of cross-test reliability. We can easily illustrate cross-test reliability using weight as a variable. A number of years ago, a British study mailed out a questionnaire in which respondents were asked to self-report their weight (among other variables). A few weeks later, they were invited to a medical clinic for further observation, at which time they were weighed on a standard scale. When the researchers correlated the self-report and the clinical scale measures, the resulting correlation was $r = .96$ (Charney et al., 1976). Obviously, this suggests that both of the two measures can be considered highly reliable and essentially substituted for one another.

Let's now consider a social science variable that has been frequently included in studies of delinquent and criminal behavior: high school grade point average (GPA). Research has consistently indicated that individuals with high GPAs are less involved in crime than those with low GPAs (Ellis et al., 2019:276-277). Because many studies of high school grades are based on self-reports, it has been worthwhile for social scientists to ask how consistent these reports are to *actual* grades. Several studies have examined this question by comparing self-reported GPAs with actual GPAs recorded by the high schools the individuals attended. Results have revealed that the correlations are fairly high, i.e., in the mid to upper .70s (Goldman et al., 1990; Hishinuma et al., 2001). Although these cross-test correlations (in the .70s) are certainly weaker than the cross-test correlations for measures of weight (in the .90s), nearly all social scientists would agree that correlations in the .70 range are "good enough" to justify continuing to use self-reported GPA in their research unless they are able to get actual recorded grades.

Intra-test reliability compares scores on part of a measure of some variable with scores on another part of the same measure. The most widely used form of this method is called the split-half method. To understand this method, consider a 30-item test designed to identify offspring who have at least one alcoholic parent. Two studies have taken the scores provided by college students on the 15 even-numbered items, totaled them, and correlated the results with the total scores for the 15 odd-numbered items (Jones, 1991; Charland & Cote, 1998). In both cases, the correlation coefficients were in the mid .90s, suggesting that the test has considerable intra-test reliability.

The fourth way of assessing reliability is called **inter-rater** (or **inter-judge**) **reliability**. It involves variables in which two or more judges offer independent assessments of a particular variable. For example, say you were interested in studying a trait that tends to be fairly common among grade school children: attention deficit hyperactivity disorder (ADHD). Incidentally, this trait has been found by numerous studies to be positively correlated with involvement in delinquency and crime later in life (Ellis et al., 2019:294).

So how would a scientist measure ADHD in children? One of the most common measurement strategies involves ratings by teachers. Are these ratings reliable? One study sought to make a determination by asking 8 teachers to observe 46 children and adolescents, and then provide ratings of each child's ADHD symptoms. The researchers then correlated each teacher's ratings of each child with the ratings provided by the other seven teachers. Correlation coefficients ranged from $r = .62$ to $r = .87$ (Danforth & DuPaul, 1996). In light of these findings, the researchers concluded that their measurement of ADHD symptoms was reasonably reliable.

How Reliable Does Reliability Have to Be?

An accepted rule is to consider correlation coefficients exceeding .75 to .80 as indicative of high reliability, at least for behavioral or social variables (Nunnally, 1978; Rossi & Freeman, 1989). In other words, using any of the four methods for assessing reliability, if you can obtain a correlation of .75 or greater, consider yourself lucky for most of the variables that criminologists or researchers in the social sciences study. If you fail to come close to a .75 correlation in assessing reliability, however, you should not assume that the measure is unreliable. Many reliable tests fail to yield a .75 test-retest correlation because many aspects of people's feelings and behavior are, in fact, unstable. People's attitudes toward political candidates in close elections, for example, may change at least a little from one news broadcast to another.

Consider a study undertaken to measure the prevalence of disruptive/ antisocial behavior exhibited by male institutionalized delinquents (Kelley, 1981). The researcher had dormitory counselors rate each juvenile twice, first at the end of one week and again at the end of three weeks of observations. The average rating given by the counselors between these two time frames was $r = .50$. Even though this coefficient is considerably less than .75, it is still indicative of acceptable reliability, given (a) the difficulty of each counselor to observe the subjects at the same time, and (b) the fact that presumably all subjects observed were on the high end of the disrupted/antisocial behavior continuum to begin with. In other words, had the rating method been used on a group of subjects exhibiting a wider range of disruptive behavior, the correlation probably would have been higher.

Students should know that a statistic can be used to estimate how well a set of items "fit together" into a single scale. It is known as **Cronbach alpha**. This statistic uses a formula for indicating how well items (or questions) seem to elicit similar response patterns by participants in a particular study. More information on Cronbach alpha can be obtained online or by consulting most statistics books.

⬤ Validity

Even though *validity* and *reliability* are related concepts, students should be able to distinguish between them. The essential difference is as follows: **Validity** refers to the degree that a variable is measuring what it is intended to

BOX 5.1 CURRENT ISSUES

Conceptualizing Intra-Test Reliability

Often, when variables are difficult to measure with just one question (or item), researchers will ask several questions that seem to "get at" the variable they are interested in, and then obtain an average score for all of the questions combined. At other times, they may give weights to each question reflecting how well each one seems to have a bearing on the variable. In either case, when one tries to measure a single variable with multiple items, the resulting measure is usually known as a scale. A major factor in determining the reliability of a scale is how well individual items comprising the scale correlate with one another ("hang together"). If all items in the scale are measuring the same trait in slightly different ways as they are intended to, they should be correlated with each other strongly.

Look at the four "fear of crime" items given in the following hypothetical scale. For each question, respondents were asked to answer in terms of five responses ranging from "not at all safe" to "extremely safe."

Item 1. How safe do you feel walking alone in your neighborhood during the day?

Item 2. How safe do you feel walking alone in your neighborhood after dark?

Item 3. How safe are children in the school zones closest to your neighborhood?

Item 4. How safe is the traffic activity in your neighborhood?

So, which of the four items would you expect to be the most strongly associated with any one of the other three? If you guessed item 1 and item 2, you would be correct, because these two items have the highest correlation coefficient. Now look at the following correlation matrix (a correlation matrix is simply an organized array of correlation coefficients). There you will see how each item is associated with each other item (based on a sample of persons answering a questionnaire). Accordingly, the correlation between item 1 and item 2 is indeed the strongest of all the correlations, but even this correlation is just $r = .399$. This is rather low (i.e., far less than 1.00, or a perfect correlation). Such a low correlation suggests that these two items are in fact not measuring the same variable. In fact, all four of these items appear to be measuring somewhat different variables, even though they are all still related to one another.

1. 2. 3. 4.

1. 1.000 .399 .212 .119

2. 1.000 .178 .224

3. 1.000 .262

4. 1.000

measure. *Reliability*, on the other hand, refers to the measurement of a variable yielding consistent results. For example, suppose you tried to measure people's tendencies to commit crime by asking them to stand on a bathroom scale and observing the readings multiple times. Even if you took readings month after month for years, you'd probably still get very high correlations. From this research, you would have to conclude that your measure was highly reliable. Of course, the *real* question anyone would want to ask you is *not* whether your measure of criminality was reliable, but whether it was *valid*. In other words, is asking people to stand on a scale a *valid* way to measure criminal tendencies? You and everyone else knows that the answer is no.

Face Validity

Face validity refers to judgments about the appropriateness of a measure based on an individual's basic understanding of a concept that one is trying to measure. The example presented earlier of someone trying to measure criminality by asking people to weigh themselves would be an example of a measure that is fundamentally lacking face validity. On the other hand, if one tried to measure criminality by asking people to report how many times they have ever been arrested, this would have much greater face validity. Although face validity is a useful concept, one should not simply dismiss ways of measuring variables that seem rather questionable from the standpoint of face validity. For instance, some have theorized that exposing the brain to testosterone (the so-called "male sex hormone") even before birth might be contributing to criminality, especially violent criminality (Blanchard & Centifanti, 2017; Eme, 2015). One difficulty in testing this theory involves testing the prediction that prenatal testosterone exposure is associated with criminal behavior.

In the late 20th century, evidence began to appear indicating that prenatal testosterone exposure could be inferred even in adulthood by measuring the relative lengths of the index finger and the ring finger, especially on the right hand (Manning et al., 1998). This measure has come to be known as the 2D:4D ratio. Although the validity of this ratio measure remains somewhat controversial (Hönekopp et al., 2007), it illustrates that sometimes strange ways are found for measuring variables, and these variables may sometime influence criminality many years later (Ellis et al., 2019:351-355). Thus, although the length of people's fingers seems on its face to not be valid for measuring events that happened before people were even born, researchers should always be open to the possibility of measuring variables in seemingly questionable ways.

Comparative Validity

Comparative (or **criterion**) **validity** involves comparing a new unestablished operational measure with an established (or widely accepted) measure. Here is an example: Finnish researchers were interested in developing an abbreviated set of questions for measuring anxiety and depression (Tambs & Moum, 1993). They used as their standard for comparison an older 23-item Finnish test battery. In their abbreviated form, they asked five questions instead of 23. Two of the questions pertained to anxiety (*feeling fearful* and *nervousness*) and three dealt with depression (*feeling hopeless about the future, feeling blue, worrying too much about things*). They administered both the 23-item test battery and their short 5-item test to the same group of subjects and correlated the resulting scores. The correlation coefficient was very high ($r = .92$).

From these results, the researchers concluded that their 5-item measure was preferable to a 23-item measure because both scales yielded almost identical scores.

Predictive Validity

Predictive (or **discriminant**) **validity** involves assessing how well values (or scores) from a particular operational measure of a variable seems to predict what it ought to predict. Suppose you wanted to measure risk-taking tendencies by asking some questions on a questionnaire. You might ask respondents how often they enjoy taking financial risks as well as physical risks in everyday life. You might then check the responses you obtained by determining how often each of your respondents had been admitted to the emergency room over the past 5 years. If your questionnaire responses are a valid measure of risk-taking tendencies, you would expect to find that respondents who were more likely emergency room patients would score higher on your questionnaire than those who had never been emergency room patients.

A specific example comes from a study of male parolees in Texas. Researchers sought to develop an objective laboratory test of aggression that might be helpful in predicting success on parole (Cherek et al., 1997). The procedure allowed each parolee willing to take part in the study to earn money, although they would be competing with an unseen person in an adjoining room. Parolees could make one of three choices each time they played: (a) they could earn money, (b) they could subtract money that was being earned by their "opponent," or (c) they could protect some of their money from being taken away by their "opponent" (their "opponent" was actually just a preprogrammed computer). As you might suspect, the option that provoked aggressive retaliation the most was the second one.

The researchers reasoned that if their game provided a valid way to measure aggressive tendencies, this second option would be pursued by parolees who had been convicted of violent offenses more than by parolees convicted of nonviolent offenses. Their prediction was correct. Specifically, throughout all six sessions, the parolees convicted of violent crimes were about three times more likely than their nonviolent counterparts to choose the option of "hurting" their "opponent." This study indicated that their gaming experiment was a valid way to measure aggressive behavior.

Additional Issues in Variable Measurement

Two more points should be made regarding measurement accuracy. One involves the issue of comparability, and the other has to do with the fact that accuracy in measuring variables is always a matter of degree rather than being an either/or situation.

Measurement Comparability. Measuring variables often must be done in a complex sociocultural context. For example, consider studies that compare homicide rates between countries and within countries over time. Though the vast majority of homicides are correctly identified in all countries that maintain homicide statistics, caution still needs to be exercised when comparing homicide rates between countries or within countries over time. As discussed in Chapter 1, studies have shown that homicide rates can be substantially reduced by improving the availability of emergency medical services (Giacopassi, 1992). Therefore, it is somewhat misleading to compare developed countries with underdeveloped countries. In other words, although homicide rates appear to be measurable in reasonably valid ways throughout the world, one can still reach inaccurate conclusions due to extraneous factors (such as the availability of well-trained first responders) (Ellis et al., 2019:4-5).

Varying Degrees of Accuracy. Even though scientists often speak of variable measurement as being either reliable or unreliable, or as valid or invalid, it is more realistic to think of reliability and validity as matters of degree rather than of type. Thus, technically speaking, it is never appropriate to declare the measurement of variables as either "reliable" or "valid." Instead, one should recognize that totally accurate measurement is simply a goal in science, and that both the reliability and the validity of measurement are never perfect. So, when scientists say that they are measuring in a reliable, or valid, way, they really mean these statements in relative, not in absolute, terms.

⊖ Precision

The precision of an operational measure may vary independently of its reliability and validity. To envision why, refer to the discussion of handedness earlier in this chapter. It could be both valid and reliable to measure handedness in terms of categorizing everyone as either right- or left-handed, but it would not be very precise in the sense that there are quite a few ambidextrous people and that quite a few people use their left hand for some tasks (e.g., writing) while they use their right hand for other tasks (e.g., brushing their teeth and throwing a ball).

Unlike validity and reliability, **precision** refers to how well variations in a variable can be detected. The precision in measuring a variable can vary from extremely refined (or precise) to very coarse (or imprecise). To illustrate, consider the variable of age. Social scientists nearly always consider it sufficiently precise to measure age according to years, unless they are studying young children (then they might use months or even weeks in their descriptions of age). Although it would certainly be more precise to measure the age of adults by asking them how many months, weeks, or even days old they are rather than just how many years old they are, it is doubtful that the extra precision would accomplish much, especially when balanced against the extra time (and irritation) it would impose on those being asked to provide the information.

When trying to measure criminal behavior by using self-reports, few criminologists simply ask people if they have ever committed a crime. Doing so would provide an extremely coarse measurement of what varies a great deal, both qualitatively and quantitatively. Consequently, most self-report measures of criminal behavior provide respondents with a list of different types of criminal and delinquent acts and then ask them to estimate as well as possible how many times they recall having done any and all of these acts (Hindelang et al., 1981; Hoskin et al., 2017). A chapter dealing with the measurement of criminal and related forms of antisocial behavior is presented later in this text.

⬤ Using Factor Analysis to Refine Measurement Accuracy

Multivariate statistics are discussed in more detail elsewhere in this text, but, for the purposes of this chapter, readers should be aware of a multivariate statistic known as **factor analysis**. This statistical method is used primarily to improve the validity and reliability of variable measurement. The way it works is quite simple, although the underlying mathematics is complex. Basically, after hundreds of individuals have completed a specific questionnaire, factor analysis can mathematically identify items (or questions) that seem to be answered similarly by the majority of respondents. Then, factor analysis specifies the degree to which these response patterns seem to "load" heavily on a specific response pattern, thereby suggesting that the items are essentially measuring the same variable.

To illustrate factor analysis, suppose you want to measure some aspect of criminality, so you make up 10 questions that seem to you intuitively to all bear on this particular aspect of criminality. Then, you give the questionnaire to a few hundred respondents, key the responses into the computer, and perform a factor analysis on the data. Basically, factor analysis will tell you how well each of your 10 questions *load* onto a single trait. Factor loadings are expressed mathematically as a type of correlation coefficient. Correlation coefficients are numbers ranging from 0.00 (meaning no relationship or no loading) to 1.00 (meaning a perfect relationship or loading). Because factor analysis is just a statistical tool, it has no way of interpreting the actual content of each item in your questionnaire. Nevertheless, it is able to help you identify items that appear to be all measuring essentially the same variable. More information will be presented in another chapter on the use of factor analysis in social science research.

⬤ Some Closing Remarks about Reliability, Validity, and Precision

Imagine that two studies attempt to answer the same question, and that they come to different conclusions. This is not an uncommon occurrence in social science, or in any science for that matter (De Los Reyes & Kazdin, 2008). Basically, there are five possible explanations:

1. Both studies may accurately reflect reality but have been based on individuals living in different cultures, subcultures, or even different periods of time.

BOX 5.2 WHAT DO YOU THINK?

Can Inaccurate Data Still Be Useful Data?

Throughout the 1990s, about 40% to 45% of adults in the United States reported attending at least one religious service during the previous 7 days (Hatch, 1989; Princeton Religious Research Center, 1992). Is this true? By compiling counts of attendees at representative community samples of actual religious services, a study estimated that the actual percentage was about 20% (Hadaway et al., 1993). Assuming that this lower estimate is closer to being correct, should the 40% figure be considered worthless data?

Although it would certainly be better to have accurate figures rather than inflated figures, if the degree of inflation is more or less constant, the figures can still be useful for the purposes of making comparisons. For example, when comparing self-reported attendance rates in the United States with rates in other developed countries, the US rates are much higher. In Canada and Australia, for instance, only about 20% of adults reported attending religious services during the previous 7 days. The residents of England reported rates of about 10%, while those in Scandinavian countries were only about 4% (Hatch, 1989). If we assume that all of these rates are substantially inflated, it is still reasonable to conclude that attendance in religious services is unusually high in the United States when compared to other Western countries.

Similar problems of overreporting have been found when people are asked if they voted in the preceding election. Political scientists have shown that only about two-thirds of those who said they voted in the last election actually did so (Silver et al., 1986; Presser & Traugott, 1992). Nevertheless, because overreporting appears to be fairly constant, these surveys can still be useful for making comparisons between jurisdictions and within jurisdictions over time.

2. Perhaps some of the data were miscalculated or erroneously interpreted in one of the two studies.

3. It is also possible that researchers in one of the two studies even faked some or all of their findings. Fraudulent scientific research appears to be rare but has occasionally been documented.

4. The sample size in one of the two studies may have been too small for detecting the correct relationship or the sample may not have been representative of any "real" population.

5. Finally, among the most likely possibilities of all is that the measurement of one of the key variables in one (or both) of the two studies may have been invalid, unreliable, or imprecise. This chapter has provided coverage of these types of problems.

Given all of the possibilities for drawing incorrect conclusions in science, one should never assume that one study ever settles an issue. This applies even to the findings from one's own research! Instead, scientists should see the findings from one (or even two) studies as (a) suggestive of what the "truth" may be and (b) a challenge to the rest of the scientific community to conduct additional replications. Only through replications do scientists come to gradually approximate truth.

Truth approximation is never in an absolute sense, but as close as scientists are able to get as they share their findings with the rest of the scientific community.

Social scientists never completely give up on improving their measurement of variables. To the extent a variable is not being measured reliably, validly, and precisely, it is said to contain **measurement error** (Skog, 1992). This type of error can be contrasted with other types of error, such as **sampling error**, which is linked to choosing research participants who are not entirely representative of a researcher's intended population.

As this chapter has revealed, there are no ironclad rules to follow in assessing reliability, validity, and precision in measurement. Reasonable judgments are an indispensable part of devising and assessing appropriate measures for scientific variables. Nevertheless, it is hard to overemphasize the importance of these three aspects of accurate measurement of variables. Another point that should be emphasized is that there are no *perfectly* reliable, valid, or precise ways to measure a variable, although some measures certainly come closer than others. Basic human traits such as age, sex, marital status, height, and body weight can be measured with high degrees of accuracy, even when based on self-reports. However, other human characteristics such as attitudes, emotions, and many types of behavior patterns are inherently difficult to measure with high degrees of precision. Nonetheless, because these latter aspects of humanity are important to social scientists, they call for careful efforts to measure them as accurately as possible.

Finally, the concepts of reliability, validity, and precision in measurement overlap. Thus, improving one of them often improves the other two. Together, these three concepts comprise what scientists term **measurement accuracy**, and all three are vital considerations in conducting social science research.

⊖ Summary

Recall that an operational measure of a variable is one that uses some consistent empirical criteria to "define" a variable. In other words, rather than simply conceiving of a variable (such as crime), scientists also seek to operationally define variables. In the case of crime, one study might operationally define crime in terms of convictions for murder while another study might rely on self-reports of thefts. Of course, neither of these operational measures is going to be entirely accurate (partly because not all murders are solved and not everyone remembers or admits to all of the thefts they have committed).

Despite the imperfections in science, scientists try to achieve as much accuracy as they can each time key variables are being measured. In this regard, there are three aspects of accuracy in scientific measurement: reliability, validity, and precision.

Reliability refers to the degree to which an operational measure of a variable can be repeated with consistent results. For example, because people's interest in sports is fairly stable over time, a reliable measure of sports interest could be expected to yield a fairly strong correlation among a sample of individuals from one month to another. If people who expressed a strong interest one month tended to indicate little interest the following month (and vice versa), the reliability of a researcher's efforts to measure such interest would have to be questioned. This would be an example of low test-retest reliability.

The other three main forms of reliability utilized in the social sciences are cross-test, inter-item, and inter-rater reliability. Cross-test reliability involves comparing tests designed to measure the same variable. Inter-item reliability compares scores for some of the items comprising a multi-item scale with scores for other items of the scale. Inter-rater reliability involves comparing two or more raters (or judges) in terms of their assessments of the same subjects regarding some variable of interest. The higher the agreement between raters, the higher the degree of reliability.

Validity refers to the degree to which an operational measure is, in fact, measuring what it is intended to measure. Three types of validity assessment methods were identified. These were face validity, comparative validity, and predictive validity. When assessing face validity, one relies predominantly on common sense. If it seems reasonable to believe that one or more questions (or other procedures) will allow a researcher to measure a particular variable, the questions (or procedures) are said to possess face validity.

In the case of comparative validity, researchers compare different supposed measures of a variable with other another. To the degree that the measures yield essentially the same results, they are considered valid; to the degree they disagree, at least one measure is considered invalid.

Regarding predictive validity, a researcher seeks to determine if a particular measurement for a variable can be used to predict another variable (or combination of variables). For example, if one sought to measure criminality but found that this new measure was totally unrelated to people's probability of ever having been arrested, one would have to be suspicious of the measure's predictive validity.

Precision is the third feature of measurement accuracy. It has to do with whether a variable is being measured (or calibrated) in a fine-grained or a coarse-grained manner. Fine-grained measurement is obviously preferable to coarse-grained measurement, although there are various practical considerations one must often take into consideration when developing fine-grained measures. Factor analysis was briefly discussed in this chapter as a statistical aid for identifying valid and reliable measurement procedures. It is a type of multivariate statistic that social scientists can often use to identify the best set of questions for measuring a particular variable. The way factor analysis helps in this regard is by pointing to clusters of items (or questions) that respondents tended to answered similarly. The degree of similarity is mathematically expressed with what are known as factor loadings. More will be revealed about factor analysis in another chapter.

Overall, students should appreciate the importance of measuring variables in valid, reliable, and precise ways. Often times, accurate measurement can be achieved by using measures that prior studies have employed. Nevertheless, one should always be open to the idea that measurement accuracy can nearly always be improved and take advantage of opportunities to do so.

⊜ Discussion Questions

1. Discuss the differences among reliability, validity, and precision in measurement.

2. Pick a phenomenon that you would like to study, and describe how you might go about measuring it. What methods could you use to test the reliability of your measure?

3. For the measures of your phenomenon, come up with two or three ways in which you could you test their validity.

4. What is correlation, and what does a correlation coefficient tell us about the relationship between two variables?

⊜ Exercises

1. Go to your institution's article database and search for an article on any topic. Pick an article and pull up a full-text version. Search the article for the words "reliability" or "validity." If these come up, describe what techniques the author(s) used to test the reliability and/or validity of their measures.

2. Think of a variable for which you could come up with varying levels of precision in its measurement. How would you measure it very coarsely and how would you measure it very finely or precisely?

Chapter 6 Surveying and Sampling

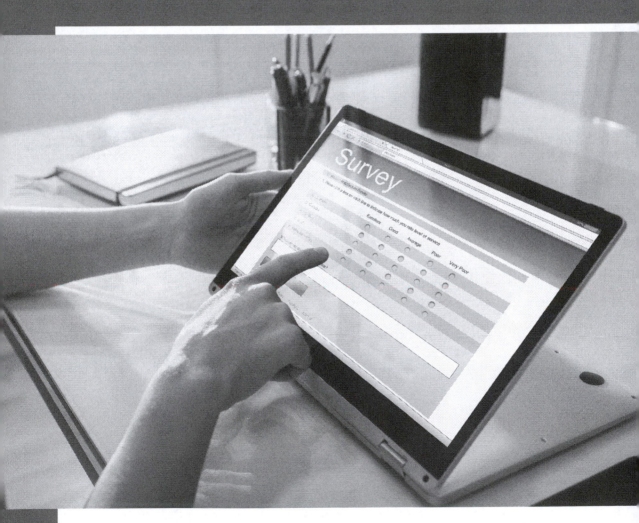

Have you ever wondered how polling organizations can predict the winner of an election before people even go to the polls? These organizations are able to predict how millions will vote based on short surveys responded *to by a couple of thousand people. Today, average predictions by most polling organizations tend to be within 1% of the actual results regarding the popular vote. As you will see in this chapter, the accuracy of these predictions depends a lot on being able to survey a small portion of the population that is representative of the population you want to make the prediction about. Maybe you have also seen advertising that claims that 9 out of 10 dentists prefer a particular brand of toothpaste. Have you ever wondered how many and which dentists they surveyed to get such favorable results for one brand of toothpaste or how many toothpastes they asked the dentists to rate? More likely than not, there was probably a disclaimer at the end of the advertisement stating that the survey was unscientific or that the sample was not representative of all dentists in the entire country. This chapter will also cover issues related to what steps need to be taken to conduct a scientific survey and how we can gauge how reliable or generalizable the results might be.*

Because of advances in sampling strategies and technology enabling large samples of people to be surveyed, polls and other public opinion surveys are commonplace, and their results have been fairly trustworthy as predictors of outcomes (Ward, 1995). Social scientists, newspaper reporters, politicians, and advertisers have learned to conduct surveys that can be accurate to within a few percentage points of the true figures. In this chapter, we will explore the various types of sampling methods that are regularly used in the social and behavioral sciences to gather information on attitudes, opinions, and behaviors.

⊖ The Nature of Scientific Surveys

In science, the term **survey** is applied to any research study that examines some empirical phenomenon without fundamentally disturbing it. The term "survey" is particularly appropriate if the aim of the study is to determine the prevalence of some phenomenon within a designated population and time frame. Surveys are conducted in virtually all the sciences. For example, astronomers survey the heavens for the positions of planets, asteroids, and the existence of previously unknown galaxies. Zoologists survey forests to assess how many members of an endangered species remain or to estimate insect infestations. Likewise, thousands of surveys related to human behavior and cultural practices are reported every year, not only by social scientists, but also by professionals in several allied fields such as education, journalism, advertising, and public administration.

These surveys inquire into people's opinions, interests, voting patterns, health and economic well-being, and criminal behaviors and victimizations. Chapter 7 discusses more in-depth self-report crime and delinquency surveys and national crime victimization surveys both aimed at uncovering the dark figure of crime. Support for these surveys comes from government agencies, nonprofit organizations, and business enterprises of all types. Numerous other surveys are undertaken each year by academic researchers motivated by a curiosity about the fascinating diversity of human activities and attitudes and uncovering the true nature and prevalence of certain types of behaviors.

Basic Terminology

In order to discuss surveying and sampling, it is important to be acquainted with several terms. One of the basic terms in surveying research is that of a **population** (sometimes called a **universe**).[1] A population or universe refers to a naturally existing collection of some phenomenon (usually a collection of people living in a designated geographic area at a given point in time). A **sample** is defined as a subset of some population. Normally, samples are very minuscule fractions of the populations from which they are drawn. For example, 3,000 US citizens constitute a large sample of people, but they are far less than 1% of the entire US population.

A **representative sample** is a fundamental concept in surveying. It refers to a sample whose members possess all characteristics in the same proportion as the population as a whole. For example, if the population being studied is the student body at a particular university and 12% of the student body at this university are females under the age of 19 majoring in criminal justice, a representative sample from that student body will comprise a similar group of persons in similar percentages as exist in the population (i.e., a sample that is roughly 12% female around the age of 19 who are majoring in criminal justice). In other words, if you want to be able to generalize the results from your small sample to the entire student body, you would want the characteristics of the students included in your sample to resemble those of the entire population of students enrolled. This is especially the case for characteristics you are interested in. Let's say you want to know whether year in school (freshman, sophomore, junior, or senior) is associated with the preferred times of day to hold classes. If you believe that it may differ, say between freshmen and seniors, then you would want to ensure that your sample is comprised of roughly the same percentage of freshmen and seniors as exist in the student population. In this way, you can be relatively confident that the responses that your sample gave related to preferred class start times actually represent the real preferred times of the entire body of freshmen and seniors. In this way you can better plan your introductory and upper-division courses at times when students would prefer to take them. (Disclaimer: We are not sure that any chair of a criminal justice department has ever conducted a scientific survey to gauge preferred class start times across these categories, but they probably have undertaken other methods to assess what times students do and do not like to take classes.) Our point is that a representative sample is basically a "miniaturized reflection" of the population that one wants to study.

Students should bear in mind that a representative sample refers to an ideal or a goal that a researcher strives to approximate in a survey. This chapter will show that there are different sampling methods used by researchers to approximate representative samples. Some of these methods have taken social scientists many years to develop and refine while others are quite old.

A term that is related to but should not be confused with representative sample is **random sample** (although some researchers carelessly use these terms interchangeably). A random sample is a sample that has been drawn from a population in which every member of the population had an equal chance of being chosen, sometimes referred to as EPSEM samples, or equal probability of selection of each member. Whereas a representative sample is an ideal toward which most surveyors strive, a random sample is the result of certain procedures that allow a representative sample to be obtained.

Each individual comprising a sample is referred to as a **sampling unit**. All random samples of sufficient size can be assumed to approximate a representative sample. However, there are ways of obtaining representative samples that do not rely entirely on random sampling methods. In order to obtain most random samples, a researcher needs to have access to what is called a **sampling frame** (Fowler, 1988). A sampling frame refers to a complete list of all members of the population. One reason these sampling procedures are not used more often is that obtaining complete lists of many populations of interest is often all but impossible. We may not even know what the real population looks like or who makes it up. For example, no one has a master list of persons who are considered the "homeless population," but many persons are interested in studying this population and have to resort to other methods to attempt to obtain a sample to survey or interview.

Another basic term used in connection with surveys is **census**. This refers to a survey that includes (or at least comes close to including) 100% of the members of a population, either directly or indirectly (such as through another household member). The word "census" got its name from the fact that most census surveys are conducted once every 10 years (at the beginning of each new decade) in virtually all literate countries (i.e., societies in which most adult citizens are able to read and write). A great deal of valuable information comes from these "nearly 100% surveys" of human populations. Recent controversies in the United States related to what types of questions should be asked on these census surveys have raised issues about the purposes and benefits and drawbacks of being able to survey the entire population, and whether certain questions might preclude a member of the population from wanting to respond to the survey, thereby rendering the census less representative. Census data can help determine the preciseness of a representative sample that has been obtained using tiny fractions of a population. Although it is proper to refer to a census as being a survey, it is normally not the custom to refer to the respondents in a census as a sample, in that a sample denotes a group of subjects comprising much less than 100% of a population.

⬔ Representative versus Nonrepresentative Samples

Samples are often chosen with the specific aim of their being representative, although this goal is sometimes unrealistic or is not central to the objective of a study. The main advantage of a representative sample is that it allows a researcher to generalize from the sample to the population once a study is completed. A nonrepresentative sample is often less time-consuming and less expensive to obtain than a representative sample but has drawbacks in that it limits the ability of the researcher to state with certainty that the results of the study from the sample are generalizable to, or representative of, the real population.

To illustrate the important distinction between a representative and a nonrepresentative sample, consider our mention of attempting to study the homeless and understand causes of their homelessness. It is conceivable that a researcher would, and many have to, go to a local foodbank or "soup kitchen" on a few days and attempt to talk with and interview all the persons there utilizing these services. Is this type of sampling method likely to yield an entirely representative sample of homeless persons? Probably not; perhaps not all persons who are homeless visit these entities, so the research would be missing segments of the homeless population that do not visit these establishments.

Likewise, could it be that this type of strategy might even include in the sample those persons who are not homeless? We know that sometimes people who do have a roof over their heads still need help with food insecurity; thus, some persons visiting a foodbank may not in fact be homeless. However, the point is that it might be very difficult to obtain a representative sample of the homeless persons in a particular city, so the choice for most researchers would be to either study persons visiting particular service-related entities or not conduct a study at all. In other words, barring the existence of some comprehensive citywide registry of homeless from which a random sample could be chosen, it would be virtually impossible for you or anyone else to obtain a representative sample of them.

Of course, in this hypothetical example, a researcher would be obliged to describe his or her sampling method so that readers are not misled into assuming that the findings are necessarily typical of a broader population of homeless persons. Over the course of time, other researchers interested in studying this population, using other sampling locations and techniques, could check the findings from this study's population. In this way, any inaccuracies in its findings would eventually become apparent.

This hypothetical example is intended to show that even though it is preferable to base all surveys on representative samples, there are legitimate reasons for not doing so. Another reason to conduct a survey even if it is not based on a representative sample has to do with the purpose of many studies. If the main reason for conducting a study is to determine how two or more variables are related to one another, the need for a representative sample is not nearly as crucial as when the main purpose is to describe the prevalence and distribution of variables within a particular population.

Probability versus Nonprobability Sampling Methods

Sampling methods that can be relied upon to approximate representative samples are called **probability sampling methods**; sampling methods that cannot be trusted to be representative of some specified population are called **nonprobability sampling methods**. Examples of these two sampling methods are described as follows.

Main Probability Sampling Methods

Probability sampling can be accomplished in two ways. One way is through random sampling and the other is through various forms of cluster sampling. Random sampling methods can be divided into three forms: pure, systematic, and stratified. Cluster sampling can be described in two forms, although their distinction is not always perfectly apparent: simple and multistage.

Random Sampling Methods

Pure random sampling must conform precisely to the definition that was stated earlier (i.e., random sampling requires that every member of the universe be given an equal chance of being selected). Some statistical "purists" also note that this includes the possibility that each member of the universe could be selected more than once, thus requiring replacement (i.e., putting a sampling unit back into the selection pool after it has been chosen). However, surveys in the social sciences are based on random sampling methods that do not usually practice replacement.

For a long time, the two most common techniques for obtaining a pure random sample involved (a) literally throwing the names of every member of the population into a hat (or some other container) and drawing out names one at a time or (b) using what is called a "table of random numbers" (which can usually be found in the back of most statistics texts). Today, however, it is much easier to use computer software programs to generate random lists of names from sampling frames or a random number generator from which to select persons from a list. Suppose a researcher wanted to get a random sample of students at some university. The registrar obviously holds the sampling frame and could generate multiple random lists of names within a very short time.

A special type of random sampling method used only in telephone surveys is called **random digit dialing** (e.g., King & Schafer, 1992; Strunin & Hingson, 1992). Once the first three digits (the prefixes) used in an area to be sampled have been entered into a computer (which has been connected to a telephone via a modem), the computer can be programmed to dial the last four digits at random. This ensures that every household with a telephone—even those not listed in the phone directory—will have an equal chance of being called. By and large, only the homeless and institutionalized persons will be underrepresented from random digit dialing sampling methods (DeKeseredy & MacLean, 1991). This has presented a problem because most of the population are now using cell phones as their primary contact and therefore not acquiring a home telephone number (landline), but many sampling frames now include cell phone numbers as well.

Systematic (or **interval sampling**) is a type of random sampling that does not perfectly meet the conditions specified in the definition of pure random sampling. However, for all practical purposes, systematic sampling is considered equivalent to random sampling. Systematic sampling takes sampling units from a sampling frame at designated intervals (such as every tenth name in a directory) or at designated positions (such as the third name from the top of each page).

The reason systematic sampling methods cannot be considered random sampling in the strictest sense is that once the interval (or the position on the page) has been designated, most members of the universe no longer have a chance of being chosen. Nevertheless, no one seriously questions that systematic sampling methods are as representative as pure random sampling methods.

Stratified random sampling is a special type of random sampling that is undertaken to allow groups with low representation in a population to be more highly represented. Users of this sampling method take a sampling frame and divide its constituents up according to one or more characteristics, and then randomly sample subjects from the resulting separate lists.

Here's an example of when to use stratified random sampling. Suppose a researcher was interested in comparing the attitudes of older-than-average students and students in their 20s on various issues at a particular college. Assume that the older-than-average students constitute only 10% of the students. This means that if a random sample of 200 students was drawn, only about 20 older-than-average students would be surveyed, a very small number from which to try to generalize. However, if the researcher were to separate the older-than-average and the regular-aged students, and then were to take 100 subjects from each of the two sampling frames, two separate random samples of equal size would be obtained. This larger sample of older-than-average students would allow the researcher to obtain enough responses to be able to better generalize the results than if they only obtained responses from 20 of these students.

Cluster Sampling Methods

Cluster sampling methods contain elements of random sampling, but they are distinguishable from random sampling in significant ways. Whereas random sampling is based on a complete sampling frame, cluster sampling is not. The word "cluster" in this context refers to what might be called "naturally occurring groups" of subjects. Examples of clusters from which subjects might be drawn would be middle-school students in school districts, inmates in prisons, or members of neighborhoods within a city. In cluster sampling, sampling frames come in two or more "layers." To get an idea of what this means, first consider the simplest form of cluster sampling.

In **simple cluster sampling**, a researcher chooses a few clusters and then collects data from many of the subjects comprising each of the clusters. For example, a researcher might be interested in studying the views of inmates related to the conditions of confinement in prison. If the researcher wanted to collect the data via personal interviews rather than by mailing out questionnaires, he or she would likely use simple cluster sampling. This could be done by choosing 10 prisons within the state (out of possibly hundreds), ensuring to select ones that are geographically dispersed throughout the state. At each of these prisons, the researcher could obtain a list of current inmates and contact a random sample of inmates at each for an interview. Note that even though the inmates are randomly selected, the congregations to be sampled are not. Nevertheless, this sampling procedure will normally approximate a representative sample.

Multistage cluster sampling has become a popular sampling method for nationwide surveys, especially when subjects are personally interviewed. The techniques involved in multistage cluster sampling were developed in the mid-1950s by private polling agencies such as Gallup International, Roper Surveys, and Harris Polls. A basic sketch of how multistage cluster sampling is commonly carried out is as follows:

1. Sampling clusters—such as counties or cities—are chosen in a way that ensures geographical diversity and roughly mirrors the mix of demographic features of the population as a whole. In other words, if an entire population contains 6% of persons over the age of 70, then the counties that are picked will collectively contain about the same percent. Choosing these main sampling clusters is done most efficiently by computer, based on state or countywide census figures.

2. Cities within each of the counties would be randomly chosen (in the case of cities, neighborhoods within the cities would be randomly chosen). Neighborhoods within the city, or blocks or streets within the neighborhood, would then be randomly chosen to send out surveys or to canvass by interviewers.

3. Starting at a random point on each block, the interviewers would conduct a designated number of interviews that would be dependent on the final sample size desired. If an interviewer cannot obtain the designated number of interviews in the chosen block or street, he or she would go to an adjacent block or street to complete the interviews.

By following these steps, a researcher could obtain a sample of a few thousand residents, depending on the number of interviews conducted in each block or street sampled. The sample obtained with this set of procedures will closely approximate a representative sample of the citizens within a city or even county.

In many surveys using multistage cluster sampling, interviewers are given guidelines to use in choosing respondents. For example, to avoid oversampling the elderly (which may happen if sampling is done during the day), interviewers might be required to conduct their interviews in the evening and/or to try to interview a certain number of various age groups. There are two major advantages that either form of cluster sampling has over random sampling. First, cluster sampling allows a researcher to confine his or her interviewing to a few manageable geographical areas. Second, cluster sampling does not require a sampling frame for the entire population.

How to Assess a Sample's Representativeness

Even if you used a probability sampling method, it is possible that your sample will not end up being representative of the population chosen for study. Fortunately, there is a way to determine how representative one's final sample is, no matter what sampling method is used. The simplest way to assess a sample's representativeness is to compare its demographics with those of the population targeted for study. For example, if one's sample includes 50% of each sex but the targeted population contains 40% female and 60% male according to the latest census, one would have to conclude that the sample underrepresents males.

How to Adjust for a Sample's Unrepresentativeness

Survey researchers sometimes impose representativeness on their samples after the data have been collected (Rust & Johnson, 1992). Although this may sound like "cooking the books," it is not, as long as the researcher is forthright in noting that such adjustments were made. The technique is called "weighting" and should only be used in surveys with large samples (i.e., over 1,000). Weighting procedures can be illustrated as follows: Assume census figures show that 12% of the subjects in a population targeted for study are Hispanic males between the ages of 35 and 50, but the sample you collected (by whatever means) contained only 10%. If the sample is large, computerized statistical procedures can be used to adjust all the results from the survey to show what the results would have been had the sample perfectly resembled the target population. Weighting procedures are technically very complicated and are only feasible using properly programmed computers.

Main Nonprobability Sampling Methods

If it is important that a research study be based on a representative sample, then a probability sampling method is strongly advised. For example, if a researcher is interested in knowing what proportion of a state's voters are currently favoring a particular political candidate, a representative sample should be obtained (either in fact or via weighing). However, if a researcher is interested in identifying campaign ads that significantly increase voters' opinions of that candidate, the answer could probably be found without obtaining a representative sample. In the first instance, the representativeness of the sample is more central to the purpose of the research project than in the second case.

Another way to look at the representativeness issue is this: No research project will be criticized for being based on a representative sample, but many are considered weak if they are *not*. Nevertheless, most social science studies are not based on representative samples. Such studies still provide valuable information, especially when considered in the context of other studies of the same topic. If the question being asked pertains more to why people behave (or think) a particular way than to identifying how many actually do so in a particular population, the representativeness of a sample is not nearly as important. The following section describes the main types of sampling methods unlikely to yield representative samples. The results of these sampling methods are often called **nonprobability samples**.

Accidental Sampling

One of the crudest methods for obtaining a sample for a research study is to stand in one location such as a shopping mall or a university student union and try to interview (or observe) whoever comes by. This is known as **accidental sampling** (or sometimes **availability sampling** because the only reason the persons are included in the sample is because they were available). Although this method is not worthless (especially for exploratory investigations), accidental samples would never be used in a study where representativeness is a major goal. Examples of accidental sampling would include a quick smattering of opinions about fear of crime or neighborhood safety obtained by news reporters for an evening news broadcast. Useful information is obtained with this sampling method, but researchers should be leery of any claim that the information is representative of all citizens in an entire neighborhood or city and can therefore be generalized to that population.

Quota Sampling

Quota sampling methods are sometimes incorporated into probability sampling procedures to help ensure representativeness. However, as a sampling method by itself, **quota sampling** is little more than accidental sampling with the added stipulation that a certain proportion of persons with certain characteristics (e.g., males versus females) are chosen. For instance, if a researcher is interested in the opinions of students at a university where two-thirds of the student population is female, when the interviews are conducted, two females could be sampled for every male. There are more sophisticated forms of quota sampling methods, but they are difficult to apply in real situations (Babbie, 1973)

Self-Selected Sampling

To some extent, all samples are self-selected because no one is ever forced to participate in a social science research project. However, in **self-selected sampling methods**, the subjects themselves actually take the initiative to be included in the study. Good examples of surveys based on self-selected samples are questionnaires that pop up on your smartphone or computer screen looking to gauge people's preference for a new product line or websites that invite people to click on a link to give their opinion on some topic.

Although the results of surveys based on self-selected samples can be informative in studying relationships among variables, rarely can such surveys be considered representative of any naturally existing population; however, given the large number of persons responding to these "pop-ups," marketing entities might generate a large enough sample to be able to speak to trends around certain products. Indeed, search engines such as Google can use the queries on their platform to examine opinions or behaviors of persons nationwide or in certain areas of the country. Google believed it could predict outbreaks of the flu quicker than public health entities by examining the areas of the country in which persons had "googled" information on flu symptoms or flu remedies—including the population of magazine subscribers or television viewers. So-called big data (data sets with millions of data points), for example, can be very powerful in providing information about which types of persons are likely to prefer which types of products, or the attitudes and opinions they are likely to have, thereby giving business entities and other organizations powerful information on who to target for certain types of advertisements. Because of the misuse of this information to target certain persons to attempt to change or sway their opinion (or vice versa to ensure that information is targeted in a way that reinforces a person's current attitudes or opinions), entities such as Facebook and Google, as well as states via public service announcements, have been educating and warning people about disinformation and reminding them to use media to *be informed, not influenced*.

Snowball Sampling

In **snowball sampling**, research subjects are recruited and then asked to recruit additional subjects. The advantage of this sampling method is that it can build up sample sizes quickly and/or it can recruit subjects who are otherwise difficult to locate. For example, if someone is interested in the behavior of the members of some secretive gang or religious cult, snowball sampling might be the only feasible way of obtaining a sizable sample. This sampling method was used in a study of homosexuality among American priests (Wolf, 1989) and in a study of criminal behavior among drug users in Scotland (Hammersley, Forsyth, & Lavelle, 1990). The likelihood is low that this sampling method will yield a representative sample.

Convenience Sampling

Convenience sampling involves obtaining a large group of subjects all at once, such as asking all the students in a criminology class to complete a questionnaire. Convenience sampling is probably the most widely used sampling method in the social sciences. Without intending any offense, a long-standing joke among social science researchers (especially psychologists) is that their two favorite groups of subjects are rats and sophomores. The fact is, however, that some social scientists have specifically criticized colleagues for relying too heavily on college students as research subjects.

It is now common for many introductory social science (especially psychology) courses to require participation in at least one research study, especially at large, research-oriented universities. In this way, professors are able to conduct many useful studies while students have an opportunity to see how social science research is conducted. Nevertheless, the mix of students cannot be relied upon to be representative of an overall university's student body, although students in a required introductory course might actually come close to representativeness in this regard.

Event Sampling

Obtaining a sample by taking every single instance of a rare event (or rare condition) is called **event sampling**. When event sampling is carried out in settings where people seek treatment, it is sometimes called **clinical sampling**.

For example, a study of child abuse was conducted a few years ago among children with cerebral palsy (Diamond & Jaudes, 1983). The sample was derived from all children diagnosed with cerebral palsy who entered a Chicago children's hospital between September 1979 and August 1980. Such a sampling method is obviously not ideal for obtaining a representative sample, but given the rarity of the disease in a general population, it would be unrealistic to ever expect random or cluster samples of children with cerebral palsy to be obtained for study.

One particularly unusual example of event sampling comes from a study of more than 1.36 million emergency (911) calls made to the Kansas City, Kansas, police department between 1986 and 1989 (Walters, 1991). The initial assumption might be that this is a self-selected sample, but such a categorization would imply that the phone call was being made for research purposes (which is not the case). Rather, sampling consecutive calls made to an emergency number is best considered a type of event sampling.

Final Comments on Nonprobability Samples

Overall, the difference between a probability sample and a nonprobability sample is that the former has a greater chance of being representative of an identifiable population than the latter. A researcher therefore is able to generalize the findings from the sample studied to the larger population with a representative sample. Thus, if a researcher has a choice between conducting a study based on either a probability sample or a nonprobability sample of equal size, and there are no differences in time and expense, the probability sample should be used. However, many circumstances make probability sampling almost impossible to obtain.

Over the years, social scientists have been at odds about employing nonprobability sampling methods. Some have argued that researchers should never attempt to generalize to any "real" population based on a nonprobability sample (Berk, 1983; Grichting, 1989). Nonetheless, some populations cannot be studied using a probablilty sampling technique, and most researchers would likely agree that although probability samples are certainly preferable, when there is a choice between using a nonprobability sampling method and not conducting a study at all, it is best to use the nonprobability sampling method (Eysenck, 1975).

⬤ Sample Size

As will be discussed in Chapters 13 and 14, statistically speaking, the larger the size of one's sample, the more likely it is that the results will accurately reflect the universe from which the sample was drawn (assuming that the same sampling methods were used). Nevertheless, there are trade-offs when sample sizes are increased. In particular, larger sample sizes nearly always require additional time and expense in data collection, coding, and data entry.

Law of Diminishing Returns

In attempting to balance the increased accuracy of a survey against the additional time and expense accompanying larger sample sizes, keep in mind the law of diminishing returns. Briefly, this mathematical law means that the larger the sample size already is, the less results are made more accurate by further increasing the number of subjects. Adding 20 subjects to a sample size of 100, for example, would increase the accuracy of a survey much more than adding 20 more subjects to a sample size of 10,000.

Over the years, statisticians have tried to develop precise guidelines for the size samples needed for a given level of accuracy. Although there is value in such estimates for planning surveys, no sampling formulas or guidelines should ever replace the following commonsense rule: Attempt to obtain as large a sample as possible within a researcher's time and expense constraints. As a rough rule of thumb, however, Table 6.1 presents figures indicating examples of the sample sizes needed to achieve accuracy within various sampling error limits.

These figures indicate that if a researcher were to obtain responses from a probability sample of 100 individuals, any percentages derived from their answers would be accurate to within 10 percentage points of the real figure. In other words, if 32% of a sample responded affirmatively to a particular question,

TABLE 6.1   Conversion of Sample Size into Percentage Confidence Intervals

Sample Size	Accuracy within a Given Percentage of the Actual Figure (Degree of Sampling Error)
100	10%
400	5%
1,500	2.5%
2,500	2.0 %
7,000	1%

the real percentage (i.e., the percentage for the entire population) would be somewhere between 22% and 42%.[2] The sample size needed for results that are within 2 percentage points of the actual percentage would be around 2,500.

Keep in mind that the figures in this table are approximations and that they only pertain to how accuracy is affected by sample size. Any inaccuracies due to invalid, unreliable, and imprecise questions (see Chapter 5), inappropriate questions and response options, or poor sampling procedures would be in addition to inaccuracies due to sampling error.

Statistical Power

The concept of **statistical power** refers to the probability that a study will yield statistically significant results when a research hypothesis is true. Obviously, this probability increases with increasing sample size. However, other factors also affect statistical power. For example, say that a researcher wanted to compare males and females for two traits. Although there is no way of ever knowing for certain, assume that for all of the people who have ever lived and died on earth, the actual difference between males and females for trait A is one-fourth of a standard deviation and for trait B it is one entire standard deviation. Stated in terms of effect size, the effect size is four times greater for trait B than for trait A.

Obviously, with a sample of a few hundred males and females, a researcher will have a much greater probability of finding a statistically significant difference in the case of trait B than in the case of trait A. This means that statistical power is not only affected by the size of one's sample but also by the extent of the "real" differences that are being assessed with one's sample. For more detailed information about statistical power, effect size, and statistical significance, you will want to obtain training in statistics and probability theory.

⊖ Surveying over Time

Sometimes researchers have a one-time interest in how a variable is distributed in a particular population. For these researchers, it is sufficient to conduct what is called a **cross-sectional survey**, meaning a survey undertaken at only one point in time. Other times, researchers may want to follow changes in a variable over two or more points in time. This requires what is termed a **longitudinal survey**. In the case of longitudinal surveys, it is useful to distinguish three different types according to how samples are drawn. These types are called panel, nonpanel, and partial panel. Longitudinal surveys are more time-consuming and costly for obvious reasons. **Panel longitudinal surveys** are ones in which the same sample is used each time the survey is conducted. These surveys allow a researcher to follow specific individuals over time to assess how they may be changing. **Nonpanel longitudinal surveys** involve selecting an entirely new sample (within the same population, of course) each time the survey is run. The advantage of this form of longitudinal survey is that a researcher is able to estimate how the population is changing without having to locate the same subjects time after time. **Partial panel longitudinal surveys** represent a compromise between the panel and nonpanel surveys.

One example of a partial panel survey is the National Crime Victimization Survey (NCVS) conducted each year by the Bureau of Justice Statistics among a representative sample of US citizens to determine if they have been recent crime victims, regardless of any calls they may have made to police (Blumstein, Cohen, & Rosenfield, 1991). The survey collects about 240,000 interviews annually on victimization, sampling about 160,000 persons in roughly 95,000 households. The NCVS will be discussed in much more detail in Chapter 7, but in general, researchers make efforts to keep the respondents in the survey for 3 consecutive years (although some will be lost due to change of residence or death). In most cases, one-third of the respondents are new each year, one-third were part of the panel the previous year, and one-third were in the panel for the two preceding years.

A lot of what criminologists know about the prevalence and correlates of offending has come from simply asking people what types of behaviors they have engaged in (Chapter 7 also discusses self-report crime surveys more in depth). These types of surveys are referred to as self-report questionnaires, and in general many thousands of people all over the world give information on various aspects of human behavior via these different types of questionnaires. The information provided by people who respond to the questionnaires, usually referred to as respondents, provides us the ability to gather knowledge about what characteristics or traits might be associated with delinquency and crime as well as how policy makers and criminal justice system officials might respond to try to prevent or curb crime in the future.

Of course, not everyone who is asked to fill out a questionnaire actually agrees to do so, and those who decline to fill it out might actually be the most criminal individuals. Furthermore, even those who do agree to fill them out might not be completely honest. This becomes especially important for questionnaires asking persons to self-report their criminal behavior. Because of this, criminologists have developed techniques for estimating the bias that might be introduced from certain persons declining to respond to self-report surveys and from possible misinformation provided by some who do agree to participate. Error in the validity of information gathered can be reduced by administering the questionnaire to a representative sample, and dishonesty can be reduced by incorporating certain techniques that can help minimize or at least detect false information.

◗ Serving as a Respondent to a Research Questionnaire

The preceding discussion of sampling and sampling error was based on the assumption that everyone who is asked to respond to a survey or questionnaire will comply with that request. Of course, this is not a reality, and because survey research is voluntary in nature, if someone decides not to participate, this must be respected. Given the nature of research participation today, the focus here is how one can increase the likelihood that those who are asked to participate in survey research agree to do so.

Under some circumstances, all subjects who are asked to be part of a survey will comply. For example, in many introductory college courses in the social sciences, especially psychology, students are expected to serve as subjects in at least one or more faculty member's research projects. In these cases, most students will agree because they will receive extra credit, and therefore there is little need to distinguish between what is called a chosen sample and an obtained (or final) sample. However, in most major studies where subjects must participate voluntarily, the distinction between these two types of samples is important.

BOX 6.1 CURRENT ISSUES

People's Unwillingness to Take the Time to Participate in Surveys

As junk mail, robo calls, and spam emails seem to be a ubiquitous part of our everyday lives, it is getting more difficult for researchers to get persons to take the time to participate in scientific research studies or to understand the importance of doing so to our continued understanding of human behavior. Most of what we know on how to best minimize attrition in surveys has been done with mail surveys, which are not as common today as phone, email, or web-based surveys. Baruch (2008) noted that response rates in academic studies had declined significantly from an average of around 65% to below 50%. Baruch and his colleague analyzed response rates in almost 500 studies and found that response rates averaged about 52% for studies soliciting information from individuals and only about 36% for those collecting information from organizations. They also found that generally incentives did not increase response rates and that phone, email, and web-based surveys had higher response rates than mail surveys (Baruch & Holtom, 2008). Calls from unknown numbers and in-boxes filled with spam and unwanted emails can have a deleterious effect on researchers' ability to garner a response rate adequate to be able to generalize results. Many people are also suspicious of what might be fraud attempts by scammers to get their personal information. As you will learn, there are several techniques researchers can employ to try to increase their response rates. Nonetheless, attrition is a pervasive problem in a world crowded with many different entities and organizations constantly attempting to solicit information about us.

In surveys conducted by mail, telephone, the internet, and face to face, the **chosen sample** refers to persons asked to participate in a study, and the **obtained sample** refers to those who actually agree to do so. The difference between these two types of samples is referred to as **sample attrition**.

Assessing Sample Attrition, Its Extent, and Causes

Researchers have identified a number of methods that might assist in increasing response rates in survey research. Four main sources of sample attrition can be identified. These are inaccessibility, inability, carelessness, and noncompliance (Rogelberg & Luong, 1998).

Inaccessibility results from difficulties in contacting or delivering a questionnaire to an intended subject. The causes of inaccessibility depend upon the precise way in which the data are being collected, but they can include people changing addresses, rarely being at home, or having unlisted phone numbers. Regarding the results of the previous study, email surveys encounter a number of problems with accessibility for certain segments of the population, and others do not trust that their information will be safe or confidential on the internet. **Inability** as a cause of sample attrition, on the other hand, refers to numerous circumstances in which a subject can be contacted but is then unable to respond due to such things as illness or an inability to understand the language in which the questionnaire is written or the interviewer is speaking. **Carelessness** as a source of sample attrition is that which comes about when an intended subject sets aside a questionnaire for completion later, but then either loses it or forgets about it. This also becomes very problematic in email and web-based surveys; many people get a lot of emails every day, and if they are busy, it is unlikely that they will go back through their email when they do have time. It is also very easy to simply hit the delete button if you are uninterested in filling out an email survey. Last, **noncompliance** (or **refusal**) comes from targeted subjects intentionally deciding not to become involved in the study. Special telephone follow-up surveys have been conducted on a few occasions to determine the reasons people fail to respond to mail questionnaires. Interestingly, respondents to these special telephone follow-ups identified both inaccessibility and carelessness as the factors for the most common reasons for not returning mail questionnaires. Noncompliance was a close third (Rogelberg & Luong, 1998).

Computer-Assisted Interviewing

As the 20th century drew to a close, researchers developed and began to test a promising a new method of obtaining data from human subjects. Instead of conducting personal or telephone interviews or contacting subjects through the mail, subjects are presented with questions in auditory form and are then allowed to respond by pressing keys on a computer. This technique has come to be known as **audio-computer-assisted self-interview** (**audio-CASI**) (Van Griensven et al., 2001; Sattah et al., 2002).

There are at least two advantages of audio-CASI relative to conventional interviewing. One is that audio-CASI presents all questions in a standardized fashion, unlike conventional interviews in which subtle variations will occur in how questions are asked. Another advantage is that audio-CASI allows subjects to input their responses directly into the computer rather than having their responses recorded by an interviewer. Not only does this reduce the risk of transcription errors, but it also allows greater assurances of privacy.

Does audio-CASI result in more accurate information being collected? The answer appears to be affirmative. One US study compared the results of a survey of illegal drug use using audio-CASI and a conventional interview. Subjects were considerably more likely to report details about illegal drug use and intimate sexual behavior when they were responding to the audio-CASI method (Turner et al., 1998).

Limiting Sample Attrition

Researchers recognize two types of error associated with sampling. One is called **random sampling error**, which is defined as error that can be reduced by increasing the size of one's sample. For example, a researcher diminishes the probability of random sampling error from a survey by increasing the number of subjects from 1,000 to 2,000. The other type of sampling error cannot be eliminated by increasing the sample size. It is called **systematic sampling error**. Systematic sampling error is caused by a segment of a population failing to be represented in a sample due to sample attrition (Rogelberg & Luong, 1998). For instance, both telephone and face-to-face surveys pertaining to sexual behavior typically result in one-fourth to one-third of prospective subjects declining to participate (Catania et al., 1992; Johnson et al., 1994; Michael et al., 1994). Are the people who decline different in any significant way from those who agree to participate? An Australian study of sexual behavior and attitudes among a large sample of adult twins found that participants had more years of education, less church attendance, and were more likely to smoke cigarettes and drink alcohol than was true for nonparticipants (Dunne et al., 1997). Notice that no matter how large the sample size might be, any error in the findings due to such a systematic sampling bias cannot be eliminated.

Studies have indicated that as long as sampling attrition in a survey is fairly small (e.g., under 15%), nearly all of the attrition can be safely attributed to random factors (e.g., people being in a bad mood, too busy, etc., when the request is made for them to participate) (Lansing & Kish, 1957; Stephan & McCarthy, 1963). When attrition exceeds 15%, however, the possibility that systematic error is confounding the results of a survey becomes increasingly likely.

Are surveys based on samples with high attrition of no scientific value? Even studies with attrition rates that are greater than half of the chosen sample can still provide useful information. To give an example, two of this text's authors conducted a professional survey to determine what criminologists considered the most important causes of crime and the best theories for explaining crime (Ellis & Walsh, 1999). Although we were disappointed that only 147 of the 500 questionnaires sent out were completed and returned (a 29% return rate), a number of the findings were still quite informative in terms of giving insight into what most criminologists think about crime causation. The next time a similar survey is conducted, it is likely that its return rate will not be much greater than ours. If so, the mix of respondents in terms of demographics will probably be similar, which should still allow for meaningful comparisons.

Basically, researchers should make every effort to obtain a high return rate, but findings based on high attrition should rarely be dismissed as uninformative. As long as the response rate is accurately disclosed and the responses appear to be valid and reliable reflections of those responding, findings can still be considered worth reporting.

Minimizing Sample Attrition in Mail Surveys

Many studies have been conducted in order to better understand attrition rates in mail surveys (Dawson & Dickinson, 1988). Return rates for mailed questionnaires have varied from lows of about 20% to highs of more than 90%, and one review of 183 mail surveys revealed that the average return rate was 48% (Heberlein & Baumgartner, 1978); however, others have argued that it is probably much closer to 30% (Arnett, 1991). Based on this research, several suggestions for increasing return rates of mail questionnaires follows. These can also apply to telephone, email or web-based, and face-to-face surveys and interviews as well.

1. *Prenotify the prospective respondent.* Numerous studies have shown that notifying prospective subjects either by letter, postcard, or telephone that they have been selected to take part in a survey before sending them the actual questionnaire will increase response rates in nearly all types of surveys (Yammarino et al., 1991; Senn et al., 2000).

2. *Attach a polite and clearly written cover letter.* Decisions about taking part in a mail survey often hinge on whether the person has confidence in the competence of those conducting the study. Sending a poorly planned cover letter will adversely affect the return rate. Helpful lists have been prepared containing information to include in a cover letter (Monette et al., 1986), but it comes down to using common sense and being able to put oneself in the place of a potential respondent.

3. *Personalize the correspondence.* Some experiments have been conducted with personalized, or personalized-appearing, cover letters. Especially in marketing surveys, computer-generated cover letters specifying a

person's name (rather than simply being addressed to occupant) yield higher response rates (Carpenter, 1975).

4. *Make the interesting/relevant features of the survey prominent.* Research has shown that people are more likely to complete and return survey questionnaires if they consider the topic to be interesting, important, and relevant to their lives (Martin, 1994). Consequently, without a monetary reward, response rates for mail surveys appear to be the highest for public health surveys (Heberlein & Baumgartner, 1978).

5. *Have a credible sponsor.* Studies have shown that the rate of questionnaire completion can be significantly increased by having the study endorsed by a respected sponsoring organization (university) than one without sponsorship (Nachmias & Nachmias, 1987; Fox et al., 1988; Yammarino et al., 1991).

6. *Keep the questionnaire short.* Researchers must recognize that, everything else being equal, as the amount of information sought increases, the likelihood that a subject will complete a questionnaire decreases (Roszkowski & Bean, 1990; Dillman et al., 1993). One review calculated that every two questions added to a mail questionnaire will reduce the return rate by roughly 1% (Heberlein & Baumgartner, 1978). However, another review of the research on questionnaire length for mail surveys concluded that effects on return rates of even doubling the number of questions is actually rather minimal (Yu & Cooper, 1983). In light of this contradictory evidence, it is probably still a good policy to keep the questionnaire as short as possible (Biner & Kidd, 1994).

7. *Make sure the questionnaire is well* **organized and neatly presented.** Questionnaires that are hurriedly constructed and poorly organized frustrate respondents and cause them to doubt the value of what they are being asked to do. The chances are then diminished that respondents will carefully complete the questionnaire and return it (Sanchez, 1992).

8. *Enclose a stamped self-addressed return envelope.* As most would suspect, higher returns are achieved if the subjects do not need to pay the postage for returning the questionnaire (Yammarino et al., 1991). Even the type of postage appears to matter. In a review of 20 studies, the return envelopes with regular first-class stamps yielded an average of 9% higher returns than envelopes with business reply postage (Armstrong & Lusk, 1987).

9. *Enclose some token compensation.* Studies have shown that enclosing as little as a dollar bill increased the percentage of returns for the average survey by 20% to 25% (James & Bolstein, 1990). Studies using both monetary compensation and "tangible" compensation of roughly equivalent value (e.g., key rings and ballpoint pens) have found monetary compensations more effective in increasing return rates (Goodstadt et al., 1977; Hansen, 1980). Researchers in one experiment included a monetary incentive of $1 accompanied by one of two different cover letters. One cover letter described the dollar as a token of appreciation, while the other cover letter

implied that the incentive obliged the recipient to complete and return the questionnaire. The latter of these two letters resulted in a significantly higher return rate (Biner & Kidd, 1994). Researchers using online surveys often entice respondents by stating that those who participate will be eligible for a drawing of some type of monetary gift card or even laptop computers or iPads.

10. *Use follow-ups.* Research has indicated that one follow-up will usually increase response rates by 10% to 20%, two follow-ups by 5% to 10% more; and three follow-ups by 3% to 5% more (Heberlein & Baumgartner, 1978; James & Bolstein, 1990). A good policy is to include a new copy of the questionnaire in at least one of the follow-up mailings (Babbie, 1983). Some also recommend the use of follow-up telephone calls in order to maximize return rates (Bailey, 1978).

Each of these 10 points can make a significant difference in both the quality and quantity of survey responses, especially in terms of minimizing attrition. Combining several of these suggestions can make an even greater difference. To illustrate, consider a longitudinal study of drug use among college students, first conducted in 1977, then in 1983, and again in 1987 (Meilman et al., 1990). The return rate in the 1977 survey was 76.7%, and 6 years later it dropped to 70.5% (Meilman et al., 1990). In the third phase, the researchers made a concerted effort to obtain the greatest possible return rate. They reduced the number of questions on the questionnaire and sent up to two follow-ups, one containing a dollar bill incentive. The response rate for the final survey was an impressive 87.25%. The researchers noted that, to the best of their knowledge, this was "a higher return rate than any previously reported" in a mail survey (Meilman et al., 1990). The higher the return rate, the better, but for most mail surveys (especially those with no follow-up mailings or compensation enclosed), return rates are less than half. Mail surveys with rates above 50% are considered adequate, and rates exceeding 70% are usually seen as very good (Monette et al., 1986).

Respondent-Completed versus Interviewer-Completed Questionnaires: Which Is More Accurate?

A few studies have sought to determine whether questionnaires completed by respondents or ones completed by interviewers are more accurate. A meta-analysis on this topic suggested that although the magnitude of the typical differences was modest, telephone and face-to-face interviews appeared to be significantly more accurate than respondent-completed questionnaires (De Leeuw, 1992). The main reason for this was not that respondents in interviews were more likely to answer honestly than those responding directly to questionnaires, but that greater proportions of interviewees actually agreed to provide data and were more likely to give complete and appropriate answers to each and every question that was asked. Basically, it appears that in interview situations, interviewers are able to make sure subjects understand each question and thereby provide reasonable responses. Overall, from the standpoint of the completeness of the data, personal interviews appear to have an advantage over respondent-completed questionnaires. However, when it comes to highly personal information, most people prefer to respond on a questionnaire rather than to an interviewer.

Inaccuracies in Self-Reports

Recall our earlier discussion of honesty in self-report surveys. There are generally four main sources of invalid and unreliable self-reported information: (1) failure to understand a question or locate an appropriate response option, (2) failure to accurately recall the answer, (3) the volatility of opinions, and (4) dishonesty.

1. *Failure to understand a question.* The extent to which respondents fail to understand the questions they are asked is unknown, but it is safe to assume that it is significant. Most researchers would prefer that respondents simply not answer questions they do not understand, but respondents may feel a social obligation to answer or they may respond to a question they do not understand simply to avoid appearing ill-informed. The most important guideline to follow to minimize such sources of error is to carefully pretest every question in a questionnaire. Another helpful suggestion is to emphasize in the instructions that questions may be left blank if they bear on subjects not relevant to the respondent's interests or knowledge.

2. *Failure to accurately recall.* Studies have been undertaken to determine how well people remember items of information about themselves and others. Two factors have been shown to have major effects on the accuracy of a subject's recall. One is the time since the event occurred, and the other is the novelty or the importance of the event. When a long time has elapsed, and the novelty or the subjective importance of the event is minimal, the recall probability is low (Bradburn, 2000). There are many items of information that most people will accurately remember even decades later. For example, if you ask your mother how much you weighed at birth, more than likely, she will recall immediately (Walton et al., 2000). Despite such impressive feats of recall, some reports will be inaccurate, particularly by mothers who have had numerous children.

    To help reduce the inaccuracy resulting from memory lapses, researchers often circumscribe their questions to recent events. For example, in national crime victimization surveys (which are based on surveys rather than on calls made to police), subjects are asked if they or a family member were a victim of a crime during the past 6 months rather than during the past year (Hilton et al., 1998). Studies have shown that asking subjects to remember a victimization event further back in time than 6 months (and especially more than a year) results in increasing errors of memory (Skogan, 1976). Not only do subjects forget instances of victimization as time goes by, but they tend to draw in events that occurred prior to the time frame specified, a phenomenon known as **telescoping** (Ellis et al., 1988; Bradburn et al., 1987).

3. *Unstable opinions*. Research has shown that people sometimes change their minds on topics during the course of completing a questionnaire (or interview). This is particularly common in **thematic surveys**, which are surveys in which in-depth coverage is given to a single topic. There is nothing that can be done about these opinion changes, but it is important to be aware that they do occur.

4. *Dishonesty*. If subjects agree to take part in a study, a researcher can generally assume that they will try to provide honest responses to the questions asked. If they do not answer honestly, it is probably because the questions are more personal or intimidating than was anticipated, or involve possible legal risks to the subjects. Similarly, when asked personal and emotionally sensitive questions, many respondents will lean toward responses considered most "socially desirable" or least embarrassing (Gendall et al., 1992; Li et al., 1993). For example, a German study found females underreporting their weight to a greater degree than males (Glaesmer & Brahler, 2002). Another study found that nearly 20% of teenagers who reported having had sexual intercourse in an initial survey reported having *not* done so 1 year later. This tendency to effectively retract previous reports of sexual intercourse was especially high among females (Rodgers et al., 1982; Kahn et al., 1988). Similarly, both men and women who have been divorced more than once tend to underreport the total number of divorces they have had (Thornton & Rodgers, 1987).

The previously mentioned studies all pertain to data directly reported on questionnaires. Regarding data provided to an interviewer, an additional factor can hinder fully honest responding. That element is the social relationship between the interviewer and the respondent. In this regard, a study of sexual assault victimization among women found that the number of assaults reported to female interviewers was nearly 25% higher than the number reported to male interviewers (Sorenson et al., 1987).

Under the category of *dishonestly* we can consider not only out-and-out lies but also slightly stretching the truth. In this regard, a public health survey conducted in England was followed by a detailed clinical examination, allowing researchers to check the accuracy of certain self-reported items against actual physical measurements. The researchers were particularly interested in the accuracy of people's reported height and weight. As you might suspect, most people reported their height and weight as being very close to the physical measurements. However, small inconsistencies were noted, with nearly all of them biased toward people being taller and lighter in weight than revealed by physical measurement (Hill & Roberts, 1998). Interestingly, men in the survey were more likely to bias their reported heights and weights than were women. Nevertheless, nearly all of the biased reporting was relatively minor.

Techniques for Minimizing and Detecting Dishonesty

A variety of techniques have been developed to promote the honesty and frankness of responses in questionnaires, or at least to be able to estimate the degree of error attributable to dishonest or incomplete disclosure. The techniques are as follows: assurance of anonymity or confidentiality; take care in asking embarrassing questions; nonjudgmental phrasing or prefacing of questions; the bogus pipeline technique; have subjects rate their honesty at the end of the questionnaire; check for internal consistency; polygraph testing; independent verification; and obtain responses to a follow-up questionnaire.

Assurance of Anonymity/Confidentiality

Probably the simplest thing a researcher can do to increase the honesty and frankness of those being surveyed is to assure them of anonymity or at least of confidentiality (Hill et al., 1988). **Anonymity** means that the researcher never knows the identity of those who completed a given questionnaire. **Confidentiality**, on the other hand, refers to a promise not to disclose any information revealed by the subjects that would cause them to be personally identified. Recall the discussion in Chapter 3 related to these concepts and research ethics. Assurance of anonymity appears to affect the honesty and frankness of subjects answering questions about behavior that is very personal and/or illegal, at least to a small degree. For instance, in a delinquent behavior study in which subjects self-reported their offending history under both anonymous and nonanonymous conditions, the overall level of delinquency correlated almost perfectly ($r = +.98$). Nevertheless, the total number of offenses reported under the anonymous condition was about 10% higher than the total number of offenses reported under the name-disclosed condition (Kulik et al., 1968).

In an interview situation, paroled child molesters admitted to more prior sex offenses and to more continuing urges to reoffend when they were assured that their responses would be kept strictly confidential than when they were not given this assurance (Kaplan et al., 1990). Similarly, drug offenders were less likely to disclose the full extent of their drug use to interviewers directly affiliated with the criminal justice system than to interviewers with no such affiliation (Joe & Gorsuch, 1977). Sometimes, responses made on a questionnaire are more honest than responses made directly to an interviewer. For instance, women were found to be more likely to disclose having had an abortion if allowed to do so in a sealed envelope rather than doing so directly to an interviewer (Jones & Forrest, 1992).

Take Care Asking Embarrassing Questions

We can all relate to having been asked questions about highly personal matters and either declining to answer or not telling the truth. To remove some of the subjective judgment surrounding possible hot-button topics of research,

TABLE 6.2 Topics That Cause People to Feel Uneasy in Research Interviews

Topic	Very Uneasy
Masturbation	56.4%
Marijuana use	42.0%
Sexual intercourse	41.5%
Stimulant/depressant use	31.3%
Intoxication	29.0%
Petting and kissing	19.7%
Income	12.5%
Gambling with friends	10.5%
Drinking	10.3%
General leisure	2.4%
Sports activities	1.3%

Source: Adapted from Blair et al., 1977:317.

Chicago researchers asked a large number of subjects to indicate which topics would cause most people to feel very uneasy in a research setting (Blair et al., 1977). Table 6.2 shows some of the findings. Note that about 40% of the respondents did not feel that even questions about masturbation would cause most people to feel "very uneasy." Presumably, these individuals would be inclined to answer honestly without embarrassment; for the majority, however, the responses may not be entirely accurate because of embarrassment.

Researchers need to make sure that such questions are sufficiently important to be asked. If asked, the questions need to be phrased as politely and unobtrusively as possible. Sometimes, questions can be prefaced with a brief warning of the personal nature of the questions about to be asked along with an explanation as to the reason. In one study, one of the authors of this text preceded a series of extremely personal questions about sexual behavior with a warning that "questions on the next page of this questionnaire are extremely personal, and you may skip them if you choose to do so and still complete the remainder of the questionnaire." About 7% of the subjects left this page blank.

Another method that was first developed by well-known sex researcher Alfred Kinsey and his research team (1948, 1953) was to not ask *whether* a particularly embarrassing behavior had been engaged in, but to simply ask how many times it had been engaged in. Of course, subjects could respond *none*, but such a questioning structure seems to make it easier for those who have engaged in a particularly embarrassing behavior to disclose doing so, both on an anonymous questionnaire and especially in an interview setting.

Nonjudgmental Phrasing or Prefacing of Questions

Studies have shown that if questions are asked in ways that imply to respondents that one type of answer is more socially or morally acceptable than another, answers will be biased toward such answers (Bradburn et al., 1978;

Hippler & Schwartz, 1987). For example, interviewers can often preface a question with a statement such as "Some people believe such-and-such, while others believe the opposite. What is your opinion regarding such-and-such?" This gives subjects some assurance that their opinion, whatever it may be, will be within reasonable bounds and will not be ridiculed. Often, questions pertaining to unusual behavior can be handled in similar ways, thereby increasing the chances that any truthful response will be respected (Catania et al., 1996).

A similar technique involves preceding questions with a statement that serves to downplay any undesirable aspect of providing an affirmative response. One study experimented along these lines by prefacing a question about whether subjects had ever been convicted of drunk driving with statements implying that drunk driving was not a very serious type of offense (Gendall et al., 1992). These statements included "Penalties for drunk driving are too harsh" and "Drinking and driving is not as dangerous as it's made out to be." The researchers found that subjects who were asked to report whether they agreed/disagreed with these statements before answering the question about ever having been convicted of drunk driving themselves reported higher rates than subjects who were asked the same question without being first asked to respond to these prefacing attitudinal statements.

Use the Bogus Pipeline Technique

A method called the bogus pipeline has been used in numerous studies to increase the honesty and frankness of questionnaire respondents. This is somewhat ironic because the bogus pipeline technique itself is effective due to being deceptive. Here is a brief sketch of how the typical bogus pipeline experiment is conducted: A subject is brought into a room and asked to complete a short questionnaire containing very basic and nonintimidating demographic and family background questions. Then the subject is told to leave the questionnaire in the first room and to follow the researcher into an adjoining room filled with sophisticated-looking computer equipment hooked up to wires and electrodes. The researcher explains to the subject that this is a recently developed device for measuring brain waves, heart rate, voice tremors, and the like that together can almost perfectly detect deception, even better than conventional "lie detectors."

With the subject's permission, he or she is hooked up to the device and asked to respond to most of the same questions just answered on the short questionnaire (that was left in the other room). Subjects are asked to lie at random on about half of the questions asked so that the researcher "can standardize the equipment." Unbeknownst to the subjects, a fellow researcher has picked up the subject's questionnaire and is using it to detect each lie. In this way, nearly all subjects are led to believe that the new lie-detecting contraption really does work. At that point, subjects are told that the researcher will be monitoring the equipment but will no longer interrupt them when any deception is detected. Subjects are then asked the really sensitive questions that were central to the study.

Studies based on the bogus pipeline design have shown that nearly all subjects are convinced of the gadget's power to detect dishonesty. And, as one

Can Researchers Accurately Assess Subjects' Honesty in Self-Report Surveys?

One method that has been used to detect dishonesty (as well as carelessness and poor memory) in responding to surveys is to simply ask subjects at the end of the questionnaire or the interview to rate their degree of honesty or carefulness. Some researchers believe that when asked this straightforward question, quite a few respondents will reveal that they were less than completely honest or careful in responding. What do you think? Will subjects who were dishonest or who just rushed through the survey actually admit to doing so at the end of it?

In a recent study (Hartley, Ellis, & Hoskin 2019), two of the authors of this book, for example, conducted a cross-national study to compare self-reported offending rates in samples of university students in the United States and Malaysia. In order to be able to state with certainty that any differences in offending in the two countries were due to real differences and not differences in honesty of the subjects in reporting their offending behavior, we included a final question on the survey that asked the following: "How carefully did you read and try to honestly answer the questions in this questionnaire? (answer from 0 to 10, with 0 meaning 'not at all honest' to 10 meaning 'extremely honest')." Results demonstrated that most of the respondents in both countries rated the carefulness and honesty with which they responded to the questions as very high despite some differences between the countries and within country between males and females. For example, the average care/honesty score for Malaysian male respondents was 8.40 whereas it was 9.42 for US males ($t = 10.572$, $p < 0.001$). Similarly, for Malaysian females, the average care/honesty rating was 8.47 compared to 9.42 for US females ($t = 16.634$, $p < 0.001$). Overall, we concluded that there was no reason to suggest that the differences we found in offending rates between the US and Malaysian university students (US students reported offending at a much higher rate) was due to dishonesty in responding to the questionnaire.

Of course, this approach to the detection of dishonesty or poor memory begs the question of what to do with questionnaires in which at least fairly high levels of deceptive or poor recall were indicated. If this happens, should researchers throw out the questionnaires of these respondents? The answer is probably yes! If this is done, however, it should be reported in the study that some surveys were thrown out due to high levels of dishonesty or lack of care in filling them out. An alternative to discarding some of the questionnaires is to conduct two separate analyses, one with and one without the questionnaires in which subjects reported being dishonest. By comparing results from these two analyses, a researcher can roughly estimate how much the suspect questionnaires might contaminate any of the findings.

might suspect, those subjected to the bogus pipeline usually give significantly less "socially desirable" (polite, politically correct) answers to questions about their attitudes and behavior than people asked the same questions in personal interviews not preceded by a bogus pipeline (reviewed by Roese & Jamieson, 1993). Researchers would obviously need IRB approval to be able to engage in this type of deception in order to elicit honest responses to a survey asking about sensitive issues or engagement in criminal behaviors.

Internal Consistency Checks

One can sometimes detect dishonest answers by asking essentially the same question more than once in the same questionnaire. This is known as checking for internal consistency (Farrington, 1973). Internal consistency checks are most often used to identify carelessness and unclear reasoning rather than out-and-out deception.

Use a Polygraph

Another method (or set of methods) that social scientists use to assess the honesty of subjects involves electronically monitoring physiological processes linked to human emotions, such as pulse, heart rate, and palm sweating. Generally, when people experience intense emotions or nervousness, these physiological indicators become elevated. Most people respond emotionally when lying, especially when important issues are involved and when they fear that the examiner may detect inconsistencies in their answers. Similar to police interrogations, researchers ask subjects a series of neutral questions to set baseline measures of pulse, heart rate, and palm sweat; the polygraph (or lie detector) is then used to look for subtle variations in stress levels. An offshoot of the polygraph test that has also been used for lie detection is a voice analyzer. This machine monitors subtle "microtremors" in the vocal cords, which tend to accompany high emotional states (Rice, 1978). Polygraph methods have been widely used in private business for detecting employee theft (Holden, 1986). They are also used in conducting criminal investigations. Only occasionally are they used for research purposes.

Independent Verification

Independent verification of self-reported information simply means that a second source for that information is obtained. For example, if we wanted to verify whether probationers were being honest in reporting avoidance of drug use, it would be important to obtain urine or hair samples. Along these lines, a household survey conducted in Puerto Rico asked people if they had ever used cocaine or heroin, teamed with assurance that the information would be kept confidential (Colon et al., 2001). At the end of the interview, subjects were asked if they would allow the interviewer to obtain a hair sample; three-fourths ($n = 152$) of them agreed. Key findings were as follows: Whereas 14 of the subjects' hair samples tested positive for "recent use" of cocaine, only 1 of these 14 subjects self-reported having used cocaine in the past three months. Regarding heroin, three subjects tested positive, but only one self-reported heroin use. This study suggests that self-reports about sensitive/illegal aspects of behavior, especially when derived from face-to-face interviews, usually provides a substantial underestimate of the actual prevalence of the behavior.

There are some very encouraging findings with respect to the accuracy of self-reports. One comes from independent verification of self-reported weight.

As mentioned earlier, studies have found very high correlations (e.g., $r = .96$) between people's self-reported weight on a questionnaire and their actual weight as indicated a few weeks later in a medical clinic (Charney et al., 1976; also see Coates et al., 1978). Obviously, nearly perfect correlations between self-reported and actual weight mean that little is gained from independent verification of this specific type of data.

Quite a number of studies have been undertaken to assess the accuracy of people's honesty in self-reported drug use. Several of these studies have obtained saliva, blood, or urine samples as a way of independently verifying earlier self-reports regarding smoking. A chemical called *cotinine* is a detectable by-product of smoking. Tests have shown that most people who smoke, even among young adolescents, honestly report doing so on questionnaires (Bauman & Koch, 1983).

Research has shown that people are more likely to report sensitive information about themselves on questionnaires than in face-to-face or telephone interviews (Siemiatycki, 1979). Why this would be true is open to speculation, but it may have to do with the tendency we all have to sometimes shade the truth so as not to cause ourselves or others to feel uneasy when socially interacting. There are ways to incorporate elements of a subject-completed questionnaire in some face-to-face interviews. One method is to provide subjects with a "mini-questionnaire" as part of the face-to-face interview. This mini-questionnaire would contain the potentially embarrassing items of information, and respondents would be told that they can send them in within the next day or two.

Conduct a Follow-Up (Retest Stability)

A very useful way to verify questionnaire data is to have subjects complete the form a second time. This method can be especially informative if the subjects are unaware at the time they fill out an initial questionnaire that they will be asked later to complete it a second time. Unfortunately, social scientists do not have many opportunities to use this type of verification. An example of the latter is the study mentioned earlier that found that roughly 20% of female teenagers who reported having had sexual intercourse on their first questionnaire stated on a questionnaire the following year that they were virgins (Rodgers et al., 1982). It would be difficult to attribute this to anything but dishonesty, although given the extremely personal nature of the question, it is certainly understandable.

⬤ Summary

In this chapter, surveys and sampling procedures were described. The two main categories of samples were identified as probability and nonprobability. Probability samples are more likely than nonprobability samples to be representative (i.e., a mirror image) of an existing population chosen for study.

There are two ways of obtaining representative samples. One way is by using a probability sampling method (one that is likely to yield a representative sample). Probability sampling methods include random sampling and cluster sampling. All but one form of random sampling require selecting sampling units (subjects) from a list of all members of the population targeted for study. These lists are referred to as sampling frames. The exception, called random digit dialing, is used in some telephone surveys. In cluster sampling, the sampling frames are in two or more "layers." The first layer may consist of clusters of subjects (e.g., all universities in some country). Within the first sampling layer, a researcher then chooses the actual subjects to be studied.

The other way to obtain a representative sample involves weighting. After the data have been collected, weighting procedures can be used to inflate the responses from the proportions of a sample that were underrepresented. In other words, if a population had exactly an equal number of males and females but a sample contained only 40% males, responses from that 40% of the sample could be inflated until their responses have a weight equal to that of the female portion of the sample. Weighting is reserved for surveys with large numbers of subject in which researchers have access to sophisticated computer programs.

Six nonprobability sampling methods were identified. These include what are termed accidental samples, quota samples, self-selected samples, snowball samples, convenience samples, and event samples. None of these sampling methods should be trusted to yield representative samples, but this does not preclude their use in scientific research, especially when probability sampling is not feasible.

Guidelines were given for deciding the size of a sample. In general, the larger the sample the better, but remember that the law of diminishing returns means that the larger the sample happens to be, the less sampling error is reduced with the addition of each new subject. Ultimately, researchers must always balance the accuracy needed in a survey against the additional time and expense of adding new subjects. More will be said about sampling issues and attempts to generalize about populations on the basis of samples in Chapter 7.

A distinction was made between cross-sectional surveys and longitudinal surveys. Longitudinal surveys are subdivided into panel, nonpanel, and partial panel according to whether the same subjects are being used each time the survey is conducted.

This chapter also looked carefully at the special problems associated with sampling human subjects, especially in terms of the accuracy of self-reported information. In the first part of this chapter, a distinction was made between a chosen sample, the sample a researcher initially selects, and an obtained sample, the subjects that a researcher actually gets. Subtracting the obtained sample from the chosen sample yields what is referred to as sample attrition, which is obviously something researchers seek to minimize. Typically, researchers feel that sample attrition that is less than 15% of the chosen sample will contain little systematic sampling error. Nevertheless, even if attrition exceeds 50% in a survey, the data can still provide useful insights. Researchers should forthrightly report the attrition rates, however.

Ways of minimizing sample attrition were discussed in greatest depth in regard to mail surveys because most of the research has involved this type of survey (as opposed to household and telephone surveys). The techniques that have been found useful in reducing attrition are as follows:

Send prenotifications to prospective respondents.

Attach a polite and clearly written cover letter.

Personalize the correspondence.

Make the most interesting/relevant features of the survey apparent.

Have a credible sponsor.

Keep the questionnaire short.

Make sure the questionnaire is neat and well organized.

Enclose a stamped self-addressed return envelope.

Enclose token compensation.

Send one or more follow-up questionnaires to nonrespondents.

Most sample attrition in household and telephone surveys is due to people not being at home and to refusals. In general, the latter is considered more of a source of potential systematic sampling error than are not-at-homes. There is little research yet on how to minimize not-at-homes and refusal. The latter portion of this chapter dealt with inaccuracies in self-reported information. Four sources of inaccuracies were identified and discussed: (1) failure to understand a question, (2) failure to accurately recall the answer, (3) unstable opinions, and (4) dishonesty. Techniques that have been used to increase frankness or to detect dishonesty in self-reported information were as follows:

Assure anonymity and confidentiality.

Take special care in asking embarrassing questions.

Phrase questions in nonjudgmental ways.

Use the bogus pipeline technique.

Have subjects self-report their degree of honesty (or level of accuracy).

Check for internal consistency within a questionnaire.

Use a polygraph.

Independently verify data.

Conduct a follow-up in which subjects re-report key data.

Discussion Questions

1. Discuss the differences between probability and nonprobability sampling techniques. Why is it important to use a probability sampling strategy if a researcher wants to generalize their findings?

2. Describe the difference between cross-sectional and longitudinal survey research. Why might longitudinal research studies be especially important for examining causal relationships in criminology?

3. What is the difference between a population and a sample?

4. Describe how a researcher can assess the representativeness of a sample. Further, are there methods that researchers can employ to adjust for a sample's unrepresentativeness?

⬭ Exercises

1. Discuss a research project for which a multistage cluster sampling strategy would be appropriate. Be sure to outline the different clusters at each stage and explain what your unit of analysis would be.

2. Plan a study for which you think a snowball sampling strategy would be the best approach. Who might your initial participants be?

⬭ Notes

[1] Technically, a distinction can be made between a *population* and a *universe,* with the latter being a more inclusive term. Specifically, a population refers to a collection of humans (or other living things), whereas a universe includes populations but also refers to collections of characteristics (or numbers representing those characteristics) exhibited by members of a population.

[2] In precise statistical terms, the error percentages presented in Table 6.1 actually represent 95% confidence limits. This means that one time out of 20, the actual percentages might exceed the confidence limits.

Chapter 7 Measuring Crime and Criminality

Have you ever done anything for which you could have been punished by time in jail or prison? Were you caught? Have you ever been the victim of a crime? Did you report it? As likely as not, most people will answer yes, no, yes, no to these questions. Despite the US government spending more money each year than the gross national product of some small nations to measure the extent of crime in the United States, there is still a tremendous amount of unknown crime. Criminologists call this the "dark figure" of crime. This chapter provides hints as to why the figure is so dark and what has and is being done to try to illuminate it through self-report and victimization surveys. Much of what we know about offending behavior is based on self-reports, and a considerable amount of research has examined the special problems surrounding the human side of sampling.

Measuring Crime and Criminal Behavior

This chapter deals with two very important issues in criminal justice and criminology: How do we measure crime and how much of it is there? The first step in coming to terms with any social problem, including the crime problem, is to discover how much of a problem it actually is. This means discovering how much of it there is, where and when it occurs most often, and among what social categories it occurs most frequently. In other words, crime has to be defined and then counted. At this point we are engaging in simple fact finding without attempting to ask theoretical questions (why does crime occur; why is it increasing or decreasing, and so on); such questions can only be properly addressed after we have reliable data on hand. But we must not forget that all social statistics are suspect to some extent, and crime statistics are perhaps the most suspect of all. Crime statistics have been collected from many different sources in many different ways and have passed through many sieves of judgment before being recorded. As Sir Josiah Stamp once cynically put it: "The government are [sic] very keen on amassing statistics. They collect them, raise them to the nth power, take the cube root and prepare wonderful diagrams. But you must never forget that every one of these figures comes in the first instance from the village watchmen, who just puts down what he damn pleases" (in Nettler, 1984:39). We don't recommend this level of cynicism because official data collection has greatly improved Stamp's observation, but we do advise you to keep a healthy skepticism about them.

Categorizing and Measuring Crime Officially

The US government provides researchers with a wide variety of crime data for their studies; all have their particular strengths and weaknesses. The major data sources that we address in this chapter are the Uniform Crime Reports (UCR), the National Crime Victimization Survey (NCVS), and the National Incident-Based Reporting System (NIBRS). The UCR and NIBRS are official statistics derived from the routine functioning of the police. These are measures of crime; we will also examine measures of criminality (the propensity of individuals to engage in criminal behavior) through self-report and clinical measures. The most basic category of official statistics comes from the calls made to police by victims or witnesses and by crimes that the police discover for themselves while on patrol. We will see later how researchers have used comparisons between each of these measures to try to resolve two contentious issues in criminology/criminal justice regarding sex and racial issues.

⬤ The Uniform Crime Reports: Counting Crime Officially

The primary source of official crime statistics in the United States since 1930 has been the annual **Uniform Crime Reports** (UCR) compiled by the Federal Bureau of Investigation (FBI). The UCR reports crimes known to the nation's police and sheriff's departments and the number of arrests made by these agencies; crimes that are the concern of the federal government (which include a wide array of white-collar crimes) are not included. Offenses known to the police are recorded whether or not an arrest is made or whether an arrested person is subsequently prosecuted and convicted. Participation in the UCR reporting program is voluntary; thus, all agencies do not participate. This is unfortunate for anyone hoping for comprehensive crime data.

In 2017, law enforcement agencies participating in the program represented approximately 308 million US residents, about 95.5% of the population (FBI, 2018). This means that crimes committed by about 4.5% of the American population (about 14.5 million people) were not included in the UCR data. UCR data are aggregated in large units of analysis to the national, state, county, city, and other geographic levels such as regions. This means that researchers cannot say much about the particular crimes they may be interested in beyond reporting their aggregated number. The only exception to this is murder, for which the FBI supplies disaggregated supplemental information. We will discuss this exception later.

What Is Crime?

The concept of crime is an abstract one because we cannot directly observe it. We can obviously witness actions that have been defined as belonging to a category called crime, such as person A stabbing person B, but not crime per se. Be that as it may, we need a conceptual definition to proceed. Perhaps the most often quoted definition of crime is that of criminologist and lawyer Paul Tappan (1947), who defined it as "an intentional act in violation of the criminal law committed without defense or excuse, and penalized by the state." A crime is thus an *act* in violation of a *criminal law* for which a *punishment* is prescribed; the person committing it must have *intended* to do so and must have done so without legally acceptable *defense* or *justification*. The only segment of Tappan's definition that we can directly observe as a discrete event is the act (we cannot observe if it was intentional); thus, if we want to ask questions about crime we must operationally define what observable acts fall under the crime umbrella.

The UCR separates crimes into two categories: **Part I offenses** (or **index crimes**), and **Part II offenses**. Part I offenses include four violent (homicide, assault, forcible rape, and robbery) and four property offenses (larceny/theft, burglary, motor vehicle theft, and arson). These crimes are all universally condemned (*mala in se* offenses) as indicated by the fact that all 125 member nations reporting their annual crime rates to the International Criminal Police Organization (Interpol) list them as major crimes (Walsh & Jorgenson, 2018). Thus, the Part I offenses apparently correspond with what most people think of as "serious" crime. The FBI's definitions of all Part I offenses follow.

> **Murder** is "the willful (nonnegligent) killing of one human being by another."
>
> **Forcible rape** used to be defined as "the carnal knowledge of a female forcibly and against her will." Beginning in 2013, the term "forcible" was removed and it became gender neutral. Thus, the definition was changed to: "penetration, no matter how slight, of the vagina or anus with any body part or object, or oral penetration by a sex organ of another person, without the consent of the victim."
>
> **Robbery** is "the taking or attempted taking of anything of value from the care, custody, or control of a person or persons by force or threat of force or violence and/or putting the victim in fear."
>
> **Aggravated assault** is "an unlawful attack by one person upon another for the purpose of inflicting severe or aggravated bodily injury."
>
> **Burglary** is "the unlawful entry of a structure to commit a felony or theft."
>
> **Larceny-Theft** is "the unlawful taking, leading, or riding away from the possession or constructive possession of another."
>
> **Motor vehicle theft** is "the theft or attempted theft of a motor vehicle."
>
> **Arson** is "any willful or malicious burning or attempting to burn, with or without intent to defraud, a dwelling house, public building, motor vehicle or aircraft, personal property of another, etc."

Note that all these definitions identify certain specific actions that must be taken by the offender in order to say that he or she qualifies as chargeable for the crime in question. Of course, all elements of the crime not directly observable (intentionality, willfulness, etc.) have to be inferred and later proven according to legal standards.

Determining Crime Rates

The UCR reports the number of each type of crime reported to the police as well as their rate of occurrence. The **rate** of a given crime is the actual number of reported (and recorded) crimes standardized by some unit of the population. We expect the raw number of crimes to increase as the population increases, so comparing the number of crimes reported today with the number reported when your parents were your age, or the number of crimes reported in California with the number reported in Louisiana, tells us next to nothing without considering population differences. For instance, California reported 1,930 murders to the FBI in 2017, and Louisiana reported 555. In which state are you most likely to be murdered? We can't say unless we take their respective populations into consideration. To obtain a crime rate, we divide the number of reported crimes in a state by its population and multiply the quotient by 100,000, as in the following comparison of California and Louisiana rates.

CA Murders = 1,930

Rate = ———— = 0.000048 × 100,000 = 4.8

CA Population = 39,780,350

LA Murders = 555

Rate = ———— = 0.000118 × 100,000 = 11.8

LA Population = 4,684,333

Thus a person in Louisiana is at over twice the risk (11.8 versus 4.8 murders per 100,000 population) of being murdered than he or she is in California. This statement is based on the statewide rates; the actual risk will vary widely from person to person based on such factors as age, race, sex, socioeconomic status (SES), neighborhood, and urban versus rural residence. In other words, some people in some places in California will be at much higher risk of being murdered than some people in some places in Louisiana.

Part II offenses are treated as less serious offenses and are recorded based on arrests made rather than cases reported to the police. Part II offense figures understate the extent of criminal offending far more than is the case with Part I figures because only a very small proportion of these crimes result in arrest. Part II offenses may not be "true" criminal offenses (e.g., runaway), or if they are, may not be particularly serious (e.g., gambling and other "victimless" crimes). However, "sex offenses" covers all offenses of a sexual nature except forcible rape, prostitution, and commercial vice. Such offenses cover everything from exhibitionism to incest. The former may be relatively harmless, but the latter can have devastating effects. This is not to say that the states will not charge incestuous or other types of child molestation offenders with serious felony crimes such as lewd and lascivious conduct or sexual battery. Table 7.1 lists the estimated number of all Part I and Part II offenses for which arrests were made in 2017 compared with 2008 and broken down by sex and age. The UCR provides numerous tables such as this.

Problems with the UCR

The UCR is useful to researchers and law enforcement agencies because it provides them with tallies of serious crimes known to the police. Rates can be compared over time and geographic locations (states, counties, and cities) going back to 1930 and thus provides data about crime trends and fluctuations. It also provides data

TABLE 7.1 Estimated Number of Arrests for Part I and Part II Crimes by Sex and Age in 2008 and 2017

| | Male | | | | | | Female | | | | | |
| | Total | | | Under 18 | | | Total | | | Under 18 | | |
Offense charged	2008	2017	Percent change	2008	2017	Percent change	2008	2017	Percent change	2008	2017	Percent change
TOTAL[1]	6,684,673	5,006,416	−25.1	911,744	380,337	−58.3	2,183,085	1,872,513	−14.2	371,761	157,996	−57.5
Murder and nonnegligent manslaughter	6,727	6,407	−4.8	662	488	−26.3	817	935	+14.4	54	42	−22.2
Rape[2]	13,445	14,341	—	2,014	2,390	—	153	418	—	28	92	—
Robbery	68,320	48,568	−28.9	18,716	9,986	−46.6	9,132	8,450	−7.5	1,892	1,166	−38.4
Aggravated assault	219,276	195,513	−10.8	27,345	13,653	−50.1	59,873	58,972	−1.5	8,460	4,968	−41.3
Burglary	172,133	105,800	−38.5	48,260	17,996	−62.7	30,796	24,815	−19.4	7,059	2,465	−65.1
Larceny-theft	485,729	378,305	−22.1	121,620	50,722	−58.3	350,042	265,548	−24.1	97,138	30,222	−68.9
Motor vehicle theft	48,194	44,239	−8.2	12,082	7,668	−36.5	10,162	12,964	+27.6	2,360	1,839	−22.1
Arson	7,987	4,908	−38.6	3,992	1,358	−66.0	1,460	1,194	−18.2	549	228	−58.5
Violent crime[3]	307,768	264,829	−14.0	48,737	26,517	−45.6	69,975	68,775	−1.7	10,434	6,268	−39.9
Property crime[3]	714,043	533,252	−25.3	185,954	77,744	−58.2	392,460	304,521	−22.4	107,106	34,754	−67.6
Other assaults	612,453	491,125	−19.8	98,121	51,063	48.0	213,142	199,319	−6.5	51,097	30,572	−40.2
Forgery and counterfeiting	36,845	24,342	−33.9	1,199	659	−45.0	22,947	12,888	−43.8	604	175	−71.0
Fraud	86,861	52,167	−39.9	3,332	1,826	−45.2	68,796	31,487	−54.2	1,807	940	−48.0

1 Does not include suspicion.

2 The 2008 rape figures are based on the legacy definition, and the 2017 rape figures are aggregate totals based on both the legacy and revised Uniform Crime Reporting definitions. For this reason, a percent change is not provided.

3 Violent crimes are offenses of murder and nonnegligent manslaughter, rape, robbery, and aggravated assault. Property crimes are offenses of burglary, larceny-theft, motor vehicle theft, and arson.

continued

Offense charged	Male Total			Male Under 18			Female Total			Female Under 18		
	2008	2017	Percent change	2008	2017	Percent change	2008	2017	Percent change	2008	2017	Percent change
Embezzlement	6,948	5,201	−25.1	502	187	−62.7	7,529	5,300	−29.6	361	185	−48.8
Stolen property: buying, receiving, possessing	59,620	51,469	−13.7	11,650	5,828	−50.0	15,782	14,567	−7.7	2,806	1,074	−61.7
Vandalism	154,800	98,927	−36.1	61,575	21,276	−65.4	31,493	28,204	−10.4	9,402	4,546	−51.6
Weapons; carrying, possessing, etc.	101,938	92,702	−9.1	22,675	10,377	−54.2	8,195	9,869	+20.4	2,292	1,262	−44.9
Prostitution and commercialized vice	11,333	7,705	−32.0	195	73	−62.6	23,154	10,427	−55.0	554	75	−86.5
Sex offenses (except rape and prostitution)	45,409	28,773	−36.6	8,469	5,082	−40.0	3,480	2,234	−35.8	899	664	−26.1
Drug abuse violations	843,915	813,824	−3.6	93,476	48,663	−47.9	200,143	263,816	+31.8	18,561	15,540	−16.3
Gambling	2,035	1,083	−46.8	259	70	−73.0	396	357	−9.8	17	13	−23.5
Offenses against the family and children	55,945	39,753	−28.9	2,293	1,603	−30.1	18,376	17,024	−7.4	1,275	955	−25.1
Driving under the influence	763,493	488,769	−36.0	8,041	3,090	−61.6	211,475	166,066	−21.5	2,623	1,014	−61.3
Liquor laws	293,557	94,685	−67.7	55,777	14,105	−74.7	117,198	43,144	−63.2	34,275	9,838	−71.3

continued

Offense charged	Male						Female					
	Total			Under 18			Total			Under 18		
	2008	2017	Percent change	2008	2017	Percent change	2008	2017	Percent change	2008	2017	Percent change
Drunkenness	342,258	182,844	–46.6	8,273	1,934	–76.6	67,886	47,517	–30.0	2,711	809	–70.2
Disorderly conduct	322,117	163,874	–49.1	82,845	27,063	–67.3	117,293	69,062	–41.1	40,315	15,242	–62.2
Vagrancy	12,512	10,594	–15.3	862	315	–63.5	3,527	3,359	–4.8	226	92	–59.3
All other offenses (except traffic)	1,869,437	1,549,710	–17.1	176,123	72,074	–59.1	569,560	569,306	*	64,118	28,647	–55.3
Suspicion	623	150	–75.9	124	31	–75.0	182	51	–72.0	28	11	–60.7
Curfew and loitering law violations	41,386	10,788	–73.9	41,386	10,788	–73.9	20,278	5,331	–73.7	20,278	5,331	–73.7

* Less than one-tenth of 1 percent.

Source: FBI (2018). Crime in the United States, 2017. Washington, DC. Government Printing Office

to law enforcement agencies to assist them in the administration, operation, and management of their agencies. However, UCR data have serious limitations that restrict their usefulness for criminological research, particularly research seeking to uncover causes of crime. Some of the more serious of these limitations follow:

- The UCR data significantly underrepresents the actual number of criminal events in the United States each year. According to a nationwide victim survey, only 49.9% of victims of violent crime and 39% of victims of property crime indicated that they reported their victimization to the police (Catalano, 2006). Victims are more likely to report violent crimes if injuries are serious and are more likely to report property crimes when losses are high. Reasons most often given for not reporting include the opinion that the police could not or would not do anything about it, that the offense was a private matter, that it "was no big deal," and fear of reprisal. An important exception to the underreporting complaint is criminal homicide, for which the UCR provides the most reliable and timely data available.

- Federal white-collar crimes are not reported, thus missing many costly crimes such as stock market fraud, hazardous waste dumping, tax evasion, and false claims for professional services. The only white-collar crimes reported in the UCR are embezzlement, fraud, and forgery/counterfeiting.

- The voluntary nature of the UCR program means that the crimes committed in the jurisdictions of nonparticipating law enforcement agencies are not included in the data. Even with full voluntary compliance, all departments would not be equally as efficient and thorough (or honest) in their record keeping.

- Crime data may be falsified by police departments for political reasons. The National Center for Policy Analysis (1998) reports that police departments in Philadelphia, New York, Atlanta, and Boca Raton, Florida, had underreported and/or downgraded crimes in their localities (and these are just the departments that we know about). With promotions, pay raises, and even continued employment based on performance, pressure is generated to "prove" such performance by presenting improved crime statistics.

- The UCR even underreports crimes that are known to the police because of the FBI's hierarchy rule. The **hierarchy rule** requires police to report only the highest (most serious) offenses committed in incidents in which multiple offenses are committed to the FBI and to ignore the others. For instance, if a man robs five patrons in a bar, pistol whips one patron who tried to resist, locks the victims in the beer cooler, rapes the female bartender, and then escapes in a stolen car, only the rape is reported to the FBI. The upshot of this is that five robberies, one aggravated assault, and one motor vehicle theft are lost to the year's tally. The rule, of course, does not prevent the state from charging the perpetrator with five counts of robbery, one count of aggravated assault, and one count of auto theft as well as one count of rape. Parenthetically, the hierarchy rule prevents criminologists from comparing cross-national data because countries such as England and Australia would record all eight crimes in their official statistics.

Supplementary Homicide Reports

Given these sorts of difficulties, why should official crime statistics be trusted at all? Many criminologists have expressed serious reservations about official crime statistics over the years (Robinson, 2005). The most frequent criticism has been that these data are too easily affected by discretionary police policies to be considered reliable. Of course, the police really have no discretion when responding to complaints by citizens or to a magistrate's warrant when it comes to felony charges. This is even more true when it comes to the most serious of all crimes—murder. It is difficult to imagine circumstances under which the police had discretionary power, or under which they would change their investigatory policies, for murder. Except for rare incidents of undiscovered bodies and homicides classified as suicides or accidents (or vice versa), we can rest assured that murder is the most reliably measured crime of all.

Murder is also the only crime the UCR provides supplemental information for in its **supplementary homicide reports**. These reports are incident-based; thus, the incident (each particular murder) is the unit of analysis. Although this additional information is only demographic in nature, with it researchers may tease out relationships among variables, such as who kills whom, under what circumstances, and what kinds of weapons are commonly used. The reports also supply data on the race, age, and sex of offenders and victims and the relationship that existed between offender and victim (spouse, lover, acquaintance, etc.). Of course, not all murders are solved, so variables such as victim/offender relationship and the age, sex, and race of the murderer in unsolved cases are not known. For instance, only 61.1% of homicides were cleared (the police had identified the probable offender regardless of whether or not he or she had been arrested) in 2017, meaning we lacked information on the offender in 38.9% of the murder incidents in the United States in 2017.

Additional Information in the Incident-Based Supplementary Homicide Reports

Victim/Offender Demographics

- Sex, Race, Age.

Victim-Offender Relationship

- **Family**—Husband, wife, common-law husband, common-law wife, mother, father, son, daughter, brother, sister, in-law, stepfather, stepmother, stepson, stepdaughter, and other family member.
- **Acquaintance**—Acquaintance, boyfriend, girlfriend, ex-husband, exwife, employee, employer, friend, homosexual relation, neighbor, and other known individual.
- **Stranger**—Stranger.
- **Unknown**—Relationship unknown.

Weapon Used

- **Firearm**—Firearm, handgun, rifle, shotgun, and other gun.
- **Knife**—Knife, cutting instrument, icepick, screwdriver, axe, etc.
- **Blunt object**—Hammer, club, etc.
- **Personal**—Hands, fists, feet, and other personal weapon.
- **Other**—Poison, pushed out window, explosives, fire, drugs, drowning, strangulation, asphyxiation, and other unknown weapon.

⊜ NIBRS: The "New and Improved" UCR

Efforts to improve the reliability and validity of official statistics are occurring all the time, with the most ambitious being the **National Incident-Based Reporting System** (NIBRS). The NIBRS began in 1982 and is designed "to enhance the quantity, quality, and timeliness of crime statistical data collected by the law enforcement community and to improve the methodology used for compiling, analyzing, auditing, and publishing the collected crime data" (FBI, 2018). NIBRS is currently a component of the UCR program and will completely replace it in 2021. As opposed to the current UCR, which monitors only a relatively few crimes and gathers few details associated with them, NIBRS collects data on 46 "Group A" offenses (grouped into 22 broad categories) and 11 "Group B" offenses. As with offenses listed under Part II in the UCR, Group B offenses in NIBRS count only if they result in an arrest.

Group A Offenses

1. Arson
2. Assault (aggravated, simple, intimidation)
3. Bribery
4. Burglary/Breaking and Entering
5. Counterfeiting/Forgery
6. Destruction/Damage/Vandalism of Property
7. Drug/Narcotic Offenses (including drug equipment violations)
8. Embezzlement
9. Extortion/Blackmail
10. Fraud (false pretenses/swindle/confidence game, credit card and ATM fraud, impersonation, welfare and wire fraud)
11. Gambling (betting, wagering, operating/promoting/assisting gambling, gambling equipment violations, sports tampering)
12. Homicide (murder and nonnegligent manslaughter, negligent manslaughter, justifiable homicide)
13. Kidnapping/Abduction

14. Larceny (pocket picking, purse snatching, shoplifting, theft and all other larceny)

15. Motor Vehicle Theft

16. Pornography/Obscene Material

17. Prostitution Offenses (prostitution, assisting or promoting prostitution)

18. Robbery

19. Sex Offenses, Forcible (forcible rape, forcible sodomy, sexual assault with an object, forcible fondling)

20. Sex Offenses, Nonforcible (incest, statutory rape)

21. Stolen Property Offenses

22. Weapon Law Violations

Group B Offenses

1. Bad Checks

2. Curfew/Loitering/Vagrancy Violations

3. Disorderly Conduct

4. Driving under the Influence

5. Drunkenness

6. Family Offenses, Nonviolent

7. Liquor Law Violations

8. Peeping Tom

9. Runaway

10. Trespass of Real Property

11. All Other Offenses

As the name implies, NIBRS is incident-based, meaning every element of each incident is recorded. There is no hierarchy rule under the NIBRS system; it reports multiple victims, multiple offenders, and multiple crimes that may be part of the same incident. It also provides information about the circumstances of the offense and about victim and offender characteristics, such as offender/victim relationship, age, sex, and race of victims and perpetrators (if known). The UCR only reports such characteristics for homicide in its Supplementary Homicide Reports. NIBRS has also made every effort to increase quality control by requiring computerized submission of data, which makes it easier for analysts to check for systematic data errors.

Despite the promise of NIBRS, it has yet to come near to realizing its full potential. Only 37 states plus the District of Columbia reported crime incidents to NIBRS in 2016 (FBI, 2017). This is because the promise of NIBRS for research purposes is its weakness in terms of agency participation. Many departments lack the workforce and technical expertise to collect and process the wide and detailed range of information that is part of each crime incident that their

BOX 7.1 CURRENT ISSUES

Using the UCR and NIBRS to Test Contending Hypotheses

What is the nature of the relationship between race and arrest rates? It has long been observed that African Americans account for about three times the total number of arrests for violent felonies (38.8% in 2005) than their percentage of the US population (about 12.8%). One school of thought maintains that blacks commit disproportionately more crimes than other racial groups and that their disproportionate appearance in the arrest statistics simply reflects this fact (the differential offending hypothesis). Another school of thought attributes elevated levels of arrest for blacks to racial discrimination among the police (the differential arrest hypothesis). These contending hypotheses cannot be tested using only UCR data because there is no verification of offenders' race from victims. If the differential arrest hypothesis is true, we should see large discrepancies between the UCR arrest data and victims' racial identifications of their assailants in the NIBRS data.

Stewart D'Alessio and Lisa Stolzenberg (2003) addressed this important question by examining NIBRS data from 17 states that included data from 335,619 arrests for rape, robbery, and aggravated and simple assault. NIBRS data is most appropriate because it allows researchers to relate a reported crime to a subsequent arrest. The researchers found that, contrary to the differential arrest hypothesis, whites were significantly more likely to be arrested for robbery, aggravated assault, and simple assault than blacks, but there was no racial difference in the probability of arrest for rape. For instance, of the 2,620 robbers described by their victims as white, 30.8% were arrested as opposed to 21.4% of the 5,278 robbers described by their victims as black. These results held after controlling for other variables (use of weapon, injury to victim, and sex and age of offender and victim). D'Alessio and Stolzenberg concluded that their study supported the differential offending hypothesis, at least for arrests for violent crimes (obviously racial differences in the probability of arrest for property crimes in which the racial and other characteristics of the offender are rarely known to the victim cannot be assessed by this method).

officers deal with, and administrators see little benefit to their department to justify the effort (Dunworth, 2001). When NIBRS replaces the UCR, many government grants will have to go to police agencies to recruit and train people about NIBRS. When or if this happens, we should see an improvement in the reliability and validity of crime data across law enforcement jurisdictions and enjoy a greater richness of information. Nevertheless, there will still be concern over what criminologists have come to call the **dark figure** of crime. The dark (or hidden) figure refers to all of the crimes committed that never come to the attention of the police (Blumstein et al., 1991).

⊖ Crime Victimization Survey Data

One way of illuminating the dark figure of crime is through crime victimization surveys. Crime victimization surveys involve asking large numbers of people if they have been criminally victimized within some specified time frame regardless of whether they reported the incident to police. The first two known victimization surveys were conducted in Scandinavia; the first one dating back to Denmark in 1720 (Clinard, 1978). At that time a concerned citizen of the city of Aarhus went door-to-door asking city residents if they had been the victim of any crime in recent years and to provide details if they had. The second known survey was carried out over two centuries later in Norway in the late 1940s (Wolfgang et al., 1972). Although these early surveys lacked scientific rigor, they provided the template for numerous international, national, and local victimization surveys conducted around the world beginning in the 1970s.

The first such survey completed in the United States in 1967 was based on interviews of adults from 10,000 households (Ennis, 1967). The first major government-sponsored survey of victimization, known as the National Crime Survey (NCS), was taken each year from 1973 to 1992 before it was redesigned in 1993. Currently, twice a year Census Bureau personnel interview a national representative sample of people age 12 or over on behalf of the Bureau of Justice Statistics (BJS). This biannual survey is the successor to the NCS and is known as the **National Crime Victimization Survey** (NCVS). In 2016, people from a total of 134,690 households were interviewed by trained interviewers (Morgan & Kena, 2018). The NCVS requests information on crimes committed against individuals and households (whether reported to the police of not) and for circumstances of the offense (time and place it occurred, perpetrator's use of a weapon, any injuries incurred, and financial loss). Additionally, interviewers request personal information about victims (age, sex, race, income, and education level) and offenders (approximate age, sex, race, and victim/offender relationship). The units of analysis are thus individuals and households.

Having collected and analyzed all this information, the data derived from the sample are extrapolated to the entire population of the United States. If the sample reveals a simple assault rate of 5 per 1,000 individuals over age 12, for instance, the NCVS will report a rate of 5 per 1,000 (or 500 per 100,000) for the United States. It is perfectly acceptable to make inferences from samples to populations like this assuming that samples are truly representative of the population, which the NCVS samples are.

The Importance of the Right Questions: Redesigning the NCVS

Figure 7.1 shows a page from the current NCVS. Note that interviewers are asked to request that respondents clarify answers to certain questions. These clarifying items were added when it became obvious to BJS researchers that the same actions on the part of offenders are perceived differently by different people. For instance, many people used the termed "robbed" to mean burglarized or cheated. Differential interpretations caused quite a problem prior to 1992 when the old NCS was redesigned and renamed the NCVS.

Note from Figure 7.2 the different ways that various questions have been changed from the old NCV to the new NCVS in order to elicit more accurate answers. From January 1992 through June 1993, the NCS/NCVS sample was divided into two parts, with half the sample respondents being administered

29.	**How were you attacked? Any other way?** *Mark (X) all that apply.* FIELD REPRESENTATIVE- *if raped, ASK—* **Do you mean forced or coerced sexual intercourse?** *If No, ASK -* **What do you mean?** *If tried to rape, ASK-* **Do you mean attempted forced or coerced sexual intercourse?** *If No, ASK-* **What do you mean?**	646 — 1☐ Raped * — 2☐ Tried to rape 3☐ Sexual assault other than rape or attempted rape 4☐ Shot 5☐ Shot at (but missed) 6☐ Hit with gun held in hand 647 — 7☐ Stabbed/cut with knife/sharp weapon * — 8☐ Attempted attack with knife/sharp weapon 9☐ Hit by object (other than gun) held in hand 10☐ Hit by thrown object 648 — 11☐ Attempted attack with weapon other than * — gun/knife/sharp weapon 12☐ Hit, slapped, knocked down 13☐ Grabbed, held, tripped, jumped, pushed, etc. 14☐ Other - *Specify*
30.	**Did the offender THREATEN to hurt you before you were actually attacked?**	649 — 1☐ Yes 2☐ No 3☐ Other-*Specify*
31.	**What were the injuries you suffered, if any? Anything else?** *Mark (X) all that apply* FIELD REPRESENTATIVE- *if raped, and box 1 in item 29 is NOT marked, ASK-* **Do you mean forced or coerced sexual intercourse?** *If No, ASK-* **What do you mean?** *It attempted rape and box 2 in term 29 is NOT marked, ASK-* **Do you mean attempted forced or coerced sexual intercourse?** *If No, ASK-* **What do you mean?**	655 — 1☐ None- *SKIP to 40* * — 2☐ Raped 3☐ Attempted rape 4☐ Sexual assault other than rape or attempted rape 5☐ Knife or stab wounds 6☐ Gun shot, bullet wounds 656 — 7☐ Broken bones or teeth knocked out * — 8☐ Internal injuries 9☐ Knocked unconscious 10☐ Bruses, black eye, cuts, scratches, swelling, chipped teeth 11☐ Other-*Specify*
32.	*ASK OR VERIFY-* **Were any of the injuries caused by a weapon other than a gun or knife?**	657 — 1☐ Yes - *ASK 33* 2☐ No - ***SKIP** to 34*
33.	**Which injuries were caused by a weapon OTHER than a gun or knife?** *Enter code(s) from 31.*	658 ☐☐☐ ☐☐☐ ☐☐☐ Code Code Code
34.	**Were you injured to the extent that you received any medical care, including self treatment?**	659 — 1☐ Yes - *ASK 35* 2☐ No - ***SKIP** to 40*
35.	**Where did you receive this care? Anywhere else?** *Mark (X) all that apply*	660 — 1☐ At the scene 2☐ At home/neighbor's/friend's 3☐ Health unit at work/school, first aid station at a stadium/park, etc. 4☐ Doctor's office/health clinic 5☐ Emergency room at hospital/emergency clinic 6☐ Hospital (other than emergency room) 7☐ Other-*Specify*

FIGURE 7.1   Example of NCVS Victimization Questions

Source: Catalano (2006) Bureau of Justice Statistics, NCVS Survey.

NCV-style questions and the other half NCVS-style questions (Kinderman, Lynch, & Cantor, 1997). This enabled researchers to compare and evaluate the results from the new and redesigned methods from information gathered in

New (NCVS, beginning January 1992)	Old (NCS, 1972-92)

1. Has anyone attacked or threatened you in any of these ways —
 	
 a. With any weapon, for instance, a gun or knife —
 b. With anything like a baseball bat, frying pan, scissors, or stick —
 c. By something thrown, such as a rock or bottle —
 d. Include any grabbing, punching, or choking,
 e. Any rape, attempted rape or other type of sexual assault —
 f. Any face to face threads —
 	
   OR
 	
 g. Any attack or threat or use of force by anyone at all?
 	
   Please mention it even if you were not certain it was a crime
 	
 2. Incidents involving forced or unwanted sexual acts are often difficult to talk about. Have you been forced or coerced to engage in unwanted sexual activity by —
 	
 a. Someone you didn't know before
 b. A casual acquaintance OR
 c. Someone you know well.
	1. Did anyone take something directly from you by using force, such as by a stickup, mugging, or threat?
	
	 2. Did anyone TRY to rob you by using force or threatening to harm you?
	
	 3. Did anyone beat you up, attack you, or hit you with something, such as a rock or bottle?
	
	 4. Were you knifed, shot at, or attacked with some other weapon by anyone at all?
	
	 5. Did anyone THREATEN to beat you up or THREATEN you with a knife, gun, or some other weapon, NOT including telephone threats?
	
	 6. Did anyone TRY to attack you in some other way?

FIGURE 7.2   Comparisons of New NCVS and Old NCS Screener Questions

Source: Kindermann, Lynch, & Cantor (1997). Bureau of Justice Statistics, Effects of the redesign on victimization estimates.

the same year. Figure 7.3 shows how the redesigned questions have produced higher crime victimization estimates. The NCVS/NCV ratio for rape victimization rates is a startling 2.57, and 1.57 for assault. Do you think that rewording questions can really have that much effect on responses because clarification usually means ruling our idiosyncratic definitions and coming closer to the legal definition? Can there be some other reason that the different strategies produced such huge differences?

Problems with the NCVS

Over the years, NCS/NCVS surveys have revealed that many more crimes occur than are reported to the police and have thus provided a valuable service to criminologists. Nevertheless, victimization surveys have their own dark figures as well as other problems that make them almost as suspect as the UCR. Some of these problems include the following:

- Crimes such as drug dealing and all "victimless" crimes such as prostitution and gambling are not revealed in such surveys for obvious reasons. And because murder victims cannot be interviewed, this most serious of crimes is not included.

- Because the unit of analysis in NCVS is households, crimes committed against commercial establishments such as stores, bars, and factories are not included. This exclusion results in a huge underestimate of crimes such as burglaries, robberies, theft, and vandalism.

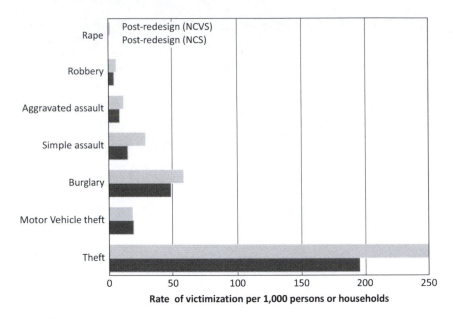

FIGURE 7.3 Increased Reporting Due to Redesigned Interviewing Procedures

Source: Kindermann, Lynch, & Cantor (1997). Bureau of Justice Statistics, Effects of the redesign on victimization estimates.

- Victimization data do not have to meet any stringent legal or evidentiary standards in order to be reported as an offense; if the respondent says he or she was robbed, a robbery will be recorded. UCR data, on the other hand, passes through the legal sieve to determine whether the reported incident was indeed a robbery. Between 5% and 20% of all crimes reported to the police are not officially recorded because the police have determined that they were unfounded (unsubstantiated) (Walsh & Jorgenson, 2018).

- Other problems associated with face-to-face interviewing involve memory lapses; an open door combined with the apparent loss of some object may be called a burglary when the only thing really lost is the "victim's" memory, and a stolen kiss may be reported as an attempted rape (notwithstanding the clarifying questions the interviewer is supposed to ask). Other problems involve providing answers the respondent thinks the interviewer wants to hear, forgetting an incident, embellishing an incident, and any number of other misunderstandings, ambiguities, and even downright lies that occur when one person is asking another about his or her life experiences.

- There are suggestions that just as underreporting plagues UCR data, over-reporting may plague NCVS data (O'Brien, 2001). Whatever the case may be, we find many anomalies when comparing the two sources of data. For instance, the 2005 UCR reports 94,635 cases of rape versus 209,880 reported in the 2005 NCVS. This presents no problem at first blush; after all, there are many reasons why more than half of all rape victims would not report their victimization. The problem is that only 35.8% (75,137) of the NCVS rape victims said they reported it to the police, and that number is 19,498 *fewer* victims than were "known to the police" that year. The same situation exists for other crimes; that is, substantially more crimes appear in police records than NCVS victims claim to have reported to the police. The discrepancy is easily explained for burglary and motor vehicle theft because the NCVS does not include commercial establishments in their reports. It is more difficult to explain the violent crime discrepancy, however. One explanation for this is that the NCVS does not include victims less than 12 years of age whereas the UCR does, although it is difficult to believe that children under 12 account for 15% to 20% of all violent crimes known to the police.

Areas of Agreement between the UCR and NCVS

Despite these and other problems, the UCR and NCVS do agree on some significant points. Both the UCR and NCVS agree on the demographics of crime; that is, they inform us that the young, the poor, and African Americans are more likely to be perpetrators and victims of crime than are females, older persons, wealthier persons, and persons of other racial or ethnic categories. Both sources also agree as to the geographic areas and times of the year and month when various crimes are more likely to occur.

There is also a high level of agreement when comparing arrest rates for violent crimes by sex and race reported in the UCR with victims' reports of the sex and race of their assailants. Examining the data over a 3-year period, O'Brien (2001) found that NCVS victims reported that 91.5% of those who robbed them and 87.7% of their aggravated assault assailants were male, as were 91.2% and 84.3%, respectively, of those arrested for those offenses. Likewise, NCVS victims reported that 64.1% of those who robbed them and 40% of their aggravated assault assailants were African American. These percentages fit the UCR arrest statistics for race almost exactly; 62.2% arrested for robbery were African American, as were 40% of those arrested for aggravated assault. O'Brien's findings provide additional support to the differential offending hypothesis tested using UCR and NIBRS data (see the D'Alessio and Stolzenberg study in Box 7.2).

⊖ Self-Reported Crime Surveys

Self-report surveys of criminal offending are a way criminologists can collect data for themselves without having to rely on government sources. These surveys involve asking people to disclose their delinquent and criminal involvement on anonymous questionnaires or in face-to-face interviews. Individuals are thus the units of analysis. Questionnaires used in these surveys typically provide a list of offenses and request subjects to check each offense they recall having committed and how often, and sometimes if they have ever been arrested, and if so many times.

The first two studies of criminal behavior using self-reports were conducted in the United States in the 1940s (Poterfield, 1946; Wallerstein & Wyle, 1947).

BOX 7.2 WHAT DO YOU THINK?

Using the UCR and NCVS to Test Alternative Hypotheses

UCR and NCVS data can be fruitfully used for more than monitoring crime trends across time, even with the limited demographic characteristics they provide. For instance, Darrell Steffensmeier and his colleagues (2006) used a comparison of the data from the two sources to test alternate views about the diminishing ratio of female to male violent crime documented from 1979 to 2003 in the UCR. Some criminologists view this convergence of arrest rates as indicative of female behavior change (the "masculinization" of female behavior); others saw it as a by-product of police policy changes (net-widening to include arrest for minor physical assaults, particularly in domestic situations). What do you think? Are these crime trends over time reflective of female behavior change of criminal justice system policy changes?

Steffensmeier et al. demonstrated that the UCR data showed little or no change in the sex gap for homicide, but a sharp rise in the percentage of females arrested for criminal assault over the period (from 20% of total arrests in 1980 to 32% in 2003). However, the increase was not borne out by NCVS data collected over the same period (i.e., the ratio of female to male arrests for criminal assault fluctuated only randomly). NCVS data are considered more reliable because it is independent of criminal justice selection bias or policy shifts. The authors' concluded that net-widening policy shifts have apparently escalated the arrest proneness of females for "criminal assault" (e.g., policing physical attacks/threats of marginal seriousness that women in relative terms are more likely to commit). In other words, women have not become more violent than in the past; rather, official data increasingly mask differences in violent offending by men and women due to policy shifts. If women had indeed become more "masculinized," we would observe significant increases in female arrests for other violent crimes that have not been subjected to police arrest policy changes, and the convergence would have been evident in the NCVS data.

With several refinements in methodology, a major study was conducted in the 1950s (Short & Nye, 1957) around which most modern studies have been modeled. Self-reported surveys have relied primarily on college and high school students for subjects, although prison inmates and probationers/parolees have also been surveyed.

Several studies have addressed the issue of the accuracy and honesty (reliability and validity) of self-reported offenses in various ways, and the results have generally been encouraging, at least for uncovering the extent of minor offenses. In one study, subjects were asked to report offenses they had committed and 2 weeks later were given back their questionnaires and told that they could amend their answers (test-retest) knowing they would subsequently undergo a polygraph ("lie detector") test (Clark & Tifft, 1966). Very little dishonesty was detected (only 20% of the subjects elicited a polygraph response), but few serious offenses were included and the study involved only 45 students.

Another study compared self-reported crimes by nondelinquent high school students with crimes reported by officially adjudicated delinquents (Kulik et al., 1968). Half of the subjects in each group were randomly assigned to receive one of two slightly different questionnaires. One required subjects to disclose their name (with assurance that they would not be prosecuted for any of their disclosures), while the other assured subjects that their answers would be completely anonymous. Regardless of which questionnaire they completed, on average the delinquent group disclosed almost four times as many offenses as the nondelinquents. Other studies have also shown that officially identified delinquents and criminals self-report substantially more offenses on anonymous questionnaires than do members of their nondelinquent peers (Cernkovich et al., 1985; Mak, 1993). Had these differences not be found, the validity of the self-report procedure would have been in doubt.

A large number of other studies have been conducted to assess the reliability and validity of self-report data. For example, one study found a high level of agreement between self-reports of the same teenage individuals completed at one time and then one month later and that their responses coincided fairly well with reports of overall behavior problems given by their parents and with police and court records (Williams & McGee, 1994). It is noteworthy that this particular study was not completed anonymously. A similar study compared self-reported delinquency with ratings of delinquent tendencies of the same adolescents by parents and teachers and found substantial (although far from perfect) agreement among all three measures (Caspi et al., 1994).

Perhaps the best study so far for assessing the reliability of self-report measures is Fergusson, Swain-Campbell, and Horwood's (2004) longitudinal study of a birth cohort ($n = 1,265$) in which self-reports were verified by police records. Juvenile and criminal offending was assessed when the cohort age was 10, 16, 18, and 21. Subjects were also assessed in terms of social class and placed into six categories with class 1 being the highest and class 6 the lowest. Subjects from class 6 self-reported a rate of offending 3.21 times greater than subjects from class 1, but the officially recorded convictions (at age 21) for class 6 subjects were 25.82 times greater than for class 1. The comparison of these two figures (3.21 and 25.82) supports the contention that those most seriously involved in offending are more likely to report a greater level of offending but are also most likely to seriously underreport their offending.

Perhaps the greatest strength of self-report research is that researchers can correlate a variety of characteristics of respondents with their admitted offenses that go beyond the demographics of age, race, and sex. For instance, they can attempt to measure various constructs thought to be associated with offending, such as impulsiveness, empathy, and sensation seeking, as well as their peer associations and their attitudes. Variation in these risk factors can be used to determine how much (if any) variation accounts for separately or together. Exceptionally ambitious longitudinal studies carried out over decades in concert with medical and biological scientists, such as the Dunedin Multidisciplinary Health and Development Study (Moffitt, 1993), the National Longitudinal Study of Adolescent Health Study (Udry, 2003), and the National Youth Survey (Menard

& Mihalic, 2001b), are able to gather a wealth of health, genetic, neurological, and physiological data that criminologists can use in their studies.

The evidence reviewed indicates that self-report crime measures provide largely accurate information about some forms of antisocial offending and reveal that almost everyone has committed some sort of illegal act in their lives. However, there are a number of reasons why self-report crime surveys also provide a distorted picture of criminal involvement.

Problems with Self-Reported Crime Surveys

- The great majority of self-reported studies (especially older studies) survey "convenience" samples of high school and college students, among whom we do not expect to find many seriously criminally involved individuals. Most self-report studies thus eliminate the very people from whom we are most interested in gathering information. One strength of the self-report method, however, is that it appears to capture the extent of illegal drug usage among high school and college students, something that neither the UCR nor the NCVS attempts to do.

- Self-report studies typically uncover only fairly trivial antisocial acts such as fighting, stealing items worth less than $5, smoking, and truancy. Almost everyone has committed one or more of these acts. These are hardly acts that help us to understand the nature of serious crime. A connected problem is that some researchers lump respondents who report one delinquent act together with adjudicated delinquents who break the law in many different ways many different times. This practice has been used to conclude that there is no relationship, for instance, between social class and delinquency (e.g., Tittle et al., 1978), a conclusion that has been called "extraordinarily senseless" (Harris & Shaw 2001:129).

- Even though most people are forthright in revealing their peccadilloes, most people do not have a serious criminal history, and those who do have a distinct tendency to underreport their crimes (Hindelang et al., 1981). As the number of crimes people commit increases, so does the proportion of offenses they withhold reporting (Hirschi et al., 1980; Cernkovich et al., 1985). For instance, researchers have asked subjects with known arrest histories whether they have ever been arrested and found that 20% to 40% replied negatively, (Hindelang et al., 1981; Petersilia, 1980), with those arrested for the most serious offenses having the greatest probability of denial (Farrington, 1982).

- There is also evidence that reporting honesty varies across race/ethnicity and sex. Specifically, males tend to report their antisocial activities less honestly than females and African Americans less honestly than other racial/ethnic groups (Kim, Fendrich, & Wislar, 2000). For instance, Cernkovich, Giordano, and Rudolph (2000) state: "Black males underreport involvement in every level of delinquency, especially at the high level of the continuum." This evidence suggests that any statements about sex or racial differences regarding antisocial behavior that are based on self-report data should be treated with great caution. When it comes to relying on self-report data to assess the nature and extent of serious crime, it is well to remember the gambler's dictum: "Never trust an animal that talks."

The Dark Figure of Crime Revisited

Recall that we defined the dark figure of crime as that portion of the total crimes committed each year that never comes to light. All three of our crime measures have their own dark areas. For the UCR, the dark figures are highly concentrated at the nonserious end of the crime seriousness spectrum, as it is for the NCVS, although to a lesser degree. The failure of victimization data to pick up these minor offenses is largely due to survey subjects not remembering all incidences of victimization. Most of the dark figures in self-report data are concentrated in the upper end of the seriousness continuum rather than the lower end. This is partly due to (a) nearly all self-report surveys excluding the most persistent serious offenders from their subject pools and (b) many of the most serious offenders who remain in self-report subject pools do not reveal the full extent of their criminal histories.

What Can We Conclude about the Three Main Measures of Crime in America?

All three main measures of crime in America are imperfect measures, but they are all that we have. Which one is "best" depends on what we want to know. Despite numerous criticisms lodged against UCR data, it is still the best single source of data for studying serious crimes nationwide and the only one for studying murder rates and circumstances. NIBRS will be a better source if it is ever able to fully replace the UCR. For studying less serious (and yet much more common) types of crimes, either victimization or self-report survey data are best. If the interest is in drug offenses or want to include certain offender characteristics in the study such as abuse, IQ, or self-control, self-reports are the only way to go. In conclusion, all three measures offer a narrow window through which we may view the extent of crime in America, but if we stand back a bit and take in the view from all three windows simultaneously, we will get a much better picture.

● Measuring Criminal Propensity: Moving from Crime to Criminality

What Is Criminality?

We have so far concentrated on measures of the prevalence (the proportion of people who are committing crimes) and incidence (the number of criminal events that occur) of crime. Criminologists also want to measure something else called **criminality**, which is people's varying propensity to commit crimes and other antisocial acts. Crimes are discrete events that violate the law and are thus properties of society. Criminality is a property of individuals and is a continuous trait that is itself an amalgam of other continuous traits that put individuals at risk for ignoring the rights and dignity of others. In other words, criminality is not a dichotomous trait that some people have and others do not. We have all done things and displayed character traits that we are not proud of, so criminality is something that ranges widely from saint to sociopath.

Given the large number of risk factors associated with the more general trait of criminality, measuring the concept is a much more involved process than measuring crime. Criminologists may embed one or two indicators of criminality such as low self-control or an empathy scale in a self-report study, but criminal justice practitioners who must deal with some very bad characters want a more comprehensive picture. To get this, they turn to constructs such as antisocial personality disorder and psychopathy, both of which are clinical rather than legal constructs.

Antisocial Personality Disorder (APD)

APD is described in the *Diagnostic and Statistical Manual* (*DSM-IV*) of the American Psychiatric Association as "a pervasive pattern of disregard for, and violation of, the rights of others that begins in childhood or early adolescence and continues into adulthood" (1994:645). APD is a clinical/legal label that psychiatrists apply to someone if he or she consistently shows three or more of the following behavioral patterns since reaching the age of 15:

1. Failure to conform to social norms with respect to lawful behaviors indicated by repeatedly performing acts that are grounds for arrest.

2. Deceitfulness, as indicated by repeated lying, use of aliases, or conning others for personal profit or pleasure.

3. Impulsivity or failing to plan ahead.

4. Irritability and aggressiveness, as indicated by repeated physical fights or assaults.

5. Reckless disregardful for safety of self or others.

6. Consistent irresponsibility, as indicated by repeated failure to sustain consistent work behavior or honor financial obligations.

7. Lack of remorse, as indicated by being indifferent to or rationalizing having hurt, mistreated, or stolen from another.

Other criteria are that the individual must be at least 18 years old, must have been diagnosed with conduct disorder prior to his or her fifteenth birthday, and his or her antisocial behavior must not occur exclusively during a schizophrenic or manic episode (APA, 1994:649–650).

The most obvious problem with the APD criteria is that it would be difficult to find any incarcerated criminal that *did not* consistently evidence three or more of them. Indeed, according to Shipley and Arrigo (2001) the base rate for APD among offenders is 50% to 80%. However, the requirement that the person must have been diagnosed with conduct disorder as a child prevents APD from being synonymous with criminal behavior. An APD diagnosis is made purely on the basis of behavior and neglects the underlying personality basis for that behavior (Arrigo & Shipley, 2001). Behavior-based criteria are very useful for guiding decision making for legal and correctional personnel, but criminologists want definitions of criminality that are independent of behavior and then determine how individuals who fall into that category are different from individuals who do not.

Measuring Psychopathy

Psychopathy is a personality disorder consisting of a cluster of traits that are anything but desirable in a mate, a friend, or a neighbor. This cluster is a laundry list of traits all of which, with the exception of "good intelligence," are associated to some degree with criminal behavior. Here is a partial list of these traits obtained from a wide variety of sources.

Insensitivity to other's feelings/lacking in empathy; Self-absorbed

Lack of emotional depth or conscience; Grandiose sense of self-worth

Extensive history of pathological lying and deception; Relatively fearless

Impulsiveness and unreliability; Good intelligence

Tendency to blame others whenever things go wrong; Superficial charm/charismatic

Failure to profit from adverse experiences; Manipulates others

A parasitic lifestyle; Lack of long-term life goals

Incapacity for love and other emotional relationships; Promiscuous sex life

High need for stimulation; Prone to boredom

Psychopaths are mercifully small in number (about 1% of the general population), but they make up 15% to 25% of the prison population (Hare, 2003), which make them very important subjects for criminological research. The "gold standard" for measuring psychopathy both for clinical and research use is the Psychopathy Checklist–Revised (PCL-R) developed by Robert Hare, arguably the leading expert in psychopathy in the world today (Bartol, 2002). To make a clinical diagnosis of an individual (the idiographic approach) using the PCL-R, the diagnostician must be a doctoral-level clinician with special training with the instrument. Once diagnoses have been made, criminologists can combine all such diagnoses with other variables of interest to make generalizations (the nomothetic approach) about extreme criminality. Diagnostic interviews may last two hours or more, and on the basis of information gleaned during that time and on the basis of file data, clinicians rate patients as either having or not having each of 20 traits such as those listed earlier. Ratings are made on a 3-point scale ranging from 0 (does not apply), 1 (applies somewhat), to 2 (definitely applies), with persons receiving a score of 30 or higher out of a possible 40 considered psychopaths (Hare, 1996a). To put this number in perspective, offenders in general have a mean PCL-R score of 22 and nonoffenders a score of 5 (Hare, 1996b).

Factor analysis of the PCL-R reveals that psychopathy is comprised of two factors, one describing a constellation of personality traits that point to insensitivity to the feelings of others and the second a generally unstable, impulsive, and deviant lifestyle (Forth et al. 1996). Although these two factors sometimes exist independently, both are often present together in the same individuals (the two factors correlate at about 0.50). It is frequently found that the physiological anomalies (such as EEG profiles) associated with psychopathy correlate with high scores on factor 1 (personality traits) but not necessarily with factor 2 (unstable and antisocial lifestyle) and that low IQ correlates with high scores on factor 2 but not on factor 1 (Harris, Skilling, & Rice, 2001; Patrick, 1994). Additionally, criminal individuals who score high on factor 1 are more likely than those who score high on factor 2 to be violent, to be more intelligent, and are less likely to improve (become less antisocial) with age (Meadows & Kuehnel, 2005).

Only about 15% to 25% of offenders diagnosed with APD fit the PCL-R criteria for psychopathy (Hare, 2000). Thus a person can be a psychopath, manipulating and exploiting others for his or her personal gain (factor 1) but may be clever and cautious enough never to violate the criminal law to the extent that he or she attracts the attention of the police (factor 2 and APD).

Reliability and Validity of the PCL-R

The PCL-R has been validated in forensic populations worldwide by a wide variety of independent research teams (Williams & Paulhus, 2004). Different meta-analyses of the reliability of the PLC-R find a mean inter-rater reliability of .86, a mean test-retest coefficient of .89, and a mean Cronbach's alpha coefficient (internal inter-item consistency) of .88 (Hare et al., 2000). These are very good reliability coefficients that hold up across races, sexes, ages, and all cultures in which it has been used (Douglas et al., 2006).

The validity of the PCL-R is equally impressive (reviewed in Hare, 2003; Kiel, 2006). It has good predictive validity in that it rather strongly predicts recidivism, violent recidivism, treatment response, and clearly discriminates among prison inmates with high, medium, and low PCL-R scores in terms of involvement in violent incidents while imprisoned. Most impressive of all is the relationships found in brain imaging studies (PET, fMRI, etc.) that find significant differences in the brains of psychopaths compared with control subjects and in metabolites (essentially waste products of metabolism) of important brain chemicals regulating approach and avoidance behavior (Walsh, 2019). Kiel (2006) sums up the reliability and validity of the PCL-R in these words: "The replicability and consistency of the neurobiological findings are a further testament to the psychometric robustness of the PCL-R and the construct of psychopathy in general."

Self-Reported Psychopathy

Psychopathy is also sometimes measured via self-report, usually as part of a broader personality assessment questionnaire. Because of their tendency to be dishonest and generally irresponsible, self-report data obtained from psychopaths must be interpreted with great caution. Self-report data are never used for diagnostic purposes.

Table 7.2 provides a partial list of self-report items modeled after the PCL-R used to measure psychopathy in a general (i.e., noninstitutionalized) population (Levenson, Kiehl, & Fitzpatrick, 1995). As is the case with clinical research, self-report studies suggest the same two major dimensions of psychopathy that are found with the PCL-R. The primary dimension points to difficulties in the affective/interpersonal domain (deceitfulness and manipulation of others), and the secondary dimension is indicative of a socially deviant lifestyle. The researchers labeled factor 1 "primary psychopathy" and factor 2 "secondary psychopathy." The alpha reliability for factor 1 was a very good 0.82; for factor 2 it was a barely adequate 0.62.

The factor loadings that you see next to each item in the table provide mathematical estimates of how well each item epitomizes or typifies the dimensions. As we saw in Chapter 5, factor loadings range from –1.0 to 1.00. A factor loading is essentially a correlation coefficient between the item and the factor of which it is a constituent part. The more a particular item comes to epitomize one of the two dimensions of psychopathy, the more its factor loading approaches 1.00, the less it typifies psychopathy the more it approaches –1.0. For example, items 1 (loading = 0.67) and 10 (loading = –0.50) are almost exact opposites. In other words, we would not expect a person agreeing with item 1 ("Success is based on survival of the fittest; I am not concerned about the losers") to agree with item 10 ("I would be upset if my success came at someone else's expense").

As with all behavioral criteria used in making clinical diagnoses, those used to identify psychopaths are based on judgments about matters of degree. Nearly everyone is occasionally at least mildly impulsive or callous toward the feelings of others, but persons who are diagnosed psychopathic exhibit these tendencies to very extreme degrees. Nevertheless, although the traits underlying these items are not criminal in and of themselves, it is not difficult to see that persons who exhibit several of them to extreme degrees will be much more disposed toward a criminal career than persons in general.

Operationalizing Crime Seriousness and Prior Record

We have seen an operational definition of a concept in terms of the operations used to measure it. Two of the most important concepts in criminal justice are the seriousness of the crime someone is being sentenced for and his or her criminal history. These are the legally relevant variables that determine sentence severity. Crime seriousness may be measured the easy way by noting the statutory penalty for a given crime (e.g., 15 years maximum for rape; 2 years for receiving stolen property) and using that as a quantitative measure. Likewise,

TABLE 7.2 Items and Factor Loadings for a Self-Report Measure of Psychopathy

Item	Factor Loading
Primary Dimension: Affective/interpersonal	
1. Success is based on survival of the fittest; I am not concerned about the losers.	.67
2. For me, what's right is whatever I can get away with.	.62
3. In today's world, I feel justified in doing anything I can get away with to succeed.	.62
4. My main purpose in life is getting as many goodies as I can.	.62
5. Making a lot of money is my most important goal.	.61
6. I let others worry about higher values; my main concern is with the bottom line.	.59
7. People who are stupid enough to get ripped off usually deserve it.	.57
8. Looking out for myself is my top priority.	.52
9. I tell other people what they want to hear so that they will do what I want them to do.	.44
10. I would be upset if my success came at someone else's expense.	−.50
11. I often admire a really clever scam.	.50
12. I make a point of trying not to hurt others in pursuit of my goals.	−.41
13. I enjoy manipulating other people's feelings.	.39
14. I feel bad if my words or actions cause someone else to feel emotional pain.	−.33
16. Even if I were trying very hard to sell something, I wouldn't lie about it.	−.33
17. Cheating is not justified because it is unfair to others.	−.32
Secondary Dimension: Socially deviant lifestyle	
18. I find myself in the same kinds of trouble, time after time.	.62
19. I am often bored.	.51
20. I find that I am able to pursue one goal for a long time.	−.49
21. I don't plan anything very far in advance.	.48
22. I quickly lose interest in tasks I start.	.48
23. Most of my problems are due to the fact that other people just don't understand me.	.46
24. Before I do anything, I carefully consider the possible consequences.	−.36
25. I have been in a lot of shouting matches with other people.	.34
26. When I get frustrated, I often "let off steam" by blowing my top.	.33
27. Love is overrated.	.32

Source: Levenson, Kiehl, & Fitzpatrick, 1995

prior record may be operationalized by assigning the maximum penalty to each prior conviction and then summing them. Better yet, we could use the weighting system, which is actually used by the courts in a given jurisdiction.

Sentencing guidelines are a way of operationalizing justice by assigning numbers to various aspects of the crime and to characteristics of the offender. Figure 7.4 presents a typical sentencing guideline, in this case, the felony sentencing worksheet (FSW) used by the courts in Ohio. The crime seriousness section of the FSW assigns points according to (1) the statutory gravity of the

FELONY SENTENCING WORKSHEET

Defendant's Name _____ Case No. _____

OFFENSE RATING

1. Degree of Offense

Assess ponts for the one most serious offense or its equivalent for which offender is being sentenced, as follows: 1st felony = 4 points; 2nd felony = 3 points; 3rd felony = 2 points; 4th felony = 1 point _____

2. Multiple Offenses

Assess 2 points if one or more of the following applies (A) offender is being sentenced for two or more offenses committed in different incidents; (B) offender is currently under a misdemeanor or felony sentence imposed by any court; or (C) present offense was committed while offender on probation or parole. _____

3. Actual or Potential Harm

Assess 2 points if one or more of the following applies: (A) serious physical harm to a person was caused; (B) property damage or loss of $300 or more was caused; (C) there was a high risk of any such harm. damage or loss, though not caused; (D) the gain or potential gain from theft offense[s] was $300 or more; or (E) dangerous ordnance or a deadly weapon was actually used in the incident, or its use was attempted or threatened. _____

4. Culpability

Assess 2 points if one or more of the following applies: (A) offender was engaging in continuing criminal activity as a source of income or livelihood; (B) offense was part of a continuing conspiracy to which offender was party; or (C) offense included shocking and deliberate cruelty in which offender participated or acquiesced. _____

5. Mitigation

Deduct 1 point for **each** of the following. as applicable: (A) there was substantial provocation. justification or excuse for offense; (B) victim induced or facilitated offense; (C) offense was committed in the heat of anger; and (D) the properly damaged loss or stolen was restored or recovered without significant cost to the victim _____

NET TOTAL = OFFENSE RATING _____

OFFENDER RATING

1. Prior Convictions

Assess ponts for **each** verified prior felony conviction, any jurisdiction. Count adjudications of delinquency for felony as convictions _____

Assess ponts for **each** verified prior felony misdemeanor conviction, any jurisdiction. Count adjudications of delinquency for misdemeanor as convictions. Do not count traffic or intoxication offenses, or disorderly conduct, disturbing the peace or equivalent offenses _____

2. Repeat Offenses

Assess 2 points if present offense is offense of violence, sex offense, theft offense, or drug abuse offense, and offender has one or more prior convictions for same type of offense _____

3. Prior Commitments

Assess 2 points if offender was committed on one or more occasions to a penitentiary, reformatory, or equivalent institution in any jurisdiction. Count commitments to Ohio Youth Commission or similar commitments in other jurisdictions. _____

4. Parole and Similar Violations

Assess 2 points if one or more of the following applies: (A) offender has previously had probation or parole for misdemeanor or felony revoked; (B) present offense committed while offender on probation or parole; (C) present offense committed while offender free on bad; or (D) present offense committed while offender in custody. _____

5. Credits

Deduct 1 point for **each** of the following as applicable: (A) offender has voluntarily made bona fide realistic arrangements for at least partial restitution; (B) offender was age 25 or older at time of first felony conviction; (C) offender has been substantially law abiding for at least 3 years; and (D) offender lives with his or her spouse or minor children or both **and** is either a breadwinner for the family or if there are minor children **a** housewife. _____

NET TOTAL = OFFENDER RATING _____

PROCEED TO DETERMINATION OF SENTENCE ON BACK

FIGURE 7.4 A Sentencing Guideline Operationalizing Crime Seriousness and Prior Record

crime (first degree, second degree, etc.), (2) whether or not the crime was committed while the defendant was on probation, parole, or bail, (3) the amount of monetary loss, and (4) a series of aggravating factors (did the crime include "shocking and deliberate cruelty"?). Points may also be deducted from the offender's score for mitigating factors (e.g., did the victim contribute to his or her victimization?). The prior record section is typically concerned with (1) number of prior felony and misdemeanor offenses, (2) previous probation, parole, or bail violations, (3) whether the defendant has previously served prison time, and (4) a series of mitigating factors such as voluntary restitution, being a family breadwinner, or being substantially law abiding over a certain period prior to the present offense. Points on both sections are added and applied to a sentencing grid on the reverse side of the FSW (not shown) at the point at which the scores intersect. These grids indicate a sentence that is typically assigned to offenders with that crime seriousness/prior record profile.

How did the designers of the FSW know what the important factors of the crime and the defendant's character are and how they should be weighted? A 2-year study of the sentencing practices of 60% of Ohio's felony judges preceded the design of the FSW (Walsh, 2006). The study determined what these judges *as a whole* considered relevant, thus ruling out any idiosyncratic opinions that individual judges may have, and determined what sentences judges gave *on average* to defendants similarly situated in terms of the guideline's criteria. Sentencing researchers using sentencing guidelines as operationalizations of crime seriousness and prior record are then quite sure that they have reliable and valid measures of the only two variables that are *supposed* to account for sentencing. If any extra-legal variable (such as the race or social class of the defendant, or the political philosophy of the judge) is able to account for variation in sentence severity after the two legally relevant variables are controlled for, then researchers have an excellent case for discriminatory treatment.

Summary

Crime and criminal behavior are measured in several ways in the United States. The oldest measure is the FBI's Uniform Crime Reports (UCR), which is a tabulation of all crimes reported to the police in most of the jurisdictions in the United States in the previous year. The UCR is divided into two parts: Part I records the eight index crimes (murder, rape, robbery, aggravated assault, burglary, larceny/theft, and arson), and Part II records arrests made for all other crimes. UCR data seriously underestimate the extent of crime because it only records reported crimes, ignores drug offenses, and only reports the most serious crime in a multiple-crime event. The problems with the UCR led to the implementation of the National Incident-Based Reporting System (NIBRS), although the system hasn't lived up to its promise.

The second major source of crime statistics is the National Crime Victimization Survey (NCVS). This survey consists of many thousands of interviews of householders throughout the United States, asking them about their crime victimization (if any) during the previous 6 months. The NCVS also has problems because it leaves out crimes against commercial establishments and relies exclusively on the memory and the word of interviewees.

The third source of crime data is self-report data collected by criminologists themselves. The advantage of self-report data is that they are derived "from the horse's mouth," and typically the questionnaires used ask about "victimless" offenses not covered in either the UCR or NCVS. The major problems with self-report data is that it does not capture serious criminal behavior and is subject to dishonesty in the form of underreporting, especially underreporting by those most seriously involved in criminal activity.

The UCR, NCVS, and self-report data come to different conclusions on a variety of points, but they agree about where, when, and among whom crime is most prevalent, and the fact that crime has fallen dramatically in the United States over the past decade. Taken together, then, we have a fairly reliable picture of the correlates of crime from which to develop our theories about explanatory mechanisms.

Measuring criminality is more complicated than measuring crime. Measuring criminality involves measuring a number of factors that put individuals at risk for committing crimes. These factors include such things as impulsiveness, low empathy, low IQ, and many other variables via self-reports and a variety of biological/physiological measures. We discussed the separate but independent constructs of antisocial personality disorder (APD) and pychopathy. The measurement of ADP primarily involves behavioral and clinical observations and, in part, reflects the legal requirement of the criminal justice system. Psychopathy, on the other hand, is measured by Hare's Psychopathy Checklist-Revised (PLC-R). The PLC-R has shown excellent reliability and validity values across cultures.

We concluded by looking at an example of a sentencing guideline, which is essentially an operational definition of crime seriousness and prior record. These are the two factors that are supposed to influence judicial sentencing. With good operational measures we can determine convicted persons who are and who are not similarly situated on these two variables, and thus any departures from the indicated sentences of people who have identical scores on the guideline can be viewed as judicial bias, either for or against a criminal defendant.

⬥ Discussion Questions

1. Do you think it wise to make "authoritative" statements or formulate theories of criminal behavior, especially serious criminal behavior, based on self-report data?

2. Can you think of other problems possibly associated with asking people about their delinquent or criminal behavior or their victimization other than discussed in the chapter?

3. What does Elliot Curry mean when he talks about criminality rather than the crime problem? What can we do about the criminality problem?

4. Defend your favored reason for why the crime rate went up so precipitously from 1963 to 1993 against an alternative reason.

⬤ Exercises

1. Consult your college library and browse one or more government documents (such as the *Sourcebook of Criminal Justice Statistics*, published annually by the US Department of Justice) for information on some crime-related topic that interests you. Examples might be "United States crime trends" or "How age is related to crime rates." Then write a 1- to 2-page summary of what the document indicates about the topic.

2. If you were the American "crime Czar," what would you do to get the various law enforcement agencies to fully implement NIBRS? No, you just can't order them to do so.

Chapter 8 Controlled Experimentation

When you were a child, did your parents let you watch violent movies, or did you play violent video games? Have you ever heard anyone proclaim that exposure to violent media causes violence in society? How could researchers go about studying whether ot not this is true? Despite a fair number of studies attempting to understand this phenomenon, it is very difficult to demonstrate that watching violent movies or playing violent video games leads to violent

behavior in individuals. Nonetheless, researchers who examine these types of relationships usually do so by utilizing a methodology referred to as controlled experimentation, which is the best method for assessing causal relationships between variables. This chapter will discuss the main components of experimental designs as well as discuss some of the research topics that have been studied using experimental approaches.

Experimental research can be distinguished from other forms of research in that it involves directly manipulating one or more of the variables being studied. In all other research designs, researchers merely observe variations in variables and record what they see. (In nonexperimental research, any manipulation of variables is carried out in the analysis phase of a study, not while data are being collected.) This chapter will demonstrate that experimentation, although often difficult, can accomplish scientific objectives that other types of research can never fully achieve.

Recall from Chapter 4 that correlation does not equal causation. What this means is that simply observing a relationship between two variables does not warrant the conclusion that one variable caused the other. This is true even when one variable clearly precedes the other in time. For instance, even if variables A and B are strongly correlated and variable A occurs in childhood while variable B occurs in adolescence, one still cannot confidently conclude that variable A causes variable B. Why? Perhaps, some third variable occurring in infancy caused both variable A and variable B.

In experimental research, a scientist systematically manipulates a suspected "causal variable" and then monitors the suspected "effect variable" to determine if it changes as expected (Stroebe & Diehl, 1991). These type of experiments are conducted more in the discipline of psychology than criminology or criminal justice because crime doesn't happen in a lab, so it is often difficult to study it there. Studies of aggression, self-control, and other concepts that are related to crime and criminality, however, can sometimes be researched using controlled experimentation. Before describing specific types of experimental designs, some terminology needs to be presented.

● Basic Experimental Terminology

Among the terms that are fundamental to experimental research are those of independent variable and dependent variable. An **independent variable** is one that is under the control of a researcher in the sense that the researcher can manipulate the level at which subjects are exposed to the variable. An independent variable is also called a **treatment variable**, especially in experiments conducted in clinical settings. A **dependent variable** is one that may be altered as a result of changes made in the independent variable (Howell, 1989). A helpful way to remember the distinction between these two terms is to state that the independent variable is considered a possible cause, and the dependent variable is considered a possible effect. Thus, the independent variable must occur first.

In most (but not all) experiments, there are at least two groups of subjects. One group, called the **experimental group**, is exposed to the independent variable or treatment to an unusual degree. The other group, called the **control group** (or **controls**), is exposed to the independent variable to a "normal" degree (or, in some cases, not at all). Distinguishing between a control group and an experimental group is sometimes arbitrary, but usually it is obvious. For example, several experimental studies have been undertaken to determine the effects of exposing males to various forms of sexually explicit mass media on aggression toward women (including the commission of sexual assault) (for reviews see Zillmann, 1984; Check & Malamuth, 1986; Donnerstein et al., 1987; Ferguson & Hartley, 2009). In most of these experiments, the independent variable would be the exposure to sexually explicit material, and the dependent variable would be aggression toward women. The experimental subjects would be those shown the sexually explicit material, and the control subjects would be those exposed to some "neutral" material, such as a nature film or perhaps those who saw no film at all.

The concept of experimental control is important in most scientific experiments; it refers to a process of assigning subjects to the experimental and control groups at random. For example, if 100 subjects are considered eligible for exposure to an independent variable, experimental control can be achieved by randomly picking 50 of them to be in the experimental group, leaving the remaining 50 for the control group. Experimental control helps to ensure that the groups to be compared are equivalent with respect to all variables except the one being manipulated, the treatment. Of course, the more subjects in each randomly selected group, the more confidence one can have that the groups are equivalent to one another.

BOX 8.1 CURRENT ISSUES

Can Reality Be Emulated with Controlled Experimentation?

Measuring dependent variables can be difficult. Researchers often measure aggression toward women with questionnaires concerning how subjects think they would respond under various hypothetical situations (Malamuth et al., 1980). In other studies, the dependent variable has involved asking male subjects about how severely men should be punished for committing various aggressive acts toward women (e.g., Donnerstein et al., 1984). The dependent variable in other studies involved confronting male subjects with a female lab assistant who hurled insults at the subjects after they had viewed either a sexually explicit video or some control video to see if the sexual material increased the likelihood that the males would respond aggressively to the affront (Malamuth & Ceniti, 1986).

In these types of experiments, researchers obviously walk a thin line between making their studies as realistic as possible while causing no significant harm to subjects or to anyone having contact with the subjects. Recall the discussion of the protection of human subjects from Chapter 3 and the requirement that researchers maximize benefits and minimize harms in line with the Belmont Report.

The time frame refers to the length of time that the dependent variable is monitored for evidence of any independent variable effects. In most of the experiments with sexually explicit videos, for example, the time frame would be the length of time between exposure to the sexually explicit material (or some control material) and when aggressive acts toward women would be expected to occur. The length of the time frame must be relevant to the dependent variable being investigated. Thus, if a particular experiment involves the use of a fast-acting medication on some aspect of alertness, the time frame might be in minutes. However, if the independent variable is a prison rehabilitation program designed to reduce recidivism, the time frame could be years following prison release.

A final term that is frequently used in experimental research is that of random assignment. Do not confuse *random assignment* with *random selection*, the latter being a concept discussed in Chapter 6 in connection with surveying. **Random assignment** means that once a pool of eligible subjects for an experiment has been identified, each subject from the pool is chosen at random to be either an experimental subject or a control subject (Levin, 1993). In most types of experimental designs, the ability to identify causes comes from the ability to take a large sample of subjects and randomly assign them to two (or sometimes more) groups. By doing so, a researcher can be confident that whatever differences appear between two groups in terms of the dependent variable can be attributed to the differential exposure to the independent variable and not differences within the groups themselves. Random assignment is also referred to as **randomization**; you have probably heard of randomized control trials in medical research where some persons with similar symptoms will receive an experimental drug and others will receive a placebo, and the selection of who will receive which is randomly assigned.

⊜ Main Types of Experimental Designs

Most experimental designs can be subsumed under one of these six categories: the *classical design*, the *after-only design*, the *before-after no control group design*, the *cross-over design*, the *Solomon four-group design*, and the *factorial design*. In describing each design, the focus will be on their simplest form, although more elaborate versions of each design are often utilized.

Classical Experimental Design

In its simplest form, the **classical design** involves subjects being randomly assigned to one of two groups, the experimental group and the control group. To ensure that subjects are randomly assigned, a coin flip might be used for each pair of subjects. For an experiment to fit the minimum requirements of a classical design, there must also be at least two time frames.

Figure 8.1 offers a graphic representation of a classical experimental design. For the moment, pay attention only to the four squares outlined with

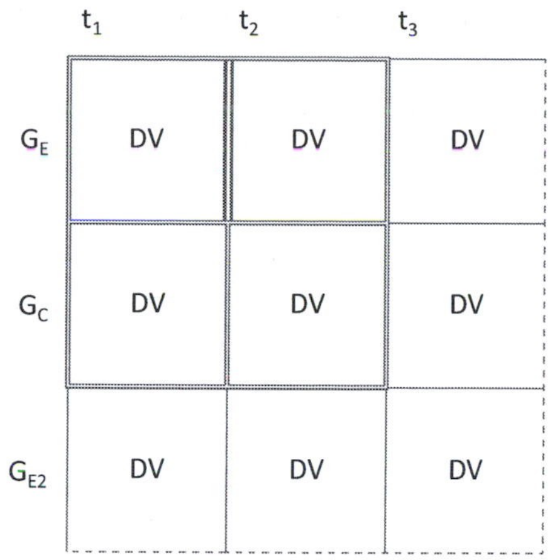

FIGURE 8.1 A Representation of a Classical Experimental Design. The Additional Cells Shown with Dashed Lines Illustrate that the Classical Design Can Be Made More Elaborate than What Is Represented by the Four Required Cells

the solid lines. Along the top of Figure 8.1, two time frames are represented: T_1 and T_2. Along the side, an experimental group (G_E) and a control group (G_C) are represented. Inside each of the four cells, observations on the dependent variable (DV) can be represented. For the experimental group, the imposition of the independent variable is represented by the double line. (Sometimes the independent variable is imposed throughout T_2, rather than simply between T_1 and T_2.)

The dashed lines at the bottom and right side of Figure 8.1 represent the fact that the classical design can be made more elaborate by adding time frames and/or groups of subjects beyond those that are minimally required. A second experimental group could be added to a classical experimental design by having two degrees of experimental exposure to the independent variable. For example, if the independent variable were a particular drug, one experimental group might get the drug once a day, whereas the second experimental group might receive it twice a day; the control group, of course, would not receive the drug at all.

Figure 8.2 illustrates a classical experimental design that involves one more time frame than the two that are minimally required. This study comes from a program designed to reduce the number of women who smoke during pregnancy (Burling et al., 1991). The time frames in this study represent the three times that a group of pregnant women who smoked visited a prenatal health clinic. Between the first and the second visits, half the mothers (chosen at random) were sent a one-page letter that briefly informed them of the possible health risks of smoking, particularly to the fetus they were carrying (e.g., low birth weight).

As one can see from viewing Figure 8.2, receipt of this letter slightly lowered the number of women who continued to smoke during pregnancy. However, it is also worth noting that some of the expectant mothers who were not sent

	t_1	t_2	t_3
G_E	100% smoked	88.4% smoked	87.0% smoked
G_C	100% smoked	98.6% smoked	94.3% smoked

FIGURE 8.2 A Study Undertaken to Reduce the Number of Women Who Smoked during Pregnancy Utilizing a Classical Experimental Design (after Burling et al., 1991)

the letter stopped smoking later on in pregnancy. Statistically, the difference between the two groups of expectant mothers during the second time frame (88.4% versus 98.6%) was significant.

After-Only Experimental Design

As in a classical design, an **after-only experimental design** must have at least two groups of subjects. However, in the after-only design, no observations occur prior to the time the independent variable is imposed on the experimental group. This is illustrated in Figure 8.3. Again as in a classical design, subjects are almost always assigned to the experimental and control groups at random. There are various reasons why researchers choose not to include pretest observations of the dependent variable in an experiment. One is that repeated measurement of the dependent variable sometimes alters this variable's subsequent levels in unacceptable ways. Another reason might pertain to the urgency with which the researcher wants the results; an after-only design often requires half the time to conduct as a classical design.

Examples of after-only experimental designs come from clinical studies of the effects of methylphenidate (Ritalin) and similar drugs on children with attention deficit hyperactivity disorder (ADHD). According to one survey in the United States, these drugs were being given to about 6% of the nation's elementary school children (predominantly boys) in the 1980s (Safer & Krager, 1988). For children with clinically significant ADHD symptoms, several studies indicate that methylphenidate improves classroom behavior (reviewed by Whalen et al., 1987; Gadow et al., 1992; Carlson & Bunner, 1993) as well as relationships with family members and peers (Barkley et al., 1985; Cunningham et al., 1985). In such experiments, researchers often randomly assigned a pool of ADHD children into an experimental group and a control group and used ratings by teachers or parents of the children's subsequent behavior. (To make sure teachers and parents are not biased in their assessments by knowing which

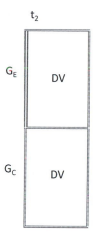

FIGURE 8.3   A Representation of a Basic After-Only Experimental Design with the Minimum Number of Cells

children were receiving methylphenidate, the control children are typically given a placebo in what is known as a double-blind experiment.) Experiments involving the treatment of ADHD children with methylphenidate have consistently found that about 80% of the experimentals exhibit significantly diminished ADHD symptoms compared to controls (Whalen et al., 1987; Carlson et al., 1992).

Before-After No Control Group Design

Although **before-after no control group design** is a cumbersome term, it precisely characterizes the nature of a widely used experimental design in social science. It is the only experimental design in which there is only one group of subjects, all of whom will be exposed to the independent variable. This design is also unique in that it can even be used with a single subject, although it is certainly preferable from a scientific standpoint to use more than one subject (Hersen & Barlow, 1976; Barlow & Hersen, 1984).

The basic structure of a before-after no control group design is shown in Figure 8.4. Note that it consists of a minimum of two periods of time during which a dependent variable is measured. These two time frames are typically separated by the imposition of an independent variable, although in some studies utilizing this design, the researcher will impose the independent variable throughout either one (but never both) of the time frames.

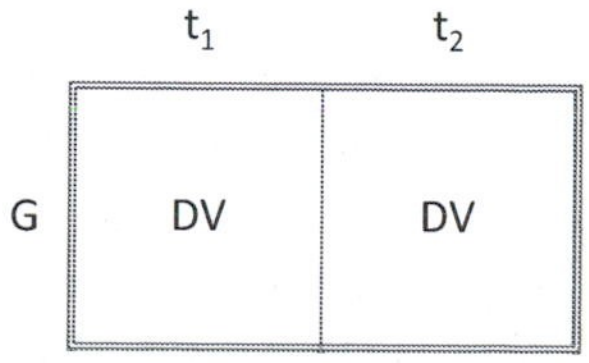

t_1 t_2

G   DV   DV

FIGURE 8.4   Basic Structure of a Before-After No Control Group Experimental Design with the Minimum Number of Cells

	t₁ Ritalin	t₂ Placebo	t-score & significance

	t$_1$ Ritalin	t$_2$ Placebo	t-score & significance
G	By Teachers: Hyperactivity B 11.2 Defiance B 10.4 By Parents: Hyperactivity B 3.8 Defiance B 7.4	By Teachers: Hyperactivity B 16.8 Defiance B 17.6 By Parents: Hyperactivity B 4.0 Defiance B 11.8	 t = 5.20, p < .0001 t = 4.64, p < .0001 t = 0.61, N.S. t = 2.14, p < .05

FIGURE 8.5   Main Results of a Before-After No Control Group Experimental Design Undertaken to Assess the Effects of Ritalin on Behavior of ADHD Children. Shading Represents the Time Frame during Which Subjects Were Taking Ritalin

Source: Adapted by authors from Zeiner, 1999.

To illustrate the before-after no control group design, let us return to the use of Ritalin for the treatment of ADHD symptoms. A Norwegian study assessed the effects of withholding treatment for ADHD children who had been taking Ritalin for several months and substituting a placebo (an inert substance) for 3 weeks instead (Zeiner, 1999). Twenty-one boys were assessed by both their teachers and parents using rating scales of hyperactive and defiant behavior. The main results are presented in Figure 8.5. The figure shows that at least in school, the hyperactive and defiant behavior of the boys while they were regularly taking Ritalin was significantly less than during the 3 weeks they were taking placebos.

Because there is no control group in a before-after no control group design, it may seem poorly equipped to provide convincing evidence of the effect of an independent variable on a dependent variable. This is certainly true regarding the most basic form of the design—as shown in Figure 8.4 and illustrated by Figure 8.5. However, there are more elaborate forms of before-after no control group experimental design that can provide very convincing evidence of experimental effects.

Consider an experiment undertaken to increase the use of seatbelts among government employees in Florida (Thyer & Geller, 1987). In a vehicle being used for highway travel, the following sign was either absent or prominently displayed on the dashboard of the vehicle: *Safety Belt Use Required in this Vehicle.* As you can see in Figure 8.6, during the two 2-week periods when the sign was present (the "imposition" weeks), seatbelt use nearly doubled that of the two 2-week periods when it was absent.

The experiment summarized in Figure 8.6 is an example of a type of before-after no control group design sometimes referred to as a **reversal design**

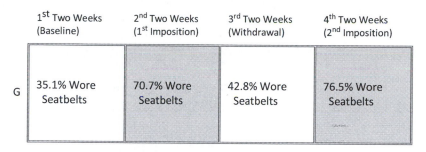

1st Two Weeks (Baseline)	2nd Two Weeks (1st Imposition)	3rd Two Weeks (Withdrawal)	4th Two Weeks (2nd Imposition)
35.1% Wore Seatbelts	70.7% Wore Seatbelts	42.8% Wore Seatbelts	76.5% Wore Seatbelts

(G)

FIGURE 8.6   Results from a Before-After No Control Group Experiment on Increasing Seatbelt Usage

Source: Adapted by authors from Thyer & Geller (1987).

because it shifts back and forth between the control and the experimental conditions. Another name for the same type of design is an **ABAB design** (Thyer et al., 1987), which is the single most widely used reversal design (Eichelman, 1992).

Had the experiment illustrated in Figure 8.6 stopped after the second week, the researcher could not have been very confident that the increase in seatbelt usage from the first to the second week was really attributable to the sign that was displayed. Along these lines is a well-known phenomenon in clinical research called **spontaneous recovery**, which refers to the tendency for people to seek treatment when the symptoms are worst. Because symptoms for most ailments fluctuate in severity, there is a reasonable probability that after patients come to a clinician, the symptoms will be less severe than at the point of first appearance. Although spontaneous recovery is not of relevance to the seatbelt usage experiment, the concept reinforces the idea that one should be cautious in interpreting before-after no control group experiments with no reversals. Before-after no control group experimental designs are especially common in clinical research. These designs are unique in being applicable to experiments with just one subject (Benjamin et al., 1983; Monette et al., 1986).

Cross-Over Design

Another type of experimental design that is often used in social science research is called a **cross-over design**. Its key feature is that, at some point in time, all participants serve as both experimental subjects and control subjects. One study that used a cross-over design was undertaken to determine if social interactions, especially with an attractive, flirtatious female, would result in elevated testosterone levels among male subjects (Dabbs et al., 1987). Testosterone levels were measured in small samples of saliva, which the subjects "donated" by spitting into a vial. Three measures of the dependent variable were taken. The first was a baseline measure obtained at the time subjects entered to laboratory. The second measure was taken after half the subjects had been isolated in a room with another male subject while the other half had been isolated in a room with an attractive and friendly female confederate. The third measure of the dependent variable was obtained about 15 minutes after the males switched rooms, with the controls becoming the experimentals and vice versa. In this study, as in most cross-over designs, each subject served under both experimental and control conditions. The experiment revealed that testosterone levels rose significantly after both forms of social interaction, but especially after interacting with the female confederates.

Another study using a cross-over design was conducted by one of the authors along with a colleague (Ellis & Mathis, 1985). We were interested in retesting earlier conclusions that students can learn as well from observing lectures on video as they can observing the same lectures face to face in a classroom (e.g., Thorman & Amb, 1974; Thorman, 1975). In our study, students were randomly selected to watch half the lectures in person and the other half live on a television monitor in an adjoining room. All students took four exams separated by four sets of six lectures. After each set of lectures, the students who had watched the lectures in person were switched to the room containing the television monitor, and those who had watched the lectures on television were switched to the lectures in person.

Did the students learn as well from being in the presence of the instructor as when they watched the instructor in an adjoining room on a television monitor? Results from the experiment are shown in Figure 8.7; results revealed that there were no significant differences in overall test scores with the exception of the first test when the students watching the lectures in person did better. After discussing the issue with the students in the television room, the reason for this initial difference was traced to poor sound quality in the

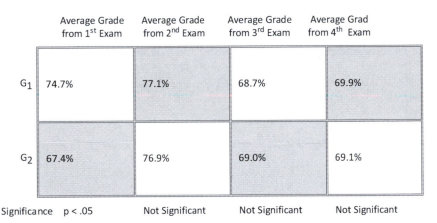

	Average Grade from 1st Exam	Average Grade from 2nd Exam	Average Grade from 3rd Exam	Average Grad from 4th Exam
G_1	74.7%	77.1%	68.7%	69.9%
G_2	67.4%	76.9%	69.0%	69.1%
Significance	p < .05	Not Significant	Not Significant	Not Significant

FIGURE 8.7 Representation of a Cross-Over Experimental Design Undertaken to Determine if College Students Learn as Well Watching Lectures In-Person as They Do Watching Lectures on Video. The Dependent Variable was the Average Test Scores; the Unshaded Cells Represent Students Attending the Lectures in Person, While the Shaded Cells Represent the Students Watching the Same Lectures on Video

Source: Adapted by authors from Ellis and Mathis (1985).

video room. After making adjustments to the sound system, test performance for two groups was virtually identical.

Notice that in Figure 8.7, the groups are simply identified as "Group 1" and "Group 2" rather than "experimental" and "controls." The reason is that in this and other cross-over experimental designs, all subjects are both experimental and control subjects at varying times throughout the study.

Solomon Four-Group Design

The **Solomon four-group design** is a specialized and rarely used design. It is discussed in courses on social and behavioral science research methods primarily to illustrate the extreme lengths to which a researcher can go to achieve experimental control over all causal contingencies. As shown in Figure 8.8, the Solomon four-group design consists of an after-only experimental design attached to a classical design. This design requires assigning subjects to a minimum of four groups, two experimental groups and two control groups. Both experimental groups receive the same level of exposure to the independent variable, and both control groups are denied anything beyond the normal level of exposure to the independent variable. The difference, however, is that one experimental group and one control group are pretested, while the other two groups are not. The purpose of this elaborate set of procedures is to see if repeated measurement of the dependent variable interacts in some way with exposure to the independent variable.

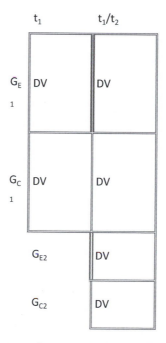

FIGURE 8.8   Representation of a Basic Solomon Four-Group Experimental Design with the Minimum Number of Cells

Experimental Factorial Design

Factorial designs are common, especially in the fields of psychology and education. They can be either experimental or nonexperimental, but the focus here will be on the former. The purpose of experimental factorial designs is to assess the possibility of two or more independent variables on a dependent variable. Note that all of the other experimental designs have focused on just one independent variable. Factorial designs not only allow researchers to look for the effects of two or more independent variables acting alone, but also interactively. **Interactive effects** refer to the effects that two or more independent variables may have on a dependent variable that neither independent variable has by itself. Interactive effects are often important to establish because in the "real world," it is common for many variables to be acting in concert rather than one at a time.

Interactive effects can be of two types. One type is an **augmenting effect**, where the effects of one variable enhance the effects of the other. The other type is an **inhibiting effect**, where increases in one variable tend to neutralize or at least dampen the effects of the other variable. Most **experimental factorial designs** involve only one time frame, so in this respect, they are a simple design. However, as shown in Figure 8.9, factorial designs have a minimum of four groups of subjects. This set of minimum conditions constitutes what is called a **two-by-two factorial design**. Figure 8.9 illustrates this point with two hypothetical variables (variables A and B), each of which is presented in a control level and an experimental level.

There are many ways to elaborate on the basic two-by-two factorial design. A factorial experiment in which subjects are exposed to two levels of one variable and three levels of another variable is called a **two-by-three factorial design**. Some factorial designs have two levels of three different variables, making it a **two-by-two-by-two factorial design**. To visualize this design, imagine Figure 8.9 having a depth dimension as well as height and length dimensions. The number of cells (and therefore groups) for a two-by-two-by-two design is eight.

Because most research about crime or the criminal justice system assumes that there are multiple variables involved in outcomes, in other words, that

		Variable A	
		Control Level	Experimental Level
Variable B	Control Level	DV for Group 1	DV for Group 2
	Experimental Level	DV for Group 3	DV for Group 4

FIGURE 8.9 A Representation of a Two-by-Two Factorial Experimental Design

there are interactive effects, these factorial designs have been undertaken in criminal justice research as well. A factorial design study about the criminal justice system, for example, is one undertaken to determine if two variables affected judgments about the appropriate sentence for persons found guilty in mock trials (Sigall & Ostrove, 1975). Each subject in the study was given one of six portfolios containing a description of two different crimes and a photograph of four different defendants. Three independent variables were manipulated in the portfolios: the physical attractiveness of the defendant (attractive or unattractive), the type of crime (burglary or swindling), and the sex of the defendant (male or female). Results were assessed separately according to the sex of the subjects, effectively adding a fourth independent variable. Thus, the design can be thought of as a two-by-two-by-two-by-two factorial design.

The main finding from the study was that regardless of the sex of the subject, attractive female defendants were sentenced less harshly than other defendants in burglary cases, but not in swindling cases. A similar study found that for both types of offenses, attractive female defendants were less harshly sentenced (Wuensch et al.,1991).

One last note: Factorial experimental designs can be combined with other basic designs. No attempt will be made here to describe these elaborate combined designs, but be aware that they are possible.

◓ Pitfalls with Human Experimentation

Experimentation, especially with human subjects, entails some special problems. These problems have both procedural and ethical ramifications.

Expectancy (Placebo) Effect

Any person who agrees to take part in an experiment is bound to be curious as to what will happen. Subtle and often unintentional cues may affect those expectations, which in turn may have major effects on the results of the experiment. Some of the best evidence for the **expectancy effect** has come from experiments involving drugs that are actually inert substances (called placebo) like sugar pills. For this reason, the expectancy effect is also referred to as the **placebo effect**, especially in experiments with drugs.

A special set of experimental procedures that are often used with human subjects to control for any possible placebo effect is called a **double-blind experiment**. Using this procedure, subjects who agree to take part in a double-blind experiment will be randomly assigned to the experimental and control groups and neither they nor persons administering the treatment to them will know whether they are receiving the real treatment or a placebo. Only a "third party" connected with the experiment will have this knowledge, and extra safeguards will be taken to ensure that this third party does not divulge this information before the experiment has been completed.

Double-blind procedures are used most often in studies involving the testing of drugs, especially drugs that may influence behavior, mood, and cognition, such as drugs used in the treatment of various forms of mental illness and behavior problems (e.g., Taylor et al., 1990). For example, a double-blind placebo-controlled study was used to assess the effectiveness of lithium (a very light metal consumed in capsule form) for treating children with conduct disorder (e.g., Silva et al., 1992). In this study, neither the children being treated nor their attending physicians knew whether the child was receiving lithium or a placebo.

To give another example, an experiment was carried out to determine whether giving young children vitamin and mineral supplements might improve their scores on intelligence tests (Benton & Cook, 1991). Forty-four subjects were randomly assigned to experimental and control groups. Neither they, their parents, nor their teachers knew which students were given capsules containing the vitamins and minerals and which were being given placebos. After 6 weeks, the children who had taken the capsules containing the vitamin and mineral supplements registered a 7.6 point gain on the test, compared to a 1.7 point loss by those who had taken the placebos. Although this difference was a statistically significant effect, a similar experiment reported in the same year found no significant effect (Todman et al., 1991).

In some clinical experiments, double-blind procedures fail. For instance, in a study of patients with persistent panic attacks, nearly all of the patients and attending physicians were able to correctly guess which patients were receiving a new experimental drug rather than a placebo because of the drug's obvious effectiveness (Margraf et al., 1991).

The Hawthorne Effect

In the late 1920s, industrial consultants were asked to recommend ways of improving work productivity in an electronics assembly plant in a district of Chicago known as Hawthorne (Diaper, 1990). The consultants explored various possibilities, and, through a series of experiments (using a before-after no control group design), they eventually concluded that improved lighting in the plant promoted worker productivity. Months later, the consultants recommended further increases in factory luminescence and found additional productivity improvements. However, they eventually lowered the luminescence and found that productivity further improved.

What could explain these findings? Operators of the plant finally came to the conclusion that the extra attention and concern given the workers during the experiment were more crucial to increasing worker productivity than was the lighting. As a result, whenever extraneous factors such as extra attention and reinforcement in an experiment with people have effects on behavior, it is referred to as the **Hawthorne effect** (Jones, 1990).

Writers have embellished the Hawthorne experiments over the years in part because careful analyses of the findings were never published (Diaper, 1990). Because it was poorly documented, several researchers have seriously questioned the reality of a Hawthorne effect (e.g., Adair, 1984; Jones, 1992), with one report going so far as to call it a "phantom phenomenon" (Granberg & Holmberg, 1992). Whether real or mythical, the concept of a Hawthorne effect is a useful vehicle from which to emphasize the importance of always being on guard against subtle unintended factors inadvertently confounding experiments involving human subjects (Gillespie, 1991).

⊖ Shortcomings of Experimental Research

Experiments are conducted with one overriding objective: to identify cause-effect relationships between variables. The need for identifying such relationships in science is of major importance in theory development. As will be apparent in the next chapter, when nonexperimental research is all that one has for understanding how variables are causally related, one is walking on thin scientific ice, even with the aid of multivariate statistics. With well-designed experimental evidence, however, one can have a great deal of confidence that causation is responsible for differences that are found.

Despite the strengths of experimental research for identifying causes, it is important to be aware of some of the shortcomings associated with it. Most problems fall into the following four interrelated categories: ethics, time and expense, lack of realism, and the fact that many questions are simply beyond the reach of experimentation.

Ethics

Ethical considerations are not confined to experimental research, but there are some unique and perplexing ethical dilemmas that must be confronted before conducting experiments, especially those involving human subjects. These were spelled out in more detail in Chapter 3; recall that they include issues surrounding the deception and informed consent of experimental subjects, and legal and moral responsibility for harm suffered by subjects. Another ethical dilemma often accompanying human experimentation involves the fact that subjects must be randomly denied treatment in order to demonstrate the treatment's effectiveness on other subjects.

Time and Expense

Experimental research is more time-consuming and expensive than nonexperimental research. Imagine how much time and money would be required to follow subjects over the course of most experiments when compared to the time and expense associated with administering a questionnaire.

Realism

Many experiments lack essential elements of realism. This has been one criticism of many criminal justice experiments, and most critics question the conclusions

Can Experiments Related to Criminal Behavior Be Emulated in a "Lab" Setting?

Many attempts to conduct experiments related to criminal behavior have been related to violence and aggression. For example, researchers have investigated whether time spent playing violent video games fostered real-world violence, and most have come to an affirmative answer (Sherry, 2001). However, the experimental designs used have largely limited measurement of "violence" to short-term effects that can only be observed in laboratory settings; then subjects have been debriefed to avoid the risk of any long-term effects. Critics of these experiments have expressed doubts that these short-term laboratory effects have any real bearing on any long-term effects that mass media may have in regard to "real life" violence. The question is should researchers ever conduct experiments designed to look for real-world effects, such as violence of an actual criminal nature? The other issue is how to explain that millions of persons watch violent movies and play violent video games but never develop or express aggressive or violent tendencies?

of these experiments. They cite that experiments are happening in a controlled setting and not in the real world, where often variables cannot be controlled or manipulated to a great degree.

Feasibility

Finally, many questions are simply beyond the reach of experimental research quite apart from considerations of ethics. Examples can be found in questions pertaining to the collective behavior of millions of people. Although it is sometimes possible to "simulate" such behavioral processes in a laboratory on a small scale, researchers are often left wondering how permanent these small-scale simulations really are to the collective behavior in naturalistic settings.

Summary

This chapter has focused attention on the concept of experimentation in social science research. The overriding distinguishing feature of experimental research is that it involves direct manipulation of an independent variable in order to assess the effects of such manipulation on a dependent variable.

Six types of experimental designs were identified and discussed: the classical design, the after-only design, the before-after no control group design, the cross-over design, the Solomon four-group design, and the factorial design.

In the classical design, subjects are divided into at least two groups: an experimental group and a control group. There is also a minimum of two time frames in a classical experiment. One time frame occurs prior to the experimental group receiving exposure to an unusual level of the independent variable, and the other after it has received this exposure. To construct an after-only design, the classical design is cut in half by removing the initial time frame. Provided a researcher has a large group of subjects randomly assigned to each of the experimental and control conditions, this removal makes the after-only design only slightly weaker than its classical counterpart. The only purpose served by the initial time frame in the classical design is to give assurance that the experimental and control groups are indeed statistically equivalent prior to exposing the experimental group to an unusual degree of exposure to the independent variable. In an after-only design, no such assurance is obtained.

The before-after no control group design can also be considered a truncated version of the classical design; in this case, the control group has been removed. With this design, a researcher can strengthen the experiment by adding more than the minimum two time frames. Within these additional time frames, the independent variable can be imposed, withheld, and then reimposed several times to confirm that it is the independent variable that is responsible for significant increases or decreases on the dependent variable.

The cross-over experimental design is unique in that two or more groups of subjects are used, with each group receiving unusual exposure to the independent variable. The sequence of this exposure, however, is different for each group.

The Solomon four-group design essentially affixes an after-only design onto a classical design. This is a rarely used design, but it illustrates the length to which a researcher can go to verify the effects an independent variable has on a dependent variable apart from any effects caused by repeated measurement of the independent variable.

Finally, in the factorial experiment design two or more independent variables are manipulated at a time. In this way it is possible to discover not only their separate effects on one or more dependent variables, but also whether there are interactive effects.

The values and the drawbacks of scientific experimentation were discussed and illustrated near the end of this chapter. Also discussed were the concepts of the expectancy effect and the Hawthorne effect. The expectancy (or placebo) effect refers to the tendency for subjects to anticipate results from experimentation, often based on subtle clues that the researcher may neither intend nor be aware of. If these clues are in any way associated with the independent variable(s) being manipulated, they can confound an experiment in ways that may be very misleading to a researcher. A set of experimental procedures specially designed to reduce the expectancy effect is called double-blind experimentation. The Hawthorne effect refers to the unintended effects that researchers may have on the results of an experiment because of the extra attention and reinforcement given to subjects.

Although there are a number of pitfalls that scientists need to watch for, the potential benefits from experimental research would be difficult to exaggerate. Whenever a researcher's primary interest is causal relationships between variables, he or she should give serious thought to experimental research.

⊖ Discussion Questions

1. Discuss the three important components of true experimental designs and how each assists in establishing causal relationships.
2. What are some of the shortcomings of experimental designs and how might a researcher overcome them?

⊖ Exercises

1. Think of a topic that you would like to study with a true experimental design. Outline the treatment and the outcome (observation) measure or measures.
2. Design an experiment that specifically includes components to help minimize the so-called placebo or Hawthorne effect.

Chapter 9 Quasi-Experimentation

Every year, hundreds of different types of programs designed to prevent future criminal behavior are implemented in jurisdictions across the country. These programs aim to reduce recidivism via interventions such as drug treatment,

mental health treatment, job training, education, and reentry initiatives to name a few. Scientifically, the surest way to find out whether these programs are successful or better at reducing recidivism compared to traditional criminal justice programs (i.e., regular probation or jail) would be to conduct an experiment in which several hundred offenders would be randomly assigned to either an experimental group that gets the intervention (attends the treatment or program) or a control group that does not get the intervention. These two groups could be studied for a year or two to determine whether there were any differences in their likelihood to reoffend. For ethical reasons, however, experiments of this type are rarely conducted. Is it ethical to randomly assign convicted offenders to either jail or treatment? Most judges and prosecutors would not agree to allow researchers to do this. So, how can researchers evaluate these programs to assess how best to reduce future offending? This chapter will discuss some powerful "almost experiments" often called quasi-experimental designs that can sometimes provide reliable answers to questions about a program's success and still meet ethical research requirements.

Thousands of experiments related to crime prevention and reduction have never been conducted, even though they would provide us with invaluable scientific information about what works. Although a few experiments have been undertaken, they usually involve some type of random assignment after the criminal justice system has already decided not to send the offender to jail, not in lieu of incarceration. Under the ethical principles of beneficence and justice, true experimental designs that would randomly assign some alternative to incarceration or harsh punishment are considered to be unethical. What do researchers do then if they want to answer questions of a causal nature but cannot conduct controlled experimentation to provide those answers? In many cases, they turn to research designs that will be the focus of this chapter: quasi-experiments.

⬤ Quasi-Experiments Compared to Controlled Experiments

The prefix *quasi* means "sort of." Accordingly, **quasi-experimental research** is similar to controlled experimentation, although it falls short in some significant way. The term quasi-experiment was first used in the 1960s to refer to studies that were not true experiments (Campbell & Stanley, 1966). In the course of learning about quasi-experimentation, keep in mind that from a methodological standpoint, the gold standard for answering all causal questions is controlled experimentation or true experiments. Therefore, if a controlled experiment is possible, there is no need for any alternative, but when ethics, time, or money makes experimentation impossible, scientists often resort to quasi-experimentation.

As summarized in Table 9.1, quasi-experiments resemble controlled experiments in that the main purpose of both is to answer questions about causation. For this reason, the terms *independent variables* and *dependent variables* are often

Table 9.1   Comparisons of Quasi-Experiments and Actual Controlled Experiments

Features	Quasi-Experiments	Controlled Experiments
Main goal is to answer one or more causal questions	Yes	Yes
Has a randomly picked control group	Never	Often
Actually manipulates exposure to the independent variable	Rarely	Nearly Always
Use terms such as *experimental group* and *control group*	Sometimes	Always
Confidence in the outcome providing an answer to the causal question (assuming adequate sample size)	High to Low	High

used in discussing quasi-experiments just as they are in controlled experiments. However, the designation of these two types of variables is not always as emphatic in the case of quasi-experimentation because in quasi-experimentation a researcher only "pretends" to manipulate an independent variable. ("Pretending" in the context of quasi-experimentation will be made clearer shortly.)

Because there is no actual experimental control in quasi-experiments, some researchers use the terms **predictor variable** instead of *independent variable*, and **criterion variable** rather than *dependent variable* (Carlo et al., 1998). In this text, the terms *independent variable* and *dependent variable* will be used. Furthermore, in most quasi-experiments, there are no genuine experimental and control groups. Therefore, it is common to use the term **exposure group** rather than "experimental group" and **comparison group** instead of "control group" (Rossi & Freeman, 1989). These latter terms are particularly helpful in maintaining the important distinction between quasi-experiments and controlled experiments and will be used throughout this chapter.

As the various types of quasi-experimental designs are examined, it will become apparent that all these designs circumvent the process of true experiments in some significant way. For example, in nearly all quasi-experimental designs, researchers bypass the process of randomly assigning subjects to experimental and control groups. They instead contrive a "control group." Despite such compromises, quasi-experimentation plays an important role in social science research and can still be a powerful tool for identifying cause-effect relationships.

Quasi-Experimental Designs in the Narrower Sense

There are both a narrow and a broad sense in which the term *quasi-experiment* is used (Rossi & Freeman, 1989). In the broadest sense of the term, quasi-experiments are all studies other than controlled experiments designed to answer causal questions. In the narrower sense, quasi-experimentation does not include research designs based simply on multivariate statistics. This chapter will use the term in the broadest sense, although it will give separate consideration to quasi-experiments that are based solely on multivariate statistics. The four types of quasi-experimental designs that fit the narrower sense are called ex post facto designs, prospective designs, linear time series designs, and event-specific alignment time series designs.

Ex Post Facto (Retrospective) Designs

Ex post facto means "after the fact." Studies that fall under the category of **ex post facto** (or **retrospective**) quasi-experiments simulate after-only experimental designs except for random assignment of subjects. Examples of ex post facto designs in criminal justice research include studies of "hot spot" policing strategies or drug court treatment programs. For example, Braga, Hureau, & Papachristos (2011) studied a program implemented by the Boston Police Department to control violent crime called Safe Street Team or SST. These researchers examined annual counts of violent crime in the areas of the city where SST was implemented and areas where it was not, essentially creating ex post facto (after the fact) treatment and control groups. Areas of the city where the SST program was implemented were the treatment group and the areas where it was not were the control group.

In this way, Braga and his colleagues could measure the effects, if any, of the SST program on violent crime. This is not considered a controlled experiment because the areas of the city where the SST program was implemented were not randomly assigned; the police department picked the areas for SST implementation. This type of quasi-experiment is usually conducted years after the program (treatment) has been implemented because it allows enough time to have elapsed to measure its effect on crime; usually researchers look at crime rates for a year or so before the program is implemented and a year or so after it commenced. Braga and his colleagues (2011) found that in the areas where the SST program was implemented, violent crime was significantly lower. Because they examined violent crime in the areas where the program was not implemented, they were able to show that violent crime was not displaced from areas where the police implemented SST to other areas where it was not implemented.

Because ex post facto quasi-experiments can always be criticized on grounds that the groups being compared may not be equivalent in all important ways *other* than their degree of exposure to the independent variable (Rossi & Freeman, 989), consider the options available in choosing comparison group members.

In ex post facto research, three different matching procedures for obtaining comparison groups have been developed. These are called group matching, individual matching, and sibling matching. **Group matching** occurs when a researcher merely ensures that, *on average*, there are no significant differences between the exposure and the comparison groups regarding a variety of demographic characteristics.

Another example of an ex post facto design using group matching was a study undertaken to examine the effectiveness of a community-based drug treatment court program. Listwan, Koetzle, and Hartman (2009) studied drug court participants who had already been through a drug treatment program but constructed their "experimental" and "control" groups by using information on the type of drug the participant had been arrested for. They were interested in whether methamphetamine users could be successful in treatment in a community-based treatment program as compared with other types of drug users. In other words, they used the individual's self-reported drug of choice to create the two groups (meth users versus non-meth users) ex post facto. The researchers assessed how well the two groups were a match by looking at a number of other important variables. For example, they compared the two groups on their prior record, employment status, education, and marital status. They reported that the two groups were similar on all of these variables except that meth users were more likely to be female than non-meth users. This is an example of group matching ex post facto.

The researchers looked at any new arrests, both new drug arrests and other types of arrest, for both groups for about 2½ years after they were participants in the drug court program. The results revealed that there was not much difference between the two groups on their measures of recidivism or whether the participants completed the treatment program. The authors therefore concluded, based on this quasi-experimental design, that meth users can be safely treated in a community-based treatment program.

Individual matching is more difficult than group matching because it requires that the researcher locate individuals in the comparison group that essentially match each individual member of an exposure group. For example, if one member of the exposure group was a middle-aged female Native American with a college degree, one should find a comparison group member with roughly identical characteristics. Obviously, individual matching ensures that the averages for the two groups will be the same, at least for all of the demographic characteristics used in carrying out the individual matching. However, individual matching is thought to give researchers greater confidence in the comparability of the two groups.

Sibling matching involves identifying individuals with some unusual trait that researchers would like to better understand from a causal standpoint and using same-sex siblings as comparison subjects. This type of matching procedure automatically controls for race/ethnicity, social status, and family background (Offord & Jones, 1976). Sibling matching has been most often used for identifying prenatal and early childhood factors potentially contributing to later problem behavior such as behavioral and psychiatric disorders (e.g., Ruff & Offord, 1971; Mura, 1974). One study that used this type of matching procedure was undertaken in Canada to better identify childhood conditions preceding antisocial behavior (Reitsma-Street et al., 1985). Several significant differences were found between the affected subjects and their unaffected siblings in terms of early life experiences, including the affected subjects being less warmly treated by parents.

BOX 9.1 CURRENT ISSUES

How Extensive Does Matching Have to Be?

Ideally, matching is performed with numerous characteristics, not just one or two. Among the most common traits used for matching are age, sex, race/ethnicity, and years of education. In criminal justice research, it is also important to match on other important variables of interest that might be related to recidivism and other outcomes like prior criminal history or prior drug use. For example, if one of the groups has more extensive average criminal histories than the other, this could be a reason that their recidivism rates are higher and not because they were the group who didn't receive the intervention or treatment. In actual experiments with control groups, researchers are able to use random assignment to control for every conceivable difference between an experimental group and a control group. Ex post facto designs are undertaken to achieve the same objective through matching procedures.

Obviously, the more characteristics one uses in matching the exposure and comparison groups, the more confidence one can have that the two groups are equivalent with the exception of the independent variable. Were it possible to match two groups of subjects on every characteristic imaginable, an ex post facto quasi-experiment would provide just as convincing a case for causal relationships as would actual controlled experiments (Rossi & Freeman, 1989).

A study involving the same research team used a similar sibling matching procedure to assess the effects of pregnancy and birth complications on antisocial behavior among adolescents (Szatmari et al., 1986). Contrary to some other studies (Drillien, 1964; McNeil et al., 1970), this one did not find pregnancy or birth complications to be significantly more prevalent among the antisocial adolescents than among their same-sex siblings.

Prospective Quasi-Experimental Designs

A **prospective quasi-experimental design** involves observing variations in the independent variable as events are unfolding, rather than reconstructing the events after the fact (as in ex post facto designs). The main advantage of measuring the independent variable as it occurs is that such measurement reduces the risk of biased recall in light of knowledge regarding the outcome (Bailey & Zucker, 1995). Otherwise, a prospective quasi-experimental design and an ex post facto design are similar. Both typically have a structure that resembles an after-only experimental design, and both use one of the three matching procedures already discussed.

An example of a prospective quasi-experiment would be one similar to the drug court treatment study but the researchers collect data on the participants while they are still in the treatment program. For example, perhaps the researchers could interview or administer surveys to the groups of participants related to any continued drug use that they had while in the program (relapse) that wouldn't be able to be gathered after they had completed the treatment.

In this way they could explore whether there are other factors that occur during treatment that might be related to future recidivism. This study would be considered a prospective quasi-experiment. Note that measurement of the independent variable will have occurred many months and perhaps years before measurement of the dependent variable. Nevertheless, the study is methodologically weaker than a controlled experiment because the participants would not be randomly assigned to an experimental and a control group.

Other prospective quasi-experimental designs have been undertaken to assess the effects of prenatal drug or alcohol exposure to the future behavior of the unborn offspring. For example, researchers could invite females who have recently confirmed their pregnancies at a health clinic to participate in a study. Those who agree to take part will be asked to keep a record of various activities, including their use of alcohol and various drugs. After their children are born, the mothers will be asked to bring their children to the clinic for testing, and the results of these tests are then correlated with the mother's drug and alcohol use history.

To give a specific example, one study was conducted in which 650 women were interviewed during each trimester of pregnancy regarding their alcohol consumption. The study found that women who gave birth to infants with the lowest birth weights and head circumferences reported drinking significantly more than mothers of normal and high-birth-weight infants, particularly during the first 2 months of pregnancy (Day et al., 1989). This evidence was particularly disturbing to the researchers because during the earliest months of pregnancy, most women are not aware that they are pregnant.

Researchers must be cautious in interpreting both prospective and ex post facto quasi-experiments. In neither case are subjects randomly assigned to the exposure and comparison groups. In the previous example, because neither the drinking mothers nor the nondrinking mothers were randomly assigned, numerous nondrinking variables could actually be responsible for the difference in birth weight and head circumference of the infants.

Generally, prospective designs are considered more persuasive than retrospective designs, especially when the independent and dependent variables are separated by long periods of time. The main drawback to a prospective design, however, is that a researcher must wait until the dependent variable manifests itself. Because this sometimes takes several years, tracking down all the subjects in order to measure the dependent variable may be difficult.

Linear Time Series Designs

Most **linear time series quasi-experiments** (also simply called time series designs) have a structure that closely resembles before-after no control group experiments, although the most powerful time series designs resemble classical experiments. The typical time series design involves tracking a dependent variable over time, observing whether the values of the dependent variable seem to change in response to changes in an independent variable.

For a simple illustration of a time series quasi-experimental design, consider a study undertaken to examine whether lowering the blood alcohol concentration (BAC) from 0.10 to 0.08 to be considered guilty of driving under the influence (DUI) had any effects on both driver and passenger fatalities stemming from auto accidents. Chamlin (2017) examined monthly crash fatality data in New Jersey from 1998 to 2011 to determine whether changes in the legal BAC level had any impact on total driver and passenger fatalities.

Time series designs can be very complex because the researcher also has to attempt to control other factors that might impact crash fatalities other than the lowering of the legal BAC level. For example, what if during this same time period, new laws regarding seat belt use or car manufacturer airbag quality also went into effect. If fatalities are lower, the researcher has to isolate that they indeed decreased due to the new BAC law change and not some other factor that might also have an effect on auto accident fatalities. Fortunately, advanced statistical modeling called ARIMA (autoregressive integrated moving average) can assist to control for other important independent variables. The previous study found that there was no significant effect on lowering the BAC level on total or driver fatalities, but they did find a significant decrease in passenger fatalities as a result (Chamlin, 2016).

There are other ways of strengthening a basic time series quasi-experimental design. One is to include one or more reversals in imposition of the independent variable. For example, let's say that the BAC law was repealed years later due to lawsuits; researchers could then study the effects of reimposing the old law. The design is therefore strengthened by looking at the effects of lowering and increasing the BAC law.

The second way to strengthen a basic time series quasi-experimental design involves adding a comparison group. This gives a time series quasi-experimental design a structure that closely resembles a classical experiment. In the New Jersey study by Chamlin, the study might be strengthened by examining auto accident fatalities in an adjacent state such as New York, where the law did not change. If passenger fatalities do not decrease in New York, the researchers can be more certain that the law had an impact. If passenger fatalities also decrease in New York where the law was not changed, researchers will have more difficulty attributing the decrease to the change in the law because passenger fatalities also went down in an adjacent state where the law was not changed.

Event-Specific Alignment Design

A type of time series design that deserves special attention is called an **event-specific alignment study**. As the name implies, this type of time series design obtains a series of average readings for some dependent variable in accordance with an independent variable that is occurring at irregular intervals over the course of time. The distinctive feature of such a design relative to a more common time series design is that all of the instances of some dependent variable are aligned according to an independent variable. Then researchers calculate the average instance of the dependent variable for each time unit leading up to and extending through the occurrence of the independent variable.

Numerous nonexperimental studies have sought evidence to either refute or support the view that the death penalty has deterrent effects (e.g., Ehrlich, 1977; Decker & Kohfeld, 1990; Forst, 1977; Cochran et al., 1994). These studies have come to inconsistent conclusions, with most but not all suggesting that the deterrent effects are minimal (Layson, 1985; Peterson & Bailey, 1991). A sociologist took a particularly innovative approach to the question by utilizing an event-specific alignment design (Phillips, 1980). He obtained historical data on executions and murders in England between 1858 and 1921. During this period of time, 22 persons were publically executed for murder. The researcher aligned each murder in England during this time according to the week in which these 22 executions took place. His time frame was between the 4 weeks preceding and 6 weeks following the week of each execution.

The main findings revealed that the number of murders was averaging just under 30 throughout the analysis period. In the week that the 22 executions took place, there was a substantial drop in the number of murders, and the number remained low for the following week. This suggests that the executions did have a deterrent effect. However, by the third and fourth weeks following these 22 executions, the number of murders rose well above the average, almost completely canceling out the apparent earlier deterring effects of the executions. A replication of this study based on contemporary US data confirmed the essential findings from this rather intriguing study (Stack, 1987).

Basically, the event-specific alignment design is similar to other time series quasi-experimental designs except that all the instances in which the independent variables are imposed are aligned at a common point. Averages for the dependent variable are then calculated for specified time intervals leading up to and following the imposition of the independent variable. Despite the limited use of the event-specific alignment design compared to the more basic time series quasi-experimental design, it is a powerful design option for assessing cause-and-effect relationships.

Quasi-Experimental Designs in the Broader Sense

In the narrow sense, quasi-experimental designs only include those just discussed, because all have design structures that resemble actual controlled experiments. In a broader sense, another type of design can also be considered a quasi-experiment. This is one in which multivariate statistics are used to "impose" comparability between two or more groups of subjects. To envision how multivariate statistics can be used to address causal hypotheses, consider a set of studies on a controversial topic: student learning in public versus private elementary schools.

An Example of Multivariate Statistics Being Used to Answer a Causal Question

Which type of school promotes greater academic achievement in grade school students: public schools or private schools? Research undertaken to address this question began to appear in the 1980s, led by a famous sociologist by the name of James Coleman, whose findings sparked controversy and have led to many subsequent studies. These studies have repeatedly demonstrated that, on average, students graduating from private schools scored higher on a variety of standardized tests of academic performance than students graduating from public schools (Coleman et al., 1981, 1982a, 1982c; Young & Fraser, 1990; Evans & Schwab, 1995; Sander, 1996).

   Although this evidence is consistent with the hypothesis that private schools better train students than public schools, there are certainly other possibilities.

BOX 9.2 WHAT DO YOU THINK?

Can Computer Software Programs Statistically Equalize Treatment and Comparison Groups in Quasi-Experimental Designs?

Why not conduct an experiment to assess whether privates schools are better than public schools? Do you think parents would be willing to allow their children to be randomly assigned to attend either private schools or public schools for the benefit of scientific knowledge? Perhaps parents who are going to send their children to public school wouldn't care, but those who decide to pay for private school would not likely agree to be part of such an experiment. Consequently, researchers like Coleman have increasingly been attempting to answer questions like which type of school is better by using computer software programs to statistically equalize students attending both types of schools.

How can one statistically equalize students? The most widely used techniques utilize multivariate statistics to determine how much of a difference exists between various demographic and family background variables (e.g., race/ethnicity, parental education, income) between students attending private school and those attending public school. These analytic techniques make statistical adjustments in the outcome variable (student achievement) on the basis of the average differences that exist in these background variables. What do you think? Can these statistical techniques emulate matched groups of private and public school students for comparative purposes?

Another technique, called propensity score matching, has been also used to create statistical matches for individuals in one's data. Although a discussion of this statistical technique is beyond the scope of this book, in criminal justice research it has been used to create offenders who are statistically similar on all variables of interest to be able to examine outcomes such as probability of incarceration or the amount of prison time handed out by a judge. In this way, a researcher can assess whether criminal justice outcomes are influenced by extra-legal factors such as race, ethnicity, and sex, all else being statistically equal.

For example, private schools tend to be selective in the students they accept and retain, whereas public schools are legally required to take every child of an appropriate age. Therefore, differences between the achievement scores of children from private schools and those from public schools might not be the result of different teaching methods, school discipline, and the like. Instead, they reflect a selection bias by private schools (Noell, 1982; Murnane et al., 1995).

Quasi-Experimental Designs for Addressing Nature-Nurture Issues

The most enduring issues in criminology center around the relative influence of learned sociocultural variables (nurture) and genetic/biological factors (nature) on human behavior (Ellis et al., 1988; Terwogt et al., 1993). With laboratory animals, controlled experiments have been conducted to assess the relative influence of nature and nurture on various types of behavior. Some of these experiments involve selectively inbreeding strains of rats or mice who exhibit some specific traits, such as unusual learning abilities, aggression, nest building, courtship patterns, and preferences for consumption of alcohol (Broadhurst & Bignami, 1965; Brush et al., 1979; Wilson et al., 1984; Wimer & Wimer, 1985).

These studies suggest that genes can and do account for substantial variation in many traits that appear to provide animal models for analogous human behavior. The way to be certain, however, would be to conduct similar breeding experiments with humans, an approach that would obviously be unethical and illegal. Fortunately, special quasi-experimental designs have been developed for addressing nature-nurture questions in humans (Pastore, 1949; Turkheimer, 1991). The most common of these designs are called twin studies and adoption studies.

Twin Studies

Twin studies take advantage of the fact that there are two types of twins, both with a known degree of genetic relatedness to one another. Identical twins are, for all intents and purposes, genetic clones of one another. Except for rare mutations occurring after conception, they share 100% of their genes in common. Therefore, any differences between pairs of identical twins regarding either physical appearance or behavior would almost certainly be attributed to environmental factors. Fraternal twins, on the other hand, are no more similar to one another than are ordinary siblings. Because all siblings receive half of their genes from each parent, they will share on average 50% of their genes, particularly if they are of the same sex.

The two-to-one ratio in the number of genes shared by sets of identical and fraternal twins makes it possible to examine behavior traits for evidence of genetic and environmental influence. To the degree genetic factors influence a trait, this rate of concordance fails to be empirically confirmed, while the influence of environmental factors must be substantial, especially if identical twins are no more concordant than fraternal twins are for the trait. A variety of twin study designs have been developed over the years (Segal, 1990), although they all rest on the fundamental logic just outlined. Behavior traits that some twin studies suggest are significantly influenced (but *not* determined) by genetic factors include intelligence and educational achievement (Tambs et al., 1989; Lykken et al., 1990), occupational status (Fulker, 1978; Tambs & Sundet, 1985), and criminality (Joseph, 2001).

Some critics of the twin study method have argued that identical twins are found to be more concordant on many behavior traits not because of the influence of genetics, but because identical twins are treated more similarly by their parents and others than are fraternal twins. However, this may be because identical twins *elicit* more similar treatment due to appearance and behavioral similarities (Rowe, 1990). Studies have generally failed to confirm that "similar treatment" is responsible for identical twins being roughly twice as concordant in numerous behavioral traits than are fraternal twins (reviewed by Segal, 1990).

Adoption Studies

Most children have only one mother and one father. However, some infants born every year are adopted at or near birth by persons unrelated to them. Such children have two sets of parents: the parents who rear them (their rearing parents) and those who gave them their genes (their genetic parents). Social scientists have used **adoption studies** to help determine how much influence genetic factors and family environment have over behavior.

Adoption studies, in fact, are very similar to a type of experimental design used with laboratory animals to address nature-nurture issues, a design referred to as **cross-fostering experiments** (Carter-Saltzman, 1980; Roubertoux & Carlier, 1988). In these experiments, offspring are removed from their genetic mothers immediately after birth and given to foster mothers for rearing. To the degree that the offspring end up more closely resembling their genetic mothers than their rearing mothers for a given behavior pattern, genetic factors are deemed important for the expressions of the behavior (Huck & Banks, 1980; Roubertoux & Carlier, 1988).

Like twin studies, adoption studies have suggested that many human behavior traits are genetically influenced. For example, adoptees reared by nongenetic relatives have been found to more closely resemble one or both of their genetic parents than either of their rearing parents for each of the following traits: alcoholism, various forms of mental illness, and hyperactivity (Cadoret et al., 1986). Adoption studies also suggest that genes contribute significantly to variations in scholastic achievement (Teasdale & Sorensen, 1983; Thompson et al., 1991) and criminality (Mednick et al., 1987; Raine & Dunkin, 1990; Ellis & Walsh, 2000; Tehrani & Mednick, 2000). One adoption study even suggested that handedness was influenced by genetic factors (Carter-Saltzman, 1980). Despite this evidence, the fact that the behavior patterns of adopted offspring are not fully explained by the influence of either set of parents makes it very likely that influences from environmental factors outside the family are important as well (Rowe, 1994).

Combined Twin/Adoption Studies and Other Designs

An especially innovative quasi-experimental design for addressing nature-nurture questions studies twins reared apart by different adoptive families (Holden, 1980; Lichtenstein, et al., 1992; Waldman et al., 1992). Although sample sizes tend to be small, twin/adoption designs have given researchers especially powerful avenues for separating the effects of genetic and environmental influences. Based on data from these combined adoption/twin studies, genetic factors have been detected for traits such as shyness/extraversion, dominance/submissiveness, intellectual ability (Holden, 1980; Bouchard et al., 1990; Waldman et al., 1992), and even occupational interests and status attainment (Moloney et al., 1991; Lichtenstein et al., 1992). Nevertheless, the effects of environmental factors, especially from outside the home, have also been quite evident (Lykken et al., 1990).

Other research designs that have been developed for sorting out the relative influence of genetic and environmental factors on behavior involve directly inspecting the DNA and the chromosomes on which DNA codes appear (Schroder et al., 1981; Ratcliffe, 1994). However, these direct approaches to behavior genetics do not easily fit into the traditional trichotomy of nonexperimental, experimental, and quasi-experimental research designs.

Although nature-nurture studies of human behavior have flourished in recent decades, they continue to be controversial. Some of the controversy has to do with details in methodology and interpretations of the findings (Loehlin, 1989). Other areas of controversy surround the moral and legal implications of some of the findings from this research (Pastore, 1949; Montagu, 1980; Snyderman & Rothman, 1988).

◒ Summary

If a scientist is interested in whether variable A causes variable B, the surest way to a confident conclusion is by way of controlled experimentation. When experimental research is impractical or unethical, it is often possible to conduct quasi-experiments that simulate experiments. In the narrow sense of the word, quasi-experiments refer to studies that take advantage of manipulations of independent variables that occur outside of the direct control of the researcher. In the broader sense of the term, quasi-experimental studies include designs that rely primarily upon multivariate statistics to achieve "control" over variables that would normally be controlled through random assignment in an actual experiment.

There are three main types of quasi-experimental designs: ex post facto, prospective, and time series. Most ex post facto designs are conceptually structured like after-only experiments. However, instead of having any true experimental groups and control groups whose membership was randomly determined, ex post facto studies have comparison groups and exposure groups. A comparison group is "constructed" by using some type of matching procedure. In ex post facto designs, the comparison group is chosen after the exposure group has received an unusual degree of exposure to an independent variable.

A prospective design is usually structured similarly to either an after-only or a classical experiment. Rather than being constructed after an unusual exposure to an independent variable has occurred, a prospective design is planned in advance of any exposure. Nevertheless, comparison subjects are again chosen through a matching process rather than by random selection.

Time series quasi-experimental designs have two distinct forms: the basic form and an event-specific alignment design. The basic time series design usually simulates a before-after no control group experiment, often with some type of reversal (e.g., ABAB) structure. Sometimes, a comparison group is used in a time series design, making it resemble a classical experimental design.

Regarding an event-specific alignment design, a researcher aligns numerous instances of a time-sequence for a dependent variable according to some specific independent variable. Then the averages for the dependent variable are calculated for each time frame leading up to and following the independent variable. From this set of statistical adjustments, one is often able to detect changes in the dependent variable associated with imposition of the independent variable.

In the broad sense of the term, some multivariate statistical studies can be classified as quasi-experiments. In a narrow sense, however, quasi-experiments based strictly on multivariate statistics simply control for "extraneous" variables statistically. Although control techniques made possible by multivariate statistics are fairly complex mathematically (i.e., propensity score matching), the basic principles underlying them are fairly easy to understand, and computer programs make them easy to perform. The key element of quasi-experiments based strictly on multivariate statistics is that the goal is to test causal hypotheses.

Special types of quasi-experimental designs have been developed for answering nature-nurture questions. The two most widely used designs are twin studies and adoption studies. Twin studies take advantage of the fact that humans have two types of twins, identical and fraternal, with known genetic relationships to one another. This makes it possible to estimate the relative influence of genetic and familial environmental factors on behavior patterns.

Adoption studies take advantage of the fact that many infants are adopted each year by nonrelatives, effectively giving them two sets of parents: their genetic parents and their rearing patents. This makes it possible to estimate the degree to which genetics and familiar environmental factors influence the behavior of adoptees.

There are, in fact, several types of both twin study designs and adoption study designs, and recently a combined twin/adoption study design has been utilized. The latter involves studying twins reared apart in order to assess the influence of both genetic and environmental factors on behavior.

⬍ Discussion Questions

1. What are some of the ways in which quasi-experimental designs attempt to emulate controlled experimentation?
2. Explain the purposes of matching in quasi-experimentation. Also, discuss the different reasons one might use group versus individual matching techniques.
3. Describe how quasi-experimental designs have been used to address nature-nuture questions.

⬍ Exercises

1. Think of a topic that one could study using an ex post facto (retrospective) design. How would you choose an appropriate comparison group?
2. Think of a topic that one could study using a time series analysis design. How would you measure the intervals for the observation points (monthly, yearly). How many observation points before and after do you think you would need to assess casual effects? What else might you want to control for in your study other than the main independent variable that might also influence the outcome studied?

Chapter 10

Data Based on Self-Reports: Guidelines for Constructing Questionnaires

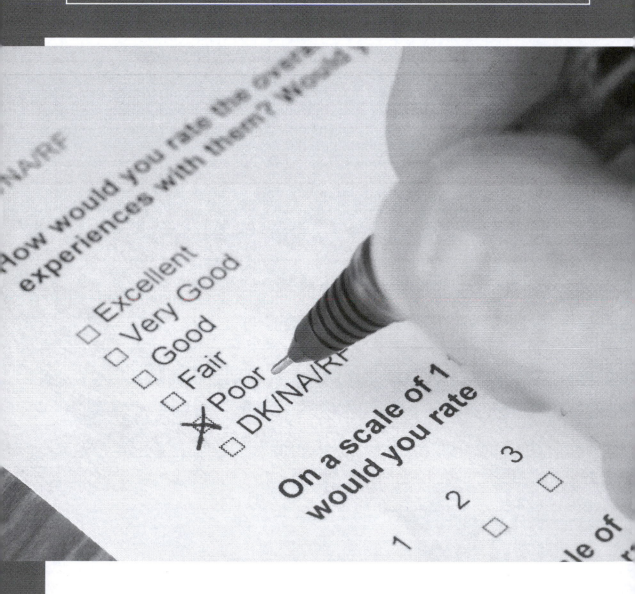

Suppose you believed like many criminologists that low self-control is somehow related to involvement in delinquent behavior. How would you go about studying whether there is any relationship between these things? Most criminologists use questionnaires to gather data on how individual (micro level) factors might be associated with crime and delinquency. What sort of questions would one ask on a questionnaire to obtain the necessary data for study? Or suppose you believe like many other criminologists that the peers that individuals hang out with, or spend time with, influence their behavior. How could you phrase questions that would provide meaningful responses related to someone's interactions with their friends or their friend's attributes and behaviors? These questions will be addressed in this chapter, which discusses self-report surveys or questionnaires.

A **research instrument** refers to any physical thing used to collect scientific data. In general, **questionnaires** are research instruments used by researchers to solicit information from potential respondents, usually in written form. In other words, a questionnaire is a research instrument through which human beings provide information about their lives and behavior, and sometimes about the lives and behavior of other persons they know, such as family members or friends. Questionnaires can be completed either by directly responding to questions on paper-and-pencil hard copies or via questions presented to participants during a telephone conversation, a face-to-face interview, or a software programs online—even through applications on a mobile device. A growing trend has involved constructing questionnaires using computer software programs that allow subjects to complete their questionnaire on line and that also compile the data into databases in real time. This saves the researcher the time and effort of having to go through each survey and construct a database of responses.

Much of what criminologists know about an individual's traits, attitudes, and opinions and their relationship to behaviors has been collected by fellow human beings graciously willing to complete questionnaires. To warrant their continued cooperation, social scientists need to take the construction and administration of questionnaires very seriously.

Basic Terminology

Before describing how to design a research questionnaire, it is useful to be acquainted with some basic terminology. First, a distinction can be made between a research *participant* and a *respondent*. The term **respondent** refers to a person who gives responses to questions on a questionnaire or in an interview. In other words, persons who are **participants** in a study are often called *respondents* if their involvement in a study is completing a questionnaire. Sometimes, respondents are asked to respond to questions not about themselves but about others who are known to the respondents. For instance, children may be asked about their parents, parents may be asked about their children, or teachers may be asked about their students. The terms *respondents*, *participants*, and *subjects* are all used interchangeably in the literature to refer to persons who agree to participate in research studies, although the term subjects has more recently fallen out of favor as an appropriate term to use.

A **question** (also called an **item** or a **questionnaire item**) refers to anything that calls for a linguistic or numeric response (in either written or oral form) from a respondent. Questions in a research questionnaire do not need to be phrased literally in the form of a question. For example, respondents might be asked to respond to the following statements:

> *How strictly did your parents enforce any religious teachings? (Rate from 1 = not at all to 10 = to an extreme degree) _____.*

> *How safe do you feel walking alone after dark in your neighborhood? (Answer from 1 meaning "not safe at all" to 10 meaning "extremely safe") _____.*

These statements constitute questions (or items) in a questionnaire. Sometimes questions consist of mere phrases. For example, participants might be instructed to indicate how they perceive themselves with respect to the following adjectives:

> *Outgoing personality*
>
> *Superstitious*
>
> *Impulsive*
>
> *Honest and trustworthy*
>
> *Have a great deal of self-control*

Each of these phrases would be considered a question or item as long as subjects were permitted to make some sort of response to each one. More will be said later in this chapter about how questions should be phrased, but let us now turn to the advantages and disadvantages of questionnaires and the types of response options that can be offered to subjects.

Advantages and Disadvantages of Data Based on Self-Reports

Before exploring options surrounding the types of self-reported information that can be collected with questionnaires, let us consider a more basic issue: the main advantages and disadvantages to the use of self-reported data.

Advantages

An obvious advantage to most self-reported data is that the data can often be collected quickly, especially if one takes advantage of computer software programs. For instance, a professor could construct a questionnaire about campus safety using a survey software program; have it sent out to all students' email addresses; give them a few days to respond; and do some initial analyses on the climate of safety on campus by the end of the week. Obviously, this is a bit exaggerated, and it would probably take months to get the survey approved by the university's IRB. Research involving human subjects must be reviewed for its adherence to ethical guidelines, but the point is that depending on the type of information being collected, this same professor might have to spend years recruiting and conducting interviews or completing observations on campus to get a sample of a comparable number of subjects.

Another advantage of self-reports, especially as they relate to criminology, is that there are many things that people know about themselves and their behaviors that no amount of observation by researchers would ever reveal. For instance, many persons have committed petty crimes or minor offenses in the past that never came to the attention of authorities; these are referred to as the dark figures of crime, and unless we ask persons to self-report, we will never know about it. If we only study as subjects those who have been caught by law enforcement, we may erroneously be attributing certain traits and factors as having relationships with crime and delinquency. Similarly, if surveys reveal that certain behaviors are much more common among the population than previously thought, petty shoplifting among teenagers, for example, might be seen as a natural occurrence in adolescent development rather than the product of poor upbringing or supervision. Many aspects of our private and intimate behavior are impractical and/or illegal for researchers to attempt to directly observe (Baldwin, 2000).

Disadvantages

The main disadvantages of self-reported data have to do with reliability. Because most people who provide self-reported information have little if any social science background, they are not likely to appreciate why the questions are being asked and thus sometimes provide very inappropriate answers. Others may read some of the questions carelessly and then provide responses that are the opposite of what they intended to report. However, there are many techniques to try to improve the accuracy of self-reported data. For the purpose of this chapter, the focus will be mainly on the mechanics of designing questions and response options to those questions. We will first consider response options.

⊖ Response Options for Questions

Response options refer to the range of answers that researchers offer subjects in connection with the questions that are asked on the survey. These options are important to a researcher because they have a major influence on the type of data that will eventually be available for analysis. Response options fall into five general categories: open-ended, fill-in-the-blank, end-anchored, all-points-anchored, and ranking. There are several forms of each of these general types.

Open-Ended Response Options

Items that present a question (or make a statement) without providing any constraints on how subjects can respond are called **open-ended**. Examples of items providing open-ended response options include the following:

> *What preventive measures do you take to avoid being a victim of crime?*
>
> *In what ways do your friends influence your behavior?*
>
> *How do you feel about current interactions between citizens and the police?*

Controversy has long surrounded the advisability of using open-ended questions (see Lazarfeld, 1944), with most researchers avoiding using any more than just a few of them in their questionnaires. The main drawback to open-ended response options is that they are time-consuming to code (Geer, 1991). **Coding** refers to the process of deciding how data will be entered into a standard format for analysis. Not only is a considerable amount of time involved in reading and then deciding how best to code each response, but responses to many open-ended questions can be ambiguous or difficult to collapse into themes or categories of responses.

The main value of open-ended questions is in getting more in-depth responses from respondents than one could by asking them to check a box or rate their agreement on some scale. A second value is in exploring areas of research that have received little prior attention (Geer, 1991). For example, gang researchers via the use of open-ended questions with former gang members have been able to provide us with a better understanding of the factors that influence gang members to desist in offending or leaving their gang life. These studies have shown that there are both "push" and "pull" factors that make gang members want to get out. One big factor pushing gang members to leave is exposure to violence, especially when it starts involving some of their friends or family members (Decker & Lauritsen, 2002; Pyrooz & Decker, 2011). Some factors pulling individuals away from gang life include having children and the increases in family responsibilities (Moloney, MacKenzie, Hunt, & Joe-Laidler, 2009). This has helped researchers to get more precise ideas of the reasons why gang members want to leave the gang. However, open-ended questions would not be able to provide precise estimates of how prevalent desistence from gang life is.

Fill-in-the-Blank Response Options

Questions that ask subjects to respond by writing in or uttering a limited number of words (usually one or two) are called **fill-in-the-blank items**. Examples of fill-in-the-blank questions are:

> *What is your religious affiliation, if any? (if Protestant, specify denomination)*
>
> _____
>
> *How many times in the past year have you been the victim of a property crime?*
>
> _____

How many times per week, on average, do you speak with your neighbors? _____

On average, how many hours per day do you spend online? _____

Items with fill-in-the-blank response options are often used for variables mis-read at the nominal level. Often, they will be coded into categories (e.g., a dozen or so religious groups or crime categories such as property crime, drug crime, or violent crime) by the researcher.

An example of a common fill-in-the-blank question comes from attempts to measure race/ethnicity. Prior to 1990, the US Census Bureau had six catego-ries into which each person was assigned (white non-Hispanic, Hispanic, black, Native American, Asian/Pacific Islander). Since then, census takers write down essentially whatever respondents answer with respect to identifying their race/ ethnicity (Rosenwaike, 1993). In the 2000 census, respondents could even iden-tify mixed-race ancestry. These changes have the advantage of better reflect-ing reality, but they mean that many racial/ethnic categories will be too few in number for meaningful analysis.

End-Anchored Continuum Response Options

The distinguishing feature of an **end-anchored continuum** is that subjects are allowed to respond along a continuum in which only the two extreme values have specific meaning. There are three forms of this response option: the **de-marcated linear form** and two numeric forms.

To give an example of the demarcated linear form, suppose a researcher is interested in attitudes toward capital punishment. In this case, the researcher might ask the following question:

To what degree do you believe it is appropriate for the state to execute persons con-victed of murder?

Extremely   *Extremely*
Inappropriate   *Appropriate*

The best known example of the demarcated linear form of the end-anchored continuum is called the semantic differential scale. Developed in the 1950s (Osgood, Suci, & Tannenbaum, 1957), these scales arrange numerous polar opposite adjectives at each end of a linear continuum (usually demarcated into seven response options) and ask subjects to respond to a single noun or phrase (e.g., life without parole, elderly abuse, recreational marijuana use) by putting an X in the appropriate space. Examples of the adjectives might include Support-Reject, Serious-Minor, Selfish-Generous, Good-Bad (Monette, Sullivan, & DeJong, 1990:379; Neuman, 1991:163). Here is an example of a semantic differential scale:

How would you characterize police–citizen relations today?

Very Bad   *Quite Good*

In the numeric form of the end-anchored continuum, the questions may be asked in the same way, but in place of the linear continuum, subjects are instructed to answer by writing in or circling a number. For the **write-in end-anchored response option**, the question might be stated as follows:

> *To what degree do you approve of the state executing persons convicted of murder? (Answer anywhere from **1** to **10**, with **1** representing strongly approve, and **10** representing strongly disapprove)* _____

An actual example comes from a study designed to more precisely measure homosexuality than by simply asking subjects whether they are homosexual, heterosexual, or bisexual (Ellis, Burke, & Ames, 1987). The question allowed subjects to answer from 0 to 100, and was phrased as follows:

> *When imagining sexual relationships, the individual with whom you imagine interacting is*
>
> > *a member of the opposite sex_____% of the time*
> >
> > *a member of the same sex_____% of the time*

The **circled end-anchored response option** of the question on the death penalty would normally appear as follows:

> *To what degree do you approve of governments executing persons convicted of murder?*
>
> *Strongly*   *Strongly*
>
> *Disapprove*   *Approve*
>
> 1   2   3   4   5   6   7   8   9   10

The main advantage of the numeric forms of the end-anchored continua compared to the demarcated line form is that numeric forms facilitate transcription for data entry.

All-Points-Anchored Response Options

The fourth type of response option is the **All-Points-Anchored Response Option**, which involves anchoring all the response options with words (usually adjectives or adverbs). Although there are no hard-and-fast rules for the number of words used, the most common scales have five points and follow this form:

> *SA–Strongly Agree (or Strongly Approve)*
>
> *A–Agree (or Approve)*

N–Neutral

D–Disagree (or Disapprove)

SD–Strongly Disagree (or Strongly Disapprove)

This and similarly worded five-point response options are called the Likert scale, after one of the first social scientists to use it (Likert, 1932). To refer to other types of all-points-anchored scales, the term Likert-type is sometimes used (e.g., Stuart & Jacobson, 1979). These similar scales have 3, 4, 6, or 7 response options instead of 5 (Stoney et al., 1998; Wyatt, 1989; Haque & Telfair, 2000). Some researchers have blended the features of a circle end-anchored and all-points anchored response option (Goldberg, 1992; Geary et al., 1995). The resulting scale is illustrated here:

To what degree are you introverted/extroverted?

Very				*Neither*				*Very*
introverted 1	2	3	4	5	6	7	8	9 *extroverted*

Ranking Response Options

A final type of response option is referred to as the **ranking response option** and is one in which respondents are given a list of items to rank in some way. This has been most often used in the study of human values, such as the relative priority people put on honesty, freedom, civic responsibility, and the like (Rokeach & Ball-Rokeach, 1989). It has also been used to gather information on the public's opinion of the relative seriousness of different crimes by having them rank-order them. Ranking the importance of such items is an alternative to rating each item (e.g., on a scale of 1 to 10).

There are two main differences between ranking and rating scales. First, ranking scales force subjects to arrange every item into a hierarchy; scales in which each item is individually rated allow subjects who so choose to give the same rating to several (or even all) items. Second, ranking items is technically ordinal measurement; rating each item separately provides an interval measure for each item. Some of the most basic statistics, such as means and correlations, require interval level of measurement; therefore, from a statistical standpoint, rating scales are better. Thus, unless there are compelling reasons to do otherwise, there are few reasons to use ranking scales instead of rating scales for the same variables.

⬤ Deciding Which Response Option to Use

A researcher should consider several factors in choosing which response option to use for each question in a survey. The following four points are particularly important:

(1) *Try to minimize the amount of coding.* Generally, the fewer items that must be read, interpreted, and coded by a researcher (or coding assistant), the

better. Of the four main types of response options just outlined, the latter two require no coding and are therefore generally preferred over the first two types. Computer survey programs have made this less of an issue than in the past because the software will code and populate responses; however, response options that are simpler for both the respondent and the researcher coding the responses are always better.

(2) *Try to measure variables at least at the interval level.* Whereas end-anchored continuum scales almost always meet the assumption of interval measurement, all-points-anchored scales are less certain in this regard. A researcher cannot be as sure that the adjectives used to anchor each point in a scale will be interpreted by respondents in equal-interval fashion, as you can be when consecutive numbers are used. In other words, how confident can we be that everyone considers the distance between *strongly agree* (*SA*) and *agree* (*A*) the same as the distance between *agree* (*A*) and *undecided/neutral* (U/N)? If you want interval-level data, you must ensure you are using response options that will deliver interval-level responses.

(3) *Avoid repeatedly switching from one type of response option to another.* Respondents are more likely to provide inaccurate responses if they are frequently confronted with different types of response options as this can be confusing. Therefore, a researcher should keep subjects focused on the content of the questions rather than continually changing the number and types of response options. Organize the questions so that all, or at least most, of those with similar response options appear together.

(4) *Give subjects considerable latitude in their responses.* Probably the most frequent error made in constructing items for research questionnaires is that of allowing insufficient response options for subjects. In other words, you want response options to be exhaustive, meaning that all potential responses are available to respondents for consideration. This error can be remedied by changing a question requiring a *yes/no* response to one that allows subjects to indicate to what degree they have a particular characteristic or attitude on a scale from 1 to 10. Researchers strive for validity in their measurement, and variables can be measured with differing degrees of precision. The use of very broad response options, therefore, might mean that researchers may not be capturing exactly what they were attempting to capture or that they are missing information that would be captured with a more refined measurement. Subtle differences in how questions are phrased can also affect people's responses.

Why would the types of responses offered to respondents make such a dramatic difference? Part of the answer may lie in the fact that most people think of themselves (correctly) as roughly average in most of their behavior and may assume that when people construct questionnaires, the response options provided reflect the typical range of responses people give (Rockwood et al., 1997). Whatever the cause may be, how can such effects be avoided? Probably the easiest solution in cases such as these would be to simply allow respondents a space into which to write the number of hours (plus minutes) of time they spend on the internet per day. As an overall take-home message, researchers should keep in mind the tremendous variability that exists in human

BOX 10.1 CURRENT ISSUES

Do Broad Questions Lead to Underestimates of Violent Victimization in Prison?

We all know that prisons can be violent places. Television shows claiming to be on "the inside" would lead you to believe that prison violence is a daily occurrence. Findings from previous research on the amount of violence in prison, however, vary considerably, with prevalence rates ranging from 1% to 40% for sexual victimization (Gaes & Goldberg, 2004) and 10% to 25% for physical victimization (Wooldredge, 1998). This leaves questions about how many inmates are actually victimized in a given year. If the true number is only 1%, maybe prison violence isn't that much of an issue. If, however, the reality is that 40% of inmates are victims, then perhaps more needs to be done to curb prison violence. Some researchers recently attempted to understand why previous findings from studies trying to measure the amount of violence in prison vary so widely.

Wolff, Shi, and Bachman (2008) undertook a study involving survey research to try to understand why the rates of violent victimization that occur in prison may not be accurate. More specifically, they wanted to examine whether the ways in which questions about victimization are asked ultimately affect whether inmates will report being victimized. These researchers administered surveys that used both general and specific questions about victimization in prison to a sample of inmates.

The general questions asked whether or not an inmate had been sexually or physically assaulted by another inmate or staff member, whereas the specific questions, for example, asked "During the past 6 months, has (another inmate or staff member) ever … touched you, felt you or grabbed you in a way that you felt was sexually threatening or made you have sex by using force or threatening to harm you or someone close to you?" (Wolff et al., 2008:1352). The results revealed that the more specific questions yielded victimization rates that were 1.1 to 9 times greater than the general questions. Further, of those inmates who responded yes to one of the specific victimization questions, 70% had responded no to the general question.

The conclusions from this example are obvious; respondents may give contradictory responses depending on how questions are asked or phrased. In a similar example, consider that the percentage of persons who support the death penalty in the United States varies on how the question is asked. If you simply ask people if they support the death penalty, well more than 60% of respondents in the United States will express support for it. If you reword the question and ask "Do you support the death penalty if there is an option of life without parole?" the percentage of respondents who express support for the death penalty decreases.

behavior and attitudes. Given this variability, researchers should construct their questions in ways that allow as much as possible this variability to be revealed.

Of course, providing a limited number of response options is appropriate for many discrete variables, such as a respondent's sex or political party affiliation. Also, there are times in the analysis of data when a researcher will be justified in collapsing some of the response options. Although not all social scientists would agree on this point, our advice is that researchers use end-anchored continuum scales as much as possible when measuring continuous variables.

Researchers used to recommend that in telephone and personal interview surveys no more than four all-points-anchored categories be given to subjects because of the difficulty people had remembering the name of each response category as the questions were being presented. This is obviously not a problem for web-based surveys, however; with end-anchored continua, subjects only need to remember the names of the two ends of the continuum and how many segments there are between the two ends. Thus, even with surveys based upon telephone and personal interviews, end-anchored continua have been increasingly recommended (Loken et al., 1987).

⊖ Types of Self-Reported Items

Four different types of self-report items are utilized in questionnaires. These are descriptive items, recall items, attitudinal items, and projective items, each of which is discussed here.

1. **Descriptive items** are those pertaining to factual information, including demographic information such as age, race/ethnicity, and marital status. Other items of a descriptive nature would be questions about year in university or religious affiliation. It is astonishing how many characteristics or traits of a descriptive nature that we can report about ourselves, but just how accurate is this information? Over the years, several studies have sought to find out, usually by asking subjects to respond to the same questions again a few weeks later (a form of test-retest reliability) or ask a similar question later on in the survey (intra-test reliability). The responses to most basic descriptive items are extremely reliable.

2. Items requiring subjects to reach back into their memories to recall some specific event, or type of event, are called **recall** (or **retrospective**) **items**. Obviously, many recall items can also be considered descriptive items, but the main distinction is that recall items are usually not of the type that people routinely use in describing themselves or their backgrounds. Recall that items in which respondents are asked about a type of specific experience people may or may not have had are called **episodic recall items** (Kessler et al., 2000; Shiffman, 2000). Here are a few examples of what would be considered episodic recall items:

   Have you ever had a near-death experience?

   How old were you when you had your first crush on a member of the opposite sex?

   Have you ever done something for which you believe you could have been arrested?

   As a child, were you ever sexually abused or molested by an adult?

   Considerable research has attempted to assess the reliability of people's responses to episodic recall items. These studies suggest that the mere occurrences of most events are more accurately reported than circumstances surrounding the events (Ayers & Reder, 1998). The further back in time one is asked to go in recalling events, the more distortion there tends to be in the details about the event.

3. **Attitudinal items** are ones asking people to express their opinions about topics. These types of questions can give researchers insight into people's views on a wide range of issues. However, as noted earlier, the way attitudinal items are phrased can often have major effects on the proportions of people agreeing or disagreeing with a particular point of view. Examples of attitudinal items, expressed both as statements and as questions, are as follows:

    Should juveniles be housed in the same prisons as adults?

    To what degree do you feel homosexual behavior is illegal?

    Indicate your agreement/disagreement with the following statements:

    Gambling should be legalized.

    Parents should be held responsible for truant behavior of their children.

4. A **projective** (or **hypothetical**) **item** is one in which subjects are asked to report what they would do under specified conditions, particularly ones that have not yet happened. A couple of examples would include:

    How would you respond if a close friend was the victim of a serious violent crime?

    Would you stand up for a close friend if they were accused of committing a serious violent crime?

Sometimes projective items require making a series of stipulations rather than just one. These projective items are usually called **scenarios** (or **vignettes**). Scenario items can be useful for comparing subjects on events that rarely occur but that can provide insight into personality. Some of the most common of these scenario-based questions have to do with studying judicial or jury decision making. In these studies, vignettes of fictional crimes and accused perpetrators are given to samples of citizens, and they are asked to determine whether or not they believe the person is guilty or, in the case of judges, asking them what type of sentence they would give if the person was found guilty. Researchers can change the race/ethnicity, sex, and age of the suspect in these vignettes to be able to also study whether people are discriminatory in their responses about guilt or punishment. If the sample of persons responding is large enough, the researcher could also examine whether there are differences in these attributions by race/ethnicity or sex of the respondent as well.

⬤ Guidelines for Item Construction

Much of the advice given by seasoned researchers about question construction falls within the realm of common sense. For example, questions should be easy to understand and arranged in the questionnaire in an easy-to-follow format. If several different types of questions are asked, it is usually a good idea to group similar questions together. Otherwise, respondents are forced to repeatedly switch their frame of mind as they proceed through the questionnaire.

Other rules for those beginning to learn questionnaire construction are to put yourself in the place of your respondent and, above all, to carefully pretest any questionnaire before it is mass produced (Diamantopoulos et al., 1994). **Pretesting** refers to the administration of a questionnaire to would-be subjects before giving it to actual subjects. It is best to pretest in four distinct steps:

> *Self-Test Phase*: Every questionnaire, once completed, should first be taken by the person who designed it to ensure that they have structured it in the way they envisioned as well as to see whether there might be any questions they want to add or delete.

> *Informed Pre-Subject Phase*: Copies of the questionnaire should then be given to three or four people, perhaps colleagues of the researcher, who are aware of the basic purpose of the study. These pre-subjects should be asked to critique each question for clarity, to ensure that there are no confusing questions, and likelihood of eliciting responses relevant to the purpose of the study.

> *Uninformed Pre-Subject Phase*: Up to a dozen or so copies of the revised questionnaire should be also administered to people who are unaware of the detailed purpose of the study. This group of respondents should be similar to the sample the researcher wants to complete the survey. After completing the questionnaire, these persons should be debriefed and asked to identify any problems with the wording of the questions. Because the designer of the questionnaire is often tempted in these debriefing sessions to correct the respondents about how they should have interpreted the questions, it is better to have someone other than the questionnaire's designer performing these interviews. None of these completed questionnaires would be used in the study.

> *Early Actual Subject Phase*: Assuming that all the questionnaires do not have to be administered at one time, it is a good idea to conduct one final pretest of the first 10 to 25 questionnaires actually administered. Unless some serious problems arise, the data from these questionnaires will be included in the study, and the researcher can continue to administer the survey to the sample.

Pretesting questionnaires is very important, whether the questionnaires are completed directly by respondents or by trained interviewers.

Clustering Items with Similar Formats

If you have several things you want your subjects to disclose to you, it is often a good idea to group a series of similar questions together under a single heading, a practice known as **item clustering**. For example, if you are interested in a wide range of behavior/personality patterns, you might present your subjects with the following statement linked to a list of specific items:

*Please rate the degree to which you enjoy the following things (Respond on a scale from **1** to **9**, with **1** being the least imaginable and **9** being the most imaginable):*

> *One-on-one competition with others* _____
>
> *Being alone and exploring nature* _____
>
> *Attending a party filled with people you have never met* _____
>
> *Taking serious risks with your life in the balance* _____
>
> *Exercising control over other people* _____

Notice how much easier it will be for subjects to answer these question in their abbreviated form than it would be if each question was separated from the others. Item clustering is a good way to obtain responses to numerous questions in a minimum space. It also has the advantage of minimizing the number of words a subject must read, which in turn minimizes the risk that a question will be misinterpreted.

⊜ Types of Questions to Avoid

Even though no ironclad rules can be made regarding exactly how to design and phrase questionnaire items, six recommendations can be made with respect to the types of questions that should *not* be used. These are as follows:

> *Avoid rhetorical and leading questions.* Leading questions are stated in such a way as to beg for a particular response. Rarely should items that are rhetorical or leading be included in a questionnaire (unless a questionnaire is simply being used as a propaganda tool rather than for scientific research). Especially when studying people's attitudes on some subject, a researcher may be tempted to try to open their minds. As a result, questions are likely to be argumentative or have a preachy tone to them. The following two questions are essentially rhetorical in character:
>
> > *Wouldn't you say it is high time that women in this country receive equal treatment under the law?*
> >
> > *How much justification can you see in the way people on welfare are being treated in today's society?*

The rhetorical nature of these questions may elicit affirmative responses from significant numbers of subjects who would not have responded affirmatively to a neutrally phrased question. However, the value of this information as reflections of people's real attitudes will have been compromised.

Avoid conjunctive items. Conjunctive items ask subjects to respond to more than one issue at a time. For example, if it is the researcher's intention to determine how favorable people's attitudes are toward a country's current president, the question might ask whether subjects consider the president to be an honest and competent leader. Although both of these personal qualities would be seen as favorable, some respondents might consider the president honest but not competent, or vice versa. Normally, if one is interested in someone's overall attitude toward something rather than in how they would objectively assess various qualities of something, the questions should be phrased in a straight-forward way, e.g., "What is your overall impression of the current president?"

Avoid yeasaying items. Social scientists have discovered that certain types of statements often elicit what are called yeasaying responses from a substantial proportion of subjects (Goldsmith, 1987). Basically, these items have a philo-sophical sounding tone that seems to compel many respondents to affirm them. Here are two examples:

> *These days, a person does not really know who they can count on.*
>
> *With the way things look for the future, it is hardly fair to bring children into the world.*

What makes these items noteworthy is that they were among the items used for years to measure *anomie*, a widely used concept roughly meaning without so-cial identity (Durkheim, 1951). In the early 1970s, the validity of such items for measuring anomie was called into question when it was discovered that many subjects who agreed with these two statements also agreed with their exact op-posite (sometimes even within the same questionnaire!) (Carr, 1971).

Items such as these have a quality about them that seems to ring true for many people regardless of any objective meaning they may convey. Other ex-amples of yeasaying items come from studying the way people express their views on highly emotional issues. Overall, items that are likely to elicit yeasay-ing responses should be avoided.

Avoid kernel of truth items. Many emphatic statements may be partially true. As a rule these should be avoided in social science questionnaires, particularly if they are obviously condescending (i.e., insulting). Examples of these ques-tions are:

> *The elderly are a burden to society.*
>
> *Ex-convicts cannot be trusted.*

Both of these statements would put many respondents in a quandary as to how to respond. They would feel uncomfortable grossly generalizing about people in ways that are obviously derogatory. Nevertheless, they might also feel that both the elderly and ex-convicts as groups do differ from people in general as the statements assert.

> *Avoid questions that have ambiguous words or phrases.* Even though the following items at first glance seem to be clear, they can be taken in a variety of ways:
>
> *Do you believe that prisons are effective?*
>
> *Are you a drug user?*

Why are these examples ambiguous? The concepts of prison effectiveness could be interpreted in several ways. It could be interpreted in the sense of keeping convicted prisoners from committing crimes as long as they are behind bars, committing new crimes after prison release, or even remaining steadily em-ployed after leaving prison. Regarding the question of drug use, would not the type of drug (including prescription drugs), the amounts, and the time frame involved all be important?

Avoid questions about behavior that are not bounded by time (and sometimes by place). For example, the following questions would be difficult for subjects to answer if their church-attending behavior had recently changed or if they just recently became eligible to vote:

How often do you go to church? _____

Do you usually vote? _____

To make the first question more meaningful, it might be bounded in time as follows, assuming that the researcher is primarily interested in recent church attendance:

Over the past 6 months, how many times did you attend church services?

_____

Or, if church-attending behavior in childhood is of primary interest, then the question might be phrased as follows:

As a child, approximately how many times did you attend church services per month? _____

Or, if both childhood and current church attendance are of interest, the question might be phrased as follows:

Please indicate about how many times you attended church services in an average month during the following times in your life:

> *From ages 1 to 10*
>
> *From ages 11 to 18*
>
> *From age 19 to the present (if applicable)*

Regarding the voting question, the researcher should assess what it is that he or she is trying to determine. Then the question should be made more specific in terms of the types of voting (presidential versus local elections) and the time frame during which subjects would have an opportunity to vote.

⊖ Combining Two or More Items to Improve Reliability

If a variable can be reliably and validly measured with a single item, there is little justification for including more than one question about it in a questionnaire. For example, researchers need not develop more than one item for measuring the sex and age of subjects. However, for variables that are difficult to measure accurately (as many variables pertaining to behavior, emotions, and attitudes

BOX 10.2 WHAT DO YOU THINK

Can You Spot Why These Questions Are Poorly Phrased?

Although many questionnaire items can only be meaningfully critiqued within the context of the overall purpose of the study for which they were designed, some items are so obviously flawed that they should not be used for any research study. Read each of the following examples, and see if you can spot problems with them:

1. *What is the size of your family?*

2. *Do you have good relations with your parents?*

3. *Is peer pressure an influence on your drinking?*

Here are some brief critiques to help you see the issues with these questions as well as some possible alternatives for each of these questions:

(1) *What is the size of your family?* Some subjects answering this question might assume that the researcher is only interested in knowing how many brothers and sisters (siblings) they have, while other respondents would probably include their parents plus their siblings in the count. Subjects whose parents are divorced might not know whether to include both parents or just one. Also, those with older siblings no longer living at home would probably not know whether to count them or not. This question is simply too vague.

Most of the ambiguities could be avoided by asking subjects: *How many brothers and sisters do you have?* Of course, a researcher interested in more detailed aspects of various family arrangements might instead ask whether all family members were presently in the home or whether subjects had any half-siblings (either in or outside the home).

(2) *Do you have good relations with your parents?* This question has two problems. First, it asks for an either/or answer to a question for which many subjects would want to give an intermediate answer. The second problem is that the question is not bounded in time (i.e., within the past year, the past 5 years, throughout childhood). Obviously, parent-child relationships are dynamic and almost certain to vary over time.

(3) *Is peer pressure an influence on your drinking?* This question is poorly phrased. Presumably, the researcher who proposed it wanted to know to what degree subjects who drank did so because of peer pressure (rather than because they liked its taste, were becoming addicted, or wanted to drink for some other reason). This question might be better broken into the following two questions:

In the past year or so, how often have you consumed alcohol? (circle one)

never

seldom

occasionally

fairly often

very often

If you do drink, indicate which of the following best explains why you do so.

*(Assign a **1** to the main reason and a **2** to the second most important reason.)*
Because my friends are doing it
Because I enjoy the taste
Because I am (or may be becoming) addicted
Because I was encouraged to do so at home
Because I like the way it makes me feel
Other (specify)

are), researchers often ask more than one question within the same questionnaire and then combine the responses to these items into a single score. These measures are called **multi-item scales** (or **multi-item tests**) and have been shown to substantially improve the reliability of difficult-to-measure variables (Mould, 1988; Neston & Safer, 1990).

An example of a multi-item scale for measuring variations in handedness has been created to get a more precise measure of whether someone is right-handed or left-handed. A number of researchers now ask subjects which hand is used in performing many different types of tasks, say five or six, and then numbers are assigned to the answers for each question and added for a single measure of handedness. Another example of a multi-item scale involves examinations that are taken by students. Although an instructor might sometimes make a determination of a student's grade based on a single question, more often numerous questions will be asked and a grade assigned on the basis of the proportion of the questions answered correctly.

Researchers should take advantage of the efforts by others to develop valid and reliable multi-item scales for the variables in which they have an interest. Nevertheless, there are sometimes good reasons for developing new multi-item scales or seeking to improve old ones. Some guidelines to keep in mind when devising multi-item scales are as follows:

1. *Make sure that all the items used in a given scale are relevant to the variable targeted for measurement.* Unfortunately, determining the relevance of items to a variable is not always easy or obvious, even for experienced researchers. Because intuitive methods of judging whether or not questions are really relevant to a particular variable can sometimes be incorrect (especially when dealing with complex intellectual and attitudinal variables), many researchers supplement their intuition with a special statistical technique called **factor analysis**. Factor analysis is a type of multivariate correlational statistic that allows researchers to locate subtle patterns in the way large numbers of subjects respond to questions. From these statistically derived patterns, questionnaire items can be grouped together in precise mathematical terms (Thompson, 1962). As with any multivariate statistics, you should get help from someone familiar with it the first time or two that you use it.

2. *The items comprising a scale are usually equally weighted.* This means that no question has more influence on the final scale score than any other question. To give each item equal weight, the structure and number of response options for each item should all be the same.

3. *Whenever possible, researchers should measure* **continuous variables** (*the opposite of* **discrete** *variables*) *at the interval or ratio levels.* Continuous variables measured at the nominal and ordinal levels make it difficult for a researcher to treat the results in statistically meaningful ways. In particular, only variables measured at the interval or ratio levels allow one to calculate means and standard deviations. In this regard, even though many treat data based on Likert scale data as interval data by calculating mean responses on these scales, statisticians point out that Likert scales are best considered ordinal, rather than interval level data (Sobel, 1992).

4. *In deriving individual scores on a scale, researchers should be sure to reverse score any items that are negatively assessing what the scale is designed to measure.* For example, suppose the following items were used to measure the degree to which adults exhibited hyperactive-disruptive symptoms in childhood:

> *To what degree do you recall being disruptive in grade school? (Answer from **1** to **9**, with **1** representing not at all and **9** representing to an extreme degree)* ____.

> *When you were a child, to what degree did you enjoy playing quietly by yourself or with a friend, rather than engaging in boisterous, rowdy play? (Answer from **1** to **9**, with **1** representing not at all and **9** representing to an extreme degree)* ____.

The researcher would need to **reverse score** one of these items because a response of 1 on the second question denotes a high degree of hyperactivity whereas a 9 on the first question denotes that same high degree of hyperactivity. In order for the possible scores on this two-item scale to range as they should from 2 to 18, the score for one of them needs to be inverted or *reverse scored*. Because this is a scale for measuring childhood hyperactivity and disruptiveness, which of the two items should be reverse scored? The answer is the second one.

⊜ Time Diaries: Special Type of Questionnaire

Most questionnaire items either ask about things that have occurred in the past or are concerned with people's attitudes. In a few types of questionnaires, however, subjects are asked to maintain daily or weekly logs of their ongoing behavior. These logs are usually called **time diaries**, and the resulting data are termed **time-use data**. The first use of time diaries on a large scale involved the Multinational Time Use Project, involving 12 industrialized countries during the 1960s (Harvey, 1993). Most time diaries ask subjects to record information about their behavior at least on a daily basis and often several times each day. In a few time diary studies, subjects wear a beeper device that tells them when to provide an entry into their log (Stone & Shiffman, 1994).

Time diaries usually provide respondents with few specific categories within which to code their activities. An Italian study indicated that respondents would rather use their own words to describe their activities and let coders fit the responses into analyzable categories (Harvey, 1993). One of the earliest ongoing activity studies was conducted among police officers while on duty (Reiss, 1971). This study found that only about 20% of the typical officer's time was spent investigating crime; the remaining time had more to do with community service activities.

Computerized Questionnaires and Use of the Internet

Two related technological developments have greatly advanced questionnaire design and administration. One is the advent of the internet, which opened up a lot of new opportunities for obtaining research subjects. The other involves recently developed computerized programs for designing virtual interactive questionnaires. These questionnaires can remind subjects that they failed to answer certain questions and even follow up on any seemingly inconsistent responses.

Because these programs can collect responses and compile them into databases in real time (some of them even have analytic capabilities), they are becoming more and more widely used. Entities such as Surveymonkey and Qualtrics have made survey construction relatively easy because, for a fee, the entity will create your survey, disseminate it via email, create a URL for your website, and even tally the results from the respondents. One of the first questions addressed by those who have been on the forefront of computer design and internet administration of questionnaires has been the type of subjects most likely to respond to internet questionnaires. The answer has been fairly reassuring in the sense that the respondents seem to be similar to college-educated young people, who have always weighed most heavily in social science research (Pasveer & Ellard, 1998; Horswill & Coster, 2001) and who comprise similar subjects that have completed social or behavioral questionnaires in the past. These programs can also guard against the same subject completing the questionnaire multiple times.

An additional advantage of using computerized internet technology in social science research is that it allows researchers to combine questionnaire data with other types of data. For example, a British study combined a questionnaire measure of risk-taking behavior with a test consisting of a series of photographs to assess preferences on driving speed, passing safety, and gaps in following other vehicles (Horswill & Coster, 2001). This study indicated that there was general agreement between the two measures.

As the use of computerized questionnaires and other internet research data opportunities become more common, one of the most promising outcomes may be the speed and accuracy with which results can be tabulated and analyzed. With subjects entering their own data in digital form, data entry is automatic, and all the researcher needs to do is to run his or her analysis when sufficient numbers of subjects have responded. These surveys are also cheaper than their mail, telephone, and face-to-face survey counterparts and can reach potentially large samples with the click of a button. Disadvantages, however, include that some of the subjects that researchers want to study may not have as easy access to computers and the internet as others, and it is relatively easy to ignore or delete a survey request with the click of a mouse. Ethical problems could also arise with the lack of anonymity through email or web-based surveys and/or trouble with consent forms and safeguards to protect confidentiality. A final point is that as more and more people across the world gain easy access to the internet, the subjects in social science research should become increasingly international.

Final Comments on Questionnaire Data

In measuring variables, it is wise to employ operational measures that have been previously developed and shown to be reliable and valid. For this reason (as well as others), those not familiar with the literature in a specific area should seek help from someone who has done prior work in that area. Having made the point in favor of using already tried-and-true operational measures when they exist, it should be quickly added that if one is familiar with a field and feels there are good reasons for defying conventional ways of measuring a variable, do so. Some of the biggest advances in knowledge have come from new approaches to operationalization of key variables.

Additional closing remarks center around not abusing the goodwill of those who agree to serve as participants in a study. One of the heartwarming aspects of social science research comes from discovering how willing most people are to cooperate as respondents in surveys. This willingness to help is greatest, of course, when the time involved seems reasonable, when they believe that the results will be worthwhile, and when they are treated courteously and in accordance with ethical guidelines and principles. Also, people are more inclined to be subjects in a research project if the questions are stated clearly and concisely and the response options are appropriate and easy to understand.

Finally, it should be noted that not all data in the social sciences are collected via questionnaires. In particular, a number of social science studies have been based on direct observations. These data collection methods are given attention in the next two chapters.

 # Summary

This chapter dealt with issues and options concerning the construction of social science research questionnaires. No one knows exactly what proportion of social science data is derived from questionnaires (either directly by having respondents read and respond to questions or indirectly by having them respond to questions asked by an interviewer), but it is safe to say that the figure is well over half. The main advantage of questionnaire data, compared to direct observation by trained researchers, is that it makes possible the collection of massive amounts of data inexpensively and quickly. However, the main potential *dis*advantage is that the data may be low in reliability. Unless both the questions and the response options are carefully phrased and pretested, and the subjects are motivated to provide honest and thoughtful answers, the results can be very misleading.

Three major topics about questionnaire construction were addressed in this chapter. The first had to do with the types of response options that can be presented to respondents. These options were subsumed under the following five categories: open-ended, fill-in-the-blank, end-anchored (both linear and numeric), all-points-anchored, and ranking. Each option has legitimate uses in the social sciences. Many factors need to be weighed by researchers in deciding which response option to use, including the degree of precision desired, the age and educational background of the subjects, and the audience for which the final report of the results is being prepared.

The second topic covered in this chapter dealt with ways of phrasing items in a questionnaire. A number of guidelines were offered while recognizing that sometimes there are legitimate reasons for deviating from some of them. About the only guideline that should never be ignored has to do with pretesting questionnaires. Ideally, questionnaire pretesting should consist of four phases: a self-test phase, an informed pre-subject phase, an uninformed pre-subject phase, and an early actual subject phase.

The third topic of this chapter pertained to the formation of multi-item scales by combining the results of two or more individual questions intended to measure the same variable. This procedure can serve to broaden the variation in scores as well as to increase the reliability of a variable's measurement.

In addition to these topics, this chapter briefly discussed time diaries and computerized questionnaires. Studies based on time diaries basically involve asking subjects to maintain logs pertaining to their daily activities. These studies have most often been used to assess cultural variations in how people allocate their time and energy.

Regarding computerized questionnaires, several programs are now available for helping researchers better design questionnaires. Some of these programs allow researchers to automatically download responses into data analysis programs. Along similar technological lines, growing numbers of studies have begun to draw research participants from visitors to sites on the worldwide web.

⊜ Discussion Questions

1. List some of the main advantages of studies that gather data using self-report measures. For what types of crime and criminological theories have these methods been essential?

2. Discuss how combining questions in a scale can improve the reliability of the measurement of variables.

3. List the advantages and disadvantages of self-report data.

4. What are some key guidelines for making determinations about which response options to use in a survey?

5. List and describe the different types of self-reported items.

6. What are the general phases that researchers should follow in order to pretest the questions on their survey?

⊜ Exercises

1. Construct a short questionnaire utilizing the different response options listed in the chapter. After the question, list the type of response option it is and the advantages and disadvantages of that type of question.

2. Construct a survey question that is a bad question for each of the six "types of questions to avoid" in the chapter. Then after each question, rewrite the question so that it is no longer a "bad question" and would elicit the type of information that the researcher would want to gather.

Chapter 11

Direct Observations: Qualitative and Quantitative Data

Have you ever spent time in a public restroom thinking about what all the graffiti scribbled on the walls means? Well, social scientists have, and they have used systematic research methodologies to try to interpret it. What about visiting a

public place where many different types of people gather and interact and say to yourself, "I wonder why these people are gathered here?" Scientists are ahead of you on that one, too. Furthermore, criminologists have hung out with gang members, observed police officers on patrol, and even lived with white supremist groups, all with the aim of better understanding the wide diversity of human behavior. And all of these studies were conducted without administering a single questionnaire.

Although it is hard to exaggerate the importance of questionnaires in the social sciences, many alternatives to this method of collecting social and behavioral science data exist. Most of these alternatives are known as **direct observations**, which means that data being collected came from a researcher (or a team of researchers) watching, listening, and recording what was observed. Most direct observations can be subsumed under two broad categories: *qualitative* and *quantitative*.

Qualitative Direct Observations

Qualitative observations are ones in which a researcher makes more or less unstructured observations of others. By unstructured observations, one means that the researcher will not be focusing attention on a few pre-identified variables. Rather, he or she will be watching and recording whatever is ocurring. The reporting of these observations often resembles reports written by a journalist. As you already learned, people (and animals) who are the focus of direct observational studies are called **research participants**, and the locations where the observations take place are usually called **study sites**. Researchers who conduct qualitative studies often rely heavily on one or two persons who befriend the researcher after arriving at a particular study site. These special subjects are called **informants** or **gatekeepers** because they are often the source of entrée and introduction to the study site or research subjects.

Another term that is often associated with qualitative research is that of **serendipitous findings**, meaning findings of importance that one happens upon, rather than explicitly setting out to discover. Although serendipitous findings occur in all aspects of scientific research, they are especially common in the case of qualitative direct observations (Gest, 1997). As shown in Table 11.1, four types of qualitative observations will be discussed: participant observations, ethnographic observations, case studies, and focus groups.

Participant Observations

Studies based on **participant observation** involve a researcher becoming enmeshed in the social processes that are being observed (Sommer & Sommer, 1991). Becoming a participant observer may occur strictly by accident or it may

TABLE 11.1   A Summary of the Main Types of Qualitative Direct Observational Data

Data Type	Description	Qualifying Remarks
Participant Observation	Researchers usually become part of the social activities being observed.	Usually occurs in a subculture of a culture familiar to the researcher.
Ethnographic Observation	Researchers usually study entire foreign cultures and carefully observe and record how people in these cultures live.	Usually occur in cultures entirely unfamiliar to the researcher.
Case Studies	Researchers provide detailed accounts of single individual, group, agency, or episode (such as a natural disaster).	Often leads to quantitative studies of similar events.
Focus Groups	Researchers lead small groups of people in discussions of specific topics.	Widely used in marketing research.

result from a researcher intentionally becoming a part of some social process with or without the knowledge and consent of those involved in the social process.

The earliest participant observation studies can be traced back to the sociology department at the University of Chicago in the early 20th century. During that time, **Robert Park**, a former newspaper reporter turned sociologist, encouraged some of his graduate students to gain greater insight into human behavior by spending less time in the library and more time out in the "real world" (Neuman, 1991). The methodology surrounding participant observation is largely unstructured and must be individually tailored to particular circumstances. For this reason, presenting any detailed guidelines on how to conduct participant observations is difficult, but some general guidelines are as follows: Be alert to both the obvious and the subtle social forces at work. Participant observers should make concerted efforts not to influence the course of events being observed.

The reporting of participant observations takes liberties with the standard scientific reporting format. Participant observers are describing unique events embedded in a complex set of social circumstances that cannot be captured by numerical coding or statistical analysis. Qualitative studies often resemble journalistic and historical accounts rather than reports in which detailed descriptions are given for how every variable was measured.

Research is replete with examples of participant observational studies that have been undertaken. These studies present a rich array of observations and insights into the lives of unusual groups of people, including prostitutes, members of gangs, and the homeless. Participant observation as a research methodology is especially suited to study little known or hard-to-reach populations. For example, it is hard to imagine that those involved in prostitution or in gangs would agree to act as respondents in a survey questionnaire. However, they might be willing to let a researcher enter their world for a time to observe their routines and daily lives and even participate in face-to-face interviews under certain circumstances. Even children can be the subjects of participant observation studies, although adult observers are obviously limited in the extent to which they can "fit" into the social interactions being observed. Researchers have been able to better understand the lives of certain groups who are ordinarily closed off to the general public through participant observational methodologies.

Ethnographic Observations

If the word **ethnography** is broken down, the prefix *ethno* means "way of life," and *graphy* refers to measurement or description (Neuman, 1991). **Ethnographic research** has been developed mainly by cultural anthropologists to obtain in-depth information about cultures and societies other than those familiar to the industrialized world (Hammersley, 1992; Scupin & DeCorse, 1992).

The methodology commonly used for obtaining ethnographic data involves observing and recording impressions of the lives and customs of a specific group of people without using formal questionnaires or other research instruments (Ember & Ember, 1988). Ethnography is among the oldest and most colorful types of research in the social sciences. Its roots go back many centuries to written accounts of European explorers and missionaries regarding their encounters with people inhabiting strange lands. As far as accounts written by trained anthropologists, ethnography is more than 150 years old.

It is depressing to note the sense of urgency many ethnographers feel about their research, given the reach of industrialization throughout the world. Virtually all preagrarian lifestyles—which are reminiscent of how all humans lived until roughly 10,000 years ago—vanished during the 20th century (Linden, 1991). Not only is this destroying the potential for social science knowledge, but it is also severing some of the last remaining links modern humans have with our past. Ethnographic research can also be conducted with modern cultures or subcultures such as gangs or particularly violent neighborhoods or urban areas (Anderson, 1999).

Reliability of Ethnographic Research

Like research based on participant observation, ethnographic research has special difficulties with reliability. These difficulties arise partly from the impressionistic nature of qualitative research methods, making whatever is reported more subject to varied interpretations than is true for most quantitative research (Bernard, 1983). Another difficulty in terms of reliability is that the sample size upon which most ethnographic generalizations are made is relatively small.

To illustrate the problem of sample size in most ethnographic research, consider the fact that ethnographers who first studied a foraging tribe in Namibia, called the *San*, concluded that these people were unusually peaceful and noncombative (Marshall, 1976). Years after this conclusion was reached, the rates of interpersonal violence were assessed in quantitative terms by asking each adult tribal member how each deceased person known to them had died. This allowed researchers to calculate the rate at which deaths were being caused by interpersonal violence among several bands of San living within the same region.

Based on the reported causes of death for thousands of deceased San, research indicates that the rate of death due to interpersonal violence was 29 per 100,000 per year (Lee, 1984; Christiansen & Winkler, 1992). This compared to an annual murder rate of about 8 per 100,000 in the United States (which has one of the highest rates among industrialized nations) (Ellis & Walsh, 2000).

How could qualitative observations bring researchers to conclusions that are very different from those of quantitative research? First, those who concluded that the San were peaceful and noncombative based their judgments on observing just one tribal band consisting of about 40 individuals for approximately a year. During this time, almost no acts of interpersonal violence were observed, and none resulting in death took place. However, note that this probably would have been true even in a society with 100 violent deaths per 100,000 in an average year. Overall, one needs larger samples than most ethnographers typically obtain to be able to generalize with confidence.

Improving the Reliability of Ethnographic and Participant Observational Data

It is noteworthy that ethnographic research has faced more than its share of challenges to its scientific reliability. Therefore, it can be instructive for all social/behavioral scientists to consider approaches to ethnographic and similar qualitative research that can diminish such challenges in the future.

One approach to improving the reliability of ethnographic data in the future would be to encourage several researchers to collect data in each culture (or subculture) studied, rather than relying exclusively on the work of a single ethnographer. Although this may lessen the romantic appeal of ethnographic research, it should provide fellow social scientists with greater confidence in the accounts that emerge. This approach reflects a general principle basic to the scientific method: Science needs to be recognized as being a social enterprise in which every scientist should both expect and encourage others to repeatedly check and recheck whatever one scientist reports as evidence (Phillips et al., 1978). Unfortunately, the rapid rate at which isolated human cultures are being absorbed into technologically advanced societies in recent decades is diminishing the opportunities to observe "uncontaminated" cultures.

Another approach that ethnographers take to improve the reliability of their data is to rely less on one or two informants for information about the nature of a specific culture. Instead, the reports of informants may be cross-checked against both qualitative and quantitative data derived from interviewing numerous members of the culture being studied. Asking some standardized questions of numerous members of a culture and recording their responses for later analysis would allow ethnographers to provide at least rough percentage estimates of how prevalent various beliefs and practices are in the culture. This in turn would reduce the use of vague adjectives such as "prevalent" and "widespread" in describing cultural beliefs and practices.

Finally, ethnographers and participant observers should have one or more specific hypotheses in mind before they begin their research. These hypotheses can be inspired by reading other research findings and can certainly be augmented or discarded after the research gets underway. However, researchers should never plan to conduct a qualitative or quantitative study with a hope that the focus of the study will simply manifest itself after they've been in the field for a while.

Overall, despite their extraordinary value, ethnographic data can be susceptible to errors of validity and reliability, and sometimes it is difficult to detect and correct these. Fortunately, anthropologists and other social scientists have developed techniques for combining the results of numerous ethnographic accounts from all over the world. This consolidation of findings from numerous ethnographic accounts has helped to improve the validity and reliability of qualitative data. Also, keep in mind that if the goal of research is to understand reality, engaging in ethnographic research, which attempts to uncover the nature and meaning of behaviors and attitudes of nonmainstream and understudied groups from the perspective of those groups, may be better at uncovering the true nature of reality. It may, therefore, be somewhat hypocritical on the part of researchers to assume that ethnographic data are somehow lacking validity.

The terms ethnographic research and participant observation are sometimes used interchangeably (Schusky & Culbert, 1987). While both involve observing and recording novel social experiences, as the terms are usually used, they can be distinguished to a degree. Unlike participant observations, many ethnographic accounts do not entail the observer becoming integrated into the sociocultural network being studied. Though it is certainly advisable for an ethnographer to learn the language, eat the food, and at least respect (if not take part in) the customs of the cultures and subcultures being studied, differences in physical appearance mean that ethnographers will be more often seen as "outsiders" than is true for participant observers.

There are also commonalities between ethnographic observations and participant observations. These commonalities include the fact that researchers often rely on gatekeepers or introduction to the group being studied from one or two key informants. Also, the subjective impressions of researchers about what is worth reporting usually play a more central role in qualitative research than in quantitative research.

⊖ Case Studies

Investigations falling under the category of **case studies** (or **case histories**) are basically narrative accounts focusing on just a few individuals, groups, or episodes (Mason & Bramble, 1989). Each case is so unique as to not warrant any attempt to assess its significance in any statistical sense.

One example of a case study undertaken by Chappell (2009) involved studying community policing in a medium-sized police department in Florida. Community policing is a philosophy that puts police officers back on the beat interacting with citizens in the community with the idea that police will be better able to problem-solve issues and prevent crime rather than just responding to crime (Walker, 1999). Many police agencies around the country have adopted the community policing model. This researcher was interested in whether or not police agencies really practice community policing; in other words, just stating or promoting publicly that you have a philosophy of community policing does not mean that your officers are actually practicing it in their daily duties.

Chappell (2009) along with several of her students conducted a case study, participating in ride-alongs with a total of 54 officers to understand and operationalize whether the officers were actually using community policing tactics. She was also interested in whether or not the police buy into community policing and think that it is a practice that achieves what it is supposed to: crime reduction and prevention.

The results of the case study were fairly interesting in that almost half of the officers stated that they believed in community policing and thought it was an effective strategy for crime prevention. However, only 35% of the officers were actually engaged in community policing tactics. Many of the officers mentioned that community policing was a good idea in theory but that the police department was too understaffed and did not have adequate resources to allow implementation of community policing strategies. In other words, the chief of police stated that the department operates under a philosophy of community policing, and half of the officers believe in the strategy, but only about one-third were actually engaging in community policing practices. This case study provides a good example of how this methodology can be used to study the behaviors of certain groups to examine the differences between policy and practice or, in this case, the philosophical versus actual practices of persons in an organization.

Because a case study usually only examines one or a few entities, generalizing the findings of a case study to other entities, in this case police departments, can be difficult. This researcher concluded, however, that the results of the study suggest that the barriers to actually adopting a community policing strategy in practice may simply be resource allocation, which is a valuable finding that is probably applicable to police departments nationwide. Departments that have enough resources may be doing community policing, but those that do not are probably not practicing community policing even though they have adopted that philosophy or have policies that mandate officers use community policing strategies.

Examples of case studies in the social sciences range from accounts of a few young children learning to read with little adult training to descriptions of increased antisocial behavior associated with damage to the frontal lobes of the brain. Case studies are unusual among qualitative research in at least three respects. First, most of those conducting the research make no effort to become socially integrated into what is being observed. Second, case studies focus on single individuals or groups. Third, case studies are often carried out as part of

BOX 11.1 CURRENT ISSUES

Are Presentence Investigation Reports Essentially Case Studies?

Each day around the country, thousands of probation officers are writing reports to assist judges and parole boards in making appropriate sentencing and release decisions. These reports contain background information on the convicted offender and are usually the culmination of information gathering from a number of sources, including an in-depth interview with the offender.

Essentially, these are case studies that are used mainly for practical, rather than strictly scholarly, purposes. The information in these reports usually includes information surrounding the crime and the victim, as well as relevant facts about the offender and his or her family, such as marital status, presence of dependents, and information on education and employment history. The report will also usually have a narrative of the defendant's version of the crime, sometimes referred to as the defendant's sentencing memorandum. There will also be a statement by the victim, if there was a victim in the crime, called the victim impact statement, outlining how the victim and his or her family have been affected by the offense (Hartley, Rabe, & Champion, 2018).

None of this information necessarily binds the judge to a particular type of sentence, but recommendations in the report for the most appropriate disposition of the case can assist in making a much more informed decision. The most common forms of these documents in legal proceedings are called **presentence investigations** or **presentence reports**.

clinical or institutional treatment, whereas other forms of qualitative research rarely have a treatment component.

As the number of case studies continues to mount, they make it possible for other researchers to review and synthesize what case studies on the same topic collectively suggest. An article reviewed several psychiatric and psychological case studies of people diagnosed with kleptomania (compulsive stealing and shoplifting) for evidence of some common underlying patterns (Goldman, 1991).

Focus Group Research

In **focus groups**, a dozen or so people are brought together to intensely discuss some topic. As a qualitative research method, focus groups can be traced back to the 1940s, although their use did not become popular until the 1970s (Massey, 2000). The individual leading these groups is called a **facilitator**, and the remaining members of the group are called **research participants** (Kerslake & Goulding, 1996).

A typical focus group session will last about 90 minutes and will sometimes have a small quantitative element, such as having participants complete a short questionnaire at the end of the session. Nevertheless, most of the information obtained from these group sessions is qualitative. The comments made by the participants are either coded by the researcher during the session or are tape recorded for later analysis (Stewart & Shamdasani, 1990). Focus groups, however, should not be thought of as mere discussion groups. The purpose of a focus group is not to debate or persuade but to explore people's thoughts and ideas. In the course of a focus group session, opinions often become clearer; sometimes, they even change as issues are probed. Also, unlike free-wheeling discussion groups, focus groups are very specifically circumscribed, and the facilitator helps to insure that the discussion remains on topic.

Focus groups are widely used in marketing research for planning new advertizing campaigns for commercial products and for helping to identify strengths and weaknesses of political candidates (Bartos, 1986). Focus groups are occasionally convened more than once in order to reassess the approaches being taken in light of new developments. In addition to being used for developing marketing strategies for commercial products and political campaigns, focus groups have been used to develop ways of informing women about the risks of cervical cancer, approaches to reducing adolescent cigarette smoking, and understanding the experiences of those who have been the victims of dating violence or domestic abuse.

One of the most novel uses of focus groups was carried out in the field of criminology. Researchers were interested in improving their understanding of the motivations for criminality, so they convened a group of habitual offenders serving time in an Oklahoma prison (Wood et al., 1997). The prisoners were assured that nothing they said would be revealed to prison or court officials. Then prisoners were asked to discuss what sorts of thoughts and emotions they recall having had in connection with the most serious crimes they had committed. Most of the offenders revealed that they typically had a rush of excitement leading up to the offense and then a sense of accomplishment afterward (as long as it appeared that they were not going to get caught). The researchers concluded that some internal, possibly neurochemical, factors may underlie the commission of crimes by many habitual offenders.

⊖ Procedures in Ethnographic/Participant Observation Data Collection

Data collection by those who conduct ethnographic and participant observations tends to be unique in sociological and criminological research. For this reason, some procedural issues need to be discussed in relationship to these types of data. To a lesser degree, these principles also apply to all types of qualitative research, especially case studies. One set of procedural issues has to do with the process of compiling "raw" data; another surrounds the analysis of the data and the writing of final reports.

Compiling Field Notes

As a rule, field notes are of two types: jottings and daily consolidations (Sanjek, 1990). **Jottings** (or **scratch notes**) should consist of note taking as close to their temporal occurrence as possible. Thus, an ethnographer or participant observer should keep a notepad handy at all times for jotting down words and phrases that will help him or her remember experiences and information acquired from the people being studied. When beginning an interview, researchers should ask interviewees for their permission to take notes. In addition to being a matter of courtesy, this request will also set a tone of seriousness and importance for the interview.

Daily consolidated note taking should occur each day and should usually be in the form of complete sentences arranged in relatively brief (2–5 sentence) paragraphs. These daily consolidations will be prompted by the words and phrases jotted down throughout the day. Nowadays, if at all possible, all daily consolidations should be entered directly into a computer.

This can be one of the most time-consuming aspects of this type of research. A survey of ethnographers sought to determine how much time they spent writing notes during a typical day of field research (Bolton, 1984). On average, the researchers reported that 2–3 hours of each working day were spent writing, editing, and organizing their field notes. If a researcher fails to commit this time on a regular basis, many of the experiences will fade from memory, and, of those experiences remembered, the details will sometimes become distorted and erroneously merged with other events.

In writing daily consolidations, it is best to jot down many short (paragraph length) accounts of significant episodes, rather than composing lengthy (a page or two) accounts (Bernard, 2002). The main reason for this is that shorter verbal accounts will be easier than long ones to organize into coherent themes when the time comes to compose the final report. Also, all daily consolidations should be dated so that researchers can later reconstruct the chronology of important events.

Some researchers choose to tape-record some of their interviews as an alternative to jotting down preliminary notes. Although tape recordings can be helpful for ensuring the accuracy of the information being collected, one should keep in mind that it adds considerable time to the data collection process. One must listen to an interview at least twice: once when it occurs and again when it is played back. Also, because it is unethical under most circumstances to tape-record people without their permission, individuals should be asked for permission prior to the interview. Knowing that a conversation is being recorded may remove some of the spontaneity and candor from interviews.

Some ethnographers recommend keeping a third type of written record, called a **diary**, while they are conducting field research. Diaries are used to maintain more personal impressions and reactions to what is being documented than will normally be included in jottings and daily consolidations (Bernard, 2002).

Analyzing and Reporting Field Notes

The methods employed in analyzing field notes involve the use of several interrelated strategies. Some researchers organize their notes around a theme or a theory that seems to tie together much of what they observed while other researchers are still searching for an underlying theme or theory throughout the time they are analyzing their data.

Fortunately, computerized programs have been developed to help researchers digest and make sense of qualitative data. Some of the most widely used programs and their websites are as follows: NVivo (www.qsrinternational.com) and ATLAS.ti (www.atlasti.com). If a researcher's notes have been entered and stored in a computer, these notes can be sorted and organized in a wide variety of ways. The simplest sorting is done on the basis of keywords or in chronological order. More complex organizing of field notes can be performed by searching or looking for combinations of words or for synonyms.

Quantitative Direct Observations

Quantitative direct observations exist in sufficient numbers and/or conditions as to make it possible for them to be counted. There are major advantages to quantitative observations. The most important advantage is that disagreements between two studies of some phenomenon can be settled more easily by conducting one or two more replications than is the case of qualitative observations. As displayed in Table 11.2, quantitative observations can be divided into two categories: **laboratory/clinical observations** and **field** (or **naturalistic**) **observations**. An intermediate category—called semi-field (or semi-natural) observations—can also be identified, although here it will be discussed simply as a type of field observations.

Laboratory/Clinical Observations

Observations in a laboratory or clinical setting are those in which researchers collect data in a physical space under the control of the researcher. Although people often think of a laboratory as consisting of test tubes or mechanical gadgets, laboratories used by social scientists can be little more than an ordinary classroom. The main advantage of a laboratory or clinical setting is that the environment can be roughly standardized, eliminating many of the factors that inadvertently affect whatever behavior is being studied.

Three types of laboratory observations can be identified. One type involves behavior that is directly observed, and the other two involves inferring behavior (as well as emotions and cognitive functioning) either on the basis of physical samples taken from subjects or on the basis of electro-physiological measurements.

Laboratory Observations in Which Behavior Is Directly Observed

A wide variety of behavior patterns have been directly observed in laboratory settings. These include a famous set of laboratory observations in which subjects were led to believe that they were inflicting electric shocks on other subjects in order to facilitate their learning (Milgram, 1963, 1974). In reality, the "learners"

Table 11.2   A Summary of the Main Types of Quantitative Direct Observational Data

Data Type	Main Subtype	Description	Qualifying Remarks
Laboratory Observations	Subject-Focused	Subjects are directly observed with respect to one or more aspects of behavior.	
	Biological Specimen	Behavior such as drug use is inferred based on samples derived from hair, urine, DNA, etc.	Mainly used in the treatment of drug offenders.
Field (and Semi-Field) Observations	Naturalistic	Quantitative naturalistic observations of one or more aspects of behavior.	Observing behavior with little or no researcher interference.
	Manipulative	Experimental research in a naturalistic (or semi-naturalistic) setting.	
Content Analysis		Interpret and code information from written or other symbolic media.	

were **confederates** in the study, meaning they were merely pretending to be subjects and were not actually being shocked by the real subject. The main purpose of these experiments was to determine what was required to get people to follow orders of an authority figure, even when doing so harmed others.

Other instances of interesting laboratory studies involved assessing persons' attitudes toward date rape after exposing them to sexually explicit videos (Milburn et al., 2000) and examining the willingness to assist others in emergencies dependent on how many persons were present in the room (Latane & Darley, 1970).

Laboratory Observations in Which Behavior Is Inferred from Physiological Specimens

Sometimes, laboratories can be used not to observe behavior directly but for making inferences about behavior based on physiological specimens obtained from subjects. Most of the behavior that has been studied via the analysis of specimens has involved the use of various drugs, including cocaine, heroin, marijuana, and nicotine (Arnold, 1990). The two main specimen sources for physiological data used in these studies have been urine and hair, although saliva and blood have also been used.

In the case of urine specimens, the most widely tested subjects have been parolees at risk of resuming use of drugs such as cocaine and heroin (McAllister & Makkai, 1991; Visher & McFadden, 1991). Several additional studies have focused on women at risk of heavy drug use during pregnancy (Neuspiel & Hamel, 1991;

Kline et al., 1997). The need for these tests was reinforced by a Boston study that revealed that 24% of poor women seeking prenatal care services at a public hospital who denied using cocaine tested positive for recent use of the drug (Frank et al., 1988). These findings were particularly disturbing in light of evidence that cocaine and other "recreational" drugs (including alcohol and tobacco) can cause permanent damage to developing fetuses (Prager et al., 1984; Sexton & Hebel, 1984). One other study used urine specimens to detect nicotine among heart disease patients who were desperately attempting to quit smoking (Wilcox et al., 1979). One drawback to the use of urine specimens for detecting drug use is that usage must have been fairly recent, usually within the past 4 to 5 days.

Hair samples are used primarily to make inferences about cocaine and heroin consumption because chemical traces of most other drugs can be quickly leached from hair shafts after washing (Leal et al., 1994). It is remarkable to note that significant chemical residues of cocaine and heroin are deposited in hair as it grows and can be detected in hair shafts several months later, no matter how often the hair is washed (Mieczkowski et al., 1991; Colon et al., 2001). Other examples of physical specimens being used to infer behavior involve the field of forensics, the branch of criminology/criminal justice that uses physical/ chemical evidence to investigate specific crimes.

⬤ Field Research

Field research consists of studies undertaken outside a laboratory setting. Two types of field research can be identified: naturalistic and manipulative. **Naturalistic** (or **nonmanipulative**) **field research** merely involves observing and recording behavior without interfering with it in any way. **Manipulative** (or **experimental**) **field research** entails systematically attempting to alter some aspect of the behavior being observed.

Naturalistic Field Research

A rather simple and early example of a field observational study was one conducted by Francis Galton (1908). During travels to various parts of England, Galton gave subjective ratings to hundreds of women that he happened to pass. Later, he calculated the average ratings given in several geographical regions and concluded that on average women in London were more attractive than those elsewhere in the country. Notice that Galton did nothing to alter that which was being observed, making it clearly a nonmanipulative field study.

Manipulative (Experimental) Field Research Data

Manipulative (or experimental) field (or naturalistic) observations are ones in which a researcher systematically controls some feature of the environment outside of a laboratory. As noted earlier, most studies that involve manipulation by researchers occurs in a confined, or laboratory, setting. Nevertheless, there are exceptions.

Examples of manipulative field research include those conducted in the 1970s where several researchers used the so-called lost letter technique mainly to study people's attitudes toward political candidates and issues (Bolton, 1974; Webb et al., 1981). The technique involves a researcher (and usually several assistants) discretely dropping hundreds of sealed, stamped, and addressed envelopes one-by-one on sidewalks in various cities or neighborhoods and then determining how many of the envelopes are eventually mailed to the addressee (the envelope included a post office box number). What is usually manipulated in the lost letter technique is the name of the organization to which the envelopes are addressed. For example, to assess people's sympathies toward the three leading American political candidates in the 1970s, researchers dropped hundreds of envelopes addressed to local campaign headquarters for different presidential candidates in various cities during the campaign (Bouchard & Stuster, 1969). Other topics covered by the lost letter technique were attitudes toward handicapped children (Cairns & Bochner, 1974) and communism (Milgram et al., 1965).

● Content Analysis

A special type of nonquestionnaire data that is only possible in literate societies is called content analysis. Studies classified as **content analyses** use written or other symbolic communication as data. The nature of the symbolic communication can either be unpublished, such as letters to loved ones or graffiti on restroom walls, or, more often, published information, such as newspaper ads and yearbook photographs. Most content analysis can be thought of as a special type of naturalistic observation that is only possible in societies where writing is common. Because content analyses are quite varied, several examples will be briefly mentioned.

Some content analyses have been based on obituaries published in newspapers in large cities that tend to cover only the deaths of prominent people. Among the conclusions reached by these studies has been that men are at least twice as likely as women to receive an obituary in such newspapers (Moremen & Cradduck, 1999).

Other studies based on content analysis have looked for trends in the use of men's and women's body parts on magazine covers (Nigro et al., 1988), especially women being portrayed as sex objects in the media (Stankiewicz & Rosselli, 2008); in portrayals of alcohol consumption on television (Pendleton et al., 1991); and in the content of television commercials (Ferrante et al., 1988). Interesting content analyses have been performed on graffiti in public restrooms (Innala & Ernulf, 1992) and even in the content of letters written by children to Santa Claus (Downs, 1983; Bradbard, 1985).

More complex content analyses have involved efforts to identify long-term trends in the weight and body proportions of fashion models. By taking careful measurements of photographs appearing since the 1930s, research-ers have documented trends toward increasing slenderness among fashion models (Morris et al., 1989; Anderson et al., 1992). Ironically, this trend has

Can Manipulating Behavior in the Field Lead to Valid Results?

Consider the lost letter technique, where a researcher discretely drop hundreds of sealed, stamped addressed envelopes in various neighborhoods and then wait to see how many of the letters are actually placed in the mail. Although clever, this technique provides only a limited amount of information for all of the time and expense involved, especially in light of the fact that no specific demographic information is obtained regarding those who do and do not mail the letter. We therefore have no information on the individuals who might have picked up the letter—only information about the neighborhood or area of the city where it was dropped. This can be problematic for drawing conclusions or inferring people's attitudes toward political candidates. For instance, maybe some persons are indifferent and so altruistic that they would drop the letter in the mail no matter who the candidate was. It also assumes that the people accidentally happening by the "lost" envelopes know who the political candidates are. In today's digital world, it may even be less likely that anyone would expend the effort to go to the post office or find a place to drop the envelope in the mail.

Similarly, several studies have been conducted over the years in which researchers attempt to study gang behavior or the behavior of subcultural groups. Although it may seem unethical to try to encourage gang members to engage in delinquent or criminal behavior in order to study and understand the inner workings of gang structure and culture, considerable information on these groups and individuals and their behavior has been recorded and written about because of field research that has attempted to manipulate their behavior to varying degrees.

What do you think? Is manipulating persons toward certain behaviors naturalistic? Can the subsequent observations of gang member behavior be considered accurate or valid? Would the gang members have acted in the same manner if the researcher had not been present? Although some skeptics might argue that crime doesn't happen in a lab, nearly all laboratory research is manipulative (experimental) in nature. Naturalistic research, however, can be both manipulative and nonmanipulative. And although others may also be skeptical of manipulative field research, both these types of direct observations have provided many insights into numerous aspects of human behavior.

occurred despite a trend toward increasing obesity in the general population of most industrialized countries (Flegal, 1999; Kirchengast & Steiner, 2001).

A quite unusual content analysis involved high school yearbooks and mental illness. The researchers compared photographs of persons who exhibited serious mental illness in adulthood to those who exhibited no symptoms (Napolean et al., 1980). Persons who were eventually diagnosed with a mental illness were rated as significantly less attractive than their relatively healthy adult counterparts by raters unaware of any adult diagnoses.

Although most content analyses pertain to written or other visual information, in a few cases oral conversations have been used. One such study was conducted early in the 20th century when a researcher jotted down the subjects of conversation he overheard on the streets of New York City (Moore, 1922). Among the conclusions reached were that in same-sex conversations females were overheard discussing males 44% of the time, while males were discussing females only 8% of the time.

⬇ Closing Comments on Direct Observations

Throughout this chapter, we have focused on direct observations as being different from questionnaire data. Nevertheless, there are times when they overlap. For example, studies have been conducted in which the behavior of children has been measured based on evaluations given by their teachers (e.g., Whalen, Henker, & Dotemoto, 1981) or by their parents (e.g., Barkley et al., 1985). In both cases, questionnaires were used to obtain the information.

Also be aware that questionnaire data and direct observations are sometimes combined in the same study. For instance, laboratory studies have been undertaken in which participants are asked to role-play and then asked to complete a questionnaire at the end of the role-playing exercise (Spencer & Taylor, 1988). Also, as a laboratory study of factors responsible for child abuse, videotapes of crying babies were played to parents to assess both the physiological and the self-reported reactions to the crying (Brewster et al., 1998).

Another example of where both direct observation and questionnaire data were combined involved a series of laboratory studies designed to determine the effects of exposing males to various forms of pornography. In some of these studies, subjects watched one or more pornography films in a controlled laboratory setting and then completed questionnaires in which they described their attitudes toward women and/or assessed their probability of behaving aggressively toward women (including the commission of rape) (e.g., Malamuth & Check, 1983, 1985).

Qualitative and quantitative data, as you might suspect, have sometimes been viewed in adversarial terms, compelling some social scientists to choose one over the other (Hammersley, 1992:161). In point of fact, there are advantages and disadvantages to each. The main disadvantage to qualitative research is that it can lack reliability if no other studies exist on the same topic. On the other hand, many aspects of human behavior and culture are so complex that quantitative data are inadequate for capturing the full breadth and color of what researchers are attempting to comprehend. In the final analysis, qualitative and quantitative research designs should be viewed as complementary rather than as antagonistic (Hammersley, 1992). Social science has certainly been enhanced by findings from both of these broad categories of research methods.

⬇ Summary

Although most social science research is based on individuals responding to questionnaires, a substantial proportion is not. This chapter categorized and described the main qualitative and quantitative methods that social scientists have developed for collecting data without questionnaires.

Four types of qualitative observations were identified: participant observations, ethnographic accounts, case studies, and focus groups. Participant observations are observations made by individuals who become intimately involved in a subculture or an institution within a society. Ethnographic accounts are narrative descriptions that social scientists provide based on visits that they make to a foreign (usually nonindustrial) society. Case studies are accounts that focus on a single individual or a single incident. Individuals and incidences are chosen either because of something very unusual about them or because they serve to illustrate what is considered an important point by the researcher. In focus group research, a dozen or so persons are brought together by a researcher to discuss some topic such as a new commercial product, a political candidate, or an organization that needs restructuring. From focus group discussions, perceived strengths and weaknesses of products, candidates, and organizational structures can often be identified. Archaeological research comes either from artifacts and fossils or from written records, and both provide insights into the lives of people who are no longer living.

In the past, reliability has been an issue in the case of ethnographic research and, to a lesser degree, participant observations. Three methods were reviewed for ways in which researchers can improve ethnographic and participant observation data. These were (1) having more than one ethnographer independently visit the same data collection site, (2) relying less on just one or two informants for data and incorporating some standardized questions directed at numerous research participants, and (3) developing specific hypotheses before beginning any data collection in order to concentrate on a few specific issues rather than simply letting events take the researcher wherever the events happen to go.

The main types of procedures used in collecting ethnographic and participant observational data were discussed, including the two main types of field notes: jottings (scratch notes) and daily consolidations. Suggestions and guidelines for analyzing and reporting field notes were also presented.

The second part of this chapter explored ways of collecting social science data via quantitative observations (without questionnaires). Such observations involve a researcher (or a trained assistant) tabulating the frequency or intensity of one or more variables. Unlike qualitative observations, quantitative observations are usually much more susceptible to statistical analysis.

Quantitative observations can be divided into two main categories: laboratory observations and field (or naturalistic) observations. (An intermediate category, called semi-field observations, was treated as a variation of field observations.) Laboratory observations give researchers maximum control over the environmental context within which a study takes place. This control can be used to gain assurance that extraneous and unforeseen factors are not responsible for research findings. Laboratory observations also allow a researcher to use technical instruments with greater precision than in most field observations.

Numerous examples were given of quantitative observations made in laboratory settings. These were subsumed under two headings: (1) observations in which behavior is directly observed and (2) observations in which behavior is inferred from biological specimens.

Regarding quantitative research that takes place in the field, its main advantage over laboratory research is that the behavior under study tends to be more spontaneous and "real" than is true for behavior in laboratory settings. Several examples of field observations were presented.

The last category of direct observations was that of content analysis. This type of research involves statistically analyzing written and sometimes other symbolic information. Examples of content analyses range from studies of obituaries and tombstones to bathroom graffiti and from television advertisements to suicide notes.

Discussion Questions

1. Discuss the major differences in making qualitative versus quantitative observations.
2. Discuss the purposes of field research as a research methodology. Further, what are the differences between naturalistic and manipulative field research?
3. Describe ethnography as a method of data collection.
4. What are the main ways in which an ethnographer could improve the reliability of his or her observational data?
5. When might a case study be an appropriate research methodology?
6. List the main procedures in participant observational data collection.

Exercises

1. Come up with a study of some crime phenomenon that could utilize qualitative observational practices. Which type of the six qualitative observation techniques would be best suited to collect your data and why?
2. Think of written or other symbolic communication for which you could conduct a content analysis. What types of research questions might you want to ask based on the content you would analyze?

Chapter 12

Archival Data Analysis, Meta-Analysis, and Evaluation Research

Have you ever heard the term evidence-based practices? If you are a criminal justice or criminology major, you should have. What does this term mean? Many jurisdictions around the country are requiring that programs implemented to

reduce or prevent crime, be evidence based. What that means is that these programs have been shown through the use of scientific research to work or achieve the intended outcomes. Traditional responses to offending— probation, jail, and prison—have not been very successful in terms of reducing the likelihood of reoffense; average recidivism rates hover around 60% for those who have been released from jail or prison. Because of this so-called revolving door of criminal justice, many citizens and local government officials are open to implementing more effective responses to crime. Governmental agencies collect data on crime and justice, and many researchers are interested in examining the outcomes of criminal justice system response. Many different types of this archival data can be utilized to examine system practices, and many different types of research methods can be used to assess effectiveness. These data and methods will be the focus of this chapter.

The final sources for social science data are those obtained primarily from organizations such as government agencies and from researchers who are able to synthesize and build on research already conducted by others. An abundance of criminal justice data is collected and stored by governmental agencies. Other research attempts to examine the effects of certain governmental and other agency programs. Many programs in the criminal justice system are adopted each year to prevent and reduce crime or to assist offenders in reintegrating back into society. Because many of these programs are funded with taxpayer dollars, the government also seeks to fund evaluations of their impact or success. The main types of methods to be explored in this chapter are archival data, cross-cultural atlases, meta-analyses, and evaluation research. Before examining these methods, it is helpful to discuss the concept of a unit of analysis.

⊜ Units of Analysis

Data compiled by governmental agencies often pertain to groups of people, rather than to individuals. For example, a study that compares the rate of poverty in numerous large cities would provide no specific information about each individual living in those cities. Instead, each city becomes what is termed the **unit of analysis**. Any units of analyses besides individuals are said to be **aggregated units of analyses**.

Although the individual is the single most widely used unit of analysis in social science research, aggregated units are still used quite often. The most common aggregated units are neighborhoods, cities, counties (parishes), and sometimes even entire countries. When these aggregated units of analyses are arranged according to their inclusiveness, they are referred to as **levels of analyses**. Thus, cities would constitute a higher level of analysis than neighborhoods, and counties would be higher than cities, with countries being the highest level of all.

An example of the use of aggregated units of analyses involves research by sociologists and public health officials who have found that people living in countries with the greatest degree of income inequality have shorter average life expectancy than people living in countries with relatively little income inequality (Wilkinson, 1989, 1997; Stanistreet et al., 1999).

Findings that have linked income inequality with poor health of populations have been particularly disturbing in light of evidence that income gaps between people living in most industrialized countries have widened considerably since around 1980 (Smeeding & Gottschalk, 1996; Juhn, 1999). Nevertheless, it needs to be noted that not all studies have found an association between income inequality and shortened average life expectancies after statistically controlling for a variety of other confounding variables (Fiscella & Franks, 2000).

From a methodological standpoint, researchers need to be aware of what their unit of analysis is. In the previous studies, the unit of analysis is clearly an aggregated one. When performing aggregated analyses, social scientists are on guard against making what is called the **ecological fallacy**. This term refers to mistakenly assuming that findings at one level of analysis will necessarily apply to another level (Robinson, 1950; Demo & Acock, 1988).

One can draw from the field of criminology to illustrate the ecological fallacy. Throughout the world, criminal/delinquent behavior is highly concentrated in the second and third decades of life (Ellis & Walsh, 2000). This would lead many to expect that if a large number of cities were compared in terms of the proportion of their citizens who were in their teens and twenties, we would find a positive correlation between these proportions and city crime rates. Simply assuming this expectation to be true would constitute an example of the ecological fallacy. In fact, studies that have compared crime rates in cities with the proportion of citizens living in those cities who are in their teens and twenties have not found consistent relationships (Ellis & Walsh, 2000).

Here is a second illustration of the ecological fallacy. A British study found that people living in districts with the heaviest voting for conservative political candidates had lower mortality rates than people living in districts where liberal candidates received most of the votes (Davy Smith, & Dorling, 1996). The same pattern was found when comparing mortality rates and voting patterns for the 50 states of the United States (Kondrichin & Lester, 1998). Does this mean that political conservatives live longer on average than liberals? Perhaps, but one should not make this assumption simply on the basis of aggregated data. You would be committing an ecological fallacy if you stated that, from these findings, an individual in a state that votes mostly liberal will not live as long as an individual who lives in a state that votes mostly conservative.

Overall, research at all levels of analysis can be informative, but one should never automatically transfer what is learned at one level to another level, except under very special circumstances (Firebaugh, 1978). Assuming otherwise is to commit the ecological fallacy.

⊜ Archival Data

As part of their everyday functioning, government agencies (or bureaus) compile information on a vast array of human activities. These data encompass people being arrested, convicted, sentenced, getting married and divorced, being committed to mental hospitals, having children, and engaging in a plethora of economic activities. In everyday discourse, the term bureaucracy often has negative connotations, but in the social sciences, both national and local governmental bureaucracies are recognized as rich sources of archival data.

When researchers use data from governmental or nongovernmental bureaucracies (such as large businesses and nonprofit organizations), the data constitutes what is often termed archival data. **Archival data** are data that have been collected by some agency without all of the specific research projects the data will be used for in mind (Mason & Bramble, 1989). This means that if a researcher has a specific interest that can be addressed by utilizing data that have already been collected (or is already being collected), he or she is using archival data. Often, the term **secondary analysis** is used to refer to the analysis of archival data. Archival data can cover all levels of analyses, ranging from comparing individuals to comparing neighborhoods, and comparing cities to comparing nations.

Examples of, and Sources for, Contemporary Archival Data Analyses

Researchers from all of the social sciences use archival data, but the greatest reliance on such data is by economists, geographers, political scientists, and sociologists and criminologists. The criminal justice system is a large source of archival data for researchers because law enforcement, the courts, and correctional systems keep many records on individuals they arrest, convict, sentence, incarcerate, or place on probation. These records become an invaluable source of information for studying how the criminal justice system operates as well as what factors affect the decisions of actors within the system. For example, researchers might be interested in whether the type of drug someone was caught with affects whether or not a prosecutor will decide to file charges or whether someone's age might be a factor in whether or not a judge sends someone to prison or gives them a term of probation. Much of what we know about decision-making practices and the administration of justice in the criminal justice system has come from secondary analyses. Other researchers have collected their own data about the administration of justice via administering surveys to police or judges by observing court dockets and sentencing hearings. If these studies used public funding, the data collected would also probably be available to other researchers through a data warehouse called the National Archive of Criminal Justice Data (NACJD), which has been a source for compiling and warehousing crime and justice data since 1978. You can search the data sets in this warehouse by going to the website listed in Table 12.1.

Conducting studies in which statistical controls are imposed is not particularly difficult when using modern computers. Multivariate statistical packages have the ability to control for all types of variables as long as those variables are a part of the data set being analyzed. Nevertheless, help from experienced researchers or statisticians should be sought when attempting to undertake a research study using multivariate statistics.

TABLE 12.1   Examples of Agencies with Massive Data Sets (in Both "Raw" and Analyzed Forms) on the Internet

Agency	Nature of Data	Web Address
Center for Disease Control Health Statistics (part of the US Department of Health and Human Services)	Physical health, mental health, fertility, birth order, pregnancies and births by age and marital status; marriage and divorce	www.cdc.gov/nchs
Statistics Canada	Statistical information about crime, health, economics, demographics, births, deaths, marriage, and divorce	https://www.statcan.gc.ca/eng/start (also available in French)
Inter-university Consortium for Political and Social Research (ICPSR)	World's largest archive of digital social science data	http://www.icpsr.umich.edu
National Archives of Criminal Justice Data (NACJD)	Domestic violence, public attitudes toward crime, self-reported drug use, and violent offending	www.icpsr.umich.eduNACJD
US Bureau of the Census (part of the US Department of Commerce)	Population distributions by geography, race/ethnicity, income, housing, poverty (many with maps, photos, and video clips)	www.census.gov
World Health Organization	Physical and mental health (often worldwide)	www.census.gov

Literally thousands of large data sets derived from routinely maintained institutional records and from institutionally sponsored surveys can now be accessed online, either through the NACJD or another archive of social science data called the Inter-university Consortium for Political and Social Research (ICPSR). Researchers can avail themselves of these data sets via the ICPSR website listed in Table 12.1. Other major sources for direct downloading of large data sets are also listed in the table.

Examples of, and Sources for, Historic Archival Data Analyses

Having considered relatively recent archival data sets, let us now consider archival data sets that are sometimes centuries old. Essentially none of these data sets can simply be downloaded from the internet or even from computer disks or thumb drives. Instead, they usually require that researchers (or their assistants) rummage through dusty records in old libraries, churches, jails, and the like.

Some fascinating studies have been conducted based on these historic treasures. For example, English studies have used old jail logs to determine the age and sex of hundreds of persons arrested and convicted for various crimes

BOX 12.1 CURRENT ISSUES

Does Changing the Law Affect Citizens' Behavior?

Researchers in the field of public health use archival data a great deal, such as when they seek to detect how changing laws might affect patterns in behavior. For example, researchers used statewide data to compare the 25 states that had mandatory helmet laws for motorcycle riders and the 25 states that had no such laws. Surprisingly, the study found an average death rate of 6.20/10,000 for registered motorcycle riders for the states with mandatory laws, compared to 5.07/10,000 in the states without such laws, with the difference being significant beyond the .01 level (Branas & Knudson, 2001). In other words, the states with the highest rates of fatal injuries were those *with* mandatory helmet laws!

Doubting that these helmet laws could actually be causing fatal motorcycle accidents, the researchers reanalyzed the data with statistical controls imposed for population density and the average temperature of each state (because both of these control variables were also positively correlated with motorcycle death rates). Imposing these statistical controls reduced the difference in death rates associated with helmet laws to nonsignificance. The inference drawn from this refined analysis was that mandatory helmet laws probably have no significant tendency to reduce fatal injuries of motorcyclists. Instead, population density and warmer average temperatures seemed to be largely responsible for increased motorcycle fatalities, and increases in these fatalities may prompt legislatures to pass laws that might protect motorcyclists.

This second example raises an important issue in archival data analysis. Because laws are not passed randomly by states, one must always be careful in simply comparing states with and without certain types of laws. In the present case, it appears that legislatures in the less populated states, especially those in colder regions of the United States, were less likely to pass mandatory helmet laws than the more populated states in warmer climates. As a result, once statistical controls for these two variables were imposed, the initial significant difference between helmet laws and motorcycle fatalities disappeared.

going back several centuries (Beattie, 1975; Weiner, 1975; Cockburn, 1977). Then, as now, offenders were shown to be predominantly males in their teens and twenties. Another example of historical archival data was a study of out-of-wedlock births in Sweden covering more than a century surrounding the 1700s (Sundin, 1992). Careful analysis revealed that the rate of such births rose and fell in concert with prosecutions for extramarital and premarital sexual behavior. Years when prosecutions were high tended to be followed by declines in out-of-wedlock births.

As one can see, many intriguing topics can be addressed with data that have already been collected. This is especially the case for criminological and criminal justice research; all law enforcement agencies keep records of those coming into contact with the criminal justice system. With the ever increasing availability of large archival data sets, one might wonder why social scientists even bother to collect any more of their own original data. Although some social scientists have become specialists in secondary analyses, most still prefer to tailor data collection for specific purposes. It is not often that researchers can find previously collected data sets measuring all the variables that they want to study. A major advantage of secondary analyses of archival data is that they often allow researchers to conduct scientific study in a matter of a few weeks, often using sample sizes in the thousands. A major disadvantage, however, is that the variables you are interested in studying may not have been collected or, if collected, may not have been measured appropriately for your analytic purposes.

Analyzing Cross-Cultural Atlases

Ethnographic observations were a major topic of coverage in the preceding chapter. Here, this topic is elaborated upon by noting that hundreds of individual ethnographic accounts have been assembled into large data banks for anthropologists and other social scientists to analyze. The most extensive versions of this cross-cultural data bank are called the **Human Relations Area Files (HRAF)**, the **Atlas of World Cultures**, and the **Ethnographic Atlas**. The latter term will be used here to refer to all three of these virtually identical data banks. The Ethnographic Atlas was first compiled for widespread use in the 1950s and 1960s by anthropologist George Murdock (1957, 1967; Murdock & White, 1969).

Murdock's interests in cross-cultural comparisons led him to set up a central repository for such data that was eventually made available for use by the social science community at large. By the 1960s, studies based on the Ethnographic Atlas began to appear in a variety of journals. These included a study that found people living in foraging societies were more likely to form monogamous marriages than those living in agrarian societies, where polygamy was considerably more prevalent (Nimkoff & Middleton, 1960). More recently, the Ethnographic Atlas has been the basis for studying cultural patterns associated with the prevalence of war (Ross, 1986), of rape (Palmer, 1989), and of varying marriage customs (Cowlishaw & Mace, 1996).

The societies/cultures covered by the Ethnographic Atlas are largely prestate, meaning that they consist of bands, villages, and communities with populations of less than a million. Large nation states, such as those encompassed by modern industrialized countries, are too diverse both ethnically and culturally to be part of the Ethnographic Atlas. Until the 1990s, the Ethnographic Atlas was available mainly in large university libraries in paper form or on microfiche (Murdock, 1981; Ember & Ember, 1988). Since the 1990s, the Ethnographic Atlas has been available online (Ferraro, 1992).

Some questions have been raised regarding the reliability of the Ethnographic Atlas, based in large part upon the accuracy of some ethnographic accounts. In other words, if unknown numbers of ethnographic accounts are unreliable, using them as a basis for building a worldwide atlas will only compound the problem (Burton & White, 1987; Ferraro, 1992). Another concern about the Ethnographic Atlas is that because there is no clear definition of what constitutes "a culture," many of the ethnographic accounts are of substantially overlapping populations of people (Cowlishaw & Mace, 1996).

Despite these problems and limitations, cross-cultural studies based on the Ethnographic Atlas have provided anthropologists and other social scientists with many important insights into both the similarity and the differences between humans living in vastly different cultures and time frames.

Review Articles and Meta-Analyses

In areas that have witnessed considerable research activity, one occasionally encounters articles (and sometimes books) that are exclusively devoted to drawing together all that has been learned up to the time the article was written. These documents are called **review articles**. Most review articles follow no specific format in terms of structure or design, although the researchers who write them are expected to have a fundamental grasp of the research in the field being reviewed and to summarize the essential knowledge clearly and objectively.

A special type of review article, called a **meta-analysis**, does conform to fairly specific rules of a statistical nature. The prefix *meta* means above or over. Accordingly, a meta-analysis is undertaken to consolidate the findings from a large number of related studies on some specific topic. Unlike research reports that simply review the literature on some topic, a meta-analysis follows procedures that help to "standardize" findings from diverse individual studies to some common statistical test (Top, 1991; Wells & Rankin, 1991).

Meta-analyses treat the studies being reviewed as if findings from each individual study were data—a sort of "studies of studies," if you will (Quinsey et al., 1993:520). The first researcher to undertake and name a meta-analysis was an American educator named **Gene Glass** (1976). A meta-analysis can be thought of as a "statistically based literature review." In a meta-analysis, the finding from each individual study is pooled with findings from similar studies, with each study usually weighted according to its particular sample size. In other words, when meta-analyzed, findings from a study based on 200 subjects would be weighted twice as heavily as a study based on 100 subjects.

Effect Size and Standardized Measurement

A concept that has come to be central to meta-analyses is called **effect size** (Mann, 1990; Bonta et al., 1998). One can conceptualize effect size by imagining that 20 studies have been conducted over the years on some important topic. At the point of conducting a meta-analysis of these 20 studies, all of the subjects are essentially pooled into one gigantic sample, thereby minimizing the risk of making either a type I or a type II error. In other words, with all the subjects from these 20 studies consolidated into a single "mega-sample," one can assume that the final pool will be much more representative of whatever is being assessed or compared than is true for any one of the individual samples used in each study.

So, if males and females were being compared in these 20 individual studies, it is likely that not all of their conclusions will agree. Suppose, for example, that one of the 20 studies found females receiving 12 months less in prison on average, while at the other extreme, one study found males receiving 6 months less in prison on average than females. In the meta-analysis of these 20 studies with all of the subjects pooled, the final result might be that females received 5 months less than males in prison on average. Presumably, this 5-month difference is closer to the "real" difference than is any difference revealed by any one of the individual studies. If so, the concept of **statistical significance** is no longer at issue in a meta-analysis; only the effect size is at issue. In other words, the effect size of 5 months is considered an approximation of the "real" difference in the sex comparison under study.

Even when studies pertain to the same phenomenon, it is common to find different scales being employed to measure that phenomenon. For example, some of the 20 hypothetical studies might be lacking one or more of the variables that most of the studies utilized. Fortunately, most studies using similar methodologies and data sets can be reviewed by looking at standardized scores—for instance, means and standard deviations. Making such conversions is a common practice in meta-analyses. As a result, effect sizes are typically expressed in terms of means and standard deviations (or their statistical derivatives) rather than in terms of actual scores.

Topics Covered by Meta-Analyses

Meta-analyses have become very popular in recent years in the social sciences and in criminal justice as the number of studies on the varying topics has increased substantially. Although there is no absolute minimum number of studies that can be subjected to a meta-analysis, few have ever been performed on fewer than 10 individual studies. Locating all (or nearly all) of the individual studies on a given topic has been made possible in recent decades as computerized searching capabilities of online journal databases have become available to researchers.

Many interesting topics have been covered by meta-analyses since the 1980s. These include the effects of divorce on the behavior problems of children, factors that best predict criminality or recidivism, and the nature of the relationship between test anxiety and performance on tests. For example, three independent meta-analyses were published on the issue of the effects of video games on subsequent "real world" aggression. Two reviews concluded that there appeared to be a slight, but measurable, positive effect (Anderson, 2001; Sherry, 2001). The third controlled for publication bias and concluded no support for the hypothesis that violent video games were associated with increased aggression (Ferguson, 2007). One type of question that has been the focus of numerous meta-analyses is that surrounding sex differences in behavior. Why would so many meta-analyses pertain to sex differences? No doubt, part of the answer is that researchers have been keenly interested in how men and women differ in their behavior. An additional reason may be that sex is an easy-to-measure variable, and many studies provide data on sex differences even when these studies were undertaken to address other issues.

For instance, since the mid-1980s, the number of females under supervision of the criminal justice system has increased rapidly (The Sentencing Project, 2007). Scholars have cited changing sentencing practices and the war on drugs as the primary drivers of the increased number of females in jail, in prison, and on probation (Chesney-Lind & Pasko, 2012). As such, researchers have been interested in the effects of sex on sentencing decisions, and there have been many studies examining this issue (Daly & Bordt, 1995). For example, researchers used meta-analysis to examine more than 40 different studies of sentencing practices published from 1960 to 1990 and concluded that the majority reveal females received more lenient treatment than males, all else being equal. Another meta-analysis looking to expand on Daly & Bordt's (1995) study of the effects of sex on sentencing severity included 58 studies published between 1991 and 2011; they concluded similarly that 65% of the studies revealed more lenient treatment of female offenders than their male counterparts (Bontrager, Barrick, & Stupi, 2013).

Vote-Counting Meta-Analyses

In the broad sense of the term, two types of meta-analysis can be identified: the one most widely used (called the **effect size meta-analysis**) and the one less often used, called a **vote-counting** (or **ballot box**) **meta-analysis** (Mayer et al., 1986; Mulvey et al., 1993). With the vote-counting method, one summarizes the results from numerous studies on some specific topic simply by showing how many significant and nonsignificant findings exist.

An example of the vote-counting meta-analysis is one undertaken by one of the authors of this text in conjunction with a former student to address a contentious issue in criminology: Is delinquent/criminal behavior related to social status (social class)? To shed light on this question, we scoured the published literature and located 273 relevant studies conducted all over the world (Ellis & McDonald, 2001). The results of these studies were summarized in two tables: one pertaining to an individual's social status and the other having to do with one's family (background) social status. Abbreviated versions of these two tables appear in Table 12.2 and Table 12.3, each of which provides a summary of how different types and measures of offending are related to social status.

In the case of individual social status (Table 12.2), one can see that nearly all of the evidence is consistent with the conclusion that crime, especially crime of a violent nature, is more common in the lower than in the upper social strata. Most of the exceptions to the tendency for offenders to be of low social status were studies based on self-reported illegal drug use, where no significant social status differences were detected (shown in the last two columns of the table).

TABLE 12.2 The Number of Studies Finding a Significant Positive or Negative Relationship between Individual Social Status and Involvement in Criminal/Antisocial Behavior or No Significant Relationship

| Nature of the Relationship | Type and Seriousness of Offenses | | | | | | Self-Reported Offenses | |
| | Official Statistics | | | | | | | |
	Violent offenses	Property offenses	Drug offenses	Delin-quency	General offenses	Recidivism	Overall offending	Illegal drug use
Negative	19	1	—	8	23	7	6	5
Not Significant	—	—	—	1	—	1	1	4
Positive	—	—	—	—	—	—	—	—

When the focus shifted from an individual's own social status to that of his or her parents, a rather different pattern emerged (Table 12.3), especially in the case of self-reported offending. Most remarkably, notice in the last column that 18 of the 29 studies of self-reported illegal drug use found a significant positive correlation and that none found a significant negative correlation. Several factors may help to explain why illegal drug use (usually marijuana) would be higher in the upper than in the lower social strata. Nonetheless, this distinct tendency has been the primary basis on which several criminologists in recent decades have questioned the idea that criminality is primarily a lower class phenomena (Tittle et al., 1978; Tittle & Meier, 1990). Basically, this vote-counting meta-analysis suggested that in the case of serious and persistent offending, there is a negative correlation between social status, while in the case of minor drug offenses, there may actually be the reverse pattern (Ellis & McDonald, 2001).

The main advantage of the vote-counting meta-analysis relative to the more widely used effect size method is simplicity plus the fact that it provides an easy-to-interpret visual picture of the collective findings from all of the studies. The main advantage of the effect size method is that it gives weight to each study according to the sample size used (while the vote-counting method treats each study equally regardless of sample size). In addition, unlike the vote-counting method the effect size method yields a final numerical estimate of the magnitude of any difference (or any relationship).

Pros and Cons of Meta-Analyses

Meta-analyses have become popular in the social sciences since the 1980s (Guzzo et al., 1987). Although popular and informative, meta-analyses are not above criticism. One criticism is that the conclusions reached from a meta-analysis can often be substantially altered by simply changing one or more of the criteria used to include/exclude studies from the final pool of those to be analyzed (Chalmers, 1989).

Another criticism is that in the interest of "objectivity," many researchers who perform meta-analyses pass few judgments about the "quality" of the studies being analyzed. This can allow numerous poorly designed studies to swamp a few well-designed studies, especially if the poorly designed ones happened to have the largest sample sizes (Wachter, 1988).

Sound advice to anyone who decides to undertake a meta-analysis for the first time would be to consult at least one of the manuals currently available (e.g., Card, 2012; Borenstein et al., 2009). It is also a good idea to locate one or two similar meta-analyses already published. Overall, it seems best for researchers to continue writing both conventional narrative reviews of the literature along with meta-analyses. When they agree with one another, one can be doubly confident that the conclusions are well established. On points of disagreement, researchers can then scrutinize any contentious results on a case-by-case basis and thereby identify where new individual studies are

TABLE 12.3 The Number of Studies Finding a Significant Positive or Negative Relationship between Parental Social Status and Involvement in Criminal/Antisocial Behavior or No Significant Relationship

| Nature of the Relationship | Type and Seriousness of Offenses | | | | | | Self-Reported Offenses | |
| | Official Statistics | | | | | | | |
	Violent offenses	Property offenses	Drug offenses	Delin-quency	General offenses	Recidivism	Overall offending	Illegal drug use
Negative	3	—	—	69	14	4	48	—
Not Significant	—	—	—	9	2	2	44	11
Positive	—	—	—	2	—	1	13	18

still needed. Thus, although a meta-analysis is not an end-all to scientific research on a topic, it is still a very powerful tool in the researcher's arsenal for extracting nature's secrets.

Conceptualizing Evaluation Research

In the early 1970s, a program for curbing juvenile delinquency was initiated in a prison in Rahway, New Jersey. This program came to be known as Scared Straight. It received much publicity and inspired similar programs in many other states (Miller & Hoelter, 1979) and even other countries (Homant & Osowski, 1982; Lewis, 1983). Scared Straight targets first-time nonviolent offenders in their early-to-mid teens (Finckenauer, 1982). The rationale behind the program is that many delinquents are oblivious to the severe legal consequences awaiting persistent criminal conduct. And, perhaps these consequences can be made clearer if young offenders visit an adult prison and receive a down-to-earth talk from inmates about what life is like behind bars.

In the typical Scared Straight program, 15 to 20 young delinquents board a bus and are driven to a maximum security prison. For an hour or so in the morning, they get a fairly standard tour of the prison. After lunch, the youth are taken to a room where they are confronted by 4 or 5 shouting, cursing prison inmates chosen for their no-nonsense attitudes and for their skills in describing the brutal realities of prison life (Lundman, 1984; Waters & Wilson, 1979). The couple of hours with the inmates typically end with stern warnings from the inmates that the youngsters themselves can expect to be behind bars in a few more years unless they change their ways. It is common for the youngsters, clowning and jovial in the morning, to be sobbing before the session with the inmates is over.

Does the Scared Straight program work? An American television documentary hailed it as "90% successful" and showed that most of the participating young believed that the experience made a big difference in their lives (Waters & Wilson, 1979; Rice, 1980). This type of anecdotal evidence is known as **testimonial evidence**, i.e., evidence based on impressionistic statements made by people closely associated with a program or treatment strategy.

Although certainly worth noting, especially in the initial stages of a program's evaluation, testimonial evidence can be unreliable and sometimes very misleading (Dewsbury, 1984). Why? Not only are there no control subjects in testimonial evidence, but the participants in treatment programs often give favorable opinions even when the programs are shown in scientific terms to be ineffective (Peele, 1983). Furthermore, for programs designed to reform delinquents, enthusiasm about whatever treatment is being administered is one of the criteria used by corrections officials to decide those ready for release. Sensing that this is part of the game that must be played, participants in Scared Straight could be misleading officials and even themselves about the program's effectiveness.

BOX 12.2 WHAT DO YOU THINK?

How Can We Find Out If Scared Straight Really Works?

Before describing findings from the research on Scared Straight, stop for a moment and think about how to objectively answer the following question: Does Scared Straight work? First, one must define what "work" means in a way that can be measured objectively. In this regard, most people agree that the main goal of correctional treatment is to reduce subsequent arrests following prison release (Petersilia & Turner, 1991). Therefore, rearrest rates of the juveniles who went through the Scared Straight program could be used to operationalize "work."

The next major step might be to find a sizable number of delinquents and randomly assign half of them to a Scared Straight experience and the other half to some sort of control condition (e.g., take them fishing for a day). If random assignment is not possible, one might use a quasi-experimental design involving two carefully matched groups of delinquents.

Many studies of the Scared Straight program have been conducted. One of these studies reported that participants had significantly lower rearrest rates than a comparison group (Langer, 1981). A second study found no difference between the exposure and comparison groups (Vreeland, 1981). A third reported significantly higher rearrest rates among the youths with the Scared Straight experience compared to those without it (Finkenauer, 1982). In a fourth study, results were presented separately by sex. For females, no significant effects were detected, while males with the Scared Straight experience had significantly higher rearrest rates than those without the experience (Buckner & Chesney-Lind, 1983).

The remaining two studies of Scared Straight involved after-only experimental designs. One study made its assessment after a 6-month follow-up (Yarborough, 1979) and the other after 12 months (Lewis, 1983). Both studies found no significant differences in overall recidivism rates between the experimentals and the controls. In summary, only 1 of the 6 studies of the effects of Scared Straight found the program to be effective in reducing recidivism rates. Additional research may still be worth undertaking, but at this point most scientific evidence does not support the view that Scared Straight reduces the probability of subsequent rearrest (McCord, 1992). Notice that this conclusion stands in stark contrast to nearly all of the anecdotal evidence.

How could these results have occurred given that testimonial evidence clearly showed Scared Straight was a success? Scientific literature contains numerous examples of empirical research confirming anecdotal impressions, but in the case of Scared Straight the bulk of the scientific evidence is contrary to all the impressions of its effectiveness in reducing future offending among participants. This is likely because the program had an immediate effect on the juveniles who went through the experience, but the effects of these programs tend to wear off over time. Evaluation research usually attempts to study effects of criminal justice programs over time because we know that as the amount of time passes since programming, the likelihood of recidivism increases. So some programs such as Scared Straight might have short-term effects that lower the likelihood of reoffense, the long-term effects may not be as pronounced, and the effects of the program diminish or may even have the opposite effect of what was intended. With this well-known example as a backdrop, it is useful to make a distinction between two types of research.

Evaluation research is concerned with empirically documenting that programs designed to create change actually do so. In criminal justice, this means that (a) some sort of human problem is identified, (b) a remedial program is conceptualized and then implemented to deal with the problem, and (c) an assessment is made as to whether the program accomplished its goal of reducing the problem.

Nearly all evaluation research attempts to answer causal questions. The best way to answer causal questions is through the use of controlled experiments. Thus, the "gold standard" for conducting an evaluation of the effectiveness of a program undertaken to alleviate a human problem is controlled experimentation (Sheldon & Parke, 1975; Glaser, 1978). The essential features of the program become the independent variable, and the hoped-for outcome constitutes the dependent variable. If controlled experimentation is not feasible, researchers then typically fall back on some sort of quasi-experimental design.

Terminology Surrounding Evaluation Research

Fundamental to the concept of **evaluation research** is the distinction between basic and applied research. **Basic** (or **pure**) **research** is undertaken to expand scientific knowledge in some area, often with no practical goal. **Applied research**, on the other hand, is for the purpose of finding solutions to an identifiable problem (Rossi & Freeman, 1989). As a major type of applied research, evaluation research is designed to assess how well a particular program designed to help alleviate an identified problem actually accomplishes its objective. The research on the effectiveness of the Scared Straight program for reducing reoffending among delinquents would be an example of evaluation research.

Although the distinction between applied and basic research is worth making, two reasons exist for recognizing that the distinction can sometimes be blurred. First, some research serves both practical and pure objectives and thus can fit into either category (Rossi & Freeman, 1989). Second, much of today's applied research is built on the foundations laid years earlier by basic research.

In program evaluation, research subjects are often referred to by other names such as clients, patients, or program participants. This renaming reflects the emphasis on a helping orientation of programs that are subjected to evaluation rather than an emphasis purely on expanding scientific understanding.

Types of Applied Research

Applied research is divided into three categories: epidemiological (or diagnostic), feasibility, and evaluation. Each is described here.

Epidemiological research assesses the prevalence of a problem. It typically consists of a survey based on a representative (or near-representative) sample that allows a researcher to estimate the proportion of a population that exhibits the problem. This may also be referred to as a needs assessment. In clinical settings, the equivalent of epidemiological research is called **diagnostic research**.

For example, many children born to mothers who consume even moderate amounts of alcohol during pregnancy have been shown to suffer major physical and neurological damage (Abel, 1984: Fried, 1984; Rosett & Weiner, 1984). As part of public health efforts to reduce alcohol drinking during pregnancy, epidemiological surveys have now been conducted in several countries to estimate the extent to which pregnant women drink and to identify women with the greatest need for intervention (Moss & Hensleigh, 1988; Rubin et al., 1988). Diagnostic research may also be used to assess the prevalence of a particular problematic behavior in the population.

The findings from epidemiological research can be used in at least four ways. First, it can help determine the full extent to which a prevention or treatment program is needed. Second, such research can help identify subpopulations that are most in need of intervention. Third, it can help researchers identify some causes of the problem and thereby devise the most effective remedies. And, fourth, when repeated over several time frames, epidemiological research can help determine the extent to which a remedial program was successful.

Feasibility research provides estimates of the time, effort, and expense involved in producing changes in whatever problems have been identified. Like epidemiological research, feasibility research often involves surveying a population. (Sometimes epidemiological and feasibility surveys are conducted together.) Feasibility research pieces together cost estimates of various courses of action and the expected benefits. This research often includes recommendations regarding the facilities and personnel that will be required to combat the problem targeted for remedy. A great many of these have been conducted to examine whether some of the public policies enacted for the betterment of society or for deterring potential offenders are cost effective ways to attempt to prevent criminal or delinquent behavior: for example, a job training program for recently released jail inmates.

Evaluation (or **evaluative**) **research** assesses the effectiveness of programs intended to alleviate social, health, or interpersonal problems. Evaluation research has been used in criminal justice on the numerous programs that have been set up to rehabilitate offenders as part of their punishment or as after-care.

⬥ Process and Impact Evaluation Research

Evaluation research may be either of a process or an impact nature (Card et al., 1992; Aultman-Bettridge, 1998). **Process** (or **ongoing**) **evaluation research** is concerned with how well a program functions. As a program functions over time, and information is accumulated regarding its effects, those administrating the program can make changes with an eye toward continual improvement.

Impact (or **summative**) **evaluation research** is applied not to continually functioning programs but to ones that have designated end points. For example, studies of the effectiveness of Scared Straight would constitute impact evaluation research. This is because each group of youth who visit the prison (or a control condition) can be independently studied. To assess such programs, researchers stipulate an objective for the program and then collect evidence as to whether such a goal had in fact been reached.

The essential difference between process evaluation research and impact evaluation research is this: The former is ongoing, and thus program assessments must be made while the program is continuing to function. Often in process evaluation research, an assessment will be made as the program functions, some adjustments are made in the program to hopefully improve it, and then at some later time, an additional round of assessments and adjustments occur. Because of the continuation of process evaluations over time, plus the fact that there is rarely a control program for comparison, the most common design is some sort of before-after, no control group design.

Impact evaluations, on the other hand, can be carried out with a wider variety of experimental and quasi-experimental design forms. For example, a study was undertaken to determine how well a welfare program for adolescent mothers with dependent children helped the mothers' transition to self-sufficiency (Lie & Moroney, 1992). This study used a classical experimental design in which mothers in the experimental group received intensive social work services and a group of control mothers received the typical amount of services. At a 2-year follow-up, significantly more experimental mothers were self-sufficient relative to the control mothers.

⊖ History of Evaluation Research

With isolated exceptions, evaluation research first began to appear in the social sciences in the 1950s (Rossi & Freeman, 1989:23). At least three unrelated events gave impetus to its emergence. They are as follows:

> One event was the publication of a review article in the 1950s by an English psychologist, **Hans Eysenck** (1952). A storm of controversy surrounded the article's suggestion that psychotherapy, which at the time was the most widely used treatment for mental illness, might have few or no beneficial effects (Barlow & Hersen, 1984). Eysenck reached two conclusions: First, despite the widespread use of psychotherapy throughout the first half of the 20th century, very little was known from a scientific standpoint about its effects. Second, what could be gleaned from the available research was that psychotherapy had few beneficial effects, except possibly for persons with the least serious forms of mental disturbances. These issues, incidentally, continue to be debated in the scientific literature (Brown, 1987; Elson, 1992).

Eysenck's conclusions were criticized in part because of the wide diversity of therapies that he and others subsumed under the category of psychotherapy (Kazdin, 1989). Critics also contended that the unfavorable scientific results could reflect more about the quality of the research than about the ineffective psychotherapy (reviewed by Barlow & Hersen, 1984). Nevertheless, more recent reviews have also concluded that the evidence is still not strong in support of claims that psychotherapy by itself has significant beneficial effects on serious forms of mental illness (Elson, 1992; Seligman, 1995).

The second event that helped bring about an increase in evaluation research was the behaviorist movement, which first began with psychology in the 1920s. **Behaviorism** is an approach to the study of behavior that focuses on observable and measurable aspects of behavior rather than on the subjective and mental aspects (Griffin, 1985; Cooper, Heron, & Herward, 1987). Most research conducted by behaviorists during the 1930s and 1940s involved recording simple behavior patterns by laboratory animals, such as lever-press in order to obtain a food pellet (Skinner, 1966). The emphasis placed on careful measurement of individual behavior became a hallmark of behaviorism (Barlow & Hersen, 1984).

Over the next couple of decades, behaviorists moved much of their research out of animal laboratories and into clinical practice, with treatments for such things as phobias and childhood behavior problems (Cooper et al., 1987). Behaviorists maintained their emphasis on careful measurement along with an insistence on documenting any claims that a particular form of treatment was effective. This type of emphasis was still fairly new to clinical practice in the social/behavioral sciences. Behaviorism heavily influenced many aspects of social learning theories that are popular in criminology today in attempting to explain criminal behavior.

In the 1960s, a major boom to evaluation research occurred in the United States when the Kennedy and Johnson administrations declared "war on poverty" and various related social problems (e.g., crime, teenage pregnancy) (Rossi & Freeman, 1989; Coleman, 1990).

Funding for these programs was usually dispensed to governmental agencies or to nonprofit organizations in the form of grants. As part of the application process, applicants had to carefully describe their program as well as how the program's effects, if there were any, would be measured. Though many of the evaluations were anecdotal or impressionistic, others were based on rigorous experimental designs in which the dependent variables were carefully measured (Dixon & Wright, 1975).

Most of the programs initiated in the 1960s were disappointing in terms of their impact on America's social problems (Sheldon & Parke, 1975; Rossi et al., 1978). As a result, many social scientists found themselves rethinking many of the theories on which these proposals were based (Alexander, 1972; Etzioni, 1973, 1977).

Types of Programs Evaluated

The types of programs subjected to evaluation research in the social sciences may be divided into three fairly distinct categories. These are prevention programs, treatment programs, and improvement-oriented programs. Because the research designs used in assessing these three types of programs are often different, each is discussed separately here.

Evaluation of Prevention Program

Prevention programs, of course, are designed to prevent some type of problem from developing or at least from becoming worse. Most of the programs targeted by social scientists for prevention have to do with various social or mental health problems such as poverty, crime, drug addiction, interpersonal conflicts, and emotional difficulties.

Two types of prevention programs are generally recognized: primary and secondary. **Primary prevention programs** are those aimed fairly indiscriminately at some population, whereas **secondary prevention programs** are more narrowly focused with respect to a high-risk population. To make this distinction more clear, suppose a program planner wanted to prevent teenagers from smoking. If he or she approached this goal by targeting all teens in a high school district, the approach would be termed primary prevention. However, if the planner targeted only teenagers who were at the highest risk of becoming smokers, such as those doing poorly in school and/or those whose parents smoke, the program would be termed secondary prevention. As readers might suspect, there are prevention programs that do not easily fit either of these conceptual categories. Nonetheless, the distinction is still a useful one to make.

Examples of primary prevention programs that have been subjected to scientific evaluation as to their effectiveness include television advertising campaigns designed to discourage youth from smoking or from using illegal drugs. Other examples come from research on programs intended to improve public safety. These include studies undertaken to determine the effects of raising and lowering the legal drinking age (Smith & Burvill, 1986), of varying the penalties for drunk driving (Ross et al., 1982; Ross, 1984; Forcier et al., 1986), and of mandating seat belt usage (Conybeare, 1980).

As with all evaluation research, the ideal design for assessing the effectiveness of prevention programs is some type of controlled experiment. Nevertheless, it is often necessary to make design compromises due to ethical, financial, or time considerations. Thus, quasi-experimental designs are used fairly often in evaluating prevention programs (Peterson & Remington, 1989).

> Examples of prevention programs of a secondary nature that have been evaluated using various experimental or quasi-experimental designs include those designed to deal with several forms of delinquency and criminality. For example, a study by Powers and Anglin (1993) examined methadone

maintenance clinics and reduction of crime among heroin addicts. Others studied whether Big Brother and Big Sister programs were effective at reducing drug use and truancy in juveniles (Grossman & Tierney, 1998) or whether a community-based substance abuse treatment program was effective at reducing recidivism among drug users (Farabee et al., 2001; Listwan et al., 2009).

Evaluation of Treatment Programs

Programs tailored to help people recover from an illness or overcome a problem are called treatment programs. Such programs can be administered to single individuals or to groups of individuals, all of whom have the same basic problem. Treatment programs that are most closely related to the social sciences are ones designed to help those with mental illness, criminality, drug dependency, poverty, and interpersonal difficulties including marital and family discord.

It goes without saying that not all programs designed to alleviate problems actually accomplish their intended goal. It fact, it may well be that the majority of treatment programs have no beneficial effects. In any case, as with prevention programs, decisions about whether or not a treatment program actually works should be based on some sort of objective measure of the dependent variable rather than on anecdotal testimonials or the good will and enthusiasm of those who designed and administered the program.

An example of a treatment program was the one discussed earlier in this chapter—Scared Straight. Notice that this program had much to be said on its behalf, including common sense (i.e., Why *shouldn't* it work?). Nevertheless, when Scared Straight was subjected to the unflinching scrutiny of evaluation research, nearly all of the evidence cast serious doubt on its ability to reduce subsequent delinquency among youth who had already gotten into legal trouble. Many types of treatment programs have been evaluated scientifically, especially in the fields of psychology, criminal justice, and social work; in criminal justice, many of these have been designed to evaluate substance abuse treatment programs as to their effects on substance abuse as well as recidivism (Hillhouse & Fiorentine, 2001). In fact, there have been so many drug treatment evaluation studies that there have now been meta-analyses of these programs' results on subsequent reoffending (Wilson, Mitchell, & MacKenzie, 2006).

Again, the best design for assessing the effectiveness of a treatment program is that of a controlled experiment. For most treatment programs, a classical design is best. In such a design, after measuring the dependent variable for randomly selected experimental and control groups, the experimental group receives exposure to a new treatment program, while the control group receives some type of conventional treatment.

Evaluation of Improvement-Oriented Programs

Evaluation research is sometimes applied to aspects of human behavior or institutional functioning for which improvement is always desired, but no specific problem has been identified. For instance, a community program designed to assist teens in getting their GED equivalent education might be interested in identifying ways of expanding outreach or reducing costs of the program even if the organization had great success in achieving its goals in recent years. Improvement-oriented evaluation research is common in the field of education, and you could state that the course evaluations you take near the end of the semester in this and other courses is a type of improvement-oriented evaluation; however, most instructors would probably question the validity of the results of these for assessing quality of instruction because scores on these evaluations tend to be correlated with student grades (Millea & Grimes, 2002) and how easy the course is as well as the instructor's popularity (Rosen, 2018) rather than quality of instruction or teaching effectiveness. Whether scientifically rigorous or not, student evaluations of instructional quality are a widely used example of evaluation research in higher education.

⊖ Locating Reports of Evaluation Research

Especially in the past 25 years, a number of journals have specialized in publishing the results of evaluation research. Nevertheless, reports of many valuable studies of evaluation programs fail to be published in conventional journals (or books). Instead, these studies are largely limited to what are called **in-house** (or **intra-agency**) **documents**. Consequently, in-house documents can be a valuable source of information about the effectiveness of many programs. Nevertheless, their marginal status as "legitimate" publications means that they have not been subjected to the normal peer-review scrutiny of articles appearing in scientific journals.

⊖ Program Evaluation: Doing It Right

Conducting an objective and meaningful program evaluation requires major commitments of time and energy. The following three steps are among the most important ones to keep in mind. First, researchers wishing to undertake a program evaluation need to become acquainted with what others working in the same or similar areas have already discovered. This means scouring libraries, surfing the web, and corresponding with agencies where prior studies might have been conducted.

Second, researchers should determine in writing the objectives of any program to be evaluated in conjunction with the program's designers and administrators, and then devise a careful plan for measuring each of those objectives. This means that program outcomes must be specific and measurable. For instance, if a program is being designed to "improve student learning," program administrators and the evaluating researchers need to agree on how such "improvements" will be objectively measured. Will the measurement be made in terms of grades, examinations, or assessments made by students?

Third, an ongoing plan for collecting the data bearing on program objectives should be devised prior to the beginning of the program. Many well-intentioned evaluation efforts have failed because collecting the data needed to objectively assess whether or not the program accomplished its intended goals began to unravel as the program got underway.

Program Evaluation: A Source of Tension

Conducting scientifically sound evaluations of programs can be challenging not just from a technical design standpoint but also because those who oversee and manage the day-to-day functioning of programs have a stake in seeing to it that the evaluations produce favorable results. Evaluators, on the other hand, need to maintain an objective impartiality in making their assessments of program effectiveness. This means that if a program does not accomplish its intended objectives, those who designed and carried out the program will need to be informed of this fact so that they can either abandon it or at least substantially modify it. Resistance to such conclusions can be substantial, especially when reputations, future funding, and even jobs are on the line (Campbell, 1969).

Some have noted that those who perform the most competent program evaluations tend to have personalities that differ substantially from the practitioners who design and manage the programs (Briar, 1980; Rothman, 1980). For this reason, some have recommended that those conducting evaluation research should never work directly for those who are managing the programs being evaluated and should even avoid sharing work space that brings them into day-to-day contact with one another (Marques et al., 1993).

Closing Thoughts about Evaluation Research

Evaluation research can be both extremely rewarding and very frustrating. Reward comes from knowing that the power of the scientific method is being harnessed to help improve the human condition. Frustration, especially in non-clinical evaluation research, can come from the difficulties experienced in securing the necessary cooperation within a large organization long enough to objectively evaluate a program. Another source of frustration is that decisions about whether to retain a program are often made without seriously considering evidence from evaluation reports (Rossi & Freeman, 1989). It should be kept in mind that agency heads and program managers often have little training in social research methods and must often make decisions on grounds having little to do with program effectiveness (Halpert, 1973).

When confronted with organizational obstacles, researchers need to remain calm and professional. The wheels of science grind slowly and finely, whereas administrative decisions often take place quickly and on the basis of very incomplete knowledge. Ultimately, researchers should remember that their main function is to provide honest and objective assessments. How those assessments are utilized is largely an administrative decision. Sometimes evaluation efforts do not have much of an impact when they first appear but may be very influential years later.

Some programs are retained far beyond the point of being cost-effective simply because of political and bureaucratic "inertia" (Arnhoff, 1975). For some of these programs, state and federal legislators have passed so-called **sunset laws**. Such laws automatically terminate the funding for programs after a specified number of years unless explicit steps are taken to maintain funding.

Social science researchers need to be cautioned against overselling the value of programs for dealing with major social problems. As noted earlier, many who proposed solutions to social problems in the 1960s lost credibility in the face of hard evidence that many of the programs instituted during those years were ineffective (Etzioni, 1973, 1977). If there is a lesson to be learned, it is that social scientists should be cautious in claiming to have solutions to the problems they study.

⊖ Summary

This chapter began by discussing the concept of units of analysis. This concept refers to the decisions of social/behavioral scientists to study human beings as individual subjects or to use some aggregated unit of analysis, such as neighborhoods, cities, or even countries.

Three categories of social science data or data analysis were discussed: archival data analysis, the Ethnographic Atlas, and meta-analysis. They share in common the fact that the researchers who conduct such research will have had little or no control over collecting the data to be used.

Most archival data were not collected with a particular research project in mind. Such data often result from the functioning of governments or large businesses or were collected for one reason but later subjected to what is called a secondary analysis. Some archival data extend back hundreds of years, such as ancient church records of births, marriages, and deaths. These are called historic archival data; records compiled over the past century or so are termed contemporary archival data.

Data used in what is variously called the Ethnographic Atlas or the Human Relations Area File (HRAF) are the result of coding from large numbers of ethnographic reports on a wide range of cultural practices and customs. These files have accumulated readings on hundreds of variables collected from relatively small nonindustrialized societies that can now be analyzed by researchers who have never visited these exotic cultures.

A meta-analysis is a "study of studies." Data used in a meta-analysis are created by converting findings from individual studies all addressing the same question into a common statistic. Then, the researcher assesses the collective picture provided by the individual studies, often describing this picture in terms of an effect size.

Applied research is research undertaken to help deal with "real world" problems. In the social sciences, most problems are of an individual, social, or health nature. The flip side of applied research is basic (or pure) research, which is undertaken to better understand a phenomenon with no immediate intention of altering it.

Three types of applied research are recognized: epidemiological, feasibility, and evaluative. Epidemiological (or diagnostic) research is undertaken to identify the extent of a problem at one or more points in time. Feasibility research is used to help develop a plan for effectively dealing with a problem. Evaluation (or evaluative) research refers to studies designed to assess how well a remedial (or treatment) program is accomplishing its intended objectives. Ideally, evaluation research is based on experimental designs, although quasi-experimental designs are also widely used.

Evaluation research can be divided into two categories: clinical and institutional. Clinical evaluation research evaluates the effectiveness of individualized treatment for persons who have voluntarily sought help. The history of clinical evaluation research can be traced back to events in the 1950s.

Methodologically, two main categories of institutional evaluation studies can be identified: process or (ongoing) and summative. Process evaluations usually involve some aspect of the continued functioning of an organization. Most process evaluation studies utilize before-after no control group experimental designs. Summative studies employ a wide range of experimental designs and are applied to programs that have a logical end point after which assessments of effectiveness are made.

Three events are associated with the emergence of evaluation research in social science. The first has to do with a widely read 1950s review article that challenged the view that scientific evidence existed to support the view that psychotherapy is effective in treating major forms of mental illness. First, this assumption was gradually replaced with more scientific and quantitative methods of assessing its effectiveness but independently and in conjunction with pharmacological treatment. Second, the behaviorist movement in the 1950s and 1960s began pushing clinical treatment in the same direction: toward more careful measurement and greater documentation of a program's effects on behavior.

Third, beginning in 1960s, two consecutive US presidential administrations (i.e., Kennedy and Johnson) sought to fund governmental programs to combat a host of social problems such as crime, illiteracy, and poverty. Funding for the functioning of these programs and provisions for documenting the effects of these programs, whether positive or negative, made program administrators accountable in ways that had never occurred before. In fact, much of the evaluation research ended up casting doubt upon the effectiveness of many, if not most, of these early programs.

Three program categories in the field of evaluation research can be identified: prevention programs, treatment programs, and improvement-oriented programs. Preventive programs are subdivided into primary and secondary prevention programs. Primary prevention has to do with population-based programs where only a small proportion of people exhibit the characteristics to be prevented. Secondary prevention targets subpopulations in which many will exhibit the characteristics to be prevented but without program exposure.

Treatment programs are aimed specifically at helping people who have the full-blown symptoms of some mental or behavioral malady. Improvement-oriented programs are geared toward improvement of behavior (e.g., teaching) or institutional functioning (e.g., serving public demands for better mail service) that are not usually in crisis but still in need of greater efficiency.

Overall, evaluation research has been popular in the social sciences since the middle of the 20th century. It is often driven not by theory and idle curiosity but by the real needs of humanity for health and comfort.

Discussion Questions

1. Define a study's units of analysis. Further, what is an ecological fallacy?
2. What are archival data, and what are some of the main sources for accessing these types of data?
3. What is a cross-cultural atlas, and what types of research are usually conducted using them?
4. What is the unit of analysis in a meta-analysis?
5. What are the main purposes of evaluation research?
6. What is the difference between primary and secondary prevention programs?

Exercises

1. Search your institution's journal databases for a meta-analytic study of a criminal justice topic. Do the authors state what criteria they used for a study to be included in their meta-analysis? What type of meta-analysis was done (vote-counting or effect size)?
2. Think of a program where you could conduct evaluation research. Do you think this program is better suited for a process or impact evaluation? Why?

Chapter 13

Univariate Statistics and the Concept of Statistical Significance

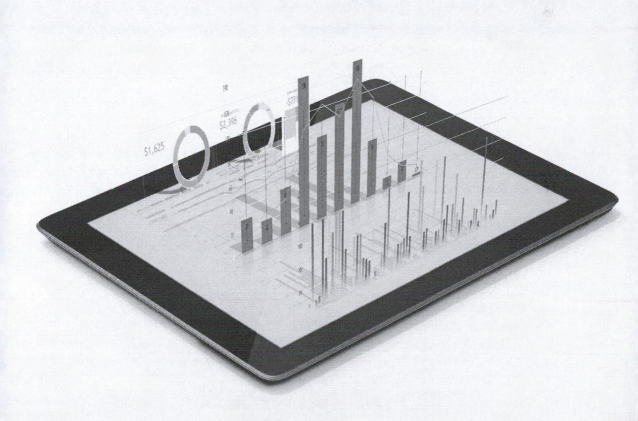

Do you know anyone with attention deficit disorder (ADD), either with hyperactivity (usually called ADHD) or without hyperactivity? Or, perhaps, it's you! In any case, according to most studies, both of these diagnoses are positively related to delinquent and criminal behavior (Ellis et al., 2019:294–296).

Of course, this is not true in any absolute sense but only in terms of statistical probability. How do scientists make such determinations? This chapter will provide a description of the normal rules that are used.

Dutch researchers recently sought to determine if recidivism (basically meaning being rearrested) was associated with both ADD and ADHD among a group of juvenile delinquents (van der Put et al., 2015). This study concluded that delinquents who had received either diagnosis were more likely to recidivate than were delinquents without ADD or ADHD. This chapter will examine the types of statistical concepts that one needs in order to draw such a conclusion.

In this chapter, you will be introduced to some of the most basic statistical concepts used by social scientists. For those who have already had a course in statistics, this chapter will build on what you have already learned. If you have not yet taken a course in statistics, this chapter will provide you with a number of concepts essential for grasping the role of statistics in social science research.

Mathematics and science are different. Science deals fundamentally with empirical phenomena (things that can be observed through the senses), while mathematics deals mainly with ideas. These mathematical ideas are mainly in the form of numbers and various ways of describing how numbers can be combined. Despite their differences, science and mathematics have become intimately linked over the past few centuries because many mathematical concepts can be useful in depicting the empirical world.

The type of mathematics that are used most in the social sciences are known as **statistics**. Statistics can be used to calculate things such averages and proportions (including percentages). It can also be used to determine how dispersed people are from whatever the averages happen to be. Finally, this chapter will discuss probabilities and how what is known as **probability theory** can be used to estimate the statistical significance of many real-world events.

⊖ The Nature of Univariate Statistical Concepts

The most basic set of statistical concepts used by social scientists is called **univariate statistics**. As the prefix *uni* implies, univariate statistics pertain to a single variable. This chapter will explore various aspects of univariate statistics. Afterward, attention will turn to understanding how scientists make judgments about the statistical significance of their findings.

Averages

Average is in the vocabulary of every English-speaking person, but many people are unaware that the term can actually have several meanings. As a result of different meanings, it is possible to be misled when discussing averages. Suppose, for example, that one is in a class of 10 students, 9 of whom are 20 years old, but the tenth student is an 80-year-old. If one were to calculate the average age by adding all of the individual ages (260) and dividing by the total number of students in class (10), the average age for students in the class would be 26. Most people would not feel quite right saying that the average age for the students in this class was 26, even though it would be technically true, at least according to one way of calculating average.

So, how do statisticians use the word? **Average** is defined as any measure of central tendency. Most measures of central tendency assume that one is dealing with interval- or ratio-level variables. In other words, it would be relatively meaningless to ask what the "average sex" or the "average religious preference" for a class is, because these are nominal variables.

To conceptualize the full range of what is meant by the word *average*, consider a simple graph, called a **frequency distribution graph**. As with nearly all graphs, a frequency distribution curve has a vertical axis (called the *y*-**axis**) and a horizontal axis (called the *x*-**axis**). The *y*-axis is used to represent the number of observations for a particular sample, and the *x*-axis is used to calibrate the variable being measured. Figure 13.1 represents a frequency distribution curve in which a special kind of curve—called a **normal** (or **bell-shaped**) **curve**—is represented.

A frequency distribution curve allows a researcher to visualize how many participants in a research study obtained each score or rating. Thus, in Figure 13.1, one can see that at point A, 75 subjects got a score of 1.5, and at point B, 125 subjects got a score of 3.3. Few frequency distribution curves have a shape that is as symmetrically shaped as this one. Nevertheless, many distributions are sufficiently close to resembling a bell shape as to warrant assuming that, if they had been based on very large samples (i.e., hundreds of thousands of subjects), they would perfectly resemble the shape of a bell. Within the context of various frequency distribution curves, three types of averages can be delineated.

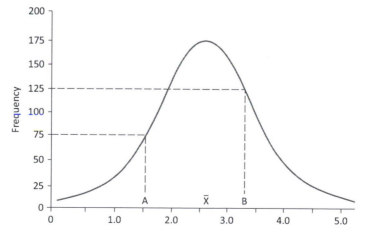

FIGURE 13.1   A Frequency Distribution Curve Based on Hypothetical Data

⬤ Measures of Central Tendency

The Mean

The type of average with which people are most familiar is called the **mean**. This type of average is defined as the result of adding up the values (or scores) pertaining to some variable for a group of subjects and then dividing the total by the number of research participants. Another name for this type of average is the **arithmetic average**. In a normal distribution (such as the one shown in Figure 13.1), the mean would be located at the highest point in the middle of the curve, directly above the X with a bar over it (sometimes the capital letter M is used to represent the mean).

The Mode

The second type of average (or measure of central tendency) is called the **mode**. Mode means "hump" or "peak." (When ordering *pie a la mode*, an individual has not asked for pie with "ice cream on top." One has literally asked for pie with "a hump on top"). The mode is defined as the most frequently observed score in a distribution curve. Obviously, for a curve that is normally distributed (as in Figure 13.1), the mode would be in the same location as the mean. So, one may wonder why there are separate concepts if the mode and the mean are in the same place. The answer is that not all distribution curves are normally distributed (bell shaped).

Look at the frequency distribution curve in Figure 13.2. This curve is said to be **bimodal** because it has two modes rather than one. Suppose a researcher conducts a survey at a strange convention of professional racehorse jockeys and basketball players. If one asks all the attendees their heights and plots the results on a frequency distribution curve, one will probably get a distribution that is bimodal.

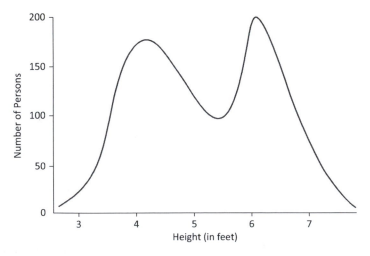

FIGURE 13.2   A Bimodal Distribution Curve Based on Hypothetical Data

If one calculates the mean height for those attending this convention, it would probably be around 5'5". Such a figure would obviously be misleading to anyone who associated "average" with what is most typical, because it is not likely that any of the attendees would be 5'5". In this case, a researcher would probably tell readers that, for this particular population, the sample was bimodally distributed, and that one mode was, say, 4'5" and the other mode was 6'2".

Although the example of a convention of racehorse jockeys and basketball players is obviously contrived, there are times when real-life variables are bimodally distributed. In the field of evolutionary biology, for example, as two new species or breeds begin to diverge from a common ancestral stock, there is often a time during the transition when some of the traits for the diverging population will take on a bimodal distribution.

The Median

The third type of average commonly recognized in science is the **median**. It is simply defined as the 50th percentile (or the midpoint) in a set of numbers that have been arranged in ascending order. More technically, the median is the point along the x-axis above and below which each half of the distribution is found. Referring back to Figure 13.1, one can see that the point above and below which half of the sample is located on the x-axis would be at exactly the same location as the mean and mode. Again, one may wonder why this third type of average is necessary. The answer is that there are certain types of distribution curves for which the concepts of the mean and the mode are not appropriate.

Figure 13.3 is an example of a distribution curve that is better described in terms of a median rather than either the mean or the mode. This curve is said to be **skewed**. Specifically, it is said to be **positively skewed**, because the *skew* (or *squished*) part of the curve is toward the higher numbers.

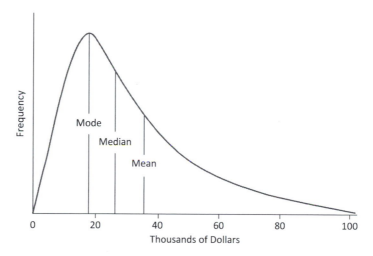

FIGURE 13.3 Positively Skewed Distribution, Which Could Represent a Hypothetical Distribution of Income in the United States

To illustrate the value of the median, think about what answer you would give to someone who asked you what the average income was for households in the United States in 2005. If Figure 13.3 was income distribution in the United States, you can see that the median income is lower than the mean income. In other words, if you add all of the household incomes (many with dual earners) and divide by the number of households (the mean), you get a higher number than the median because the incomes of a relatively few very high-income households are inflating the mean.

Alternatively, you might decide to use the mode or the peak in the income distribution to describe the average household income. Doing so would put the average even lower. The main problem with this modal income figure is that it can be highly volatile. Factors such as changes in the minimum wage and in the number of low-wage jobs can whipsaw the modal income substantially from one year to the next.

Therefore, nearly all social scientists have agreed that the best single indicator of income distributions (whether for individuals or households) is the median. This average reveals the income where half of all households in the United States earned less than and the other half earned more than this amount. Notice that the distribution curve is highly skewed.

Skewed frequency distribution curves are fairly common. Variables linked to age—such as the age distribution of persons in the workforce or of persons involved in crime—tend to be highly skewed. The length of time prisoners must spend behind bars is also nearly always skewed, i.e., most prisoners are incarcerated just 1 or 2 years; somewhat fewer serve 3 to 5 years behind bars; and very few persons get 20, 30, or even life sentences.

Measures of Dispersion

The other major feature of a frequency distribution curve is called **dispersion**. This concept refers to the degree to which scores are tightly or loosely scattered about the measure of central tendency (i.e., mean, mode, or median). Various ways of measuring dispersion have been developed, but the most widely used method is standard deviation.

Standard Deviation

For variables that are normally distributed, a useful shorthand way of describing dispersion has been devised. Because normally distributed variables are so prevalent, this standardized measure of dispersion has numerous statistical applications. To conceive of this measure, look at Figure 13.4, and imagine that it is a slippery slide and that someone is located at its summit (the mean). Notice that, as this person descends down the slope (in either direction), he or she would reach a point when the curve stops bending outward (convexed) and begins bending inward (concaved). If a vertical line were to be drawn through that point until the line intersects the x-axis, the distance between that point of intersect and the mean is called **standard deviation**.

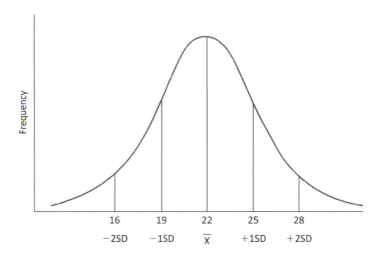

16   19   22   25   28
−2SD −1SD x̄ +1SD +2SD

FIGURE 13.4 Frequency Distribution Curve Based on Hypothetical Data

The most common symbols used to represent the standard deviation are s and SD. In statistics, there are general rules for differentiating these symbols that are not relevant to the present discussion. For this text, we will use the symbol *SD*. There are specific mathematical formulas in statistics that are used to calculate the standard deviation.

However, for purposes of this text, readers only need to have a mental picture of standard deviations. Using the numbers shown along the *x*-axis for Figure 13.4, note that the mean is at approximately 22, and the standard deviation is about 3. Thus, if you start at the mean and begin counting forward, you encounter +1SD at 25, +2SD at 28, etc. Similarly, counting back from the mean (i.e., to the left), one encounters –1SD at 19, –2SD at 16, etc.

To understand the power of standard deviation in conjunction with the mean, one should know that it is possible to construct any normal curve simply by knowing the curve's mean and standard deviation. Figure 13.5 makes this point clear. Mathematically, it has been determined that 34% (approximately one-third) of an entire population will have a score between the mean and the first standard deviation on either side of the mean. Thus, two-thirds of the scores for a normally distributed variable will fall between the first standard deviation on both sides of the mean. Close to 95% of the scores will fall within the first two standard deviations. And, for all practical purposes, all scores for a normally distributed variable are captured by three standard deviations. (Theoretically, a normal curve of distribution never intersects with the *x*-axis.)

By knowing the few numbers represented in Figure 13.5, it is possible to make several deductions about scores for a normally distributed variable by simply knowing the mean and the standard deviation. Consider the following simple illustration. Say that the mean is 30 and the standard deviation is 5 for scores on a social science exam. If 200 students took the exam, one can now estimate how many students received a score higher than 40. The answer is roughly 2% of 200, or 5. This answer is derived by inserting 30 as the mean for the normal curve and noting that 40 comes at the second positive standard deviation (because the standard deviation is 5). Because only 2.5% of the

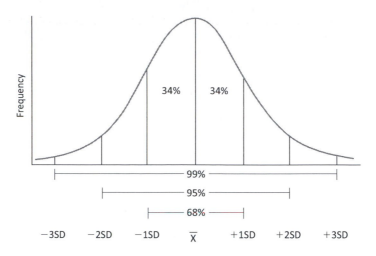

FIGURE 13.5   Frequency Distribution Curve Based on Hypothetical Data

population remains beyond the second standard deviation, one multiplies .025 times 200 students. Of course, because a variable may not be perfectly normally distributed, one may find that there are actually a few more or a few less than 5 students who got scores higher than 40.

The mean and standard deviation are fundamental concepts in the social sciences. The terms are used in most research reports. In fact, many of the much more complex statistics used in the social sciences (and the biological sciences as well) incorporate these two concepts as underlying elements.

Other Measures of Dispersion

There are other measures of dispersion that one encounters when reading research reports. One is called the **range**. If the variable is being measured at the interval or ratio level, the range is defined as the top value for a variable minus the bottom value. This simple concept of dispersion has limited utility because it is quickly altered by one unusually high or low value. Any extremely unusual score in a variable's distribution is called an **outlier**.

Another measure of dispersion is called the **variance**. It is defined as the standard deviation squared. Scientists use the concept of variance as a conservative indicator of the entire spread of a population with respect to scores on a variable. Describing the dispersion of scores for variables that are skewed, bimodally distributed, or otherwise not bell shaped is less standardized than for normally distributed variables. The most common measure of dispersion of nonnormally distributed variables divides the distribution into **quartiles**. Quartiles are calculated by arranging all the scores in order and then counting until one reaches intervals containing one-fourth, one-half, and three-fourths of the population. If this sounds reminiscent of procedures used to determine the median, it is because the median and the second quartile are the same thing, i.e., the 50th percentile. Although quartiles are a cruder measure of dispersion than standard deviation (and variance), the concept of quartiles can be applied in meaningful ways to distribution curves that do not conform to normal distributions.

Illustrating the Concepts of Averages and Dispersions

To provide you with a little practice interpreting the concepts of *mean* and *standard deviation*, consider a study conducted in Canada. It involved seeking to determine if middle school students would behave differently toward a teacher depending on how the teacher was dressed (Davis et al., 1992). All of the students sampled were boys. To make the assessment, 92 boys were shown a teacher dressed in a business suit and tie, while 92 other boys were shown the very same teacher only dressed in a T-shirt and jeans.

To measure "respect," all the boys were asked 12 specific questions about how they thought a good friend or classmate would respond to the teacher. The questions included "Would your friend do assignments given by him?" "Make smart remarks to him?" "Disrupt the class?" "Pay attention in his class?" etc. Students answered each question on a 5-point scale ranging from "definitely not" to "definitely."

In coding the questionnaires, the researchers assigned numbers from 1 to 5 to the responses (with 5 meaning the most respect); then they totaled these 12 responses for each boy as a final "index of respect." The scores on each student's respect rating ranged from a low of 12 to a high of 60. A summary of the average "respect" ratings is presented in Table 13.1.

TABLE 13.1   Respect Scores for Teacher Who Was "Formally" Attired and "Casually" Attired

	Type of Attire	
	Formal Attire	Casual Attire
Mean respect rating	36.6	33.6
Standard deviation	6.6	7.3
N	92	96

To give yourself a little practice with the concepts of means and standard deviation, try to answer the following question based on information presented in Table 13.1: *Focusing just on the casual attire rating, what percentage of students rated the casual attire with a rating greater than 41?* Here is how to make a quick estimate: If one adds one standard deviation to the mean rating, one gets 40.9, which is very close to 41. That means that 34% of the ratings will lie between 33.6 and 40.9, leaving essentially 16% of the ratings above a rating of 41.

Here are two similar questions for readers to answer. First, concerning the formal attire ratings, the top 16% of the ratings would have begun with what number? Second, the bottom 16% of the ratings would have begun with what number? (For the answers, see Note 1 at the end of this chapter.)

⊖ Building the Concept of Statistical Significance

Having become acquainted with the concepts of averages and dispersions, let us now move to the important concept of statistical significance. The value of this latter concept can be made apparent by asking the following question: What if someone asserted that the two averages presented in Table 13.1 (36.6 and 33.6) are essentially the same? In other words, they are the sort of averages that would have occurred by chance, which means that, in fact, the typical student does *not* react any differently to teachers based on how well they dress. Now, suppose that someone else makes the opposite argument, asserting that these two averages *are* obviously different from one another, and therefore one's manner of dress *does* matter. The bone of contention is this: Is it reasonable to consider a difference of 3 rating points more than would simply occur by chance?

Can the disagreement be settled peacefully? Fortunately, the answer is yes, provided that those involved are willing to agree on certain statistical principles (which nearly all social scientists do). These statistical principles have to do with what are called rules of probability. When these rules are combined in certain ways, they can be used to create a concept known as **statistical significance**. Without this simple concept, and the rules upon which it is grounded, science would be chaotic.

The Concept of Probability

There are ways to "bias" a coin so that it will fall to one side more times than to the other. For instance, the "heads" side could be made of a heavier metal than the "tails" or the edge of the coin could be beveled inward ever so slightly toward the "heads" side.

Suppose that someone gave you two coins and asked you to determine if either of them had been made in a biased fashion, but you were not allowed to actually do a physical inspection of either coin. All you could do is toss each coin 10 times. Assume you did this and got the following results:

Coin 1 = 6 heads and 4 tails

Coin 2 = 8 heads and 2 tails

Obviously, you would be more likely to suspect that coin 2 was the biased one, but how confident would (or should) you be? Statisticians have developed some basic rules that can aid your intuition.

One rule of probability is called the **multiplicative rule**. It states in part that one can multiply the probabilities of several similar individual events (like coin flipping) to derive an estimate of the probability of any combined number of those events. To illustrate, using a completely "fair coin," the probability of getting heads the first time it is tossed is 50:50 or .5, and the probability of getting heads in the second toss is also .5. So, the multiplicative rule states that the possible outcome for a two-coin toss is .5 × .5 = .25 for 2 heads, and the probability of getting one of each is .50. Using this sort of logic, one can also calculate the probability of getting 6 heads or more out of 10 tosses and 8 heads or more out of 10 tosses. For those who are curious, the answers are .2051 and .0439, respectively. The likelihood of getting 8 out of 10 heads (with a fair coin, of course) is considerably less than the likelihood of getting 6 out of 10.

Probability in a statistical sense refers to mathematical estimates of the likelihood of various events taking place. In thinking about probability, one should keep in mind that all probabilities range from 0.00 (0%) to 1.00 (100%). Also, many more complex events than coin tossing and dice rolling can be estimated using rules of probability. One of the main reasons for this is that the probability of many types of events conforms almost perfectly with normal curves of distribution (Hinkle et al., 1988).

Providing the actual mathematical proof that many statistical probabilities can be expressed as normal curves of distribution would carry us far from the focus of this chapter, so it will not be presented here. Nevertheless, for those who are still a little reluctant to believe that scientists can often use probability-based statistics to make reliable judgments of a probabilistic nature, consider the following example.

Thinking Scientifically, Thinking Statistically

Almost every conclusion reached by scientists has at least some probability of being incorrect. Scientists seek to estimate what that probability is and then attempt to keep it at a minimum when drawing conclusions. As we have just seen, it is possible to make probability estimates using some basic mathematical rules.

Because of the probabilistic nature of science, scientific writing contains few emphatic statements. Table 13.2 contains some examples of the sort of nonprobabilistic statements that rarely appear in scientific reports. Alongside these statements are similar statements that acknowledge the fact that nearly all scientific findings are tentative. This tentativeness is due not only to errors that are sometimes made in measurement but also to the fact that nearly all scientific research is based on samples, and samples do not necessarily reflect what is the case in an entire population. Often times, samples are not collected in a manner that makes them representative of the population from which they were drawn. Recall the discussion of how to obtain samples that are representative from Chapter 6.

BOX 13.1 CURRENT ISSUES

An Amazing Example of Probability in Real Life

In a room with 30 people, there is approximately a 70% chance that at least 2 of the room's occupants have the same birthday (but not necessarily the same year). Don't believe it? To get a sense of why this is true, assume we pick you and one of the other 29 persons (we will set aside leap year births for simplicity's sake). The probability that you and this person will have the same birthday is 1/365 or .0027. Actually, it is a little higher because births are concentrated in some months more than in others (Bobak, 2001).

A probability of .0027 is obviously not much of a chance, but note that both you and this other person have the same probability of matching birth dates with the remaining 28 people in the room; thus .0027 × 28 = .0810 (or 8.1%). If a third person is chosen at random, there is a .0027 × 27 probability that he or she will have the same birthday as any one of the remaining 27 people, i.e., .0729. Add this probability to .0027 and .0810, and one is now up to a probability of .1566 (or 15.66%). Then the fourth person that is chosen has a .0027 × 26 probability of having the same birthday as the remaining 26 people, and so on. When finished multiplying and adding all these probabilities, one comes to .71.

Each person added to the room beyond 30 raises the odds of matching birthdays considerably. With 60 people in the room, the chances are virtual certainty (.994), although one will not actually reach 1.00 until 366 people are in the room. To increase the odds of a match to about 90% certainty, one needs to have about 40 birthdays picked at random.

Still skeptical? Test it empirically. If there are fewer than 30 people in the room you select, have some of them throw in the birthday of their mothers to get your sample of birth dates up to at least 30. (Hint: Comparisons of birthdays can be done most quickly by asking how many were born in each month and then having those born in a given month state the actual day they were born.)

TABLE 13.2   Types of Statements Scientists Rarely and Frequently Make in Reference to Research Findings

Rare (Inappropriate) Scientific Statements	Frequent (Appropriate) Scientific Statements
Such-and-such has now been proven.	Such-and-such has a great deal of empirical support.
There is no doubt that such-and-such occurs.	There is a high probability that such-and-such occurs.
There is no reason to doubt such-and-such.	Evidence has consistently indicated such-and-such.
Such-and-such is true.	Numerous studies have found such-and-such.

In thinking about writing for a scientific audience, it is important to notice the difference between the statements in these two columns. Remember to use statements similar to those in the second column rather than those in the first.

In addition to being less emphatic, statements in the second column also direct the reader to the evidence, rather than simply to the conclusion.

Why are scientific statements so guarded and unemphatic? In part, scientific knowledge is always tentative and nearly always stated in statistical terms. As one delves deeply into most areas of science, especially social science, it is not uncommon for research findings to disagree with one another. The confusion associated with these inconsistencies is minimized when each researcher explicitly acknowledges that his or her findings are definitive and are associated with at least some probability of being incorrect (which, in fact, is always the case).

One needs to accept the fact that science creeps, rather than leaps, to "the truth." It is a grindingly slow social process, in which no single researcher simply *proves* something once and for all. When thinking and writing for scientific audiences, be careful not to overstate the weight of evidence derived from any one study. So, never say that any study you conduct proves anything to be true. Instead, you can state that your findings provide evidence *supporting* a particular conclusion.

The .05 Probability of Error and the Concept of Statistical Significance

We have now established that essentially all scientific research findings run at least some risk of being inaccurate, and we have shown that rules of probability can be used to estimate the chances of such inaccuracies. Let us now consider how much of a chance of inaccuracy should be considered acceptable, keeping in mind that a zero chance is essentially not an option.[2]

Nearly all scientists use a 5% cut-off for judging statistical significance. This means that they will consider a finding "statistically significant" if there is only a 5% chance (or less) of a finding being simply a random event, and they will not declare it significant if the probability exceeds 5%. When researchers present these probabilities in research reports, the numbers are usually expressed as decimals (e.g., .05) rather than as percentages (e.g., 5%).

Probabilities of error are often preceded with the letter p (called a **p-value**), which is followed by an equal sign (=), a greater-than sign (>) or a less-than sign (<), and then the probability estimate itself. Therefore, if one reads $p > .05$, one knows that what was reported fell short of being considered statistically significant. When reading $p < .001$, one knows that the finding was very significant, because there was less than one chance out of a thousand that its occurrence would be a statistical fluke.

Returning to the findings summarized in Table 13.1, recall that an unresolved issue was whether a mean rating of 36.3 was significantly higher than a mean of 33.6. Now for the solution: Using a statistical test that will soon be described, the researchers who conducted the study (Davis et al., 1992) determined that by declaring the two means significantly different, they risked only a 1% chance of doing so in error. Therefore, they concluded that the junior high school students gave significantly higher respect ratings to the formally attired teacher than to the casually attired teacher. Nevertheless, the differences were obviously still only modest. Thus, statistical "significance" means "reliably present" rather than "important" or "strong."

Hypothesis Testing and the Concept of the Null Hypothesis

A **hypothesis** is a tentative statement about empirical reality, which may or may not be true. A **null hypothesis** simply posits that no relationship or no difference exists in whatever is being studied. In other words, when researchers put forth a null hypothesis about two or more variables, they are hypothesizing that the variables are not related to one another or that there are no differences between two or more groups with reference to the variables under scrutiny.

The null hypothesis is usually implied rather than stated. Thus, even though a researcher does not explicitly state the null hypothesis, it looms as an implied alternative to any hypothesis that is stated. Researchers normally state and test what are called **alternative** or **research hypotheses**. These hypotheses assert that there *are* relationships or differences among whatever variables are being studied.

To illustrate the null versus the alternative hypothesis, consider a personality-attitude study (Kish & Donnenwerth, 1972). The researchers found a significant relationship between sensation seeking and dogmatism-authoritarianism for males, but not for females. What these researchers found can now be stated as follows: The null hypothesis was rejected in the case of males, but it could not be rejected for females. Because the null hypothesis is normally only implied, researchers often speak of retaining it by "failing to reject it."

Whenever an alternative to the null hypothesis is accepted, by implication, the null hypothesis is "rejected." Conversely, whenever the null hypothesis cannot be rejected, all alternative hypotheses must be rejected.

Inferential Statistics

Mathematicians (and other number-orientated intellectuals) have been toying with probability estimates for centuries (Hacking, 1991). Such tinkering is often of no practical utility because applications have been incorporated into some valuable statistical tools that social scientists often use in their research. A few of the most widely used of these statistical tools will be considered here. The statistical tools that one should be most aware of are those used for assessing statistical significance. These tools are collectively known as **inferential statistics**, because they allow researchers to make inferences about rejecting and accepting hypotheses. In this chapter, the focus will be on three of the most widely used inferential statistics: the *t*-test and ANOVA, which are used for comparing means, and chi-square, which is used for comparing proportions.

The *t*-Test: Comparing Two Means

One of the simplest and most widely used applications of mathematical probability is one called the **t-test**. It is a relatively simple test that can be used for comparing two means to determine if they can be considered significantly different from one another. The *t*-test is also occasionally referred to as **student's t**. The *t*-test was developed by a statistician named William Gosset, who worked for the Guiness Brewery in Dublin, Ireland. Brewery policy prevented him from publishing the paper introducing the *t*-test under his own name, so he published it under the pseudonym "Student."

How does the *t*-test work? As noted earlier, many probability estimates conform almost perfectly to normal curves of distribution. This makes it possible to apply these probability estimates to the study of many real-world events that also resemble normal curves of distribution. The *t*-test was developed for this purpose.

Without delving into the mathematical details, the *t*-test is relatively easy to understand. To use it, a researcher basically needs to determine the two means to be compared, their respective standard deviations (SDs), and the sample size upon which each mean and SD was based. The square root of each SD is then used to derive what is called a **standard error** of the mean (SE). An SE provides a mathematical estimate for the stability of one or both means.

One can visualize the final steps in deriving an estimate of statistical significance using a *t*-test by comparing Figures 13.6a and 13.6b. In the case of Figure 13.6a, one can see that the means are very close to each other, and that their respective SEs (represented with shading) overlap one another. Performing a *t*-test on the results of the data set shown in Figure 13.6a reveals that these two means cannot be considered significantly different from one another.

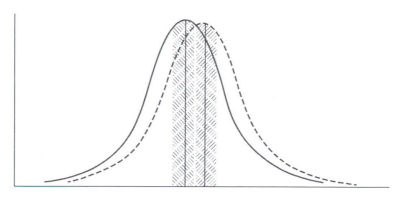

FIGURE 13.6a Two Overlapping Normal Curves That Would Not Be Considered Different to a Statistically Significant Degree According to a *t*-Test

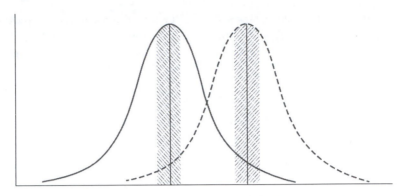

FIGURE 13.6b   Two Overlapping Normal Curves That Would Be Considered Different to a Statistically Significant Degree according to a *t*-Test

In contrast, consider Figure 13.6b. There, the reader can see that the means are much further apart, and that the SEs do not overlap. This is clear evidence that the means should be considered significantly different from each other. Without generating graphs such as those shown in Figure 13.6a, a *t*-test will yield a simple number (usually called a *t*-value), along with an associated probability that the *t*-value occurred by chance. If the *p*-value is less than .05, then the two means are declared different from one another to a statistically significant degree.

Here is an illustration of the *t*-test in action, beginning with a question. Who receives better grades in college, men or women? Over the years, several studies have investigated this question, and most have concluded that women get better grades (e.g., Summerskill & Darling, 1955; Olds & Shaver, 1980; Caldas & Bankston, 1999), although the fact that males and females gravitate toward different majors complicates making direct comparisons. To eliminate variability in sex differences in the courses taken, one can compare the grades men and women receive when taking the same course. Two US studies have compared the grades of men and women with reference to courses in introductory statistics. One study found that females obtained slightly higher grades, but not significantly so (Buck, 1985), while the other found that females received significantly higher grades than males (Brooks, 1987).

Now focus on the second of these two studies. To obtain his data, Brooks (1987) went back over the grades he had given to more than 300 students who had taken a statistics course from him over the previous 10 years. He assigned all As a 4, all Bs a 3, and so forth. The average grade for the men was 2.21, and the average grade for the women was 2.74. The question that then needs to be answered is whether these two means are different enough from one another to be considered statistically significant. Based on their respective SDs (converted to SEs) and the sample size, Brooks performed a *t*-test. The result was $t = 5.30$, $p < .001$. Guess what he concluded.

If one is following the logic so far, one will notice that the *p*-value in Brooks's study is very, very small (less than one in a thousand). This means that if Brooks were to declare the two means significantly different from one another, he would be risking less than one chance out of a thousand of doing so in error. In light of those statistical odds, one should have no doubt about what Brooks concluded regarding which sex did best in his statistics course. (In case you are curious about how to interpret the t-value itself, it can be roughly translated as stating that the two averages were 5.3 standard errors away from one another. Standard error is a concept akin to standard deviation that is explained in most statistics texts or online.)

For another illustration of the t-test, let us return one more time to the Canadian study of student ratings for teachers based on formal versus casual dress. The average differences were shown in Table 13.1, and we have already noted that the findings were considered statistically significant. Here are the actual numbers reported: $t = 2.982$, $p < .0032$. Take a moment to write out a sentence that would essentially summarize what anyone knowledgeable in inferential statistics would conclude from these numbers. (See Note 3 at the end of this chapter to check your answer.)

ANOVA: Comparing Two or More Averages

To compare more than two means at a time, another inferential statistic, called **analysis of variance** (**ANOVA**), is widely used. ANOVA is a bit more complicated mathematically, but the underlying statistical principles of probability are very similar to those developed for the t-test (Howell, 1989). Depending on the exact nature of the data being analyzed and the types of questions being addressed, there are advantages to ANOVA that will not be discussed here.

To illustrate ANOVA, consider a study undertaken by two educational psychologists to compare three different approaches to teaching artistic expression to young school children (Cox & Rowlands, 2000). The three approaches they chose to compare were a conventional one used in Canadian public grade schools and two experimental approaches, one taught according to the Montessori (1912, 1965) method and the other by the Steiner (1909/1965) method. In order to maintain our focus on how the researchers analyzed their data, we will not discuss the nature of the differences among these three educational approaches.

Two people were used to judge the quality of the artistic works created by the 60 children involved in the study (20 children having been taught by each of the three approaches). The average ratings by the two judges of each student's artistic works are presented in Table 13.3. One can see that the average rating for the artistic creations of children from one of the three approaches was rated quite a bit higher than the other two, but is the difference statistically significant?

The ANOVA statistic is expressed with the letter F; it and its accompanying p-value were as follows: $F = 6.27$, $p < .01$. Look at these numbers, and formulate in your mind what they would allow the researchers to conclude. If you are focusing on the low p-value, you are on the right track. If this number suggests to you that there is very little chance that the three means are

TABLE 13.3   Comparison of Three Different Approaches to Teaching Artistic Expression

Assessed Quality of Artistic Expression	Teaching Approaches		
	Traditional	Montessori	Steiner
Mean respect rating	2.58	2.68	3.58
Standard deviation	0.94	0.94	0.95
N	20	20	20

equivalent, you are reasoning as you should. If you conclude, therefore, that one of these means must be significantly different from one or both of the other two, your conclusion would be the same as that of the researchers who undertook the study.

There is more to the study on teaching artistic expression than the comparisons shown in Table 13.3, and questions can be raised about how comparable the three groups of children were and about the appropriateness of the ratings given by the two judges. Nevertheless, the study illustrates the essential logic of ANOVA, which has several additional elements that can be used with even more complex data.

Chi-Square: Comparing Proportions

Thus far, the concept of statistical significance has been illustrated by discussing examples in which means are compared. However, researchers sometimes want to compare proportions instead. For this task, the most widely used statistical test is one known as **chi-square** (X^2). To see how chi-square works, consider a study published quite a few years ago to determine whether people who commit suicide are more likely to do so during the full moon than during other phases of lunar cycle (Lester et al., 1969). Here is how the study was designed. The researchers used records from a New York coroner's office to determine when 399 suicides occurred relative to the four phases of the 28-day lunar cycle (each phase consisting of 7 days).

The researchers reasoned that 99.75 of these suicides would have occurred by chance during each of the four phases of the lunar cycle. They then sought to determine if more than 99.75 suicides occurred during the full moon phase of the lunar cycle. Indeed, 102 suicides occurred during that time. But, was this significantly more than one would have expected to occur by chance? To answer this question, the researchers entered their observations for the four lunar phases, along with the numbers expected by chance, into a chi-square formula. Manipulating the numbers in accordance with the formula yielded the following: $X^2 = 1.07$, df $= 2$, $p > .25$.

Had this study's researchers declared 102 significantly different from 99.75, they would have risked a 25% probability of doing so in error. This risk, of course, far exceeds the .05 error limit normally set in scientific research. Thus, the researchers concluded that there was no significant tendency for suicides to

BOX 13.2 WHAT DO YOU THINK?

Is a 5% Chance of Being Wrong Too High?

If the instructor of this course told you on the first day of class that there was a 5% chance that the course would be canceled within the first month of the semester and that if it were canceled it would be very difficult for you to enroll in another course that late in the semester, would you take your chances and stay in the course knowing that there is a small likelihood that you could wake up one morning and have an email notifying you that the course had been canceled? Most of you would probably take that risk and stay enrolled in the course.

Scientists who conduct research are not simply interested in the nature of what they find but also in whether their findings are of a sufficient magnitude to surpass what would be expected by chance. To address this important issue in an objective way, most research studies incorporate at least one inferential statistic as part of their design.

This chapter has explored three widely used inferential statistics: the t-test, analysis of variance, and chi-square. Several types of each of these inferential statistics have been developed, and there are several subtle features of each one with which readers should become acquainted. Also, there are many other types of inferential statistics that have been developed that are less commonly used, and many are considerably more complicated. You should, however, understand two important purposes of inferential statistics. First, understanding inferential statistics allows one to make sense of them when reading the numerous scientific studies in which they are utilized. Second, when thinking about designing research projects, one should always have in mind some notion of how the data will be analyzed, and nearly all studies that test hypotheses utilize some type of inferential statistic.

As an incidental note, one should know that not all social scientists are in agreement about the appropriateness of using tests of statistical significance (Berk, 2004; Falk & Greenbaum, 1995). Most of the criticisms are technical in nature and based on questions about the true randomness of most samples used in social science research (Shaver, 1992; Harris, 1997).

The bottom line of any discussion regarding a scientific finding is whether it is of sufficient magnitude to be considered significant. In order to remove potentially biased subjective judgments from the decision-making process as much as possible, the concept of statistical significance has been developed. In most cases, scientists allow themselves up to a 5% chance of making a decision in error when they declare findings significantly different from one another.[3] Now what do you think? Is it reasonable for scientists to make decisions based on a 5% chance they could be wrong? Again referring to the 5% chance of the course being canceled, most of you would probably agree that it is fairly judicious for scientists to risk no more than a 5% chance of being wrong when utilizing tests of significance.

occur more often during the full moon than during the moon's remaining three phases. (The chi-square value itself along with its associated degrees of freedom are central to the calculation of statistical significance but are not essential to the present nonstatistical discussion of chi-square.)

⬤ Summary

This chapter was written to familiarize readers with several fundamental statistical concepts in terms of how these concepts are used in scientific research, rather than in terms of their underlying mathematics. The focus was on the measurement of a single variable, and two overarching sets of concepts were also considered. The first set had to do with averages and dispersion. The second involved probability and statistical significance.

The existence of three main types of averages were noted: the mean, the median, and the mode. In the case of normally distributed variables, all three refer to exactly the same location along the x-axis of a frequency distribution curve. However, for skewed or bimodal distribution curves, types of averages can vary substantially, depending on the specific measure used.

The mean is derived by adding all the scores obtained for a variable and then dividing the sum by the number of individuals in the study. This is the preferred measure of central tendency as long as the variable under consideration is close to being normally distributed.

In the case of dispersion, the most widely used measure in the social sciences is standard deviation. Along the x-axis, the first standard deviation from the mean on each side will capture 34% of a normally distributed population. If one extends further out from the mean to the second standard deviation on both sides of the mean, one will capture 95% of a normally distributed population. Other measures of dispersion include the range and various tiles (e.g., quartiles). Variance is also a type of dispersion measure; it is mathematically defined as the standard deviation squared.

Turning to the concepts of probability and chance, the probability of anything happening ranges from .00 to 1.00. For a set of scientific observations, the lower the probability that a finding is due to chance, the more statistically significant it is said to be. Rarely will researchers declare a finding statistically significant if it has more than a .05 probability of having occurred by chance. Various statistical procedures have been developed for estimating chance probabilities associated with the comparisons of means and proportions. These procedures, collectively known as inferential statistics, are based on ingenious combinations of simple rules of probability and on the fact that probability estimates can often be represented by normal curves of distribution.

The three most widely used types of inferential statistics in the social sciences are the t-test, ANOVA (analysis of variance), and chi-square. The t-test allows researchers to estimate the likelihood that the means from two groups of subjects (or the same subjects under different conditions) can be considered different. The lower the p-value associated with this estimate, the greater the confidence researchers can have that the differences are "real." An ANOVA test functions similarly but can be used to compare several means, rather than just two. To determine if two or more proportions are significantly different from one another, the most widely used test is chi-square.

Many inferential statistical concepts cannot be given attention here. None-theless, with what has been discussed in this chapter, one should have a basic understanding of how most scientists make decisions about the statistical significance when testing hypotheses. Additional statistical concepts will be presented in the next chapter.

⊜ Discussion Questions

1. What are univariate statistics?
2. What is a frequency distribution curve, and what is special about the normal curve?
3. List and describe the three main measures of central tendency.
4. What do we mean when we say that a distribution is bimodal?
5. List and describe the main measures of dispersion.
6. Describe statistical significance and the concept of probability.
7. What is the multiplicative rule?
8. Think of an example of a research question for which you could use each of the following statistical tests: t-test, ANOVA, and chi-square.

⊜ Exercises

1. Get a quarter, toss it 10 times, and record whether it lands on heads or tails each of the 10 times. Did you get 5 heads and 5 tails? If not, toss the coin 10 more times and record the number of heads and tails. Do this three or four times, and average the numbers of heads and tails. Do you get closer to a 50–50 percentage split of heads and tails than with either of the single 10-toss trials?
2. Search for an empirical article on some topic of criminal justice in one of your institution's journal databases. Scroll to the methodology section. Do the researchers state null or research hypotheses? Do they explain why they used either null or research hypotheses?

⊜ Notes

[1] Regarding formal attire ratings, the top 16% of the ratings would begin around 43. The bottom 16% of the ratings would begin at 30.

[2] In the context of the article, "$t = 2.982, p < .0032$" would be interpreted as very significant (with only about 3/1,000 of a chance of having occurred by chance). Therefore, one can confidently conclude that high school students believe that

their fellow students assign modestly higher levels of "respect scores" to male teachers who are more formally dressed (dress shirt and tie) than more casually dressed (jeans and a T-shirt).

[3] Two concepts that are closely related to that of statistical significance are effect size and statistical power. Recall that effect size was discussed in Chapter 12 as part of a broader discussion of meta-analysis, and statistical power was dealt with in Chapter 6 when dealing with issues surrounding sample size.

Chapter 14

Bi/Multivariate Statistics: The Concept of Correlation

Is your heart rate fast, slow, or somewhere in between? Of course, most people have no idea, and, in fact, an individual's heart rate varies quite a bit, depending on such things as how much physical exercise or emotional stress

may have been recently experienced. Nonetheless, research has repeatedly shown that individuals whose heartbeats are relatively slow (under standard testing conditions) are more likely to become involved in delinquent and criminal behavior than individuals with comparatively rapid heartbeats (under the same testing conditions) (reviewed by Ellis et al., 2019:347-350). How would a researcher conduct a study to check or elaborate on this finding? The basic statistical logic (but not the actual statistical formulas) of a likely research design will be described in this chapter.

The types of statistics covered in the preceding chapter are primarily used to describe how single variables are distributed, either in one population or in two subsamples of a given population (e.g., males and females). However, sometimes researchers are interested in doing more than describing how variables are distributed. Instead, they want to know how two variables might be related to one another. For example, say you wanted to know if people with many years of education are less likely to commit crime than those with fewer years of education. Assuming that you had the necessary data, what sort of analysis could you perform to give you an objective answer? A class of statistics known as bivariate statistics can be used.

Researchers can go even further and compare three, four, or more variables at the same time. For example, a researcher might have an interest not only in how crime and years of education are related, but in how this relationship might also be correlated with income. To deal with such questions, one will usually employ what are known as multivariate statistics. In this text, we will only touch on multivariate statistics, but it is good to keep in mind that most of the principles behind multivariate statistics are akin to those used in bivariate statistics. Therefore, although this chapter will focus on bivariate statistics, most of what you learn will be applicable to multivariate statistics as well.

⊖ Background for Bivariate Statistics

In the mid-1700s, a French philosopher-mathematician named **Rene Descartes** (pronounced *da cart'*) cleverly deduced that one could describe geometric shapes with equations. This revolutionary idea helped bring about fields of mathematics such as algebra, trigonometry, and calculus. Descartes' ideas also laid some of the intellectual foundation for a type of statistic that has come to be widely used in the social sciences known as **bivariate statistics**.

Two English social scientists are credited with having applied Descartes' idea to the field of statistics. The first of these scientists was **Francis Galton**, a cousin of Charles Darwin, who had an interest in comparing traits for sets of identical twins to help assess the influence of genes on human behavior. Late in the 1800s, Galton demonstrated that these comparisons could be illustrated with graphs, but he wanted to reduce each graph down to a single number. A few years later, a friend of Galton's named **Karl Pearson** also became interested in converting graphs depicting relationships into numbers. Pearson eventually developed a formula for making the conversion. To his credit, this formula, called **Pearson's** r, is still the most widely used one in correlational statistics today.

Constructing Scattergrams

To begin exploring the concept of correlation, it is best to think about relationships between variables in graphic terms. The graphs to be considered here are called **scattergrams** (or **scatterplots**), and the sorts of variables we will confine most of our attention to will be those measured at the interval or ratio levels. To envision how scattergrams are constructed, pretend that you were desperate for something to do and decided to conduct a study to find out whether people's shoe size and age are related. Because sex is also related to shoe size, assume that you confined your study to males, and that you were very eager to know the results so you stopped collecting data after five subjects. Suppose that you got the results shown in Table 14.1.

If you were to construct a scattergram using this set of data, you would first draw the axes and assign one of the variables (shoe size) to the y-axis (vertical axis) and the other variable (age) to the x-axis (horizontal axis). Next, calibrate each axis to include the entire range of scores for the two variables. This is shown in Figure 14.1. Also shown in this graph is the data plotted with the name of each subject beside the point representing his location with reference to the two variables. (The number appearing after the "r" can be ignored for the moment. It will be explained later in this chapter.)

From this scattergram, consider the following question: Does there appear to be a relationship between shoe size and age? Hopefully, you answered "yes" because you noticed that there is a strong tendency for those who scored low on the variable of *shoe size* (Mike and Jim) to have also scored low on the variable of *age*. Likewise, those who scored high on shoe size (Dave and especially Bill) were those who scored high on age. This sort of pattern is referred to as a **positive relationship** (or a **positive correlation**). More precisely, a positive relationship is one in which increasing values of one variable are associated with increasing values of another variable.

TABLE 14.1   Results of a Silly Hypothetical Study of Shoe Size and Age

Subjects	Shoe Size	Age
Sam	8	15
Bill	13	20
Mike	5	10
Jim	5	13
Dave	10	18

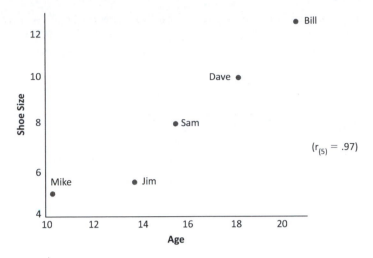

FIGURE 14.1 Scattergram Based on Five Hypothetical Observations between Shoe Size and Age

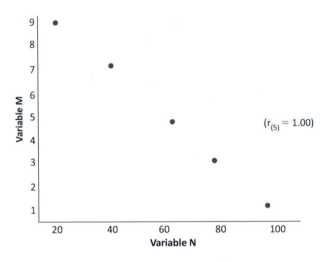

FIGURE 14.2 Scattergram Based on Five Hypothetical Observations of Scores on Variables M and N

Let us now turn to another set of hypothetical data, this time going directly to the scattergram instead of beginning with a table of numbers showing the observations themselves. Figure 14.2 represents the relationship between variable M and variable N. As with Figure 14.1, the question that should be answered after examining this graph is: Does there appear to be a relationship between these two variables? Your answer again should be "yes." However, notice that in Figure 14.2 the individuals who scored high on variable M scored low on variable N and vice versa. This relationship is said to be **negative** (or **inverse**). Stated more formally, an inverse (or negative) correlation is one in which increasing values of one variable are associated with decreasing values of the other variable.

Something else is noteworthy about Figure 14.2: All five observations fall *perfectly* along a straight line (as opposed to simply coming close as in Figure 14.1). When this occurs, the correlation is said to be perfect.

Converting Scattergrams into Correlation Coefficients

Numbers used to represent correlations are called **correlation coefficients**. The coefficient used to represent a perfect negative correlation is –1.00 and for a perfect positive correlation, a +1.00 (the plus sign is normally just understood rather than specified). As one might suspect, there are few perfect correlations in the "real world," either positive or negative.

As illustrated in Table 14.2, all correlations range from –1.00 to 1.00, with 0.00 marking the midway point. Correlation coefficients at either end are described as "perfect correlations," whereas those near zero are said to be devoid of any relationship.

Figure 14.3 shows how a scattergram would look with a set of data represented by a 0.00 correlation coefficient. The points on this graph might be compared to a shotgun blast. Notice how the scores on one variable seem to have no relationship with scores on the other variable. To keep this hypothetical example simple, the axes on Figure 14.3 have had the calibrations omitted. Instead, arrows are used to represent increasing values for variables X and Y.

TABLE 14.2 A Diagram Representing the Entire Range of Correlation Coefficients

The Full Range of Correlation Coefficients

–1.00 ««««««««««« 0.00 »»»»»»»»»»> +1.00

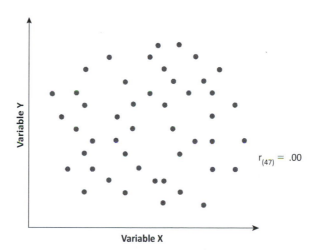

$r_{(47)} = .00$

FIGURE 14.3 Scattergram Based on 47 Hypothetical Observations of Scores on Variables X and Y

The Concept of a Regression Line

The set of points in Figure 14.3 suggests no correlation between the variables because the figure lacks a discernable regression line. A **regression line** is defined as the line that comes the closest to intersecting all the points in a scattergram. Notice that in Figures 14.1 and 14.2, one could easily approximate where the regression line would be, but in Figure 14.3, it is difficult even to decide whether the regression line should run in a positive or a negative direction.

In statistics, students learn two formulas for determining regression lines, but here it is only necessary to be able to visually estimate these lines. From this, one can estimate the numbers used to represent the configuration of points in scattergrams, as will be done in the next section.

Estimating Correlation Coefficients from Scattergrams

Although every scattergram can be represented by a correlation coefficient, the only way to determine the coefficient accurately is by a statistical formula. This text will not teach the formula, but it will teach the reader how to interpret correlation coefficients when they are encountered in a research report. Correlation coefficients in the scientific literature are rarely accompanied by scattergrams, so one should get accustomed to comprehending the correlation coefficients whenever one is encountered in a scientific report.

The symbol used to represent correlation coefficients is *r*. Sometimes this symbol is followed with a subscript indicating the size of the sample upon which it is based. For example, Figure 14.1 is represented as $r_{(5)}$, because there were five individuals in this hypothetical study. Three scattergrams have been presented thus far, and each of them would be associated with a very different correlation coefficient. If one looks back on Figure 14.1, one will see that it represents a strong positive correlation, with a correspondingly strong (nearly perfect) correlation coefficient ($r = .97$). Figure 14.2, of course, represents a perfect negative correlation ($r = -1.00$), and Figure 14.3 reflects the essential absence of a correlation ($r = .00$).

To challenge your current comprehension of correlations, attempt to estimate the correlation coefficient for Figure 14.4. In other words, estimate how well these data points cluster along a regression line as opposed to being randomly scattered like a shotgun blast.

The first step you should take in coming to an estimate is to eliminate half the possible coefficients automatically by deciding whether the correlation is positive or negative. Figure 14.4 is obviously negative because the high values for variable Y are associated with low values for variable X and vice versa. Therefore, the correlation must be somewhere between 0.00 and −1.00. In narrowing your estimate further, try to answer the following question: Is the pattern created by the points more like a random scattering, i.e., a shotgun blast, or more like a straight line? This should tell you whether the coefficient is

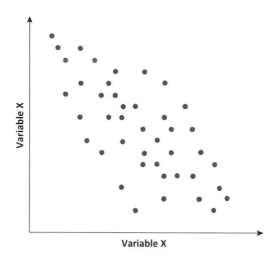

Variable X

FIGURE 14.4   Scattergram of the Relationship between Variables Y and X, Based on 43 Hypothetical Observations

above .50 (closer to a straight line) or below .50 (closer to a shotgun blast); if you really cannot decide, the coefficient is probably close to .50 itself. Do not read the following paragraph until you have made your guess.

The answer is $r = -.65$. This would be considered a strong correlation, although it is still far from perfect, as in Figure 14.1. (For the time being, pay no attention to the different numbers of observation points in the two graphs.)

If your guess was between −.50 and −.80, you made a good guess and must understand the basic concept. If your guess was outside that range, or you didn't even try, go back to Figure 14.4 and pencil in a regression line. Notice that the points are distinctly packed about the line; they are definitely far from being randomly scattered (like a shotgun blast). When a pattern is almost equally split between conforming to an inverse regression line and being randomly scattered, the correlation coefficient will be in the neighborhood of −.50. In the case of Figure 14.4, the points are in fact packed a bit more tightly around the regression line than they are randomly scattered. Therefore, the correlation is a bit higher than −.50; it is precisely −65.

Let's do one more: Estimate the correlation coefficient for Figure 14.5. Again, the first step should be to eliminate half the possibilities by determining whether the direction of the scatter is positive or negative. Do this by visualizing the regression line. Then determine whether the scattering of points better conforms to the regression line or to a shotgun blast. If it is former, the correlation coefficient is probably above .50; if the latter, it is probably below .50. Make your estimate before reading further.

The correlation coefficient for Figure 14.5 is .32. If your estimate was close to this value, you are understanding the basic concept of correlation, at least as it relates to what is called a linear relationship. The following section introduces you to the concept of linearity.

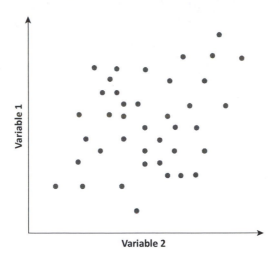

FIGURE 14.5 Scattergram of the Relationship between Variables 1 and 2, Based on Hypothetical Data

Curvilinear versus Linear Correlations

Our discussion of correlations so far has followed a basic assumption: The best fitting regression line for a set of points is straight. This is called a **linear assumption**, but there are cases in which such an assumption is inappropriate. Fortunately, most of the variables considered by criminologists and social scientists (at least within their ranges of variation that they study) warrant a linear assumption. If in doubt, however, the safest approach is to look at the scattergram. By applying the most common correlational formula (i.e., Pearson correlation) to a set of data, one assumes that the best fitting regression line is straight.

To appreciate the significance of the assumption of linearity, consider Figure 14.6. If the best fitting straight line is drawn through these points, it would be a line ascending at about a 30° angle along the y-axis starting at about 4. If the actual correlation coefficient for these data points is calculated based on this straight regression line, one gets a low positive correlation ($r = .25$). In fact, the relationship between variables M and N is best considered much stronger than .25. The problem lies with the mistaken assumption that a straight regression line is appropriate for this set of data.

When relationships are curvilinear rather than linear, researchers typically present the data in a scattergram rather than with a correlation coefficient. Nevertheless, special correlational formulas can be applied to a wide variety of curved lines. There is no need for students in introductory research methods (or even introductory statistics) to know how to interpret nonlinear correlations, but it is worth noting that they exist.

The most common shapes of nonlinear relationships are U-shapes and "initial rise (or decline) then level" shapes, all of which can be inverted. These are illustrated in simplified form in Figure 14.7. One example of a U-shape

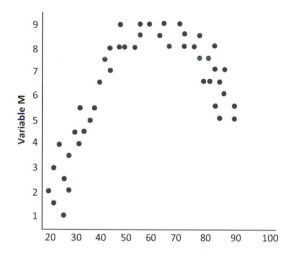

FIGURE 14.6 Scattergram Representing the Relationship between Variables M and N, Based on Hypothetical Data

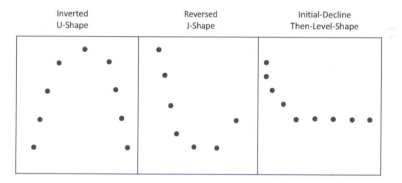

FIGURE 14.7 Samples of Some of the Most Common Shapes of Curvilinear Correlational Patterns

relationship has to do with the relationship between the number of children a couple has and the couple's marital stability. At least two studies have found that couples with no children and those with 10 or more have the greatest probabilities of divorce. Couples with one or two children have the lowest divorce probabilities (Thornton, 1977; Maneker & Rankin, 1987).

Another example of a U-shape relationship is between alcohol consumption and mortality rates due to heart disease. People who are most likely to die from heart disease either report that they are abstainers or that they are among the heaviest drinkers (reviewed by Marmot, 1984; Moore & Pearson, 1986). This U-shaped correlation has been interpreted as showing that moderate consumption of alcohol is helpful in preventing diseases of the cardiovascular system (e.g., Turner et al., 1981). However, a review of the evidence points out that, compared to moderate drinkers, many abstainers are former heavy drinkers and that their death rate from heart disease is even higher than that of currently heavy drinkers, mainly because they are older (Sharper, 1990). This plus other evidence raises questions about the beneficial effects of moderate levels of alcohol consumption in preventing heart disease, although the detrimental effects of heavy drinking are not in doubt. Besides being an example of a curvilinear relationship, this line of research also illustrated a point that will be made later in this chapter: Be very careful when making deductions about causation when all of the evidence is of a correlational nature.

An example of an initial decline, then a level curve is the relationship between a mother's age when pregnant and her chances of having a low birth weight infant. The average birth weight of babies born to mothers between the ages of 13 and 15 was lower than babies born to mothers older than 16. Beyond the age of 16, however, teenage mothers were no more likely to give birth to low birth weight infants than mothers in their 20s or 30s (Ketterlinus et al., 1990).

The concept of curvilinearity helps to underscore a point made earlier: Correlational statistics, like all statistics, are based on assumptions, and the researcher needs to be assured that the data being analyzed matches those assumptions. In Figure 14.6, for instance, there is clearly a strong relationship between variables M and N. The fact that a Pearson correlational formula assumes linearity, however, means that it would yield only a slight positive correlation coefficient when applied to Figure 14.6. Note that had the measurement of variable N stopped at 60, the Pearson correlation coefficient would have been much stronger (i.e., $r = .94$).

The Pearson correlation also assumes that variables were measured at interval or ratio levels. There are other types of correlational formulas, however, and there are ways of adapting Pearson correlation for use with nominal level variables, but these issues will not be covered in this text.

⊖ Interpreting Statements about the Strength of Correlations

Research reports using correlations are often accompanied by narrative accounts with statements such as "A strong relationship was found between this variable and that variable." What does a researcher mean when making such statements? Here are some general guidelines:

1. Correlation coefficients that are .80 or higher would reflect very strong relationships (regardless of whether the coefficients were positive or negative).
2. Coefficients between the .60s and .70s would be considered strong or quite strong.
3. Coefficients between the .40s and .50s would be regarded as moderate to substantial.
4. Those in the .20s and the .30s would be termed weak to modest.
5. Finally, coefficients in the teens or below would usually be of little or no practical importance, even if they happen to be statistically significant because of very large sample size.

These ranges are not presented for memorization; they merely depict what should be intuitively obvious. In other words, it would be unreasonable for a researcher to describe a correlation coefficient of .25 as very strong or a coefficient of .93 as modest.

Variability and Correlations

As a rule, researchers should try to maximize the variability in each variable that is correlated. By so doing, they increase the chances of observing any relationship that may exist. Figure 14.8 illustrates this point by presenting a scattergram with a substantial negative correlation between variables A and B (i.e., $r_{(44)} = -.61$). However, if the range on variable A is limited to between 0 to 5 instead of 0 to 15 (i.e., just the bold points), the correlation would be virtually zero and would actually switch signs from negative to positive ($r_{(13)} = .12$).

One more feature of Figure 14.8 is that it contains one observation point that would be termed an outlier. As mentioned earlier, an outlier refers to any observation that is extremely deviant relative to the overall pattern of observations. The outlier on Figure 14.8 is located at 1 on the y-axis and at about 20 on the x-axis. The magnitude of a correlation coefficient is affected more by outliers than by observations falling within the general pattern of points. The more points there are that conform to the general pattern, however, the less of an effect one or two outliers have on a correlation coefficient. In Figure 14.8, the coefficient is depressed from $r_{(43)} = -.61$ by the inclusion of the outlier. Although researchers should never remove observations without explicitly stating that they did so, sometimes extreme outliers are removed in a separate analysis in order to show the relationship for the bulk of the sample.

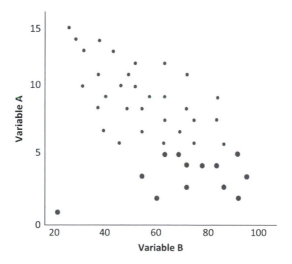

FIGURE 14.8   Scattergram of the Relationship between Variables A and B, Based on Hypothetical Data

An example in which an extreme outlier was removed was in a study of statewide rape rates and sales of adult/pornographic magazines (e.g., Scott & Schwalm, 1988a, 1988b). One state—Alaska—had a rape rate that was nearly four times greater than that of the next leading state. Consequently, the researcher presented results with and without Alaska as an outlier.

The Statistical Significance of Correlation Coefficients

Just as when comparing means and proportions, when correlating variables, a researcher eventually comes to the question of statistical significance. In other words, if two studies are conducted, and one finds a correlation of $r_{(14)} = .41$ and the other finds $r_{(450)} = .25$, a judgment will have to be made about whether one or both of these studies are statistically significant correlations. Because of the tremendous difference in sample size, one can instinctively deduce that if only one of these two correlations is significant, it would be the second one.

The methods used to estimate the probability of correlation coefficients being statistically significant are similar to those used to assess the statistical significance for t-tests, ANOVAs, and chi-squares. Statisticians have developed methods for estimating the probability of any correlation coefficient reflecting a real relationship given the number of observations used to derive the coefficients.

It is not the purpose here to examine the logic behind their derivations, but a hint for those who are curious is as follows: Most variables that researchers correlate come fairly close to being normally distributed. Because many probabilities can also be represented in terms of normal distributions, it is possible to derive probability estimates for the intersection of two normally distributed variables by squaring their separate probabilities.

What one should know in order to make sense of research reports based on correlation is that just about every correlation coefficient that appears in print will be followed by its p-value. Thus, the p-value associated with $r_{(14)} = .41$ is $p > .05$, and that for $r_{(450)} = .25$ is $p < .001$ (with some qualifying remarks about one-tailed vs. two-tailed assumptions that will not be dealt with here). To make sense of the expression "$r_{(14)} = .41, p > .05$," you would say that the correlation is not statistically significant because the probability that it occurred by chance is greater than .05. Before reading the next paragraph, try to interpret the expression "$r_{(450)} = .25$ is $p < .001$" on your own.

One's interpretation should be roughly as follows: A modest, but highly significant correlation was found, because $r = .25$ based on a sample size of more than 400 is associated with less than a 1/1,000 chance of being a statistical fluke. If you wonder how statisticians have determined the p-values that are associated with a particular correlation coefficient and sample size, the answer is that it is ultimately based on the same principles of probability that were briefly discussed in Chapter 13.

Interpreting Two Studies Based on Correlation

Here are two examples of actual published studies that have used correlations to address empirical questions. As you read them, mainly pay attention to the underlying logic of (a) identifying the variables to be correlated, (b) performing the correlation, noting its strength and direction, (c) determining the p-value associated with the correlation coefficient, and (d) making a deduction about the nature of the relationship and whether it can be considered statistically significant.

Example 1: A psychological study conducted several decades ago sought to determine if there was a relationship between a personality trait called sensation seeking and a type of attitude known as dogmatism/authoritarianism (Kish & Donnenwerth, 1972). The researchers gave 13 males and 29 females a questionnaire that was designed to measure both variables. The analyses revealed one relationship that was statistically significant and one that was not. Before reading the next paragraph, see if you can answer the following questions based simply on the two correlation coefficients and their p-values: Which was the significant correlation? What was the direction of both correlations, and how would this be translated into a statement about the relationship between sensation seeking and dogmatism/authoritarianism?

For Males: $r_{(13)} = -.81\ (p < .01)$
For Females: $r_{(29)} = -.29\ (p > .05)$

If you conclude that the study suggests that there is a significant negative (inverse) relationship between sensation seeking and dogmatism/authoritarianism among the males, but not among females, you are on the right track. Regarding the direction of the correlation, it is negative in both cases, suggesting that people who are sensation seekers tend to be less dogmatic/authoritarian than nonsensation seekers.

Example 2: Now consider a study that is a little more complicated. It was undertaken by an anthropologist to determine whether wealthy males have more wives and consequently more children than poor males. Rather than being conducted in an industrialized society where results might be quite different, this anthropological study was carried out among a tribal people living in Kenya (Borgerhoff Mulder, 1988). Marriage and birth records for the tribe had been maintained for decades by staff at a local mission. Unlike industrial societies where having multiple wives is illegal, the practice of polygamy is acceptable and fairly common among this tribal group.

The researcher correlated two indicators of "wealth" among the tribal males (size of landholding and number of cows owned) with both the number of wives and number of surviving offspring for each male. Because there may have been changes over time, the correlations were performed for three marriage cohorts.

The term **cohort** is worth knowing. It is used by social scientists to refer to a group of individuals with some significant time-dependent event in common (such as a time frame during which they were born or got married). One cohort consisted of males who got married between 1918 and 1929; the second cohort were those who got married between 1930 and 1939; and the third cohort were those married between 1940 and 1953 (Borgerhoff Mulder, 1988).

Table 14.3 summarizes findings from this study. Notice that the fertility measures are listed in the first column and the wealth measures appear in the last five columns (the number of cows was not measured for the first marriage cohort). It is fairly common in tabular presentations of correlation coefficients to use asterisks to denote statistical significance. In looking at the bottom of Table 14.3, notice that a legend denoting the three most common statistical significance levels is displayed.

Try answering the following two questions based on your examination of Table 14.3. First, are wealth and fertility among males significantly correlated or does the answer vary depending on what measure of wealth is used or what time period is studied? Second, for which of the three cohorts is the relationship strongest and most statistically significant?

If you answered the first question by concluding that, in all cases, the correlations were statistically significant, you would be correct. Regarding the second question, the strongest correlations were found in the case of the second marriage cohort (i.e., those married between 1930 and 1939).

One guideline that can be used in speculating about the causal significance of a correlation has to do with the temporal sequence, which refers to the time order in which two variables occurred. Thus, in Box 14.1, if child abuse and later alcohol and drug abuse are correlated, the alcohol and drug abuse cannot possibly be the causal variable because it takes place several years following any child abuse. Nevertheless, this does not mean the child abuse per se must be a cause in order to explain why it is correlated with later alcohol and drug abuse.

TABLE 14.3 Correlation between Wealth (Size of Landholding and Number of Cows Owned) and Male Fertility (Number of Wives and Number of Surviving Offspring)

Measures of Male Fertility	Marriage Cohorts				
	1918–1929	1930–1939		1940–1953	
	Acres	Acres	Cows	Acres	Cows
Number of wives	.70**	.91***	.84***	.49**	.62**
Number of surviving offspring	.72***	.92***	.86***	.42**	.50**
N	11	25	25	37	34

*p < .05; **p < .01; ***p < .005 (Adapted from Borgerhoff Mulder, 1988.)

BOX 14.1 CURRENT ISSUES

Caution: Correlation Does Not Equal Causation

An important issue surrounding correlation is bound up in a brief, but long-repeated, sentence: *"Correlation does not equal causation"* (e.g., Ezekiel, 1941:451; Alland, 1967:208; Games, 1990). This adage means that you should not be fooled into thinking that a cause-effect relationship has been found simply because two variables are correlated. The same note of caution is sometimes referred to as the third variable problem, meaning that there could be many other influential factors responsible for a statistical relationship than those being measured.

To illustrate, we noted that in one African tribe, wealth is associated with fertility among males. From this finding, can we conclude that wealth causes fertility to rise in males? Perhaps. But before reaching this conclusion, it would be wise to check the customs of the society and the ecology of the region. For example, parental pressure or extreme poverty may force women to marry the few wealthiest men in a particular tribal community. Under other cultural or ecological conditions, other types of relationship between wealth and fertility might be found.

Consider another example. Studies have repeatedly shown that to the degree a person is subjected to physical abuse as children, he or she is more likely to abuse drugs and/or alcohol later in life (Cohen & Densen-Gerber, 1981; Wright, 1985). Does this mean that child abuse causes drug abuse? Possibly. However, another possibility is that drug abuse and alcoholism are both genetically influenced (Grove et al., 1990; Tsuang et al., 1996) and therefore will be frequently transmitted from parent to child. People who struggle with substance abuse problems may be more prone to abuse their children when they misbehave compared to parents with no substance abuse problems. Therefore, the statistical correlation between being abused as a child and later drug and/or alcohol abuse problems may be explained without assuming that child abuse causes drug abuse.

The adage that "correlation does not equal causation" should not discourage researchers from speculating about why variables might be correlated. Such speculation serves vital functions in science. However, as conjectures are made, they need to be couched in words such as "may be" and "possibly," rather than "it is obvious" and "no other explanation is possible." Remember that among the hallmarks of science are caution and objectivity. Among the tell-tale signs that someone is not being cautious and objective is to read claims that only one causal interpretation of a particular correlation is possible.

With regard to temporal sequences, it is useful to keep in mind that when scattergrams are used to illustrate correlations, the common practice is to put the antecedent (and *possible* causal) variable on the x-axis and the subsequent (and *possible* effect) variable on the y-axis (Howell, 1989:101). In the case of child abuse and drug abuse, for example, child abuse would normally appear on the x-axis, and drug abuse on the y-axis.

Another important point regarding temporal sequences is that if a researcher has a variable that he or she believes is a cause of some other variable (the effect), he or she will often refer to the presumed cause as the **independent variable** and the presumed effect as the **dependent variable**.

Reflections on the Importance of Statistics in the Research Process

As we bring our formal discussion of statistics to a close, it is important to keep in mind that these mathematical tools are fundamental to the social sciences. Very few articles or books pertaining to social science disciplines (except for philosophy and history) are devoid of statistical concepts, and, in many cases, several statistical concepts are used together to draw conclusions. At the same time, it is worth noting that the appearance of numerous and complex statistical concepts in a scientific article does not automatically make that article more scientifically worthy than an article with few or relatively simple statistics.

In a book cleverly titled *Lies, Damn Lies, and Statistics* (Wheeler, 1976), the author made the point that statistics can not only be used to enlighten, but they can also be used to confuse and deceive, both intentionally and unintentionally. You need to be aware that not all social scientists are simply interested in the truth. Some are at least sometimes driven by political agendas that incline them to pick their facts or bend the truth in order to reach some preordained conclusion.

As part of your training in criminology, keep in mind that *you* are "the final authority" as to what does and does not rise to the level of "making sense." To make informed decisions, it helps to be familiar with the rules that underlie the statistics being used. In brief, statistics and research methods are inextricably linked. This chapter can provide you with some background for understanding some of the statistical principles upon which most social science research is based.

Multivariate Statistics: When Bivariate Statistics Are Not Enough

So far in this chapter, the focus has been on correlating two variables at a time, i.e., bivariate statistics. Although correlating two variables at a time can provide valuable information, we have just noted that it is not a trustworthy way to answer questions about causation. In other words, knowing that variable A is correlated with variable B does not tell us anything specific about the causal nature of their relationship, even when the temporal sequence for the two variables is clear.

What if you could correlate three, four, or even more variables all at once? Could that give you a better idea about the causal nature of any relationships that might be found? The answer is that it can sometimes help, particularly when multiple correlations are combined with knowledge about the temporal sequences in which the variables occur.

To illustrate, consider a relationship that has received much research attention since the 1990s. Numerous studies have found a positive correlation between maternal smoking during pregnancy and offspring involvement in delinquent and criminal behavior (reviewed by Ellis et al., 2019:326-327). However, because this is merely a correlation, it is scientifically risky to conclude that maternal smoking actually *caused* the offending behavior of offspring later in life. Other possibilities need to be considered.

One possibility comes from noting that smoking tends to be more prevalent in the lower than in the upper social strata (Flay et al., 1983; Morales et al., 1997; Lindstrom et al., 2000). Also, involvement in serious criminal offending has been found to be associated with low social status among parents (reviewed by Ellis et al., 2019:97). If one considers these factors together, it is reasonable to suspect that living in low social status conditions might elevate a mother's chances of becoming a smoker as well as the chances of her offspring becoming a criminal.

Scientists often refer to correlations that seem to be of no causal significance as **spurious correlations**. Fortunately, if the real causal variables are measured along with the variables involved in a spurious relationship, researchers can use multivariate statistics to eliminate much of the spurious relationship. The statistical process for eliminating spurious relationships is usually called **statistical control**.

Achieving Statistical Control

Understanding how statistical control works in detail requires an advanced course in statistics. Here, you should simply know that the capacity to statistically control variables is part of most computerized statistical programs.

An Example of Partialling as a Multivariate Statistic

Say you were interested in how two variables were related to one another and that you suspected that much of their relationship was due to a third factor affecting both of these two variables. There is a fairly widely used multivariate statistic that can help you explore such a possibility. This statistic is known as **partialling**. Without dealing with any of the actual statistical features of partialling, it works by removing one variable (by giving it a fixed value) so as to identify the extent to which any other variables one has measured remain correlated with one another.

To envision how partialling works, consider a study undertaken to examine the relationship between religiosity and delinquency. In fact, numerous studies have been published on the topic of how religiosity is related to criminality and delinquency. Due in part to the many different ways that religiosity can be conceptualized, the findings have been mixed. Nevertheless, most of the research findings have indicated that religiosity and offending are negatively correlated, i.e., individuals who are more religious are less likely to violate criminal statutes (reviewed by Ellis et al., 2019:112-125).

In an article published quite some time ago, two researchers speculated that the negative correlation between religiosity and delinquency was largely

BOX 14.2 WHAT DO YOU THINK?

Can We Blame Criminal Offending on a Mother's Smoking Behavior While She Was Pregnant?

To get a better sense of how statistical controls are imposed in data analysis, let's return to the evidence of a positive correlation between maternal smoking during pregnancy and offspring criminality later in life. For the sake of argument, *assume* that the correlation between how many cigarettes a mother smokes during pregnancy and the probability of her offspring being convicted of a crime 20 years later is .25. Also assume the negative correlation between the mother's social status and the offspring being convicted 20 years later is –.25. You now would like to know if the first correlation is simply the result of the second. If this is the case, it would mean that the relationship between maternal smoking and offspring offending is actually spurious.

Here is what can be done to address such a question. To keep things simple, assume that there are only three social strata: upper, middle, and lower. You can tell the computer to separate the mothers into three groups according to social status and then to run separate correlations between smoking and offending for each of the three strata. Suppose this is done with the following resulting correlations: .02, .05 and –.07. If you add these three coefficients together and divide by three, your *average* correlation between smoking and offending is .00.

The most reasonable interpretation of this average coefficient is that once the variable of social status is eliminated (controlled), the .25 correlation between maternal smoking and offending disappears. Therefore, the correlation between maternal smoking and offspring offending would be considered spurious rather than "real" in a causal sense.

On the other hand, if a positive correlation between maternal smoking and offending is found at all three levels of social status, then it would be more reasonable to conclude that the smoking-offending relationship is not spurious, at least regarding parental social status. It is important to emphasize that this illustration is hypothetical. In reality, scientists still do not know why maternal smoking and offspring involvement in delinquency and crime are positively correlated as the vast majority of studies have found (Ellis et al., 2019:326). One study that made a special effort to statistically control for one important aspect of social status—maternal education—concluded that this did not significantly reduce the smoking-offending correlation (Gibson et al., 2000). Nonetheless, we always have to keep in the back of our mind that some of the effects on the dependent variable by the independent variables we studied might also be at least partially due to some other independent variable that we didn't include in our study.

due to both variables being influenced by a third variable: boredom (Ellis & Thompson, 1989). Specifically, they hypothesized that tendencies toward boredom would not only lead to greater delinquency, but it would also lead to lower attendance at religious services, which, in turn, would diminish most religious beliefs.

To test this hypothesis, the researchers administered a questionnaire to hundreds of college students. Among the questions asked were ones having to do with their religiosity, their involvement in delinquency, and their tendencies to often feel bored. The researchers then analyzed the responses they obtained in two ways. First, they correlated their measures of religiosity with their measures of delinquency using conventional Pearson correlation. Second, they ran these correlations again after partialling out their measure of boredom susceptibility. The results of these two analyses are shown in Table 14.4 for males only (a separate table for females revealed similar patterns, but for brevity are not presented here).

If you compare the correlations without and with boredom being statistically controlled, you can see that there is considerable support for the hypothesis. In other words, most of the significant correlations (identified with asterixes) were reduced to nonsignificance once self-reported boredom was partialled out. This provides an illustration of how one type of multivariate statistic—partialling—can be used to answer questions about how "third variables" may be impacting some relationships of interest.

Table 14.4   Bivariate and Partial Correlation Coefficients Linking Various Aspects of Religiosity to Involvement in Delinquency (and Some Adult Offending)

Aspects of Religiosity	Type of Correlation	Types of Offenses				
		Official Contact	Serious Crime	Delin-quency	Drug Offenses	School/Family Offenses
Belief in creator god	Bivariate	−.04	−.00	−.09	−.17*	−.05
	Partial	.05	.11	.03	−.01	.03
Belief in personal god	Bivariate	−.13	−.06	−.10	−.20**	−.07
	Partial	−.06	.03	−.00	.01	.01
Belief that praying can influence worldly events	Bivariate	−.19*	−.17*	−.20*	−.22*	−.09
	Partial	−.09	−.04	−.04	.01	.03
Belief in personal immortality	Bivariate	−.08	.10	−.06	−.11	−.01
	Partial	−.01	.19*	.05	.03	.06
Belief in punishment hereafter	Bivariate	−.17*	−.13	−.23**	−.32***	−.13
	Partial	−.10	−.04	−.13	−.19*	−.05
Belief that a guardian angel watches me	Bivariate	−.12	−.18*	−.14	−.16*	−.14
	Partial	−.03	−.08	−.00	.03	−.06
Religion personally important	Bivariate	−.19*	−.19*	−.25**	−.34***	−.15*
	Partial	−.06	−.02	−.03	−.07	.00
Christian orthodoxy scale	Bivariate	−.18*	−.11	−.18*	−.22**	−.10
	Partial	−.11	.00	−.06	−.05	−.01
Number of religious services attended the past year	Bivariate	−.12	−.20*	−.14	−.33***	−.13
	Partial	−.00	−.06	.05	−.11	−.00

*p < .05; **p < .01; ***p < .001

⬛ Closing Comments on Multivariate Statistics

Multivariate statistics are widely used in criminal justice research, where many research ideas are tested using large data sets derived from governmental agencies. Besides partialling, among the most widely used multivariate statistics in the social sciences are ones known as ordinary least squares regression, logistic regression, and path analysis. Before you use any of these statistical analyses, you will want to get some fairly extensive statistical training. Another helpful source of information about multivariate statistics can be obtained from colleagues or professors who have used them in the past.

Despite their widespread use, multivariate statistics have limitations. Among these limitations is that the statistics only provide valid results if the variables being studied are accurately measured (Frankfort-Nachmias & Nachmias, 1992). Unfortunately, many variables of interest to social scientists have problems regarding their reliability and precision. Despite the caution social scientists should use in applying multivariate statistics to their data, studies based on these procedures have provided researchers with many insights that are very difficult to achieve in any other way.

⬛ Summary

The concept of correlation was developed by social scientists to have a standardized mathematical shorthand for describing how two variables are related to one another. Although caution must always be exercised in interpreting correlation coefficients, these bivariate statistics are widely used in the social sciences.

To learn exactly how correlation coefficients are calculated, training in statistics is necessary. However, just a few principles are needed to properly interpret correlation coefficients. These principles are as follows:

1. A correlation coefficient is a number that will always range between –1.00 and 1.00, with .00 representing the complete lack of a relationship.

2. A coefficient at or near –1.00 would indicate that as one variable increases in the value, there is a strong tendency for the other variable to decrease in value. This would be termed a strong negative (or inverse) correlation (or relationship).

3. Conversely, a coefficient at or near 1.00 denotes a relationship in which increases in the value of one variable are strongly associated with increases in the value of the second variable. This would be termed a strong positive correlation (or relationship).

Criminologists and other social scientists shy away from interpreting correlations in any causal sense. In other words, even strong correlations (e.g., $r = .80$) should not be interpreted as suggesting that one of the two variables is "the cause" of the other. Both variables could be the result of some third variable that may not have even been measured. So, although it is often interesting and helpful to know that two variables are correlated, caution must be exercised in interpreting correlations.

Sometimes researchers effectively correlate several variables at once or they hold some variables constant while correlating others. These are examples of what are known as multivariate statistical analyses. Such analyses are mathematically complex, but the basic principles can be traced back to simpler bivariate statistics. Often, the purpose of multivariate statistics is to narrow the possibilities regarding causal relationships between variables.

Discussion Questions

1. How do bivariate and multivariate statistics differ from univariate statistics?
2. What is the difference between a positive and a negative correlation of two variables?
3. What do researchers mean when they say that correlation does not equal causation?
4. What is the main purpose of using multivariate statistics?
5. How does partialling achieve statistical control?

Exercises

1. Search for an empirical article on some topic of criminal justice using the keywords "empirical" and "correlation" in one of your institution's journal databases. Try to find the correlation matrix or the correlation coefficients for the study's variable relationships. Using the guidelines from the chapter related to the strength of relationships, list whether the correlations are weak or strong.

2. Search for an article on some criminal justice topic using the keyword "multivariate statistics" and scroll to the results section. How do the researchers explain the effects of each of their independent variables on their dependent variable? Did some of the independent variables have no statistically significant effect? Do they mention which had the largest effects?

Glossary

abstract A short paragraph at the beginning of an article that gives a brief summary of the article related to the topic, methodology, sampling strategy, results, and conclusions.

Academy of Criminal Justice Sciences (ACJS) An international organization for cultivation of professional and scholarly activities in the field of criminal justice. ACJS membership includes both educators and practitioners who support education, research, and policy analysis within criminal justice education.

accidental (or availability) sampling One of the crudest methods for obtaining a sample for a research study is to stand in one location such as parking lot or university student union and try to interview (or observe) whoever comes by. Accidental sampling is a nonprobability sampling technique because the only reason the persons are included in the sample is because they were available at the location.

adolescent-limited offenders Offenders who are prone to engaging in criminal activity only during their adolescent years. Adolescent-limited offenders make up the majority of offenders who eventually desist in offending in early adulthood.

adoption studies Studies that attempt to determine how much influence genetic factors and environmental factors have on behavior by examining whether infants adopted at birth by persons unrelated to them exhibit behaviors that are more like their genetic or adoptive parents.

aesthetic appeal An element of assessing the merit of a theory that involves a sense of beauty. Aesthetic appeal alone is not very helpful for scientifically explaining the empirical world, but when combined with other components of merit, an aesthetic sense can be valuable in theory construction.

after-only experimental design Experimental design that has at least two groups of subjects but there are no observations prior to the time the independent variable is imposed on the experimental group.

aggravated assault An unlawful attack by one person upon another for the purpose of inflicting severe or aggravated bodily injury.

aggregated units of analyses Any units of analyses besides individuals.

all-points-anchored response option A type of end-anchored response option that involves anchoring all the response options with words (usually adjectives or adverbs). The most common scales have five points.

American Society of Criminology (ASC) An international professional organization in criminology and criminal justice made up of members who pursue scholarly, scientific, and professional knowledge related to aspects of crime and delinquency to include measurement, etiology, consequences, prevention, control, and treatment.

analysis of variance (ANOVA) Similar to the t-test but allows the comparison of more than two means at a time. ANOVA is a bit more complicated mathematically, but the underlying statistical principles of probability are very similar to those developed for the t-test.

animal model A scientific model that results from locating behavior in nonhuman animal species that appears to resemble some aspect of human behavior. These models are used to demonstrate that some type of behavior is at least roughly equivalent across various species and usually involves combining science with intuition.

anonymity   A special type of confidentiality that refers to the practice of insuring that no identifying information of participants will be obtained in the course of collecting data. This means that the researcher never knows the identity of those who completed the questionnaire.

anthropology   The study of man (or humankind) which began in the mid-1800s as the academic/intellectual community of Europe became increasingly interested in human origins and in studying the ethnic and cultural diversity of the human species.

applied research   Research undertaken with the purpose of finding solutions to an identifiable problem.

archival data   Data that have been collected by some agency without reference to the persons who might analyze the data in research studies.

arithmetic average (or mean or average)   The measure of central tendency calculated by summing all the scores and dividing by the total number of scores.

arson   Any willful or malicious burning or attempting to burn, with or without intent to defraud, a dwelling house, public building, motor vehicle or aircraft, or personal property of another.

artifactual cultural variables   Variables that have to do with the wide variety of material things that characterize most human societies, such as neighborhoods and dwellings we live in or the types of media we consume.

atavistic   Basically meaning "evolutionary throw-back traits" from Cesare Lombroso whose idea that individuals possessing "primitive physical traits" that were better adapted to living in times before industrialization than in modern societies might be more prone to criminality.

Atlas of World Cultures   A type of ethnographic atlas, or databank of ethnographic accounts.

attitudinal item   Questions asking people to express their opinions about topics.

audio-computer-assisted self-interview (audio-CASI)   A method of administering a survey via computer; subjects are presented with questions in auditory form and are allowed to respond by pressing keys that correspond with various answers on the computer.

augmenting effect   An interactive effect where the effects of one variable enhance the effects of the other.

basic (or pure) research   Research undertaken to expand scientific knowledge in some area, often with no practical goal.

before-after no control group design   The only experimental design in which there is only one group of subjects, all of whom will be exposed to the independent (treatment) variable.

behavioral/personality variables   Variables having to do with how we act as individuals. Behavioral variables relate to specific acts like smoking or drinking whereas personality variables relate to more consistent characteristics of a person like agreeableness, attention seeking, or introverted versus extroverted.

behaviorism   An approach to the study of behavior that focuses on observable and measurable aspects of behavior rather than on subjective or mental aspects. The hallmark is the emphasis on precisely measuring individual behavior.

Belmont Report   A report issued in 1979 by the National Commission for the Protection of Human Subjects of Biomedical and Behavioral Research. This report outlined three main principles for ethics in research involving human participants. These were respect for persons, beneficence, and justice. Respect for persons encompassed the idea that participants must be treated as having autonomy; the principle of beneficence was related to protecting participants from harm; and justice refers to the notion that the benefits and burdens of a research study should be distributed fairly across all participants.

bimodal   A distribution curve that has two modes rather than one.

bivariate statistics   Statistics that describe the relationship between two variables.

blind peer review   A peer review process where the author's name does not appear on the manuscript; this is so the author's identity is not known to the reviewers. Also, the reviewers' identities are not known to the author, hence blind review. In this review process, far more scientific articles are rejected than accepted, especially the first time they are submitted.

burglary   The unlawful entry of a structure to commit a felony or theft.

carelessness   A source of sample attrition where an intended subject sets aside a questionnaire for completion later, but then either loses it or forgets about it.

cartographic criminology   Attributed to an 18th-century French astronomer named Adolpe Quetelet, who devoted much of his career to mapping the prevalence of crime in several European countries. Today, cartographic criminology is better known as crime mapping and has had a major resurgence with the emergence of global positioning system (GPS) technology combined with modern computer graphics. Basically, GPS uses multiple satellites to obtain and keep track of objects and events anywhere on earth.

case study (or case history)   Narrative accounts focusing on just a few individuals or groups. Each case is so unique as to not warrant any attempt to assess its significance in any statistical sense.

categorical measurement   Mainly nominal and ordinal level variables that are consolidated into categories.

causation   A concept that is central to scientific theorizing and involves the idea that variation in a phenomenon is the result of variation in other phenomena, and that effects often result not from just one causal variable. Essentially, if we say that variable A is a cause of variable B, we mean that variable A precedes variable B

in time and that variable A is nearly always present wherever variable B is present.

census   Refers to a survey that includes (or at least comes close to including) 100% of the members of a population, either directly or indirectly (such as through another household member).

certificate of confidentiality   A document issued by funding agencies that protects researchers from having to disclose participant identities or information in criminal proceedings. The government would have to convince a grand jury or judge to compel a researcher to provide this information.

chi-square (X^2)   Statistical test used for comparing proportions.

chosen sample   Refers to persons asked to participate in a study.

circled end-anchored response option   A numeric form of the end-anchored continuum where instead of a linear continuum, subjects are instructed to answer by circling a number.

classical experimental design   The classical design involves subjects being randomly assigned to one of two groups, the experimental group and the control group. For an experiment to fit the minimum requirements of a classical design, there must also be at least two time frames.

cleared offenses   A crime is cleared by the arrest of a suspect or by exceptional means (cases in which a suspect has been identified but he/she is not immediately available for arrest).

clinical sampling   Event sampling that is carried out in settings where people seek treatment.

coding   Refers to the process of deciding how data will be entered into a standard format for analysis.

cognitive variables   Variables that encompass the emotions we feel, the individual attitudes we hold, the thoughts and intellectual abilities we possess, and the mental health/illness with which we are either blessed or cursed.

cohort   Term used by social scientists to refer to a group of individuals with some significant time-dependent event in common (such as a time frame during which they were born or got married).

comparison group   Term used in quasi-experiments to refer to the control group because there are no genuine experimental and control groups.

comparative (or criterion) validity   Involves comparing a new unestablished operational measure with an established (or widely accepted) measure.

compatibility   An element of assessing the merit of a theory; refers to how agreeable a particular theory is with other theories of related phenomena that have been found to generate accurate hypotheses.

Comte, Auguste   French philosopher/scientist who argued for the scientific study of human societies and social relationships. Comte coined the term *sociology* to describe the discipline that would study societies and social relationships upon which societies are based.

conceptual definition   The definition of a phenomenon or variable that one would typically find in a dictionary. Such a definition uses familiar terms to describe a word (or phrase) that is unfamiliar.

confederates   Persons that are part of the research team but are pretending to be participants in a study in order to observe the behavior of other "real" participants.

confidentiality   Refers to the assurance given by a researcher not to reveal the identity of those who provide information as participants of research; the researcher will not disclose any information revealed by the subjects that would cause them to be personally identified.

constant   Any phenomenon that always takes on the same value or intensity.

content analysis   A special type of non-questionnaire data that is only possible in literate societies. These studies examine written or other symbolic communication as data.

continuous variable   A variable that does not exist in segments, but instead varies gradually from low to high or weak to strong, etc.

control group   In an experiment, the control group (or controls) is the group exposed to the independent variable (treatment) to a "normal" degree or, in some cases, not at all.

convenience sampling   Nonprobability sampling technique that involves obtaining a large group of subjects all at once, such as asking all the students in a criminology class to complete a questionnaire. The subjects are obtained out of convenience.

correlation   Refers to how variables are related to one another, especially if those variables are measured on a continuous scale.

correlation coefficient   A number between −1 and 1 that indicates the direction and strength of a relationship between two variables.

crime rate   The rate of a given crime is the actual number of reported crimes standardized by some unit of the population.

criminal anthropology   From Lombroso, the idea that humans can be born criminal or that human criminals have physical or cognitive defects, which he called atavisms.

criminal justice   As a discipline, the study of the system of administration of criminal law to include police, courts, and corrections.

criminality   The propensity for an individual to engage in criminal behavior.

criminologist   Someone who studies criminology, or the causes and treatment or prevention of crime and criminal behavior. Criminologists tend to hold doctorates in criminology, criminal justice, sociology, or other related fields.

criminology   The scientific study of the causes and treatment or prevention of crime and criminal behavior.

criterion variable   Term used in quasi-experimental research to refer to the dependent variable.

Cronbach alpha   A statistic that is used to estimate how well a set of items "fit together" into a single scale. This statistic uses a formula for indicating how well items (or questions) seem to elicit similar response patterns by participants in a particular study.

cross-fostering experiments   Studies similar to adoption studies used with laboratory animals to address nature-nurture issues. In these experiments, offspring are removed from their genetic mothers immediately after birth and given to foster mothers for rearing. To the degree that the offspring end up more closely resembling their genetic mothers than their rearing mothers for a given behavior pattern, genetic factors are deemed important for the expressions of the behavior.

cross-over design   An experimental design where all participants serve as both experimental subjects and control subjects at some point during the experiment.

cross-sectional survey   A survey undertaken at only one point in time.

cross-test reliability   A method of assessing the reliability of measurement that involves correlating the results of two different operational measures of the same variable.

cultural anthropology   A type of anthropology that focuses on studying the vast array of human cultures and social customs exhibited by people throughout the world.

cumulative   The idea that scientific knowledge is continually derived through building on what others have already learned. Researchers in any area of social science are attempting to add results and findings to an ever-growing "knowledge base" in an effort to better understand phenomena.

customary cultural variables   Variables that measure the values and practices that most members of a particular society share such as the languages spoken, day-to-day social customs, and rules we (usually) follow.

daily consolidated field notes   Data collection technique in ethnographic or participant observation research involving compiling of jottings each day that should usually be in the form of complete sentences arranged in relatively brief (two-to five-sentence) paragraphs.

dark figure of crime   The dark (or hidden) figure of crime refers to all of the crimes committed that never come to official attention.

debriefing   At the end of any study involving some deception, the researcher will usually meet with the participants involved to inform them of the true nature of the study. These debriefings are considered important in order to reduce the risk of any long-term adverse effects that might result from participation in the study.

deception   In the context of social science research, deception involves providing misleading information to prospective participants. There are two forms: deception by omission and orchestrated deception.

deception by omission   Involves a researcher deceiving participants by not giving them complete information about a study.

demarcated linear form   An end-anchored continuum response option that arranges numerous polar opposite adjectives at each end of a linear continuum (usually demarcated into seven response options) and asks subjects to respond to a single noun or phrase by putting an X in the appropriate space. The best known example of the demarcated linear form of the end-anchored continuum is called the semantic differential scale.

demographic variables   Variables pertaining to basic human characteristics such as age, sex, race, ethnicity, marital status, years of education, and income, and are widely used to describe human populations.

dependent variable: In an experiment, the variable that might change as a result of manipulation of the independent variable. The dependent variable is the outcome a researcher is trying to predict or explain.

Descartes (pronounced da cart'), Rene   French philosopher-mathematician who cleverly deduced that one could describe geometric shapes with equations. This revolutionary idea helped bring about fields of mathematics such as algebra, trigonometry, and calculus. Descartes' ideas also laid some of the intellectual foundation for a type of statistic that has come to be widely used in the social sciences known as bivariate statistics.

descriptive item Questions soliciting factual information from respondents, including demographic information such as age, race/ethnicity, and marital status.

determinism An unproven (and unprovable) philosophical assumption that any explanation given for a phenomenon must entail only empirical (or natural), as opposed to supernatural, factors. Although there is no way to prove that supernatural entities (God, the devil, etc.) are not actually causing whatever is being observed, by removing the supernatural from consideration, scientists can at least hope to identify and comprehend natural cause(s) of phenomena.

diagnostic research Epidemiological research in a clinical setting.

diagrammatic (or structural) model A geometric sketch (or sometimes an actual physical object) that is used to help illustrate a theory.

diary Record kept by researchers while they are conducting field research. Diaries are used to maintain impressions and broader reactions to what is being observed than would be present in jottings and daily consolidations.

direct observations Method where the data are collected by the researcher (or a team of researchers) by watching, listening, and recording what is observed.

discrete variable A variable that exists in two or more segments. Normally, discrete variables are measured at either the nominal or the ordinal level.

dispersion Refers to the degree to which scores are tightly or loosely scattered about the measure of central tendency (i.e., mean, mode, or median).

double-blind experiment A procedure where participants are randomly assigned to the experimental and control groups, and neither they nor persons administering the treatment to them know whether they are receiving the real treatment or a placebo. Only a "third party" connected with the experiment will have this knowledge, and extra safeguards will be taken to ensure that this third party does not divulge this information before the experiment has been completed.

ecological fallacy Refers to erroneously assuming that findings at one level of analysis will necessarily apply to another level. For example, if a study finds that neighborhoods with higher unemployment rates have higher crime rates, an ecological fallacy would be to assume that individuals in these neighborhoods who are unemployed are more likely to be criminal. This could be true, but research cannot conclude that because the unit of analysis in the study was the neighborhood, not the individuals living in the neighborhoods.

economics A social science discipline related to understanding all aspects of human financial affairs, ranging from individual and family finances (microeconomics) to the financial activities of states, nations, and the world as a whole (macroeconomics). Economics is closely related to the fields of business and finance.

education the study of the process of acquiring and transmitting knowledge and facilitating learning, usually in an academic setting. Many educational researchers examine ways to improve teaching techniques and to determine why students vary in learning abilities and interests.

effect size The quantitative measure of the size of the difference between two groups. Often the main statistic used in meta-analysis rather than statistical significance.

effect size meta-analysis A type of meta-analysis that gives weight to each study according to the sample size used (the vote-counting method treats each study equally regardless of sample size). In addition, unlike the vote-counting method the effect size method yields a final numerical estimate of the magnitude of any difference (or any relationship).

empiricism/empirical The idea in science that knowledge is derived from using our senses to observe phenomena (i.e., sight, hearing, tough, taste, or smell). In other words, all scientific knowledge rests on what can be perceived through the senses, with sight and sound being the most frequently used.

end-anchored continuum response option Item that allows respondents to respond along a continuum in which only the two extreme values have specific meaning.

epidemiological research Research with the purpose of assessing the prevalence of a problem. It typically consists of a survey based on a representative (or near-representative) sample that allows a researcher to estimate the proportion of a population that exhibits the problem.

episodic recall item Recall item in which respondents are asked about a type of specific experience they may or may not have had.

equational (or mathematical) model Scientific models that use mathematical formulas and equations to represent some aspect of a theory.

ethical/ideological neutrality The idea that scientists should not allow ethics and ideology to influence what they observe and report.

Ethnographic Atlas A cross-cultural data bank including hundreds of individual ethnographic accounts that have been assembled for anthropologists and other social scientists to analyze. Other similar data banks include the Human Relations Area Files (HRAF) and the Atlas of World Cultures.

ethnographic research A method developed mainly by cultural anthropologists to obtain in-depth information about cultures and societies other than those familiar to the industrialized world.

ethnography Literally measurement or description of the way of life. A methodology commonly used for obtaining ethnographic data involves observing and recording impressions of the lives and customs of a specific group of people without using formal questionnaires or other research instruments.

evaluation (or evaluative) research Research that assesses the effectiveness of programs intended to alleviate social, health, or interpersonal problems. Evaluation research has been used in criminal justice on the numerous programs that have been set up to rehabilitate offenders as part of their punishment or as after-care.

event sampling Obtaining a sample by taking every single instance of a rare event (or rare condition).

event-specific alignment design A type of time series design that obtains a series of average readings for some criterion variable in accordance with a predictor variable that is occurring at irregular intervals over the course of time.

expectancy (placebo) effect Subtle, often unintentional clues affecting participants' expectations of participating in an experimental study, which in turn may have major effects on the results of the experiment. Some of the best evidence for the expectancy effect has come from experiments involving drugs that are actually inert substances (called placebo) like sugar pills. For this reason, the expectancy effect is also referred to as the placebo effect, especially in experiments with drugs.

experimental factorial design A design whose purpose is to assess the possibility of two or more independent variables on a dependent variable, as well as allow researchers to examine the interactive effects of two or more independent variables.

experimental group In an experiment, the group that is exposed to the independent variable or treatment, or exposed to an unusual degree.

experimental research A research method that involves directly manipulating one or more of the variables being studied.

ex post facto (retrospective) designs Quasi-experimental design that simulates after-only experimental designs except does not use randomization to assign subjects.

exposure group Term used in quasi-experiments to refer to the experimental group because there are no genuine experimental and control groups.

Eysenck, Hans An English psychologist who wrote a controversial article suggesting that psychotherapy, which at the time was the most widely used treatment for mental illness, might have few or no beneficial effects. Eysenck reached two conclusions. First, despite the widespread use of psychotherapy throughout the first half of the 20th century, very little was known from a scientific standpoint about its effects. Second, what could be gleaned from the available research was that psychotherapy had few beneficial effects, except possibly for persons with the least serious forms of mental disturbances.

face validity Refers to judgments about the appropriateness of a measure based on an individual's basic understanding of a concept that one is trying to measure.

facilitator Refers to the individual leading a focus group discussion.

factor analysis A statistical method used primarily to improve the validity and reliability of variable measurement. Basically, after hundreds of individuals have completed a specific questionnaire, factor analysis can mathematically identify items (or questions) that seem to be answered similarly by the majority of respondents. Then, factor analysis specifies the degree to which these response patterns seem to "load" heavily on a specific response pattern, thereby suggesting that the items are essentially measuring the same variable.

falsifiability As an element to assess the merit of a theory, refers to how easily a theory can be disproved. Falsifiability is important because it demonstrates that a theory can be tested and shown to be false or not supported with empirical data.

falsifying data Involves fabricating or misrepresenting data or findings from a study's analysis.

feasibility research Research aimed at providing estimates of the time, effort, and expense involved in producing changes in whatever problems have been identified. Feasibility research pieces together cost estimates of various courses of action and the expected benefits. This research often includes recommendations regarding the facilities and personnel that will be required to combat the problem targeted for remedy.

field notes Method of data collection utilized in ethnographic and participant observation research.

field observations Studies undertaken outside a laboratory setting that involve observing and recording behavior without interfering with it in any way.

field research Consists of studies undertaken outside a laboratory setting.

fill-in-the-blank response option Questions that ask subjects to respond by writing in or uttering a limited number of words (usually one or two).

focus group A qualitative methodology where a dozen or so people are brought together to intensely discuss some topic.

forcible rape The carnal knowledge of a female forcibly and against her will.

forensic anthropology An applied branch of physical anthropology used in many crime investigations.

frequency distribution graph A graph with a vertical axis (called the y-**axis**) and a horizontal axis (called the x-**axis**). The y-axis represents the number of observations for a particular sample, and the x-axis represents the calibration of the variable being measured.

Galton, Francis English scientist who had an interest in comparing traits for sets of identical twins to help assess the influence of genes on human behavior. Late in the 1800s, Galton demonstrated that these comparisons could be illustrated with graphs.

geography Literally "earth measurement" but is a discipline focused on how politically drawn boundaries impact, and are affected by, features of the earth's surface. Although geography is considered a social science, it has close ties with geology, a physical science dealing with physical features of the earth and the formation of those features, and meteorology, which studies the earth's weather patterns.

Glass, Gene An American educator who was the first researcher to undertake and name a meta-analysis.

Google Scholar (http://scholar.google. com) A search engine that allows one to search for academic articles on specific topics, or researchers, and usually identifies the names and referencing information for the academic articles.

group matching Procedure in quasi-experimental designs for obtaining comparison groups where the researcher merely ensures that, on average, there are no significant differences between the exposure and the comparison groups regarding a variety of demographic characteristics.

Hawthorne Effect Named after an experiment in the late 1920s involving examining methods to improve work productivity in an electronics assembly plant in a district of Chicago known as Hawthorne; those conducting the experiment, using a before-after no control group design, found that improved lighting in the plant promoted worker productivity. Months later, the consultants recommended further increases in factory luminescence and found additional productivity improvements. However, they eventually lowered the luminescence and found that productivity also further improved. After this finding, the persons conducting the experiments concluded that the extra attention and concern given to the workers during the experiment were influencing productivity levels, not the lighting. As a result, when extraneous factors such as extra attention and reinforcement in an experiment with people have effects on behavior, it is referred to as the Hawthorne effect

hierarchy rule A rule requiring the police to report only the most serious offense committed in a multiple offense–single incident to the FBI and to ignore the others.

history The study of the past through written or oral accounts of past events, especially events that were especially consequential in human affairs.

homicide/murder The willful (nonnegligent) killing of one human being by another.

Human Relations Area Files (HRAF) A type of ethnographic atlas or databank of ethnographic accounts.

hypothesis A statement about empirical reality derived from theory that may or may not be true.

impact (or summative) evaluation research Applied not to continually functioning programs, but to ones that have designated end points. To assess such programs, researchers stipulate an objective for the program and then collect evidence as to whether such a goal had in fact been reached. For example, studies of the effectiveness of Scared Straight would constitute impact evaluation research. This is because each group of youth who visit the prison (or a control condition) can be independently studied.

inability A source of sample attrition that refers to numerous circumstances in which a subject can be contacted but is then unable to respond due to such things as illness or an inability to understand the language in which the questionnaire is written or the interviewer is speaking.

inaccessibility A source of sample attrition that results from difficulties in contacting or delivering a questionnaire to an intended subject (e.g., people changing addresses, rarely being at home, or having unlisted phone numbers).

independent (treatment) variable In experiments, the variable under the control of a researcher in the sense that the researcher can manipulate the level at which participants are exposed to the variable. Also, the variable that a researcher believes is predicting or is a possible cause of changes in the dependent variable or outcome being studied.

individual matching Procedure in quasi-experimental designs for obtaining comparison groups requiring the researcher to locate individuals in the comparison group that match each individual in the exposure group.

inferential statistics The ability to make statements about population parameters based on sample statistics. They allow researchers to make inferences about rejecting and accepting hypotheses.

informants (or gatekeepers) Persons at study sites who befriend a researcher. These special participants are called such because they are often the source of entrée and introduction to other research participants at the study site.

informed consent Entails informing prospective research participants of the basic purposes of a study and then obtaining their permission to be a participant (with the understanding that their participation is voluntary, and they are free to withdraw at any time).

inhibiting effect An interactive effect where increases in one variable tend to neutralize or at least dampen the effects of the other variable.

in-house (or intra-agency) documents Reports of studies of evaluation programs that are not published in conventional journals (or books) and therefore are not widely disseminated or subject to peer review processes. Instead, these studies are largely limited to being available to persons within the agency.

Institutional Review Board (IRB) Committees that oversee all research, especially that involving human subjects, and are mandatory at institutions that receive federal research funds (primarily universities and hospitals).

interactive effects Refers to the effects that two or more independent variables may have on a dependent variable that neither independent variable has by itself.

inter-rater (or inter-judge) reliability A method of assessing the reliability of measurement that involves two or more judges offering independent assessments of a particular variable and then comparing those assessments.

interval level of measurement Level of measurement of a variable that involves not only having an order to the calibrating units (as in ordinal measurement), but that the intervals are equidistant, or the distance between each successive unit is equal. For example, scores on academic achievement tests or sentence lengths in months for those sent to prison.

intra-test reliability A method of assessing the reliability of measurement that involves comparing scores on part of a measure of some variable with scores on another part of the same variable. The most widely used form of this method is called the split-half method.

item clustering Grouping a series of similar questions together under a single heading.

jottings (or scratch notes) Field notes that consist of note taking as close to their temporal occurrence as possible. Thus, an ethnographer or participant observer should keep a notepad handy at all times for jotting down words and phrases that will help him or her remember experiences and information acquired from the people being studied.

kin selection An idea proposed by William Hamilton in attempts to explain altruism in species and an extension of Darwin's natural selection, which described reproducing indirectly by helping close relatives reproduce.

laboratory/clinical observations Observations in a laboratory or clinical setting where the researcher collects data in a physical space under the control of the researcher.

larceny-theft The unlawful taking, leading, or riding away from the possession or constructive possession of another.

levels of analyses When aggregated units of analyses are arranged according to their inclusiveness.

levels of measurement Any of the four specified levels (nominal, ordinal, interval, and ratio) that describe how the variability in an operational definition is measured. The level at which a variable is measured is important to the types of analyses that can be utilized in studying it.

life-course persistent offenders Offenders who are more prone toward career criminality, in other words, engaging in criminal activity throughout their life course.

linear assumption The assumption that the best fitting regression line for a set of points is straight.

linear time series quasi-experimental design Closely resembles before-after no control group experiment and involves tracking a criterion variable over time, observing whether the values of it change in response to changes in a predictor variable.

longitudinal survey A survey that is administered over two or more points in time.

manipulative (or experimental) field research Field research that entails systematically attempting to alter some aspect of the behavior being observed.

measurement accuracy The extent to which measures are reliable, valid, and precise. Improving one usually improves the other two for better measurement accuracy.

measurement error The extent to which a variable is not being measured reliably, validly, and precisely.

median The measure of central tendency that represents the 50th percentile (or the midpoint) in a distribution curve or a set of numbers that have been arranged in ascending order.

meta-analysis A special type of review article that is undertaken to consolidate findings from a large number of related studies on some specific topic. A meta-analysis follows procedures that help to "standardize" findings from diverse individual studies to some common statistical test. To this extent, it is a statistically based literature review. The unit of analysis is the individual study, and therefore a meta-analysis is a study of studies.

mode The measure of central tendency that is defined as the most frequently observed score in a distribution.

model The representation of some aspect of a theory in a more tangible/physical form. A model is often used to illustrate or clarify some aspect of a theory and could be a diagrammatic (or structural) model, an equational model, or an animal model.

motor vehicle theft The theft or attempted theft of a motor vehicle.

multi-item scales (or multi-item tests) The practice where researchers ask more than one question within the same questionnaire and then combine the responses to these items into a single score. This is often done to improve the reliability of difficult-to-measure variables.

multiplicative rule States in part that one can multiply the probabilities of several similar individual events (like coin flipping) to derive an estimate of the probability of any combined number of those events.

multistage cluster sampling Sampling where the sampling frames come in two or more "layers." This may involve selecting a cluster from which to sample (counties) and then from those counties selected, selecting a random sample of cities within the counties; then within those cities, neighborhoods would be randomly chosen. Finally, blocks or streets within the neighborhoods would be randomly selected to send out surveys to the addresses on the street or block. The sample obtained with this set of procedures will closely approximate a representative sample of the citizens within the county.

National Crime Victimization Survey (NCVS) A biannual survey of a large number of people and households requesting information on crimes committed against individuals and households (whether reported to the police or not) and for circumstances of the offense (time and place it occurred, perpetrator's use of a weapon, any injuries incurred, and financial loss).

National Incident-Based Reporting System (NIBRS)   A comprehensive crime statistic collection system that is currently a component of the UCR program and is eventually expected to replace it entirely.

natural selection   A theory of evolution proposed by Charles Darwin outlining the processes by which organisms adapt in order to survive in changing environments and that explains the diversity of life on earth.

naturalistic (or nonmanipulative) field research   Field research that involves observing and recording behavior without interfering with it in any way.

negative (or inverse) relationship   Relationship between two variables where increasing values of one variable are associated with decreasing values of the other variable.

negatively skewed distribution   A distribution where the scores accumulate toward the left end of the distribution.

noncompliance (or refusal)   A source of sample attrition that stems from targeted participants intentionally deciding not to become involved in the study.

nominal level of measurement   The level of measurement of a variable that simply involves naming the calibrating units without any ordered meaning to them. Nominal-level measures are simply names given to variables for distinction purposes. For example, sex, race, political affiliation, and college major.

nonpanel longitudinal surveys   Surveys that involve selecting an entirely new sample (within the same population) each time the survey is run. The advantage of this form of longitudinal survey is that a researcher is able to estimate how the population is changing without having to locate the same subjects time after time.

nonprobability sampling methods   Any sampling method that cannot be trusted to obtain a sample that is representative of some specified population.

normal (or bell-shaped) curve   A theoretical distribution where the mean, median, and mode are all in the same place at the center of the distribution, and that has asymptotic properties meaning that the tails of the distribution taper off toward the base of the horizontal axis but never reach it.

null hypothesis   A standard benchmark hypothesis that asserts that there is no difference or no relationship with respect to whatever is being studied.

obtained sample   Refers to persons asked to participate in a study who actually agree to do so.

Occam's razor   A principle that encompasses the idea that the simpler the explanation, the better. The principle is named after William of Occam, who was an 18th-century scientist who attempted to distill scientific theories proposed by others down to their core principles (Dewsbury, 1984).

open-ended response option   Items that present a question (or make a statement) without providing any constraints on how subjects can respond.

operational definition   A definition that specifies in empirical terms precisely what should be done to observe variations in some variable or exactly how that variable ought to be measured.

orchestrated deception   Involves concocting instructions or circumstances so as to lead subjects to believe something that is not true.

ordinal level of measurement   The level of measurement of a variable that involves arranging the calibrating units into a logical order or rank. For example, we could measure a person's fear of crime on a scale ranging from not fearful to somewhat fearful to fearful and finally, very fearful.

outlier   Any extremely unusual score in a variable's distribution.

panel longitudinal surveys   Surveys in which the same sample is used each time the survey is conducted. These surveys allow a researcher to follow specific individuals over time to assess how they may be changing.

paradigm Broad perspectives from which theories emanate and refers to assumptions about the nature of phenomena.

Park, Robert A former newspaper reporter turned sociologist who was a faculty member at the University of Chicago in the early 20th century. He encouraged his graduate students to gain greater insight into human behavior by spending less time in the library and more time out in the "real world." This participant observation methodology became synonymous with what was called the Chicago School of Criminology.

parsimony An element of assessing the merit of a theory; refers to how simple and understandable a theory is: the simpler the theory, the better it is said to be. Also called Occam's razor for the 18th-century scientist William of Occam.

Part I offenses (or index crimes) The four violent (homicide, assault, forcible rape, and robbery) and four property offenses (larceny/theft, burglary, motor vehicle theft, and arson) reported in the Uniform Crime Reports.

Part II offenses The less serious offenses reported in the Uniform Crime Reports and are recorded based on arrests made rather than cases reported to the police.

partialling A widely used multivariate statistic for assessing the effect that a third variable is contributing to the relationship between two variables that works by removing one variable (by giving it a fixed value) so as to identify the extent to which any other variables one has measured remain correlated with one another.

partial panel longitudinal surveys A survey that represent a compromise between panel and nonpanel surveys. Essentially, some of the participants from the original sample are kept in the administration of the survey and some participants are drawn as a new sample. For example, the National Crime Victimization survey is a partial panel longitudinal survey in which one-third of the respondents are new each year, one-third were part of the panel the previous year, and one-third were in the panel for the two preceding years.

participant Refers to persons who agree to participate in research studies.

participant observation: Involves a researcher becoming involved in the social processes of participants that are being observed.

Pearson, Karl English scientist and firend of Francis Galton who also became interested in converting graphs depicting relationships into numerical form. Pearson eventually developed a formula for making the conversion. To his credit, this formula called Pearson's r is still the most widely used one in correlational statistics today.

peer review The process of reviewing the merit of manuscripts for publication in academic journals. Basically an editor sends the manuscript to two, three, or four individuals who are qualified to pass judgment on the merit of the article. Each peer reviewer (also called a referee) is expected to read and comment on the manuscript. Based on the comments received, and often the editor's own reading of the manuscript, one of three decisions for publication is made: rejection, acceptance, or varying degrees of revise-and-resubmit.

philosophy The prefix *philo* means "to love" and the suffix *sophia* denotes wisdom or knowledge. Philosophy refers to intellectual efforts to understand the meaning of life, the nature of good and evil, and the breaths and limits of human knowledge. It should be noted that today that most doctoral degrees awarded in science—from the physical sciences to the biological sciences to the social sciences—are PhDs, meaning doctorates of philosophy.

physical (or biological) anthropology A type of anthropology that attempts to piece together fossil evidence of the physical evolution of humans. It also tries to link the emergence of the human species from several extinct ancestral forms of human-like creatures based on fossil evidence.

plagiarism The intentional representation of someone else's writings or ideas as your own.

political science A social science discipline focusing on studying governments and the political forces that drive them. Political scientists also analyze voting patterns and shifts in public opinion, and the dynamics of international relationships. Political science issues are often interwoven with issues of economics, geography, sociology, and history.

population Refers to a naturally existing collection of some phenomenon (usually a collection of people living in a designated geographic area at a given point in time).

positive relationship (or a positive correlation) A relationship between variables where increasing values of one variable is associated with increasing values of another variable.

positively skewed distribution A distribution where the scores accumulate toward the right end of the distribution.

precision Refers to how well variations in a variable can be detected. The precision in measuring a variable can vary from extremely refined (or precise) to very coarse (or imprecise).

predictive accuracy One of the most important bases for assessing the merit of a theory; involves how accurately the theory predicts what researchers observe.

predictive scope As an element for assessing the merit of a theory, refers to the number of hypotheses that can be accurately predicted by a theory.

predictive (or discriminant) validity Involves assessing how well values (or scores) from a particular operational measure of a variable seem to predict what it ought to predict.

predictor variable Term used in quasi-experimental research instead of independent variable because there is no actual experimental control.

presentence investigations or presentence reports Reports that contain background information on the defendant and the nature of the offense they were convicted of with the purpose of providing the sentencing judge with information to determine an appropriate punishment.

pretesting Refers to the administration of a questionnaire to would-be respondents before giving it to actual respondents.

primary prevention programs Prevention programs focused fairly indiscriminately at some population, such as all teenagers in a school district.

probability In a statistical sense refers to mathematical estimates of the likelihood of various events taking place.

probability sampling methods Any method of sampling that can be relied upon to approximate representative samples.

probability theory The branch of mathematics that deals with probabilities. The general theoretical principles governing statistical decision making where estimates are assigned measures between 0 and 1. It is used to estimate the statistical significance of many real-world events.

process (or ongoing) evaluation research Evaluation research that is concerned with how well a program functions. As a program functions over time, and information is accumulated regarding its effects, those administrating the program can make changes with an eye toward continual improvement.

projective (or hypothetical) item One in which respondents are asked to report what they would do under specified conditions, particularly ones that have not yet happened.

prospective quasi-experimental design Involves observing variations in the predictor variable as events are unfolding, rather than reconstructing the events after the fact. Otherwise, a prospective quasi-experimental design and an ex post facto design are similar.

psychiatry Literally means "correcting the mind." Psychiatrists have a background in both medicine and psychology and usually work toward providing treatment to persons with some form of mental illness or disability.

psychology Literally the study of the mind (or psyche or spirit) which emphasizes examining human behavior and cognitive processes, such as thoughts and emotions. More recently, psychology as also been linked with biology, especially neurology; however, psychology is still a social science particularly in terms of research methodology that psychologists use.

public health A discipline involved in studying the health of large populations, rather than individual patients. Public health officials work closely with social scientists and several efforts have been made in recent years to deal with neighborhood concentrations of crime using what is known as a "public health model." This model confronts crime much as one would deal with a communicable disease outbreak.

p-**value** Represents the probability value.

qualitative observations Data collection where a researcher makes more or less unstructured observations of others. By unstructured observations, one means that the researcher will not be focusing attention on a few preidentified variables. Rather, he or she will be watching and recording whatever seems interesting.

quantitative direct observation Observation that allows data to exist in sufficient numbers and/or conditions to make it possible for them to be counted.

quartiles Measure of dispersion that represents the 25% points in a distribution; calculated by arranging all the scores in order, and then counting until one reaches intervals containing one-fourth, one-half, and three-fourths of the population.

quasi-experimental research Similar to controlled experimentation, although it is lacking one or more of the three main components of a true experiment.

question (also called an item or a questionnaire item) Refers to anything that calls for a linguistic or numeric response (in either written or oral form) from a respondent.

questionnaire Research instruments used to solicit information from potential respondents, usually in written form. In other words, a questionnaire is a research instrument through which human beings provide information about their lives and behavior, and sometimes about the lives and behavior of other persons they know.

quota sampling Nonprobability sampling technique where a researcher attempts to choose a certain proportion of persons with certain characteristics (e.g., males versus females) into the sample.

random assignment (randomization) In experimental designs, the process of randomly assigning participants to be in either the experimental group or the control group. By doing so, a researcher can be confident that whatever differences appear between the two groups in terms of the dependent variable can be attributed to the differential exposure to the independent variable and not differences in the groups themselves.

random digit dialing A method of obtaining a random sample in a telephone survey where once the first three digits (the prefixes) used in an area to be sampled have been entered into a computer (that has been connected to a telephone via a modem), the computer can be programmed to dial the last four digits at random. This ensures that every household with a telephone—even those not listed in the phone directory—will have an equal chance of being called.

random sample A sample that has been drawn from a population in which every member of the population had an equal chance of being chosen, sometimes referred to as EPSEM samples, or equal probability of selection of each member.

random sampling error Differences between characteristics of the obtained sample and those of the population that are due to chance, and can be reduced by increasing the sample size.

range The simplest measure of dispersion and defined as the top value for a variable minus the bottom value.

ranking response option A response option in which respondents are given a list of items to rank in some way.

ratio level of measurement The level of measurement of a variable that has equidistance between each successive calibration units, but also assumes that there is a point at which the variable is nonexistent, or has a meaningful zero point—for example, height and weight, as well as income in dollars, and number of prior arrests.

recall (or retrospective) item Questions requiring respondents to reach back into their memories to recall some specific event.

regression line Defined as the line that comes the closest to intersecting all the points in a scattergram.

reliability Refers to the tendency for a variable to yield stable and consistent scores when it is being measured.

replication Verifying the findings of others through repeating their original study.

representative sample Refers to a sample whose members possess all characteristics in the same proportion as the population as a whole.

research (or alternative) hypothesis A hypothesis that specifies a directional relationship between two or more variables being studied.

research instrument Refers to any physical thing used to collect scientific data.

research participants The people (and animals) who are the focus of research studies.

respondent Refers to a person who gives responses to questions on a questionnaire or in an interview. In other words, persons who are participants in a study are often called respondents if their involvement in a study simply involves completing a questionnaire.

response option Refers to the range of answers that researchers offer subjects in connection with the questions that are asked on the survey. These options are important to a researcher because they have a major influence on the type of data that will eventually be available for analysis.

reversal (ABAB) design An experimental design where the experiment is set up to shift back and forth between control and experimental conditions.

reverse score Items whose scores need to be inverted to measure them on a scale.

review articles Articles exclusively utilized to encompass all that has been learned about a specific topic up to the time the article was written.

robbery The taking or attempted taking of anything of value from the care, custody, or control of a person or persons by force or threat of force or violence and/or putting the victim in fear.

sample A subset of some population studied to understand the population itself.

sample attrition The difference between the chosen and the obtained samples.

sampling error The extent to which a sample of research participants is representative of the population from which they were drawn.

sampling frame Refers to a complete list of all members of the population.

sampling unit Each individual comprising a sample.

scale measurement Mainly interval and ratio level variables where the measures can be subject to calculations such as averages.

scattergrams (or scatterplots) Graphs that depict the relationships or correlation between variables.

scenarios (or vignettes) Projective (or hypothetical) items requiring respondents to make a series of stipulations rather than just one. Some of the most common of these scenario-based questions have to do with studying judicial or jury decision making where vignettes of fictional crimes and accused perpetrators are given to samples of persons. Then they are asked to determine whether or not they believe the person is guilty or asked to determine what type of sentence they would give if the person was found guilty.

scientific fraud In science, fraud refers to intentional misrepresentation of scientific ideas or findings.

scientific law A statement about what should always occur under a precise set of conditions. The best known scientific laws come from the physical sciences, such as Newton's law of gravity.

scientific method A set of methodological rules and assumptions that scientists use to answer their questions.

scientific model refers to some type of simplified representation of some aspect of a theory.

scientific paradigm Refers to a set of assumptions about the nature of the phenomenon to be explained and the approach that will be taken to obtain those explanations. Paradigms are best thought of as more general and encompassing than theories.

secondary analysis Refers to the analysis of archival data.

secondary prevention programs Prevention programs more narrowly focused with respect to a high-risk population, such as targeting teenagers in a school district who are at the highest risk of becoming smokers, such as those doing poorly in school and/or those whose parents smoke.

self-correcting In science, the idea that when errors in observations are made, sooner or later the mistakes will be identified.

self-report surveys The collecting of data by criminologists themselves, asking people to disclose their delinquent and criminal involvement on anonymous questionnaires.

self-selected sampling Sampling method where the subjects themselves take the initiative to be included in the study. Good examples of surveys based on self-selected samples are questionnaires that pop up on your smart phone or computer screen, looking to gauge people's preference for a new product line, or websites that invite people to click on a link to give their opinion on some topic.

serendipitous findings Findings that a researcher did not anticipate at the outset of a study. These are findings that are often surprising because a researcher was not explicitly intending the discovery of them.

sibling matching Involves identifying individuals with some unusual trait that researchers would like to better understand from a causal standpoint and using same-sex siblings as comparison subjects. This type of matching procedure automatically controls for race/ethnicity, social status, and family background.

simple cluster sampling Sampling method where a researcher chooses a few clusters of naturally occurring groups of subjects from a population and then collects data from many of the subjects comprising each of the clusters.

skewed distribution Distribution where the scores are accumulated in one end or the other.

snowball sampling Nonprobability sampling technique where research subjects are recruited and then asked to recruit additional subjects. The advantage of this sampling method is that it can build up sample sizes quickly (like a snowball) and/or it can recruit subjects who are otherwise difficult to locate.

social (including behavioral) science Disciplines whose primary objective is to understand behavioral and sociocultural phenomena.

social work A specialized discipline for assisting those in need of assistance or welfare (the poor, disabled, and otherwise disadvantaged). Social workers attempt to restore and enable their clients to be as physically and mentally healthy and self-sufficient as possible.

sociology A major social science established in the mid-1800s after a French philosopher/scientist named Auguste Comte, who argued that a special science was needed to study human societies and social relationships. He coined the term *sociology* to describe the discipline that would study societies and social relationships upon which societies are based. As sociology began to take root in North America in the late 19th century, many of its adherents developed an interest in understanding criminal behavior.

Solomon four-group design   A specialized and rarely-used experimental design that consists of an after-only experimental design attached to a classical design. This design requires assigning subjects to a minimum of four groups, two experimental groups and two control groups. Both experimental groups receive the same level of exposure to the independent variable, and both control groups are denied anything beyond the normal level of exposure to the independent variable. The difference is that one experimental group and one control group are pretested, while the other two groups are not. The purpose of this elaborate set of procedures is to see if repeated measurement of the dependent variable interacts in some way with exposure to the independent variable.

spontaneous recovery   A phenomenon in clinical research that refers to the tendency for people to seek treatment when their symptoms are worst. It is a potential threat to the validity of a before-after no control group experiments with no reversals.

spurious correlation   Term scientists use to refer to correlations that seem to be of no causal significance.

standard deviation   Measure of dispersion that is the most stable measure and can be used to compare scores across samples. Mathematically, it is the square root of the variance.

standard error   The standard deviation of any sampling distribution of any statistic.

statistical control   The statistical process for eliminating spurious relationships.

statistical generalizability   Using statistical inference and probability theory; the ability of a researcher to state that the findings from their analysis of a sample are also true for the population from which the sample was drawn. The process of inferring sample statistics as estimates of population parameters.

statistical power   Refers to the probability that a study will yield statistically significant results when a research hypothesis is true.

statistical significance   The probabilistic importance of a hypothesis test.

statistics   In general, the type of mathematics that are used most in the social sciences. Specifically, the methods and procedures used to describe and infer facts from data, as well as the numerical, tabular, and graphic descriptions of collected data, and the characteristics of a sample drawn from a larger population.

stratified random sampling   A special type of random sampling that is undertaken to allow groups with low representation in a population to be more highly represented. Involves taking a sampling frame and dividing its constituents up according to one or more characteristics and then randomly sampling subjects from the resulting separate lists.

study sites   The locations where qualitative observations take place.

sunset laws   State and federal legislation that automatically terminates funding for programs after a specified number of years unless explicit steps are taken to maintain funding.

supplementary homicide reports   Additional information provided in the Uniform Crime Reports for the crime of homicide. The information is incident based and includes information on what kinds of weapons were used; the race, age, and sex of offenders and victims; and the relationship that existed between offender and victim (spouse, lover, acquaintance, etc.).

survey   A widely used technique in the social sciences; refers to studies that examine empirical phenomenon without disturbing it. Most often used to determine the prevalence of some phenomenon within a designated population and time frame.

systematic (or interval) sampling   A type of random sampling that does not perfectly meet the conditions specified in the definition of pure random sampling.

Systematic sampling takes sampling units from a sampling frame at designated intervals (such as every tenth name in a directory) or at designated positions (such as the third name from the top of each page).

systematic sampling error Differences between characteristics of the obtained sample and those of the population that are caused by a segment of a population failing to be represented in a sample due to sample attrition.

telescoping The phenomenon where subjects report events occurring to them outside the time frame specified by the researcher. For example, asking a subject to report any victimizations that have occurred in the last 6 months, and they report victimizations that have occurred in the past year.

testimonial evidence Evidence based on impressionistic statements made by people closely associated with a program or treatment strategy.

test-retest reliability A method of assessing the reliability of measurement that involves administering the same instrument to a sample twice and comparing the consistency of scores.

thematic surveys Surveys where in-depth coverage is given to a single topic.

theory A plausible explanation of reality; scientifically, a set of logically related propositions or statements from which hypotheses can be derived.

time diary Questionnaire where respondents are asked to maintain daily or weekly logs of their ongoing behavior.

time-use data The data that result from a time diary.

t-**test (or student's *t*)** A relatively simple test that can be used to compare two means to determine if they can be considered significantly different from one another. The *t*-test was developed by a statistician named William Gosset who worked for the Guiness Brewery in Dublin, Ireland. Brewery policy prevented him from publishing the

paper introducing the *t*-test under his own name, so he published it under the pseudonym "Student."

twin studies Studies that attempt to determine how much influence genetic factors and environmental factors have on behavior by examining identical twins, who share 100% of their genes in common, and fraternal twins, who share on average 50% of their genes. The two-to-one ratio in the number of genes shared by sets of identical and fraternal twins makes it possible to examine behavior traits for evidence of genetic and environmental influence, because any differences between pairs of identical twins regarding either physical appearance or behavior would almost certainly be attributed to environmental factors.

two-by-three factorial design An experimental factorial design in which subjects are exposed to two levels of one variable and three levels of another variable.

two-by-two factorial design An experimental factorial design where subjects are exposed to two levels of two different variables.

two-by-two-by-two factorial design An experimental factorial design having two levels of three different variables.

type I error Involves rejecting the null hypothesis when it is in fact true.

type II error Defined as accepting the null hypothesis when it is actually false.

Uniform Crime Reports (UCR): Annual report compiled by the Federal Bureau of Investigation (FBI) containing crimes known to the nation's police and sheriff's departments; the number of arrests made by these agencies; and other crime-related information.

unit of analysis The entity that is the unit being studied. Examples are individuals, groups, neighborhoods, or schools.

univariate statistics The prefix *uni* implies statistics pertaining to a single variable. Also referred to as descriptive statistics.

universe A more inclusive term than population; a population refers to a collection of humans (or other living things) and a universe includes populations but also refers to collections of characteristics (or numbers representing those characteristics) exhibited by members of a population.

validity Refers to the degree that a variable is measuring what it is intended to measure.

variable Empirical phenomena that take on different values or intensities.

variance Measure of dispersion that is a conservative indicator of the entire spread of a population with respect to scores on a variable. Mathematically, it is the average sum of the squared deviation scores about the mean.

verifiability Using our own empirical observations to confirm or refute the empirical observations of others, and vice versa. Verifying the findings of other researchers is achieved through replication.

vote-counting (or ballot box) meta-analysis A type of meta-analysis where the researcher summarizes the results from numerous studies on some specific topic simply by showing how many significant and nonsignificant findings exist.

write-in end-anchored response option A numeric form of the end-anchored continuum where, instead of a linear continuum, subjects are instructed to answer by writing in a number.

References

Abel, E. L. (1984). *Fetal alcohol syndrome and fetal alcohol effects*. New York: Plenum.

Abelson, P. H. (1992). Diet and cancer in humans and rodents. *Science*, 255, 141.

Adair, J. G. (1984). The Hawthorn effect: A reconsideration of the methodological artifact. *Journal of Applied Psychology*, 69, 334–345.

Adams, R. (1976). Criminal justice: An emerging academic profession and discipline. *Journal of Criminal Justice*, 4, 303–314.

Ahlburg, D. A. (1986). A relative cohort size forecasting model of Canadian total live births. *Social Biology*, 33, 51–56.

Alcock, J. (1993). *Animal behavior: An evolutionary approach* (5th ed.). Sunderland, MA: Sinauer.

Alexander, K. L., & Pallas, A. M. (1985). School sector and cognitive performance: When is a little a little? *Sociology of Education*, 58, 115–128.

Alexander, T. (1972 October). The social engineers retreat under fire. *Fortune*, 86, 132–148.

Alland, A. (1967). *Evolution and human behavior*. London, England: Tavistock.

Allis, S. (1991 May). Can Catholic schools do it better? *Time*, 48–49.

Alonso, S. J., Castellano, M. A., Afonso, D., & Rodriquez, M. (1991). Sex differences in behavioral despair: Relationships between behavioral despair and open field activity. *Physiology and Behavior*, 49, 69–72.

Alonso, S. J., Castellano, M. A., & Rodriguez, M. (1991). Behavioral lateralization in rats: Prenatal stress effects on sex differences. *Brain Research*, 539, 45–50.

Althausen, J. D., & Mieczkowski, T. M. (2001). The merging of criminology and geography into a course on spatial crime analysis. *Journal of Criminal Justice Education*, 12, 367–383.

American Psychiatric Association. (1994). *Diagnostic and statistical manual of mental disorders* (4th ed.). Washington, DC: Author.

Anastasi, A. (1976). *Psychological testing*. New York: Macmillan.

Anda, R. F., Williamson, D. F., Escobedo, L. G., Mast, E. E., Giovino, G. A., & Remington, P. L. (1990). Depression and the dynamics of smoking: A national perspective. *Journal of the American Medical Association*, 264, 1541–1545.

Anderson, A. E., & DiDomenico, L. (1992). Diet versus shape content of popular male and female magazines: A dose-response relationship to the incidence of eating disorders? *International Journal of Eating Disorders*, 11, 283–287.

Anderson, B. A., Silver, B. D., & Abramson, P. R. (1988). The effects of race of interviewer on measures of electoral participation by blacks in SRC National Election Studies. *Public Opinion Quarterly*, 52, 52–83.

Anderson, C. A. (2001). Effects of violent video games on aggressive behavior, aggressive cognition, aggressive effect, physiological arousal, and prosocial behavior: A meta-analytic review of the scientific literature. *Psychological Science*, 12, 353–359.

Anderson, E. (1999). *Code of the street: Decency, violence, and the moral life of the inner city.* New York. Norton.

Anderson, G. S. (2007). *Biological influences on criminal behavior.* Boca Raton, FL: CRC Press (Taylor & Francis Group).

Anderson, J. L., Crawford, C. B., Nadeau, J., & Lindberg, T. (1992). Was the Duchess of Windsor right? A cross-cultural review of the socioecology of ideals of female body shape. *Ethology and Sociobiology*, 13(3), 197–227.

Aquilino, W. S. (1993). Effects of spouse presence during the interview on survey responses concerning marriage. *Public Opinion Quarterly*, 57, 358–376.

Ardila, A., Ardila, O., Bryden, M. P., Ostrosky, F., Rosselli, M., & Steenhuis, R. (1989). Effects of cultural background and education on handedness. *Neuropsychologia*, 27, 893–897.

Armstrong, J. S. (1975). Monetary incentives in mail surveys. *Public Opinion Quarterly*, 39, 112–116.

Armstrong, J. S., & Lusk, E. J. (1987). Return postage in mail surveys. *Public Opinion Quarterly*, 51, 233–248.

Arnett, J. (1991). Still crazy after all these years: Reckless behavior among young adults aged 23–27. *Personality and Individual Differences*, 12, 1305–1313.

Arney, W. R. (1990). *Understanding statistics in the social sciences.* New York: Freeman.

Arnhoff, F. N. (1975). Social consequences of policy toward mental illness. *Science*, 188, 1277–1281.

Arnold, W. (1990). The determination of drugs and their substitutes in human hairs. *Forensic Science International*, 46, 17–18.

Arrigo, B., & Shipley, S. (2001). The confusion over psychopathy (1): Historical considerations. *International Journal of Offender Therapy and Comparative Criminology*, 45(3), 325–344.

Aultman-Bettridge, T. (1998 January/February). Evaluation tips: Process evaluation. *Program Evaluation Newsletter*, 1, 7.

Ayers, M. S., & Reder, L. M. (1998). A theoretical review of the misinformation effect: Predictions from an activation-based memory model. *Psychonomic Bulletin and Review*, 5, 1–21.

Babbie, E. (1983). *The practice of social research* (5th ed.). Belmont, CA: Wadsworth.

Babbie, E. R. (1973). *Survey research methods.* Belmont, CA: Wadsworth.

Bagley, C. (1992). Maternal smoking and deviant behavior in 16 year olds: A personality hypothesis. *Personality and Individual Differences*, 13, 377–378.

Bailar, B. (1988). An enterprise in social science. *Science*, 240, 1057–1059.

Bailey, J. M., & Zucker, K. J. (1995). Childhood sex-typed behavior and sexual orientation: A conceptual analysis and quantitative review. *Developmental Psychology*, 31, 43–55.

Bailey, K. D. (1978). *Methods of social research.* New York: Free Press.

Baldwin, W. (2000). Information no one else knows: The value of self-report. In A. A. Stone, J. S. Turkkan, C. A. Bachrach, J. B. Jobe, H. S. Kurtzman & V. S. Cain (Eds.), *The science of self-report: Implications for research and practice* (pp. 3–7). Mahwah, NJ: Lawrence Erlbaum Associates.

Barbaree, H. E., Baxter, D. J., & Marshall, W. L. (1989). The reliability of the rape index in a sample of rapists and nonrapists. *Violence Victims*, 4, 299–306.

Barkley, R. A., Karlsson, J., Pollard, S., & Murphy, J. V. (1985). Developmental changes in the mother-child interactions of hyperactive boys: Effects of two dose levels of Ritalin. *Journal of Child Psychology and Psychiatry*, 26, 705–715.

Barkow, K., Heun, R., Ustun, T. B., Gansicke, M., Wittchen, H.-U., & Maier, W. (2002). Test-retest reliability of self-reported age at onset of selected psychiatric diagnoses in general health care. *Acta Psychiatrica Scandinavia*, 106, 117–125.

Barlow, D. H., & Hersen, M. (1984). *Single case experimental designs: Strategies for studying behavior change* (2nd ed.). New York: Pergamon.

Barnouw, V. (1989). *Physical anthropology and archaeology*. Chicago: Dorsey.

Bartol, C. (2002). *Criminal behavior: A psychosocial approach* (6th ed.). Upper Saddle River, NJ: Prentice Hall.

Bartos, R. (1986). Qualitative research: What it is and where it came from. *Journal of Advertising Research*, 26, RC-3–RC-6.

Baruch, Y., & Holtom, B. C. (2008). Survey response rate levels and trends in organizational research. *Human Relations*, 61, 1139–1160.

Bauer, H. H. (1992). *Scientific literacy and the myth of the scientific method*. Urbana: University of Illinois Press.

Bauman, K. E., & Koch, G. G. (1983). Validity of self-reports and descriptive and analytical conclusions: The case of cigarette smoking by adolescents and their mothers. *American Journal of Epidemiology*, 118, 90–98.

Baumrind, D. (1971). Principles of ethical conduct in the treatment of subjects: Reaction to the draft report of the Committee on Ethical Standards in Psychological Research. *American Psychologist*, 26, 887–896.

Beattie, J. M. (1975). The criminality of women in eighteenth-century England. *Journal of Social History*, 9, 80–116.

Beattie, J. M. (1977). Crime and the courts in Surrey: 1737–1753. In S. Cockburn (Ed.), *Crime in England: 1550–1800* (pp. 155–186). Princeton, NJ: Princeton University Press.

Beattie, J. M. (1986). *Crime and the courts in England, 1660–1800*. Princeton, NJ: Princeton University Press.

Becker, M. B. (1976). Changing patterns of violence and justice in fourteenth- and fifteenth-century Florence. *Comparative Studies in Society and History*, 18, 288.

Benjamin, R., Mazzarins, H., & Kupfersmid, J. (1983). The effect of time-out (TO) duration on assaultiveness in psychiatrically hospitalized children. *Aggressive Behavior*, 9, 21–27.

Benton, D., & Cook, R. (1991). Vitamin and mineral supplements improve the intelligence scores and concentration of six-year-old children. *Personality and Individual Differences*, 12, 1151–1158.

Berk, R. A. (2004). *Regression analysis: A constructive critique*. Thousand Oaks, CA: Sage.

Berk, R. A. (1983). An introduction to sample selection bias in sociological data. *American Sociological Review*, 48, 386–398.

Bernard, H. R. (1983). *Research methods in anthropology: Qualitative and quantitative approaches*. Walnut Creek, CA: AltaMira Press.

Bernard, H. R. (2002). *Research methods in anthropology: Qualitative and quantitative methods* (3rd ed.). New York: AltaMira Press.

Begley, S., & Seward, D. (1986 May). Back from the stone age? *Newsweek*, 69.

Bersoff, D. M., & Bersoff, D. N. (2000). Ethical issues in the collection of self-report data. In A. A. Stone, J. S. Turkkan, C. A. Bachrach, J. B. Jobe, H. S. Kurtzman & V. S. Cain (Eds.), *The science of self-report: Implications for research and practice* (pp. 9–24). Mahwah, NJ: Lawrence Erlbaum Associates.

Biner, P. M., & Kidd, H. J. (1994). The interactive effects of monetary incentive justification and questionnaire length on mail survey responses rates. *Psychology and Marketing*, 11, 483–492.

Blair, E., Sudman, S., Bradburn, N., & Stocking, C. (1977). How to ask questions about drinking and sex: Response effects in measuring consumer behavior. *Journal of Marketing Research*, 14, 316–321.

Blanchard, A., & Centifanti, L. C. M. (2017). Callous-unemotional traits moderate the relation between prenatal testosterone (2D:4D) and externalising behaviours in children. *Child Psychiatry & Human Development*, 48, 668–677.

Blum, D. E. (1989). A dean is charged with plagiarizing a dissertation for his book on Muzak. *Chronicle of Higher Education*, 35, A17.

Blumstein, A., Cohen, J., & Rosenfeld, R. (1991). Trend and deviation in crime rates: A comparison of VCR and NCS data for burglary and robbery. *Criminology*, 29, 237–263.

Bobak, M. (2001). The seasonality of live birth is strongly influenced by sociodemographic factors. *Human Reproduction*, 16, 1512–1517.

Bolton, G. M. (1974). The lost letter technique as a measure of community attitudes towards a major social issue. *Sociological Quarterly*, 15, 567–570.

Bolton, R. (1984). We all do it, but how? A survey of contemporary field note procedure. In Final report: Computers on ethnographic research. Washington, DC: National Institute of Education (ERIC, no. ED 1. 310/2:248173).

Bonta, J., Law, M., & Hanson, K. (1998). The prediction of criminal and violent recidivism among mentally disordered offenders: A meta-analysis. *Psychological Bulletin*, 123, 123–142.

Bontrager, S., Barrick, K., and Stupi, E. (2013). Gender and sentencing: A meta-analysis of contemporary research. *The Journal of Gender, Race, and Justice*, 16, 349–372.

Borgerhoff Mulder, M. (1988). Reproductive success in three Kipsigis cohorts. In T. H. Clutton Brock (Ed.), *Reproductive success* (pp. 419–438). Chicago: University of Chicago Press.

Borenstein, M., Hedges, L. V., Higgins, J. P. T., & Rothstein, H. R. (2009). *Introduction to meta-analysis*. Chichester, UK: Wiley.

Bornstein, R. F. (1990). Publications politics, experimenter bias, and the replication process in social science research. *Journal of Social Behavior and Personality*, 5, 71–81.

Bouchard, T. J., Jr., Lykken, D. T., McGue, M., Segal, N. L., & Tellegen, A. (1990). Sources of human psychological differences: The Minnesota Study of Twins Reared Apart. *Science*, 250, 223–228.

Bouchard, T. J., Jr., & Stuster, J. (1969). The lost letter technique: Predicting elections. *Psychological Reports*, 25, 231–234.

Boyle, M. H., Offord, D. R., Racine, Y., Fleming, J. E., Szatmari, P., & Sanford, M. (1993). Evaluation of the revised Ontario Child Health Study scales. *Journal of Child Psychology and Psychiatry*, 34, 189–213.

Brackett, J. K. (1994). *Criminal justice and crime in late Renaissance Florence, 1537–1609*. Westport, CT: Greenwood.

Bradbard, M. R. (1985). Sex differences in adults' gifts and children's toy requests at Christmas. *Psychological Reports*, 56, 969–970.

Bradburn, N. M. (2000). Temporal representation and event dating. In A. A. Stone, J. S. Turkkan, C. A. Bachrach, J. B. Jobe, H. S. Kurtzman & V. S. Cain (Eds.), *The science of self-report: Implications for research and practice* (pp. 49–61). Mahwah, NJ: Lawrence Erlbaum.

Bradburn, N. M., & Sudman, S. (1979). *Improving interview method and questionnaire design: Response effect to threatening questions in survey research*. San Francisco: Jossey-Bass.

Bradburn, N. M., Rips, L. J., & Shevell, S. K. (1987). Answering autobiographical questions: The impact of memory and inference on surveys. *Science*, 236, 157–161.

Bradburn, N., Sudman, S., Blair, E., & Stocking, C. (1978). Question threat and response bias. *Public Opinion Quarterly*, 42, 221–234.

Bradley, J., Gerald, J. F., & Kearney, I. (1993). Modelling supply in an open economy using a restricted cost function. *Economic Modeling*, 10, 11–21.

Braga, A. A., Hureau, D. A., & Papachristos, A. V. (2011). The relevance of micro places to citywide robbery trends: A longitudinal analysis of robbery incidents at street corners and block faces in boston. *Journal of Research in Crime and Delinquency*, 48, 7–32.

Branas, C. C., & Knudson, M. M. (2001). Helmet laws and motorcycle rider death rates. *Accident Analysis and Prevention*, 33, 641–648.

Brandt, A. (1978). Racism and research: The case of the Tuskegee Syphilis Study. *The Hastings Center Report*, 8, 21–29.

Brennan, M. T., & Fox, P. C. (1999). Sex differences in primary Sjogren's syndrome. *Journal of Rheumatology*, 26, 2373–2376.

Breslau, N., Kilbey, M., & Andreski, P. (1991). Nicotine dependence and anxiety in young adults. *Archives of General Psychiatry*, 48, 1069–1074.

Breslau, N., Peterson, E. L., Schultz, L. R., Chilcoat, H. D., & Andreski, P. (1998). Major depression and stages of smoking: A longitudinal investigation. *Archives of General Psychiatry*, 55, 161–166.

Brewster, A. L., Nelson, J. P., McCanne, T. R., Lucas, D. R., & Milner, J. S. (1998). Gender differences in physiological reactivity to infant cries and smiles in military families. *Child Abuse and Neglect*, 22, 775–788.

Briar, S. (1980). Toward the integration of practice and research. In D. Fanshel (Ed.), *The future of social work research* (pp. 31–37). Washington, DC: National Association of Social Workers.

Bridges, G., Gillmore, G., Pershing, J., & Bates, K. (1998). Teaching quantitative research methods: A quasi-experimental analysis. *Teaching Sociology*, 26, 14–28.

Brittain, J. M. (1990). Cultural boundaries of the social sciences in the 1990s: New policies for documentation, information and knowledge creation. *International Social Science Journal*, 41, 105–117.

Broad, W., & Wade, N. (1982). *Betrayers of the truth*. Simon & Schuster.

Broadhurst, P. L., & Bigami, G. (1965). Correlative effects of psychogenetic selection: A study of the Roman high and low avoidance strains of rats. *Behaviour Research and Therapy*, 2, 273–280.

Brook & Brook (1990). The psychosocial etiology of adolescent drug use: A family interactional approach. *Genetic, Social, and General Psychology Monographs*, 116, 159.

Brook, J. S., Brook, D. W., Gordon, A. S., Whiteman, M., & Cohen, P. (1990). The psychological etiology of adolescent drug use: A family interactional approach. *Genetic, Social, and General Psychology Monograph*, 116, 111–267.

Brooks, C. I. (1987). Superiority of women in statistics achievement. *Teaching of Psychology*, 14, 45–46.

Brown, D. (1991). *Human universals*. New York: McGraw-Hill.

Brown, J. (1987). A review of meta-analyses conducted on psychotherapy outcome research. *Clinical Psychology Review*, 7, 1–23.

Brozek, J. (1990). Contributions to the history of psychology, XVII: Early uses of the term "objective psychology." *Perceptual and Motor Skills*, 70, 377–378.

Brush, F. R., Froehlich, J. C., & Sakellaris, P. C. (1979). Genetic selection for avoidance behavior in the rat. *Behavior Genetics*, 9, 309–316.

Bryden, M. P. (1987). Handedness and cerebral organization: Data from clinical and normal populations. In D. Ottoson (Ed.), *Duality and unity of the brain*. (pp. 55–70). Boston, MA: Springer.

Buck, J. L. (1985). A failure to find gender differences in statistics achievement. *Teaching of Psychology*, 12, 100.

Buckner, J. C., & Chesney-Lind, M. (1983). Dramatic cures for juvenile crime: An evaluation of a prisoner-run delinquency prevention program. *Criminal Justice and Behavior*, 10, 227–247.

Bunge, M. (1990). What kind of discipline is psychology: Autonomous or dependent, humanistic or scientific, biological or sociological? *New Ideas in Psychology*, 8, 121–137.

Burling, T. A., Bigelow, G. E., Robinson, J. C., & Mead, A. M. (1991). Smoking during pregnancy: Reduction via objective assessment and directive advice. *Behavior Therapy*, 22, 31–40.

Burris, V. (1983). States in the development of economic concepts. *Human Relations*, 36, 791–812.

Burton, M. L., & White, D. R. (1987). Cross-cultural surveys today. *Annual Review in Anthropology*, 16, 143–160.

Buss, D. M. (1994). *The evolution of desire*. New York: Basic Books.

Buttell, F. P., & Pike, C. K. (2003). Investigating the differential effectiveness of a batterer treatment program on outcomes for African American and Caucasian batterers. *Research on Social Work Practice*, 13, 675–692.

Byers, S. N. (2005). *Introduction to forensic anthropology: A textbook* (2nd ed.). New York: Pearson Professional.

Cadoret, R. J., Troughton, E., O'Gorman, T. W., & Heywood, E. (1986). An adoption study of genetic and environmental factors in drug abuse. *Archives of General Psychiatry*, 43, 1131–1136.

Cairns, L. G., & Bochner, S. (1974). Measuring sympathy toward handicapped children with the "lost-letter" technique. *Australian Journal of Psychology*, 26, 89–91.

Caldas, S. J., & Bankston, C. I. (1999). Black and white TV: Race, television viewing, and academic achievement. *Sociological Spectrum*, 19, 39–61.

Cameron, G. T., Lariscy, R. W., & Sweep, D. D. (1992). Predictors of systematic public relations research in higher education. *Journalism Quarterly*, 69, 466–470.

Campbell, D. T. (1969). Reforms as experiments. *American Psychologist*, 24, 409–429.

Campbell, D. T., & Stanley, J. C. (1966). *Experimental and quasi-experimental designs for research*. Skokie, IL: Rand McNally.

Cano-Urbina, J., & Lochner, L. (2019). The effect of education and school quality on female crime. *Journal of Human Capital*, 13(2), 188–235.

Card, J. J., Greeno, C., & Peterson, J. L. (1992). Planning an evaluation and estimating its cost. *Evaluation and The Health Professions*, 15, 75–89.

Card, N. A. (2012). *Applied meta-analysis for social science research*. New York, NY: Guilford.

Carlo, G., Roesch, S. C., & Melby, J. (1998). The multiplicative relations of parenting and temperament to prosocial and antisocial behaviors in adolescence. *Journal of Early Adolescence*, 18, 266–290.

Carlson, C. L., & Bunner, M. R. (1993). Effects of methylphenidate on the academic performance of children with attention-deficit hyperactivity disorder and learning disabilities. *School Psychology Review*, 22, 184–198.

Carlson, C. L., Pelham, W. E., Milich, R., & Dixon, J. (1992). Single and combined effects of methylphenidate and behavior therapy on the classroom performance of children with attention-deficit hyperactive disorder. *Journal of Abnormal Child Psychology*, 20, 213–232.

Carney, M. M., & Buttell, F. P. (2006). An evaluation of a court-mandated batterer intervention program: Investigating differential program effect for African American and white women. *Research on Social Work Practice*, 16, 571–581.

Carpenter, E. H. (1975). Personalizing mail surveys: A replication and reassessment. *Public Opinion Quarterly*, 38, 614–620.

Carr, E. H. (1962). *What is history?* New York: Knopf.

Carr, L. G. (1971). The Strole items and acquiesce. *American Sociological Review*, 36, 287–293.

Carter-Saltzman, L. (1980). Biological and sociocultural effects on handedness: Comparison between biological and adoptive families. *Science*, 209, 1263–1265.

Caspi, A., Elder, G. H., & Bem, D. J. (1987). Moving against the world: Life-course patterns of explosive children. *Developmental Psychology*, 23, 308–313.

Caspi, A., Moffitt, T. E., Silva, P. A., Southamer-Loeber, M., Krueger, R. F., & Schmutte, P. S. (1994). Are some people crime-prone? Replications of the personality-crime relationship across countries, genders, races, and methods. *Criminology*, 32, 163–195.

Castonguay, L. G., Proulx, J., Aubut, J., McKibben, A., & Campbell, M. (1993). Sexual preference assessment of sexual aggressors: Predictors of penile response magnitude. *Archives of Sexual Behavior*, 22, 325–334.

Catalano, R. T., Bruckner, J., Marks, A. R., & Eskenazi, B. (2006). Exogenous shocks to the human sex ratio: The case of September 11, 2001, in New York City. *Human Reproduction*, 21, 3127–3131.

Catalano, S. (2006). *NCVS survey*. Bureau of Justice Statistics. Washington, DC: US Department of Justice.

Catania, J. A., Binson, D., Canchola, J., Pollack, L. M., Hauck, W., & Coates, T. J. (1996). Effects of interviewer gender, interviewer choice, and item wording on responses to questions concerning sexual behavior. *Public Opinion Quarterly*, 60, 345–375.

Catania, J. A., Coates, T. J., Stall, R., Turner, H., Peterson, J., Hearst, N., et al. (1992). Prevalence of AIDS-related risk factors and condom use in the United States. *Science*, 258, 1101–1106.

Cernkovich, S. A., Giordano, P. C., & Pugh, M. D. (1985). Chronic offenders: The missing cases in self-report delinquency research. *Journal of Criminal Law and Criminology*, 76, 705–732.

Cernkovich, S. A., Giordano, P. C., & Rudolph, J. (2000). Race, crime, and the American dream. *Journal of Research in Crime and Delinquency*, 37(2), 131–170.

Chalmers, T. C. (1989). Meta-analysis (letter). *Science*, 243, 283–284.

Chambliss, W. J. (1974). The state, the law and the definition of behavior as criminal or delinquent. In D. Glaser (Ed.), *Handbook of criminology* (pp. 24–46). Chicago: Rand McNally.

Chamlin, M. B. (2017). An interrupted time series analysis of the differential impact of New Jersey's BAC legislation on driver and passenger crash fatalities. *Journal of Crime and Justice*, 40(4), 542–549.

Chandrasekhar, S. (1987). *Truth and beauty: Aesthetics and motivations in science*. Chicago, Illinois: University of Chicago Press.

Chappell, A. T. (2009). The philosophical versus actual adoption of community policing: A case study. *Criminal justice Review*, 34, 5–28.

Charland, H., & Cote, G. (1998). The children of alcoholics screening test (CAST): Test-retest reliability of concordance validity. *Journal of Clinical Psychology*, 54, 995–1003.

Charney, E., Goodman, H., McBride, M., Lyon, B., & Pratt, R. (1976). Childhood antecedents of adult obesity: Do chubby infants become obese adults? *New England Journal of Medicine*, 295, 6–9.

Chase, I. D. (1980). Social process and hierarchy formation in small groups: A comparative perspective. *American Sociological Review*, 45, 905–924

Chaudhary, N. K., Solomon, M. G., & Cosgrove, L. A. (2004). The relationship between perceived risk of being ticketed and self-reported seat belt use. *Journal of Safety Research*, 35, 383–390.

Check, J. V. P., & Malamuth, N. M. (1986). Pornography and sexual aggression: A social learning theory analysis. *Communication Yearbook*, 9, 181–213.

Cherek, D. R., Moeller, F. G., Schnapp, W., & Dougherty, D. M. (1997). Studies of violent and nonviolent male parolees: I. Laboratory and psychometric measurements of aggression. *Biological Psychiatry*, 41, 514–522.

Chesney-Lind, M., and Pasko, L. (2012). *The female offender: Girls, women, and crime* (3rd ed.). Thousand Oaks, CA: Sage.

Christiansen, K., & Winkler, E. M. (1992). Hormonal, anthropometrical, and behavioral correlates of physical aggression in Kung San men of Namibia. *Aggressive Behavior*, 18, 271–280.

Church, A. H. (1993 Spring). Estimating the effect of incentives on mail survey response rates: A meta-analysis. *Public Opinion Quarterly*, 57(1),62–79.

Clark, J., & Tifft, L. (1966). Polygraph and interview validations of self-reported deviant behavior. *American Sociological Review*, 31, 516–523.

Clinard, M. B. (1978). Comparative crime victimization surveys: Some problems and results. *International Journal of Criminology and Penology*, 6, 221–231.

Coates, T., Jeffrey, R., & Wing, R. (1978). The relationship between persons' relative body weights and the quality and quantity of food stored in their homes. *Addictive Behaviors*, 3, 179–185.

Cochran, J. K., Chamlin, M. B., & Seth, M. (1994). Deterrence or brutalization? An impact assessment of Oklahoma's return to capital punishment. *Criminology*, 32, 107–134.

Cochran, J. K., Wood, P. B., & Arneklev, B. J. (1994). Is the religiosity delinquency relationship spurious? A test of arousal and social control theories. *Journal of Research in Crime and Delinquency*, 31, 92–123.

Cochrane, R., & Howell, M. (1995). Drinking patterns of black and white men in the West Midlands. *Social Psychiatry and Psychiatric Epidemiology*, 30, 139–146.

Cockburn, J. S. (Ed.). (1977). *Crime in England 1500–1800*. Princeton, NJ: Princeton University Press.

Cohen, F. S., & Densen-Gerber, J. (1981). A study of the relationship between child abuse and drug addiction in 178 patients: Preliminary results. *Child Abuse and Neglect*, 6, 383–387.

Coleman, J. S. (1964). *Introduction to mathematical sociology*. Glencoe, NY: Free Press.

Coleman, J. S. (1990). *Equality and achievement in education*. Boulder, CO: Westview Press.

Coleman, J. S., Hoffer, T., & Kilgore, S. (1981). *Public and private schools*. Chicago: National Opinion Research Center.

Coleman, J. S., Hoffer, T., & Kilgore, S. (1982a). Achievement and segregation in secondary schools: A further look at public and private school differences. *Sociology of Education*, 55, 162–182.

Coleman, J. S., Hoffer, T., & Kilgore, S. (1982b). Cognitive outcomes in public and private schools. *Sociology of Education*, 55, 65–76.

Coleman, J. S., Hoffer, T., & Kilgore, S. (1982c). *High school achievement*. New York: Basic.

Coleman, R., & Thorson, E. (2002). The effects of news stories that put crime and violence into context: Testing the public health method model of reporting. *Journal of Health Communication*, 7, 401–425.

Colon, H. M., Robles, R. R., & Sahai, H. (2001). The validity of drug use responses in a household survey in Puerto Rico: Comparison of survey responses of cocaine and heroin use with hair tests. *International Journal of Epidemiology*, 30, 1042–1049.

Conklin, J. E. (1986). *Criminology* (2nd ed.). New York: Macmillan.

Conybeare, J. A. C. (1980). Evaluation of automobile safety regulations: The case of compulsory seat belt legislation in Australia. *Policy Sciences*, 12, 27–39.

Cooper, J. O., Heron, T. E., & Herward, W. L. (1987). *Applied behavior analysis*. Columbus, OH: Merrill.

Cordner, G. W. (1991). A problem oriented approach to community-oriented policing. In J. R. Greene & S. D. Mastrofksi (Eds.), *Community policing: Rhetoric or reality?* (pp. 135–152). New York: Praeger.

Cormier, D. T., Berry, A. B., Rhodes, M., & Copeland, J. (2017). What makes humans human? a review of important genetic differences between chimpanzees and humans. *Journal of Student Research*, 6(2), 1–6. https://jofsr.org/index.php/path/article/view/291.

Cornwell, C., & Trumbull, W. N. (1994). Estimating the economic model of crime with panel data. *Review of Economics and Statistics*, 76, 360–366.

Coser, L. (1975). Two methods in search of substance. *American Sociological Review*, 40, 691–700.

Cowlishaw, G., & Mace, R. (1996). Cross-cultural patterns of marriage and inheritance: phylogenetic approach. *Ethology and Sociobiology*, 17, 87–97.

Cox, M. V., & Rowlands, A. (2000). The effect of three different educational approaches on children's drawing ability: Steiner, Montessori, and traditional. *British Journal of Educational Psychology*, 70, 485–503.

Craig, R. J. (1987). MMPI-derived prevalence estimates of homosexuality among drug dependent patients. *International Journal of the Addictions*, 22, 1139–1145.

Cuenot, R. G., & Fugita, S. S. (1982). Perceived homosexuality: Measuring heterosexual attitudinal and nonverbal reactions. *Personality and Social Psychology Bulletin*, 8, 100–106.

Culliton, B. J. (1983a). Fraud inquiry spreads blame. *Science*, 219, 937.

Culliton, B. J. (1988a). Authorship, data ownership examined. *Science*, 242, 658.

Culliton, B. J. (1988b). A bitter battle over error (II). *Science*, 241, 18–21.

Cunningham, C. E., Siegel, L. S., & Offord, D. R. (1985). A developmental dose-response analysis of the effects of methylphenidate on the peer interactions of attention deficit disordered boys. *Journal of Child Psychology and Psychiatry*, 26, 955–972.

D'Alessio, S., & Stolzenberg, L. (2003). Race and the probability of arrest. *Social Forces*, 81, 1381–1397.

D'Antonio, W. V. (1989 August). Executive office report: Sociology on the move. *ASA Footnotes*, 17, 2.

Dabbs, J. M., Frady, R. L., Carr, T. S., & Besch, N. F. (1987). Saliva testosterone and criminal violence in young adult prison inmates. *Psychosomatic Medicine*, 49, 174–182.

Dabbs, J. M., Jr., Ruback, R. B., & Besch, N. F. (1987). *Males' saliva testosterone following conversations with male and female partners*. American Psychological Association Poster Session. New York.

Daly, K., & Bordt, R. (1995). Sex effects and sentencing: A review of the statistical literature. *Justice Quarterly*, 12, 141–175.

Danforth, J. S., & DuPaul, G. J. (1996). Interrater reliability of teacher rating scales for children with attention-deficit hyperactivity disorder. *Journal of Psychopathy and Behavioral Assessment*, 18, 227–237.

Davey Smith, G., & Dorling, D. (1996). I'm all right John. *British Medical Journal*, 313, 1573–1577.

Davis, B., Clarke, A. R. B., Francis, J., Hughes, G., MacMillan, J., McNeil, J., et al. (1992). Dress for respect: The effect of teacher dress on student expectations of deference behavior. *Alberta Journal of Educational Research*, 38, 27–31.

Davis, H., & Gergen, P. J. (1994). The weights and heights of Mexican-American adolescents: The accuracy of self-reports. *American Journal of Public Health*, 84, 459–462.

Davis, H. P., Rosenzweig, M. R., Becker, L. A., & Sather, K. J. (1988). Biological psychology's relationship to psychology and neuroscience. *American Psychologist*, 43, 359–371.

Dawson, J. L. B. (1977). Alaskan Eskimo hand, eye, auditory dominance and cognitive style. *Psychologia*, 20, 121–135.

Dawson, S., & Dickinson, D. (1988). Conducting international mail surveys: The effect of incentives on response rates within an industrial population. *Journal of International Business Studies*, 19, 491–496.

Day, N. L., Jasperse, D., Richardson, G., Robles, N., Sambamoorthi, U., Taylor, P., et al. (1989). Prenatal exposure to alcohol: Effect on infant growth and morphologic characteristics. *Pediatrics*, 84, 536–541.

De Beer, J. (1991). Births and cohort size. *Social Biology*, 38, 146–153.

De Leeuw, E. D. (1992). Data quality in mail, telephone, and face to face surveys (Unpublished doctoral dissertation). T T Publikaties, Amsterdam.

De Los Reyes, A., & Kazdin, A. E. (2008). When the evidence says,"yes, no, and maybe so" attending to and interpreting inconsistent findings among evidence-based interventions. *Current Directions in Psychological Science*, 17(1), 47–51.

Dean, R. S. (1982). Assessing patterns of lateral preference. *Clinical Neuropsychology*, 4, 124–128.

Decker, S. H., & Kohfeld, C. W. (1990). The deterrent effect of capital punishment in the five most active execution states: A time series analysis. *Criminal Justice Review*, 15, 173–191.

Decker, S. H., and Lauritsen, J. L. (2002). Breaking the bonds of membership: Leaving the gang. In C. R. Huff (Ed.), *Gangs in America III* (pp. 103–122). Thousand Oaks, California: Sage Publications, Inc.

DeKeseredy, W. S., & MacLean, B. D. (1991). Exploring the gender, race, and class dimensions of victimization: A left realist critique of the Canadian Urban Victimization Survey. *International Journal of Offender Therapy and Comparative Criminology*, 35, 143–161.

Demo, D. H., & Acock, A. C. (1988). The impact of divorce on children. *Journal of Marriage and the Family*, 50, 619–648.

Derzon, J. H. (2010). The correspondence of family features with problem, aggressive, criminal, and violent behavior: A meta-analysis. *Journal of Experimental Criminology*, 6, 263–292. https://doi.org/10.1007/s11292-010-9098-0.

Dewsbury, D. A., ed. (1984). *Foundations of comparative psychology*. New York: Van Nostrand Reinhold

Dewsbury, D. A. (1984). *Comparative psychology in the twentieth century*. Stroudsburg, PA: Hutchinson Ross.

Diamantopoulos, A., Reynolds, N., & Schlegelmilch, B. (1994). Pretesting in questionnaire design: The impact of respondent characteristics on error detection. *Journal of the Market Research Society*, 36, 295–313.

Diamond, L. J., & Jaudes, P. K. (1983). Child abuse in a cerebral-palsied population. *Developmental Medicine and Child Neurology*, 25, 169–174.

Diaper, G. (1990). The Hawthorne effect: A fresh examination. *Educational Studies*, 16, 261–267.

Dickinson, W. R. (1971). Letter to the editor. *Science*, 173, 1191–1192.

Dillman, D. A. (1991). The design and administration of mail surveys. *Annual Review of Sociology*, 17, 225–249.

Dillman, D. A., Sinclair, S. M. D., & Clark, J. R. (1993). Effects of questionnaire length, respondent-friendly design, and a difficult question on response rates for occupant addressed census mail surveys. *Public Opinion Quarterly*, 57, 289–304.

Dixon, M., & Wright, W. C. (1975). *Juvenile delinquency prevention programs*. Nashville, TN: Peabody College for Teachers.

Dong, E. (1991). Confronting scientific fraud. *Chronicle of Higher Education*, 38, A52.

Donnerstein, E., Linz, D., & Penrod, S. (1984). The effects of multiple exposures to filmed violence against women. *Journal of Communications*, 34, 130–147.

Donnerstein, E., Linz, D., & Penrod, S. (1987). *The question of pornography*. New York: Free Press.

Douglas, K., Vincent, G., & Edens, J. (2006). Risk for criminal recidivism: The role of psychopathy. In C. Patrick (Ed.), *Handbook of Psychopathy* (pp. 533–554). New York: Guilford.

Downs, A. C. (1983). Letters to Santa Claus: Elementary school-age children's toy preferences in a natural setting. *Sex Roles*, 9, 159–163.

Drillien, C. M., & Wilkinson, E. M. (1964). Emotional stress and mongoloid births. *Developmental Medicine and Child Neurology*, 6, 140–143.

Drost, E. A. (2011). Validity and reliability in social science research. *Education Research and Perspectives*, 38(1), 105–123.

Dunne, M. P., Martin, N. G., Bailey, J. M., Heath, A. C., Bucholz, K. K., Madden, P. A., et al. (1997). Participation bias in a sexuality survey: Psychological and behavioural characteristics of responders and non-responders. *International Journal of Epidemiology*, 26, 844–854.

Dunworth, T. (2001). Criminal justice and the IT revolution. Federal Probation. http://search.epnet.com/citation.asp?tb=1.

Durkheim, E. (1951). *The division of labor in society*. Glencoe, IL: Free Press.

Echeburua, E., Fernandez-Montalvo, J., & Amor, P. J. (2006). Psychological treatment of men convicted of gender violence: A pilot study. *International Journal of Offender Therapy and Comparative Criminology*, 50, 57–70.

Ehrlich, I. (1977). Capital punishment and deterrence: Some further thought and additional evidence. *Journal of Political Economics*, 85, 741–788.

Eichelman, B. (1992). Aggressive behavior: From laboratory to clinic. *Archives of General Psychiatry*, 49, 488–492.

Ekman, J. (1990). Alliances in winter flocks of willow tits: Effects of rank on survival and reproductive success in male–female associations. *Behavioral Ecology and Sociobiology*, 26, 239–245.

Ellis, L. (1969). Time variations in interview quality (Unpublished master's thesis). Pittsburg State University, Pittsburg, KS.

Ellis, L. (1989). *Theories of rape: Inquiries into the causes of sexual aggression*. New York: Hemisphere.

Ellis, L. (1998). NeoDarwinian theories of violent criminality and antisocial behavior: Photographic evidence from nonhuman animals and a review of the literature. *Aggression and Violent Behavior*, 3, 61–110.

Ellis, L., Beaver, K., & Wright, J. (2009). *Handbook of crime correlates*. Amsterdam: Elsevier (Academic Press).

Ellis, L., Burke, D., & Ames, A. (1987). Sexual orientation as a continuous variable: A comparison between the sexes. *Archives of Sexual Behavior*, 16, 523–529.

Ellis, L., Cooper, J. A., & Walsh, A. (2008 May/June). Criminologists' opinions about causes and theories of crime and delinquency: A follow-up. *The Criminologist*, 33, 23–26.

Ellis, L., & Engh, T. (2000). Handedness and age of death: New evidence on a puzzling relationship. *Journal of Health Psychology*, 5, 561–565.

Ellis, L., Farrington, D., & Hoskin, A. (2019). *Handbook of crime correlates* (2nd ed.). Amsterdam: Elsevier (Academic Press).

Ellis, L., Hershberger, S., Filed, E., Wersinger, S., Pellis, S., Geary, D., et al. (2008). *Sex differences: Summarizing more than a century of scientific research*. New York: Psychology Press.

Ellis, L., & Mathis, D. (1985). College student learning from televised versus conventional classroom lectures: A controlled experiment. *Higher Education*, 14, 165–173.

Ellis, L., & McDonald, J. N. (2001). Crime, delinquency, and social status: A reconsideration. *Journal of Offender Rehabilitation, 32*, 23–52.

Ellis, L., Miller, C., & Widmayer, A. (1988). Content analysis of biological approaches in psychology: 1894–1985. *Sociology and Social Research, 72*, 145–149.

Ellis, L., & Thompson, R. (1989). Relating religion, crime, arousal, and boredom. *Sociology and Social Research, 73*, 132–139.

Ellis, L., & Walsh, A. (1999). Criminologists' opinions about causes and theories of crime and delinquency. *The Criminologist, 24*, 3–6.

Ellis, L., & Walsh, A. (2000). *Criminology: A global perspective*. Boston, MA: Allyn and Bacon.

Elson, J. (1992). Is Freud finished? *Newsweek*, 60.

Eme, R. (2015). Greater male exposure to prenatal testosterone. *Violence and Gender, 2*(1), 19–23.

Ember, C. R., & Ember, M. (1988). *Anthropology* (5th ed.). Englewood Cliffs, NJ: Prentice-Hall.

Ennis, P. H. (1967). *Criminal victimization in the United States: A report of a national survey*. Washington DC: US Government Printing Office.

Etzioni, A. (1973). Faulty engineers or neglected experts. *Science, 181*, 13.

Etzioni, A. (1977 December). One and a half cheers for social science. *Psychology Today*, 168.

Evans, W. N., & Schwab, R. M. (1995). Finishing high school and starting college: Do Catholic schools make a difference? *The Quarterly Journal of Economics, 110*, 941–974.

Evanschitzky, H., Baumgarth, C., Hubbard, R., & Armstrong, J. S. (2007). Replication research in marketing revisited: A note on a disturbing trend. *Journal of Business Research, 60*, 411–415.

Eysenck, H. J. (1952). The effects of psychotherapy: An evaluation. *Journal of Consulting Psychology, 16*, 319–324.

Eysenck, H. J. (1975). Who needs random samples? *Bulletin of the British Psychological Society, 28*, 195–198.

Eysenck, H. J. (1994). Personality theory and the problem of criminality. In B. J. McGurk, D. M. Thornton, & M. Williams (Eds.), *Applying psychology to imprisonment: Theory and practice* (pp. 29–57). London: Her Majesty's Stationary Office.

Eysenck, S. B., & Eysenck, H. J. (1975). *Manual of the Eysenck personality questionnaire: Adult version and children's version*. Kent, UK: Hodder & Stoughton.

Ezekiel, M. (1941). *Methods of correlational analysis* (2nd ed.). New York: Wiley.

Falk, R., & Greenbaum, C. W. (1995). Significance tests die hard: The amazing persistence of a probabilistic misconception. *Theory and Psychology, 5*, 75–98.

Farabee, D., Shen, H., Hser, Y.-I., Grella, C. E., & Anglin, M. D. (2001). The effect of drug treatment on criminal behavior among adolescents in DATOS-A. *Journal of Adolescent Research, 16*, 679–696.

Farrington, D. P. (1973). Self-reports of deviant behavior: Productive and stable? *Journal of Criminal Law and Criminology, 64*, 99–110.

Farrington, D. P. (1982). Longitudinal analyses of criminal violence. In M. E. Wolfgang & N. A. Weiner (Eds.), *Criminal violence (pp. 171–200)*. Beverly Hills, CA: Sage.

Feather, N. (1974). Explanations of poverty in Australia and American samples: The person, society and fate. *Australian Journal of Psychology, 26*, 199–226.

Federal Bureau of Investigation. (2001). *Crime in the United States, 2002: Uniform crime reports*. Washington, DC: US Government Printing Office.

Federal Bureau of Investigation (2017). NIBRS overview. https://ucr.fbi.gov/nibrs-overview.

Federal Bureau of Investigation (2018). *Crime in the United States, 2017: Uniform Crime Reports*. Washington, DC: US Government Printing Office.

Ferguson, C. (2007). The good, the bad and the ugly: A meta-analytic review of positive and negative effects of violent video games. *Psychiatric Quarterly*, 78(4), 309–316.

Ferguson, C. & Hartley, R. D. (2009). The pleasure is momentary … the expense damnable? The influence of pornography on rape and sexual assault. *Aggression and Violent Behavior*, 14, 323–329.

Fergusson, D. M., & Horwood, L. J. (2002). Male and female offending trajectories. *Development and Psychopathology*, 14, 159–177.

Fergusson, D., Swain-Campbell, N., & Horwood, J. (2004). How does childhood economic disadvantage lead to crime? *Journal of Child Psychology and Psychiatry*, 45(5), 956–966.

Fernandez-Rhodes, L., Robinson, W. R., Sotres-Alvarez, D., et al. (2017). Accuracy of self-reported weight in Hispanic/Latino adults of the Hispanic Community Health Study/Study of Latinos. *Epidemiology* 28, 847–853.

Ferrante, C., Haynes, A., & Kingsley, S. (1988). Image of women in television advertising. *Journal of Broadcasting & Electronic Media*, 32(2), 231–237.

Ferraro, G. (1992). *Cultural anthropology: An applied perspective*. St. Paul, MN: West.

Finckenauer, J. O. (1982). *Scared straight! and the panacea phenomenon*. Englewood Cliffs, NJ: Prentice-Hall.

Finkel, S. E., Guterbock, T. M., & Borg, M. J. (1991). Race-of-interviewer effects in a pre-election pool. *Public Opinion Quarterly*, 55, 313–330.

Finkelhor, D., & Ormrod, R. (2004 June). Prostitution of juveniles: Patterns from NIBRS. Juvenile Justice Bulletin.

Finkenauer, J. O. (1982). *Scared straight! and the panacea phenomenon*. Englewood Cliffs, NJ: Prentice-Hall.

Firebaugh, G. (1978). A rule for inferring individual-level relationships from aggregate data. *American Sociological Review*, 43, 557–572.

Fiscella, K., & Franks, P. (2000). Individual income, income inequality, health, and mortality: What are the relationships? *Health Services Research*, 35(1), 307–318.

Fisher, H. (1991). Monogamy, adultery, and divorce in cross-species perspective. In M. H. Robinson & L. Tiger (Eds.), *Man and beast revisited* (pp. 95–126). Washington, DC: Smithsonian.

Flaskerud, J. H., & Hu, L.-T. (1992). Relationship of ethnicity to psychiatric diagnosis. *The Journal of Nervous and Mental Disease*, 180, 296–303.

Flay, B. R., d'Avernas, J. R., Best, J. A., Kersell, M. W., & Ryan, K. B. (1983). Cigarette smoking: Why young people do it and ways of preventing it. In P. J. McGrath & P. Firestone (Eds.), *Pediatric and adolescent behavioral medicine: Issues in treatment* (pp. 132–183). New York: Springer.

Flegal, K. (1999). The obesity epidemic in children and adults: Current evidence and research issues. *Medicine and Science in Sports and Exercise, Supplement*, S509–S514.

Fluehr-Lobban, C. (2000 October 6). How anthropology should respond to an ethical crisis. *Chronicle of Higher Education*.

Forcier, M. W., Kurtz, N. R., Parent, D. G., & Corrigan, M. D. (1986). Deterrence of drunk driving in Massachusetts: Criminal justice system impacts. *The International Journal of Addictions*, 21, 1197–1220.

Forgas, J. P., Morris, S. L., & Furnham, A. (1982). Lay explanations of wealth: Attributions for economic success. *Journal of Applied Social Psychology*, 12, 381–397.

Forst, B. (1977). The deterrent effect of capital punishment: A cross-state analysis of the 1960s. *Minnesota Law Review*, 61, 743–767.

Forsyth, D. R. (1991). A psychological perspective on ethical uncertainties in research. In A. J. Kimmel (Ed.), *New directions in methodology of social and behavioral science* (pp. 91–100). San Francisco, CA: Jossey-Bass.

Forth, A. E., Brown, S. L., Hart, S. D., & Hare, R. D. (1996). The assessment of psychopathy in male and female noncriminals: Reliability and validity. *Personality and Individual Differences, 20,* 531–543.

Forward, R. L. (1980 December). Spinning new realities. *Science, 80*(1) 40–49.

Foster, S. L., & Cone, J. D. (1995). Validity issues in clinical assessment. *Psychological Assessment, 7,* 248–260.

Fowler, F. J., Jr. (1988). *Survey research methods* (Rev. ed.). Newbury Park, CA: Sage.

Fox, R. J., Crask, M. R., & Kim, J. (1988). Mail survey response rate: A meta-analysis of selected techniques for inducing response. *Public Opinion Quarterly, 52,* 467–491.

Frank, D. A., Zuckerman, B. S., & Amaro, H. (1988). Cocaine use during pregnancy: Prevalence and correlates. *Pediatrics, 82,* 888–895.

Frankfort-Nachmias, C., & Nachmias, D. (1992). *Research methods in the social sciences* (4th ed.). New York: St. Martin's Press.

Freeman, D. (1999). *The fateful hoaxing of Margaret Mead: A historical analysis of her Samoan research.* Boulder, CO: Westview.

Freund, K. (1963). A laboratory method for diagnosing predominance of homo- or hetero-erotic interest in the male. *Behavioral Research and Therapy, 1,* 85–93.

Fried, P. A. (1984). Alcohol and the newborn infant. In S. Kacew & M. J. Reasor (Eds.), *Toxicology and the newborn* (pp. 86–100). The Netherlands: Elsevier.

Fuchs, S., & Turner, J. H. (1986). What makes a science "mature"? Patterns of organizational control in scientific production. *Sociological Theory, 4,* 143–150.

Fulker, D. W. (1978). Multivariate extensions of a biometrical model of twin data. In W. E. Nancy (Ed.), *Progress in clinical and biological research (pp. 217–236).* New York: A. R. Liss.

Furnham, A. (1982). The perception of poverty among adolescents. *Journal of Adolescence, 5,* 135–147.

Futrell, R., & Simi, P. (2004). Free spaces, collective identity, and the persistence of US white power activism. *Social Problems, 51*(1), 16–42.

Gadow, K. D., Paolicelli, L. M., Nolan, E. E., Schwartz, J., Sprafkin, J., & Sverd, J. (1992). Methylphenidate in aggressive hyperactive boys: II. Indirect effects of medication treatment on peer behavior. *Journal of Child and Adolescent Psychopharmacology, 2,* 49–61.

Gaes, G. G., & Goldberg, A. L. (2004). *Prison rape: A critical review of the literature.* Washington, DC: National Institute of Justice.

Galton, F. (1908). *Memories of my life.* London: Methuen.

Games, P. A. (1990). Correlation and causation: A logical snafu. *Journal of Experimental Education, 58,* 239–246.

Garcia, E., & Herrero, J. (2007). Perceived neighborhood social disorder and attitudes toward reporting domestic violence against women. *Journal of Interpersonal Violence, 22,* 737–752.

Geary, D. C., Rumsey, M., Bow-Thomas, C. C., & Hoard, M. K. (1995). Sexual jealousy as a facultative trait: Evidence from the pattern of sex differences in adults from China to the United States. *Ethology and Sociobiology, 16,* 355–383.

Geer, J. G. (1991). Do open-ended questions measure "salient" issues? *Public Opinion Quarterly, 55,* 360–370.

Gendall, P., Hoek, J., & Blakeley, M. (1992). Estimating a socially undesirable behaviour. *Marketing Bulletin, 3,* 1–8.

George, D., & Mallery, P. (2003). *SPSS for Windows step by step: A simple guide and reference. 11.0 update* (4th ed.). Boston: Allyn & Bacon.

Gerald, M. S., & Higley, J. D. (2002). Evolutionary underpinnings of excessive alcohol consumption. *Addiction*, 97, 415–425.

Gest, H. (1997). Serendipity in scientific discovery: A closer look. *Perspectives in Biology and Medicine*, 41, 21–28.

Giacchi, M., Mattei, R., & Rossi, S. (1998). Correction of the self-reported BMI in a teenage population. *International Journal of Obesity and Related Metabolism Disorders*, 22, 673–677.

Giacopassi, D. J. (1992). The effects of emergency medical care. *Journal of Criminal Justice*, 20, 249–259.

Gibson, C. L., Piquero, A. R., & Tibbetts, S. G. (2000). Assessing the relationship between maternal cigarette smoking during pregnancy and age at first police contact. *Justice Quarterly*, 17, 519–542.

Gibson, M. S. (1982). The "female offender" and the Italian School of criminal anthropology. *Journal of European Studies*, 12, 155–165.

Gillespie, R. (1991). *Manufacturing knowledge: A history of the Hawthorne experiments*. New York: Cambridge University Press.

Glaesmer, H., & Brahler, E. (2002). Schatzung der pravelnz von ubergewicht und adipositas auf der grundlage subjektiver daten zum body-mass-index (BMI) (Prevalence estimation of overweight and obesity based on subjective data of body-mass-index). *Gesundheitswesen*, 64, 133–138.

Glaser, D. (1978). Evaluation of sex offender treatment programs. In E. M. Brecher (Ed.), *Treatment programs for sex offenders* (pp. 85–92, Appendix B). Washington, DC: US Government Printing Office.

Glass, G. (1976). Primary, secondary, and meta-analysis of research. *Educational Researcher*, 5, 3–8.

Glass, G. V., McGaw, B., & Smith, M. L. (1981). *Meta-analysis in social research*. Beverly Hills, CA: Sage.

Glassman, A. H., Helzer, J. E., Convey, L. S., Cottler, L. B., Stetner, F., Tipp, J. E., & Johnson, J. (1990). Smoking, smoking cessation, and major depression. *Journal of the American Medical Association*, 264, 1546–1549.

Goist, K. C., Jr., & Sutker, P. B. (1985). Acute alcohol intoxication and body composition in women and men. *Pharmacology, Biochemistry, and Behavior*, 22, 811–814.

Goldberg, L. R. (1992). The development of markers for the big-five factor structure. *Psychological Assessment*, 4, 26–42.

Golden, F. (1981). Fudging data for fun and profit. *Time*, 118, 83.

Goldman, B. A., Flake, W. L., & Matheson, M. B. (1990). Accuracy of college students' perceptions of their SAT scores, high school and college grade point averages relative to their ability. *Perceptual and Motor Skills*, 70, 514.

Goldman, M. J. (1991). Kleptomania: Making sense of the nonsensical. *American Journal of Psychiatry*, 148, 986–996.

Goldsmith, R. E. (1987). Two studies of yeasaying. *Psychological Reports*, 60, 239–244.

Goodall, J. (1977). Infant killing and cannibalism in free-living chimpanzees. *Folia Primatol*, 28, 259–282.

Goodall, J. (1990). *Through a window: My thirty years with the chimpanzees of Gombe*. Boston: Houghton Mifflin Company.

Goodman, E., Hinden, B. R., & Khandelwal, S. (2000). Accuracy of teen and parental reports of obesity and body mass index. *Pediatrics* 106, 52–58.

Goodstadt, M. S., Chung, L., Kronitz, R., & Cook, G. (1977). Mail survey response rates: Their manipulation and impact. *Journal of Marketing Research*, 14, 391–395.

Goodyear, R. K., Crego, C. A., & Johnson, M. W. (1992). Ethical issues in the supervision of student research: A study of critical incidents. *Professional Psychology: Research and Practice*, 23, 203–210.

Gordon, R. A. (1967). Issues in the ecological study of delinquency. *American Sociological Review*, 32, 927–944.

Gordon, R. A. (1993). *The battle to establish a sociology of intelligence: A case study in the sociology of politicized disciplines*. Baltimore, MD: John Hopkins University Department of Sociology.

Gottfredson, L. S. (1994). Egalitarian fiction and collective fraud. *Society*, 31, 53–59.

Gottfredson, M. R., & Hirschi, T. (1990). *A general theory of crime*. Stanford, CA: Stanford University Press.

Gould, R. J., & Slone, C. G. (1982). The "feminine modesty" effect: A self-presentational interpretation of sex differences in causal attribution. *Personality and Social Psychology Bulletin*, 8, 477–485.

Graham, J. R. (1990). *MMPI-2: Assessing personality and psychopathology*. New York: Oxford University Press.

Granberg, D., & Holmberg, S. (1992). The Hawthorne effect in election studies: The impact of survey participation on voting. *British Journal of Political Science*, 22, 240–247.

Grande, C. G. (1988). Delinquency: The learning disabled student's reaction to academic school failure? *Adolescence*, 89, 209–219.

Green, P. (1971). The obligations of American social scientists. *Annals of the American Academy of Political and Social Science*, 394, 13–27.

Greenfield, T. K., & Weisner, C. (1995). Drinking problems and self-reported criminal behavior, arrests and convictions: 1990 US alcohol and 1989 county surveys. *Addiction*, 90, 361–373.

Greenland, C. (1988). The treatment and maltreatment of sexual offenders: Ethical issues. *Annals of the New York Academy of Sciences*, 528, 373–378.

Grichting, W. L. (1989). Psychology and sociology in Australia: The published evidence. *Australian Psychologist*, 24, 115–126.

Griffin, D. R. (1985). Animal consciousness. *Neuroscience and Biobehavioral Reviews*, 9, 615–622.

Grossman, J. B., & Tierney, J. P. (1998). Does mentoring work? An impact study of the Big Brothers Big Sisters Program. *Evaluation Review*, 22, 403–426.

Grove, W. M., Eckert, E. D., Heston, L., Bouchard, T. J., Segal, N., & Lykken, D. T. (1990). Heritability of substance abuse and antisocial behavior: A study of monozygotic twins reared apart. *Biological Psychiatry*, 27, 1293–1304.

Guzzo, R. A., Jackson, S. E., & Katzell, R. A. (1987). Meta-analysis analysis. *Research in Organizational Behavior*, 9, 407–442.

Hacking, I. (1991). *The taming of chance*. New York: Cambridge University Press.

Hadaway, C. K., Marler, P. L., & Chaves, M. (1993). What the polls don't show: A closer look at US church attendance. *American Sociological Review*, 58, 741–752.

Hall, G. C. N., & Hirschman, R. (1991). Toward a theory of sexual aggression: A quadripartite model. *Journal of Consulting and Clinical Psychology*, 59, 662–669.

Halperin, J. M., Matier, K., Bedi, G., Sharma, V., & Newcorn, J. H. (1992). Specificity of inattention, impulsivity and hyperactivity to the diagnosis of attention-deficit hyperactivity disorder. *Journal of the Academy of Child and Adolescent Psychiatry*, 31, 190–196.

Halperin, J. M., Newcorn, J. H., Matier, K., Sharma, V., McKay, K. E., & Schwartz, S. (1993). Discriminant validity of attention-deficit hyperactivity disorder. *Journal of the Academy of Child and Adolescent Psychiatry*, 32, 1038–1043.

Halpern, D. F., & Coren, S. (1991). Handedness and life span. *New England Journal of Medicine*, 354, 998.

Halpert, H. P. (1973). Research utilization, a problem in goal setting: What is the question. *American Journal of Public Health*, 63, 377–378.

Hamilton, W. D. (1963). The evolution of altruistic behavior. *American Naturalist*, 96, 354–356.

Hamilton, W. D. (1964). The genetical evolution of social behavior. *Journal of Theoretical Biology*, 37, 1–16, 17–52.

Hammersley, M. (1992). *What's wrong with ethnography?* London: Routledge.

Hammersley, R., Forsyth, A., & Lavelle, T. (1990). The criminality of new drug users in Glasgow. *British Journal of Addiction*, 85, 1583–1594.

Hansen, R. A. (1980). A self-perception interpretation of the effect of monetary and non-monetary incentives on mail survey respondent behavior. *Journal of Marketing Research*, 17, 77–83.

Hapke, R. (1972 May). The limits to growth: Implications for the United States. *Zero Population Growth National Reporter*, 4, 8–9.

Haque, A., & Telfair, J. (2000). Socioeconomic distress and health status: The urban-rural dichotomy of services utilization for people with sickle cell disorder in North Carolina. *Journal of Rural Health*, 16(1), 43–55.

Hare, R. (1993). *Without conscience: The disturbing world of the psychopaths among us*. New York: Pocket books.

Hare, R. (2000). *Assessing psychopathy with the PCL-R*. San Diego: Sinclair Seminars.

Hare, R. (2003). *Manual for the revised psychopathology checklist* (2nd ed.). Toronto, ON: Multi-Health Systems.

Hare, R. D. (1996a). Psychopathy: A clinical construct whose time has come. *Criminal Justice and Behavior*, 23, 25–54.

Hare, R. (1996b), Psychopathy and antisocial personality disorder: A case of diagnostic confusion. *Psychiatric Times*, 13, 1–8.

Hare, R. D., Clark, D., Grann, M., & Thornton, D. (2000). Psychopathy and the predictive validity of the PLC-R: An international perspective. *Behavioral Sciences and the Law*, 18, 623–645.

Harris, A., & Shaw, J. (2001). Looking for patterns: Race, class, and crime. In J. Sheley (Ed.), *Criminology: A contemporary handbook* (pp. 129–163). Belmont, CA: Wadsworth.

Harris, A. R., Thomas, S. H., Fisher, G. A., & Hirsch, D. J. (2002). Murder and medicine: The lethality of criminal assault 1960–1999. *Homicide Studies*, 6, 128–166.

Harris, G. T., & Rice, M. E. (1996). The science in phallometric measurement of male sexual interest. *Current Directions in Psychological Science*, 5, 156–157, 160.

Harris, J. A. (1997). The relationship between aggression and employment integrity. *Journal of Business Psychology*, 12, 39–44.

Harris, P., Skilling, T., & Rice, M. (2001). The construct of psychopathy. In M. Tonry (Ed.), *Crime and justice: A review of research* (pp. 197–264). Chicago: University of Chicago Press.

Harrison, P., & A. Beck (2005). Prison and jail inmates at midyear 2004. *Bureau of Justice Statistics Bulletin*, US Department of Justice, April, 2005.

Hartley, R. D., Ellis, L., & Hoskin, A. (2019). Self-reported offending in the United States and Malaysia: Does east meet west? *International Journal of Offender Therapy and Comparative Criminology*.https://doi.org/10.1177/0306624X19883753.

Hartley, R. D., Maddan, S., & Spohn, C. C. (2007). Concerning conceptualization and operationalization: Sentencing data and the focal concerns perspective. *The Southwest Journal of Criminal Justice*, 4(1), 58–78.

Hartley, R. D., Rabe, G., & Champion, D. (2018). *Criminal courts: Structure, process, and issues*. New York: Pearson.

Harvey, A. S. (1993). Guidelines for time use data collection. *Social Indicators Research*, 30, 197–228.

Hatch, N. O. (1989). *The democratization of American Christianity*. New Haven, CT: Yale University Press.

Haviland, W. A. (2000). *Anthropology* (9th ed.). Fort Worth, TX: Harcourt.

Hawkins, J. D., & Weis, J. G. (1985). The social development model: An integrated approach to delinquency prevention. *Journal of Primary Prevention*, 6, 73–97.

Hebb, D. O., & Thompson, W. R. (1954). The social significance of animal studies. In G. Lindzey (Ed.), *Handbook of social psychology, Vol. 1: Theory and method* (pp. 532–561). Cambridge: Addison-Wesley.

Heberlein, T. A., & Baumgartner, R. (1978). Factors affecting response rates to mailed questionnaires: A quantitative analysis of the published literature. *American Sociological Review*, 43, 447–471.

Henggeler, S. W., Melton, G. B., Smith, L. A., Schoenwald, S. K., & Hanley, J. H. (1993). Family preservation using multisystemic treatment: Long-term follow-up to a clinical trial with serious juvenile offenders. *Journal of Child and Family Studies*, 2, 283–293.

Hersen, M., & Barlow, D. H. (1976). *Single case experimental designs*. New York: Pergamon.

Hill, A., & Roberts, J. (1998). Body mass index: A comparison between self-reported and measured height and weight. *Journal of Public Health Medicine*, 20, 206–210.

Hill, P. C., Dill, C. A., & Davenport, E. C., Jr. (1988). A reexamination of the bogus pipeline. *Educational and Psychological Measurement*, 48, 587–601.

Hillhouse, M. P., & Fiorentine, R. (2001). 12-step program participation and effectiveness: Do gender and ethnic differences exist? *Journal of Drug Issues*, 31, 767–780.

Hilton, N. Z., Haris, G. T., & Rice, M. E. (1998). On the validity of self-reported rates of interpersonal violence. *Journal of Interpersonal Violence*, 13, 58–72.

Hindelang, M. J., Hirschi, T., & Weis, J. G. (1981). *Measuring delinquency*. Beverly Hills, CA: Sage.

Hinkle, D. E., Weirsma, W., & Jurs, S. G. (1988). *Applied statistics for the behavioral sciences*. Boston, MA: Houghton Mifflin.

Hippler, H., & Schwartz, N. (1987). Response effects in surveys. In H. Hippler, N. Schwartz, & S. Sudman (Eds.), *Social information processing and survey methodology* (pp. 102–122). New York: Springer.

Hirschi, T. (1969). *Causes of delinquency*. Berkeley, CA: University of California Press.

Hirschi, T., Hindelang, M. J., & Weis, J. G. (1980). The status of self-report measures. In M. W. Klein & K. S. Teilman (Eds.), *Handbook of criminal justice evaluation* (pp. 473–488). Beverly Hills, CA: Sage.

Hishinuma, E. S., Johnson, R. C., Foster, J. E., Nishimura, S. T., Miyamoto, R. H., Yuen, N. Y. C., et al. (2001). Association between actual and self-reported grades for ethnically diverse Asian/Pacific Islander adolescents. *Research in Education*, 65, 53–69.

Hoffer, T., Greeley, A. M., & Coleman, J. S. (1985). Achievement growth in public and Catholic schools. *Sociology of Education*, 58, 74–97.

Holden, C. (1986). Days may be numbered for polygraphs in the private sector. *Science*, 232, 705.

Homant, R. J., & Osowski, G. (1982). The politics of juvenile awareness programs: A case study of JOLT. *Criminal Justice and Behavior*, 9, 55–68.

Hönekopp, J., Bartholdt, L., Beier, L., & Liebert, A. (2007). Second to fourth digit length ratio (2D: 4D) and adult sex hormone levels: New data and a meta-analytic review. *Psychoneuroendocrinology*, 32(4), 313–321.

Horswill, M. S., & Coster, M. E. (2001). User-controlled photographic animations, photograph-based questions, and questionnaires: Three internet-based instruments for measuring drivers' risk-taking behavior. *Behavior Research Methods, Instruments, and Computers*, 33, 46–58.

Hoskin, A. W., Hartley, R. D., Ellis, L., & McMurray, H. (2017). Does religiosity explain cross-national differences in crime? The case of the United States versus Malaysian university students. *Journal of Religion & Society*, 19, 1–17.

Howell, D. C. (1989). *Fundamental statistics for the behavioral sciences* (2nd ed.). Boston, MA: PWS-Kent.

Huck, W., & Banks, E. M. (1980). The effects of cross-fostering on the behaviour of two species of North American lemmings, Dicrostonyx Groenlandicus and Lemmus Trimucronatus: II. Sexual behaviour. *Animal Behaviour*, 28, 1053–1062.

Hudson, R. P. (1998). Book review. *Bulletin of the History of Medicine*, 72, 131–132.

Hunt, E. (1983). On the nature of intelligence. *Science*, 219, 141–146.

Hunter, J. E. (2001). The desperate need for replications. *Journal of Consumer Research*, 28, 149–158.

Hunter, J. E., & Hunter, R. G. (1984). Validity and utility of alternative predictors of job performance. *Psychological Bulletin*, 96, 72–98.

Hurwitz, S., & Christiansen, K. O. (1983). *Criminology*. London, England: Fairleigh Dickonson University Press.

Idler, E. L., & Benyamini, Y. (1997). Self-rated health and mortality: A review of twenty-seven community studies. *Journal of Health and Social Behavior*, 38, 21–37.

Imrohoroglu, A., Merlo, A., & Rupert, P. (2000). On the political economy of income redistribution and crime. *International Economic Review*, 41, 1–25.

Innala, S. M., & Ernulf, K. E. (1992). Understanding male homosexual attraction: An analysis of restroom graffiti. *Journal of Social Behavior and Personality*, 7, 503–510.

Innes, J., & Styles, J. (1986). The crime wave: Recent writing on crime and criminal justice in eighteenth-century England. *The Journal of British Studies*, 25, 380–435.

Inter-University Consortium for Political and Social Research. (1984). *Guide to resources and services—1983–1984*. Ann Arbor, MI: University of Michigan's Institute for Social Research.

Jaakkola, M. S., & Jaakkola, J. J. K. (1997). Assessment of exposure to environmental tobacco smoke. *European Respiratory Journal*, 78(10), 2384–2397.

Jackson, J., Strauss, C. C., Lee, A. A., & Hunter, K. (1990). Parent's accuracy in estimating child weight status. *Addictive Behaviors*, 15, 65–68.

Jacoby, A. (2018). Social service organizations, discretionary funding, and neighborhood crime rates. *Crime & Delinquency*, 64(9), 1193–1214. https://doi.org/10.1177/0011128716688884.

James, J. M., & Bolstein, R. (1990). The effect of monetary incentives and follow-up mailings on the response quality in mail surveys. *Public Opinion Quarterly*, 54, 346–361.

Jarausch, K. H., & Hardy, K. A. (1991). *Quantitative methods for historians: A guide to research, data, and statistics*. Chapel Hill, NC: University of North Carolina Press.

Joe, G., & Gorsuch, R. (1977). Issues in evaluation of drug abuse treatment. *Professional Psychology*, 8, 609–640.

Johnson, A. M., Wadsworth, J., Wellings, K., & Field, J. (1994). *Sexual attitudes and lifestyles*. London, England: Blackwell Publications.

Johnson, E. A. (1982). The roots of crime in imperial Germany. *Central European History*, 15, 351–376.

Johnson, R. B., & Onwuegbuzie, A. J. (2004). Mixed methods research: A research paradigm whose time has come. *Educational Researcher*, 33, 14–26.

Jones, E. F., & Forrest, J. D. (1992). Under reporting of abortion in surveys of US women: 1976 to 1988. *Demography*, 29, 113–126.

Jones, J. (1971). First glimpse of a stone age tribe. *National Geographic*, 140, 880–882.

Jones, J. W. (1991). *The children of alcoholics screening test*. Chicago: Camelot.

Jones, S. R. G. (1990). Worker interdependence and output: The Hawthorne studies re-evaluated. *American Sociological Review*, 55, 176–190.

Jones, S. R. G. (1992). Was there a Hawthorne effect? *American Journal of Sociology*, 98, 451–468.

Jordan-Bychkov, T. G., & Domosh, M. (1999). *The human mosaic: A thematic introduction to cultural geography* (8th ed.). New York: Addison Wesley Longman, Inc.

Jørgensen, M. H., Curtis, T., Christensen, P. H., & Grønbæk, M. (2007). Harm minimization among teenage drinkers: Findings from an ethnographic study on teenage alcohol use in a rural Danish community. *Addiction*, 102, 554–559.

Joseph, J. (2001). Is crime in the genes? A critical review of twin and adoption studies of criminality and antisocial behavior. *Journal of Mind and Behavior*, 22, 179–218.

Judson, H. F. (1980 November 17). Where Einstein and Picasso meet. *Newsweek*, 23.

Juhn, C. (1999). Wage inequality and demand for skill: Evidence from five decades. *Industrial and Labor Relations Review*, 52, 424–443.

Junger-Tas, J. (2012). Delinquent behaviour in 30 countries. In Junger-Tas et al., *The many faces of youth crime: Contrasting theoretical perspectives on juvenile delinquency across countries and cultures (pp 69–93)*. New York: Springer.

Junger-Tas, J., & Marshall, I. H. (2012). Introduction to the International Self-Report Study of Delinquency (ISRD-2). In Junger-Tas et al., *The many faces of youth crime: Contrasting theoretical perspectives on juvenile delinquency across countries and cultures* (pp. 3–20). New York: Springer.

Junger-Tas, J., Marshall, I. H., & Ribeaud, D. (2003). Delinquency in an international perspective. In *The International Self-Reported Delinquency (ISRD) Study*. Kugler: Amsterdam.

Kahn, J. R., Kalsbeek, W. D., & Hofferth, S. L. (1988). National estimates of teenage sexual activity: Evaluating the comparability of three national surveys. *Demography*, 25, 189–204.

Kane, E. W., & Macaulay, L. J. (1993). Interviewer gender and gender attitudes. *Public Opinion Quarterly*, 57, 1–28.

Kaplan G. A., Pamuk, E. R., Lynch, J. W., Cohen, R. D., & Balfour, J. L. (1996) Inequality in income and mortality in the United States: Analysis of mortality and potential pathways. *British Medical Journal*, 312, 999–1003.

Kaplan, S. L., Busner, J., Kupietz, S., Wassermann, E., & Segal, B. (1990). Effects of methylphenidate on adolescents with aggressive conduct disorder and ADDH: A preliminary report. *Journal of the American Academy of Child and Adolescent Psychiatry*, 29, 719–723.

Kass, S. J., & Vodanovich, S. J. (1990). Boredom proneness: Its relationship to type A behavior pattern and sensation seeking. *Psychology*, 27, 7–16.

Kater, M. (1983). *The Nazi Party: A social profit of members and leaders, 1919–1945*. New York: Oxford University Press.

Kazdin, A. E. (1989). *Behavior modification in applied setting* (4th ed.). Pacific Grove, CA: Brooks/Cole.

Kelley, C. (1981). Reliability of the behavior problem checklist with institutionalized male delinquents. *Journal of Abnormal Child Psychology*, 9, 243–250.

Kemph, B. T., & Kasser, T. (1996). Effects of sexual orientation of interviewer on expressed attitudes toward male homosexuality. *Journal of Social Psychology*, 136, 401–404.

Kendler, K. S., Neale, M. C., MacLean, C. J., Heath, A. C., Eaves, L. J., & Kessler, R. C. (1993). Smoking and major depression: A causal analysis. *Archives of General Psychiatry*, 50, 36–43.

Kerslake, E., & Goulding, A. (1996). Focus groups: Their use in LIS research data collection. *Education for Information*, 14, 225–232.

Kessler, R. C., Wittchen, H.-U., Abelson, J., & Zhao, S. (2000). Methodological issues in assessing psychiatric disorders with self-reports. In A. A. Stone, J. S. Turkkan, C. A. Bachrach, J. B. Jobe, H. S. Kurtzman, & V. S. Cain (Eds.), *The science of self-report: Implications for research and practice* (pp. 229–255). Mahwah, NJ: Lawrence Erlbaum Associates.

Ketterlinus, R. D., Henderson, S. H., & Lamb, M. E. (1990). Maternal age, sociodemographics, prenatal health and behavior: Influences on neonatal risk status. *Journal of Adolescent Health Care*, 11, 423–431.

Kiehl, K. (2006). A cognitive neuroscience perspective on psychopathy: Evidence for paralimbic system dysfunction. *Psychiatry Research*, 142, 107–128.

Kim, J., Fendrich, M., & Wislar, J. (2000). The validity of juvenile arrestees' drug use reporting: A gender comparison. *Journal of Research in Crime and Delinquency*, 37, 429–432.

Kindermann, C., Lynch, J. P., & Cantor, D. (1997). *Effects of the redesign on victimization estimates*. Washington, DC: US Department of Justice.

King, M., & Schafer, W. E. (1992). Religiosity and perceived stress: A community survey. *Sociological Analysis*, 53, 37–47.

Kinsey, A. C., Pomeroy, W. B., & Martin, C. E. (1948). *Sexual behavior in the human male*. Philadelphia: Saunders.

Kinsey, A. C., Pomeroy, W. B., Martin, C. E., & Gebhard, P. H. (1953). *Sexual behavior in the human female*. Philadelphia, PA: W. B. Saunders.

Kirchengast, S., & Steiner, V. (2001). Sexual dimorphism in body composition, weight status and growth in prepubertal school children from rural areas of Eastern Austria. *Collegium Antropoligicum*, 25, 21–30.

Kish, G. B., & Donnenwerth, G. V. (1972). Sex differences in the correlates of stimulus seeking. *Journal of Consulting and Clinical Psychology*, 38, 42–49.

Kleck, G., & Gertz, M. (1995). Armed resistance to crime: The prevalence and nature of self-defense with a gun. *Journal of Criminal Law and Criminology*, 86, 150–182.

Kline, J., Ng, S. K. C., Schittini, M., Levin, B., & Susser, M. (1997). Cocaine use during pregnancy: Sensitive detection by hair assay. *American Journal of Public Health*, 87, 352–358.

Kloppenberg, J. T. (1989). Objectivity and historicism: A century of American historical writing. *American Historical Review*, 42, 1011–1030.

Kondrichin, S. V., & Lester, D. (1998). Voting conservative and mortality. *Perceptual and Motor Skills*, 87, 466.

Krebs, D. L. (1971). Infrahuman altruism. *Psychological Bulletin*, 76, 411–414.

Kuhn, T. S. (1962). *The structure of scientific revolutions*. Chicago, IL: University of Chicago Press.

Kulik, J. A., Stein, K. B., & Sarbin, T. R. (1968). Disclosure of delinquent behavior under conditions of anonymity and nonanonymity. *Journal of Consulting and Clinical Psychology*, 32, 506–509.

Kummer, H. (1971). *Primate societies: Group techniques of ecological adaptation*. Arlington Heights: Harlan Davidson.

Lakatos, I. (1970). Falsification and the methodology of scientific research programmes. In I. Lakatos & A. Musgrave (Eds.), *Criticism and the growth of knowledge*. Cambridge: Cambridge University Press.

Lambert, M. C., Knight, F., Taylor, R., & Newell, A. L. (1993). Further comparisons of teacher and parent ratings of behavior and emotional problems in Jamaican children. *International Journal of Intercultural Relations*, 17, 1–18.

Langer, S. (1981). *"Scared straight"? Fear in the deterrence of delinquency*. Lanham, MD: University Press of America.

Langevin, R. (1990). Sexual anomalies and the brain. In W. Marshall, D. Laws, & H. Barbaree (Eds.), *Handbook of sexual assault: Issues, theories and treatment of the offender* (pp. 103–113). New York: Plenum.

Lansing, J. B., & Kish, L. (1957). Family life cycle as an independent variable. *American Sociological Review*, 22, 512–516.

Larsen, C. S., Matter, R. M., & Gebo, D. L. (1991*). Human origins: The fossil record* (2nd ed.). Prospect Heights, IL: Waveland.

Latane, B., & Darley, J. M. (1970). Social determinants of bystander intervention in emergencies. In J. Macaulay & L. Berkowitz (Eds.), *Altruism and helping behavior: Social psychological studies of some antecedents and consequences* (pp. 13–27). New York: Academic Press.

Laughlin, C. D. (1991). Womb = woman = world: Gender and transcendence in Tibetan Tantric Buddhism. *Pre- and Peri-Natal Psychology Journal*, 5, 147–165.

Lawson, P. (1986). Property crime and hard times in England, 1559–1624. *Law and History Review*, 4, 95–127.

Layson, S. K. (1985). Homicide and deterrence: A reexamination of the United States time-series evidence. *Southern Economic Journal*, 52, 68–89.

Lazarfeld, P. F. (1944). The controversy over detailed interviews: An offer for negotiation. *Public Opinion Quarterly*, 8, 38–60.

Leal, J., Ziedonis, D., & Kosten, T. (1994). Antisocial personality disorder as a prognostic factor for pharmacotherapy of cocaine dependence. *Drug and Alcohol Dependence*, 35, 31–35.

Lee, R. B. (1984). *The Dobe !Kung*. New York: Holt, Rinehart & Winston.

Leger, D. W. (1992). *Biological foundations of behavior: An integrated approach*. New York: Harper Collins.

Leohlin, J. C. (1989). Partitioning environmental and genetic contributions to behavioral development. *American Psychologist*, 44, 1285–1292.

Leone, P. E., Rutherford, R. B., & Nelson, C. M. (1991). *Special education in juvenile corrections*. Reston, VA: Council for Exceptional Children.

Lester, D., Brackopp, G. W., & Priebe, K. (1969). Association between a full moon and completed suicide. *Psychological Reports*, 25, 598.

Levenson, M. R., Kiehl, K. A., & Fitzpatrick, C. M. (1995). Assessing psychopathic attributes in a noninstitutionalized population. *Journal of Personality and Social Psychology*, 68, 151–158.

Levin, J. R. (1993). Statistical significance testing from three perspectives. *Journal of Experimental Education*, 61, 378–382.

Lewin, R. (1988). Linguists search for the mother tongue. *Science*, 242, 1128–1129.

Lewis, R. V. (1983). Scared straight—California style: Evaluation of the San Quentin Squires program. *Criminal Justice and Behavior*, 10, 209–226.

Li, C. Q., Windsor, R. A., Perkins, L., Godenberg, R. L., & Lowe, J. B. (1993). The impact on infant birth weight and gestational age of cotinine-validated smoking reduction during pregnancy. *Journal of the American Medical Association*, 269, 1519–1524.

Lichtenstein, P., Harris, J. R., Pedersen, N. L., & McClearn, G. E. (1992). Socioeconomic status and physical health, how are they related? An empirical study based on twins reared apart and twins reared together. *Social Science and Medicine*, 36, 441–450.

Lie, G.-Y., & Moroney, R. M. (1992). A controlled evaluation of comprehensive social services provided to teenage mothers receiving AFDC. *Research on Social Work Practice*, 2, 429–447.

Lieberman, L. (1989). A discipline divided: Acceptance of human sociobiological concepts in anthropology. *Current Anthropology*, 30, 676–682.

Likert, R. (1932). A technique for the measurement of attitudes. *Archives of Psychology*, 21, 1–55.

Linden, E. (1991 September). Lost tribes, lost knowledge. *Time*, 138, 46–56.

Lindstrom, M., Hanson, B. S., Ostergren, P. O., & Berglund, G. (2000). Socioeconomic differences in smoking cessation: The role of social participation. *Scandinavian Journal of Public Health*, 28, 200–208.

Linsky, A. S. (1975). Stimulating responses to mailed questionnaires: A review. *Public Opinion Quarterly*, 38, 82–101.

Listwan, S., Shaffer, D., and Hartman, J. (2009). Combating methamphetamine use in the community: The efficacy of the drug court model. *Crime & Delinquency*, 55, 627–644.

Loehlin, J. C. (1992). *Genes and environment in personality development*. Newbury Park, CA: Sage.

Loken, B., Pirie, P., Virnig, K. A., Hinkle, R. L., & Salmon, C. T. (1987). The use of 0–10 scales in telephone surveys. *Journal of the Market Research Society*, 29, 353–362.

Lombroso, C. (1899). Le crime; causes et remedes. English translation, 1911. *Crime, its causes and remedies*. Boston: HP Horton.

Lonsway, K. A., & Fitzgerald, L. F. (1994). Rape myths. *Psychology of Woman Quarterly*, 18, 133–164.

Lott, J. R., Jr., & Mustard, D. B. (1997). Crime, deterrence, and right-to-carry concealed handguns. *Journal Legal Studies*, 26, 1–68.

Lundman, R. J. (1984). *Prevention and control of juvenile delinquency*. New York: Oxford University Press.

Lykken, D. T., Bouchard, T. J., Jr., McGue, M., & Tellegen, A. (1990). The Minnesota twin family registry: Some initial findings. *Acta Genetic and Medical Gemellology*, 39, 35–70.

Mahoney, M. J. (1987). Scientific publication and knowledge politics. *Journal of Social Behavior and Personality*, 2, 165–176.

Mak, A. S. (1993). A self-report delinquency scale for Australian adolescents. *Australian Journal of Psychology*, 45, 75–79.

Malamuth, N. M., & Ceniti, J. (1986). Repeated exposure to violent and nonviolent pornography: Likelihood of raping ratings and laboratory aggression against women. *Aggressive Behavior*, 12, 129–137.

Malamuth, N. M., & Check, J. V. P. (1981). The effects of mass media exposure on acceptance of violence against women: A field experiment. *Journal of Research in Personality*, 15, 436–446.

Malamuth, N. M., & Check, J. V. P. (1983). Sexual arousal to rape depictions: Individual differences. *Journal of Abnormal Psychology*, 92, 55–67.

Malamuth, N. M., & Check, J. V. P. (1984). Debriefing effectiveness following exposure to rape depictions. *Journal of Sex Research, 20,* 1–13.

Malamuth, N. M., & Check, J. V. P. (1985). The effects of aggressive pornography on beliefs in rape myths: Individual difference. *Journal of Research in Personality, 19,* 299–320.

Malamuth, N. M., Harber, S., & Feshbach, S. (1980). Testing hypotheses regarding rape: Exposure to sexual violence, sex differences, and the "normality" of rapists. *Journal of Research in Personality, 14,* 121–137.

Maneker, J. S., & Rankin, R. P. (1987). Correlate of marital duration among those who file for divorce: Selected characteristics in California, 1966–1976. *Journal of Divorce, 10,* 97–107.

Mann, C. (1990). Meta-analysis in the breech. *Science, 249,* 476–480.

Manning, J. T., Scutt, D., Wilson, J., & Lewis-Jones, D. I. (1998). The ratio of 2nd to 4th digit length: A predictor of sperm numbers and concentrations of testosterone, luteinizing hormone and oestrogen. *Human Reproduction, 13,* 3000–3004.

Margraf, J., Ehlers, A., Roth, W. T., Clark, D. B., Sheikh, J., Agras, W. S., et al. (1991). How "blind" are double-blind studies? *Journal of Consulting and Clinical Psychology, 59,* 184–187.

Marks, P., & Carter, B. (2000, November 9). The 2000 elections: The network predictions; Media rethink an urge to say who's first. *New York Times,* B2.

Marmot, M. G. (1984). Alcohol and coronary heart disease. *International Journal of Epidemiology, 13,* 160–166.

Marques, J. K., Day, D. M., Nelson, C., & West, M. A. (1993). Findings and recommendations from California's experimental treatment program. In G. C. N. Hall, R. Hirsch-Man, J. R. Graham, & M. S. Zaragoza (Eds.), *Sexual aggression: Issues in etiology, assessment, and treatment.* Washington, DC: Taylor and Francis.

Marshall, E. (1991). Sullivan overrules NIH on sex survey. *Science, 253,* 502.

Marshall, L. (1976). *The Kung of Nyae Nyae.* Cambridge: Harvard University Press.

Martin, C. L. (1994). The impact of topic interest on mail survey response behaviour. *Journal of the Market Research Society, 36,* 327–338.

Mason, E. J., & Bramble, W. J. (1989). *Understanding and conducting research* (2nd ed.). New York: McGraw-Hill.

Massey, D. S. (2000). When surveys fail: An alternative for data collection. In A. A. Stone, J. S. Turkkan, C. A. Bachrach, J. B. Jobe, H. S. Kurtzman, & V. S. Cain (Eds.), *The science of self-report: Implications for research and practice* (pp. 145–160). Mahwah, NJ: Lawrence Erlbaum Associates.

Masters, R. D., & Roberson, C. (1990). *Inside criminology.* Englewood Cliffs, NJ: Prentice-Hall.

Matthews, K., Shepherd, J. P., & Sivarajasingham, V. (2006). Violence-related injury and the price of beer in England and Wales. *Applied Economics, 38,* 661–670.

Mayer, J. P., Gensheimer, L. K., Davidson, W. S., II, & Gottschalk, R. (1986). Social learning treatment within juvenile justice: A meta-analysis of impact in the natural environment. In S. J. Apter & A. P. Goldstein (Eds.), *Youth violence: Programs and prospects* (pp. 24–38). New York: Pergamon.

McAllister, I., & Makkai, T. (1991). Correcting for the under-reporting of drug use in opinion surveys. *International Journal of the Addictions, 26,* 945–961.

McBroom, P. (1980). *Behavioral genetics.* Washington, DC: National Institute of Mental Health Monograph.

McCann, H. G. (1978). *Chemistry transformed: The paradigmatic shift from phlogiston on oxygen.* Norwood, NJ: Ablex.

McConaghy, M., & Blaszczynski, A. (1991). Initial stages of validation by penile volume assessment that sexual orientation is distributed dimensionally. *Comprehensive Psychiatry*, 32, 52–58.

McCord, J. (1992). Deterrence of domestic violence: A critical view of research. *Journal of Research in Crime and Delinquency*, 29, 229–239.

McCubbin, J. A., Wilson, J. F., Bruehl, S., Brady, M., Clark, K., & Kort, E. (1991). Gender effects on blood pressures obtained during an on-campus screening. *Psychosomatic Medicine*, 53, 90–100.

McLeod, S. (2018). The Stanford Prison Experiment. https://www.simplypsychology.org/zimbardo.html.

McNeil, T. F., Wiegerink, R., & Dozier, J. E. (1970). Pregnancy and birth complications in the births of seriously, moderately, and mildly behaviorally disturbed children. *The Journal of Nervous and Mental Disease*, 151, 24–34.

McNeill, P. M., Berglund, C. A., & Webster, I. W. (1992). Do Australian researchers accept committee review and conduct ethical research? *Social Science and Medicine*, 35, 317–322.

Meadows, R., & Kuehnel, J. (2005). *Evil minds: Understanding and responding to violent predators*. Upper Saddle River, NJ: Prentice Hall.

Mednick, B., Reznick, C., Hocevar, D., & Baker, R. (1987). Long-term effects of parental divorce on young adult male crime. *Youth and Adolescence*, 16, 31–45.

Meilman, P. W., Gaylor, M. S., Turco, J. H., & Stone, J. E. (1990). Drug use among college undergraduates: Current use and 10-year trends. *International Journal of the Addictions*, 25, 1025–1036.

Melancon, T. F. (1982). *Marriage and reproduction among the Yanomamo Indians of Venezuela*. Ann Arbor, MI: University Microfilms.

Menard, S., & Mihalic, S. (2001a). Drugs and crime revisited. *Justice Quarterly*, 18, 269–299.

Menard, S., & Mihalic, S. (2001b). The tripartite conceptual framework in adolescence and adulthood: Evidence from a national sample. *Journal of Drug Issues*, 31, 905–940.

Merton, R. K. (1938). Social structure and anomie. *American Sociological Review*, 3, 672–682.

Merton, R. K. (1965). *On the shoulders of giants: A shandean postscript*. New York: Free Press.

Michael, R. T., Gagnon, J. H., Laumann, E. O., & Kolata, G. (1994). *Sex in America: A definitive survey*. Boston, MA: Little, Brown, and Company.

Mieczkowski, T. M., Barzelay, D., Gropper, B., & Wish, E. (1991). Concordance of three measures of cocaine use in an arrestee population: Hair, urine, and self-report. *Journal of Psychoactive Drugs*, 23, 241–249.

Milburn, M. A., Mather, R., & Conrad, S. D. (2000). The effects of viewing R-rated movie scenes that objectify women on perceptions of date rape. *Sex Roles*, 43, 645–664.

Milgram, S. (1963). Behavioral study of obedience. *Journal of Abnormal and Social Psychology*, 67, 371–378.

Milgram, S. (1964). Issues in the study of obedience: A reply to Baumrind. *American Psychologist*, 19, 848–852.

Milgram, S. (1974). *Obedience to authority*. New York: Harper & Row.

Milgram, S., Mann, L., & Harter, S. (1965). The lost letter technique: A tool of social research. *Public Opinion Quarterly*, 29, 437–438.

Millea, M., and Grimes, P. W. (2002). Grade expectations and student evaluations of teaching. *College Student Journal*, 36, 582.

Miller, J. G., & Hoelter, H. H. (1979). *Oversight on scared straight*. Washington, DC: US Government Printing Office.

Mitani, J. C., Watts, D. P., & Muller, M. N. (2002). Recent developments in the study of wild chimpanzee behavior. *Evolutionary Anthropology: Issues, News, and Reviews*, 11, 9–25.

Moffitt, T. E. (1993). Adolescent-limited and life-course-persistent antisocial behavior: A developmental taxonomy. *Psychological Review*, 100, 674–701.

Moffitt, T. E., Caspi, A., Rudder, M. & Silva, P. A. (2001). *Sex differences in antisocial behavior: Conduct disorder, delinquency, and violence in the Dunedin Longitudinal Study*. Cambridge: Cambridge University Press.

Moffitt, T. E., & Walsh, A. (2003). The adolescent limited/life course persistent theory of antisocial behavior: What have we learned. In A. Walsh & L. Ellis (Eds.), *Biosocial criminology: Challenging environmentalism's supremacy (pp. 125–144)*. Hauppauge, NY: Nova Science.

Moll, J., Oliveira-Souza, R., Eslinger, P. J., Bramanti, B. E., Mourao-Miranda, J., Andreiuolo, P. A., et al. (2002). The neural correlates of moral sensitivity: A functional magnetic resonance imaging investigation of basic and moral emotions. *Journal of Neuroscience*, 22, 2730–2736.

Moloney, D. P., Bouchard, T. J., Jr., & Segal, N. L. (1991). A genetic and environmental analysis of the vocational interests of monozygotic and dizygotic twins reared apart. *Journal of Vocational Behavior*, 39, 76–109.

Moloney, M., MacKenzie, K., Hunt, G., & Joe-Laidler, K. (2009). The path and promise of fatherhood for gang members. *British Journal of Criminology*, 49, 305–325.

Monaghan, P. (1993 April 7). Facing jail, a sociologist raises questions about a scholar's right to protect sources. *Chronicle of Higher Education*, 39(31), A10.

Monette, D. R., Sullivan, T. J., & DeJong, C. R. (1986). *Applied social research: Tool for the human services*. New York: Holt, Rinehart & Winston.

Monette, D. R., Sullivan, T. J., & DeJong, C. R. (1990). *Applied social research: Tool for the human services*. Fort Worth, TX: Holt, Rinehart, & Winston.

Montagu, A. (1980). *Sociobiology examined*. New York: Oxford University Press.

Montessori, M. (1912). *The Montessori method*. London, England: Heinemann.

Montessori, M. (1965). *Spontaneous activity in education*. New York: Schoken Books.

Moore, H. T. (1922). Further data concerning sex differences. *Journal of Abnormal and Social Psychology*, 17, 210–214.

Moore, R. D., & Pearson, T. (1986). Moderate alcohol consumption and coronary artery disease: A review. *Medicine*, 65, 242–267.

Morales, A. W., Marks, M. N., & Kumar, R. (1997). Smoking in pregnancy: A study of psychosocial and reproductive risk factors. *Journal of Psychosomatic Obstetrics and Gynecology*, 18, 247–254.

Moremen, R. D., & Cradduck, C. (1999). How will you be remembered after you die? Gender discrimination after death twenty years later. *Omega*, 38, 241–254.

Morgan, R. & G. Kena (2018). *Criminal victimization, 2016: Revised*. Washington, DC: Bureau of Justice Statistics.

Morris, A., Cooper, T., & Cooper, P. J. (1989). The changing shape of female fashion models. *International Journal of Eating Disorders*, 8, 593–596.

Moss, N., & Hensleigh, P. A. (1988). Substance use by Hispanic and white non-Hispanic pregnant adolescents: A preliminary survey. *Journal of Youth and Adolescence*, 17, 531–541.

Mould, D. E. (1988). A critical analysis of recent research on violent erotica. *Journal of Sex Research*, 24, 326–340.

Mulvey, E. P., Arthur, M. W., & Reppucci, N. D. (1993). The prevention and treatment of juvenile delinquency: A review of the research. *Clinical Psychology Review*, 13, 133–167.

Mura, E. L. (1974). Perinatal differences: A comparison of child psychiatric patients and their siblings. *Psychiatric Quarterly*, 48, 239–255.

Murdock, G. P. (1957). World ethnographic sample. *American Anthropologist*, 59, 644–687.

Murdock, G. P. (1967). *Ethnographic atlas*. Pittsburgh, PA: University of Pittsburgh Press.

Murdock, G. P. (1981). *Atlas of world cultures*. Pittsburgh, PA: University of Pittsburgh Press.

Murdock, G. P., & White, D. (1969). Standard cross-cultural sample. *Ethnology*, 8, 329–369.

Murnane, R. J., Newstead, S., & Olsen, R. J. (1995). Comparing public and private schools: The puzzling role of selectivity bias. *Journal of Business and Economic Statistics*, 3, 23–35.

Murphy, W. D., Krisak, J., Stalgaitis, S., & Anderson, K. (1984). The use of penile tumescence measures with incarcerated rapists: Further validity issues. *Archives of Sexual Behavior*, 13, 545–554.

Nachmias, D., & Nachmias, C. (1987). *Research methods in the social sciences*. New York: St. Martin's Press.

Napolean, T., Chassin, L., & Young, R. (1980). A replication and extension of "physical attractiveness." *Journal of Abnormal Psychology*, 89, 250–253.

Nellis, M. (2005). Out of this world: The advent of satellite tracking of offenders in England and Wales. *Howard Journal of Criminal Justice*, 44, 125–150.

Neston, P. G., & Safer, M. A. (1990). A multi-method investigation of individual differences in hemisphericity. *Cortex*, 26, 409–421.

Nettler, G. (1984). *Explaining crime* (3rd ed.). New York: McGraw-Hill.

Neubauer, D., & Fradella, H. F. (2018). *America's Courts and The Criminal Justice System*. Boston, MA: Cengage Publishing.

Neuman, W. L. (1991). *Social research methods: Qualitative and quantitative approaches*. Boston, MA: Allyn & Bacon.

Neuspiel & Hamel (1991). Cocaine and infant behavior. *Journal of Developmental and Behavior Pediatrics*, 12, 55–64.

Nigro, G. N., Hill, D. E., Gelbein, M. E., & Clark, C. L. (1988). Changes in the facial prominence of women and men over the last decade. *Psychology of Women Quarterly*, 12, 225–235.

Nimkoff, M. F., & Middleton, R. (1960). Types of family and types of economy. *American Journal of Sociology*, 66, 215–225.

Noell, J. (1982). Public and Catholic schools: A reanalysis of public and private schools. *Sociology of Education*, 55, 123–132.

Norman, C. (1984). Reduce fraud in seven easy steps. *Science*, 224, 581.

Norman, T. T., Chamberlain, M. A., French, M. A., & Burrows, G. F. (1982). Platelet monoamine oxidase activity and cigarette smoking. *Journal of Affective Disorders*, 4, 73–77.

Nunnally, J. C. (1978). *Psychometric theory* (2nd ed.). New York: McGraw Hill.

O'Brien, R. (2001). Crime facts: Victim and offender data. In J. Sheley (Ed.), *Criminology: A contemporary handbook* (pp. 59–83). Belmont, CA: Wadsworth.

Offord, D. R., & Jones, M. B. (1976). The proband-sibling design in psychiatry with two technical notes. *Canadian Journal of Psychiatry*, 21, 101–107.

Olds, D. E., & Shaver, P. (1980). Masculinity, femininity, academic performance, and health: Further evidence concerning the androgyny controversy. *Journal of Personality*, 48, 323–341.

Osgood, C. E., Suci, G. J., & Tannenbaum, P. H. (1957). *The measurement of meaning*. Urbana: University of Illinois Press.

Padgett, K. G., Bales, W. D., & Blomberg, T. (2006). Under surveillance: An empirical test of the effectiveness and consequences of electronic monitoring. *Criminology & Public Policy*, 5, 61–91.

Palmer, C. (1989). Is rape a cultural universal? A reexamination of the ethnographic data. *Ethnology*, 28, 1–16.

Pastore, N. (1949). *The nature-nurture controversy*. New York: King's Crown Press.

Pasveer, K. A., & Ellard, J. H. (1998). The making of a personality inventory: Help from the WWW. *Behavior Research Methods, Instruments, and Computers*, 30, 309–313.

Patrick, C. J. (1994). Emotion and psychopathy: Startling new insights. *Psychophysiology*, 31, 319–330.

Pearlman, K., Schmidt, F. L., & Hunter, J. E. (1980). Validity generalization results for tests used to predict job proficiency and training success in clerical occupations. *Journal of Applied Psychology*, 65, 373–406.

Peck, J. R., & Feldman, M. W. (1988). Kin selection and the evolution of monogamy. *Science*, 240, 1672–1674.

Peele, S. (1983 April). Through a glass darkly. *Psychology Today*, 38–42.

Pendleton, L. L., Smith, C., & Roberts, J. L. (1991). Drinking on television: A content analysis of recent alcohol portrayal. *British Journal of Addiction*, 86, 769–774.

Peoples, J., & Bailey, G. (1991). *Humanity: An introduction to cultural anthropology*. St. Paul, MN: West.

Peters, M., Thomas, D., & Zamberlan, C. (1997). *Boot camps for juvenile offenders: Program summary*. Washington, DC: ICF International.

Petersilia, J. (1980). Criminal career research: A review of recent evidence In N. Morris and M. Tonry (Eds.), *Crime and Justice: Annual Review of Research*, (pp. 321–379). Vol. II, Chicago: University of Chicago Press.

Petersilia, J., & Turner, S. (1991). An evaluation of intensive probation in California. *The Journal of Criminal Law and Criminology*, 82, 610–658.

Peterson, D. E., & Remington, P. (1989 November). Publicity, policy, and trends in cigarette smoking: Wisconsin 1950–1988. *Wisconsin Medical Journal*, 40–41.

Peterson, R. D., & Bailey, W. C. (1991). Felony murder and capital punishment: An examination of the deterrence question. *Criminology*, 29, 367–395.

Phillips, D. P. (1980). The deterrent effect of capital punishment: New evidence on an old controversy. *American Journal of Sociology*, 86, 139–148.

Phillips, D. P., E. J. Kanter, B. Bednarczyk, and P. L. Tastad. (1991). Importance of the lay press in the transmission of medical knowledge to the scientific community. *New England Journal of Medicine*, 325, 1180–1183.

Phillips, S., King, S., & DuBois, L. (1978). Spontaneous activities of female versus male newborns. *Child Development*, 49, 590–597.

Pierce, J. P., Aldrich, R. N., & Hanratty, S. (1987). Uptake and quitting smoking trends in Australia, 1974–1984. *Preventative Medicine*, 16, 252–260.

Pope, C. & Mays, N. (1995). Reaching the parts other methods cannot reach: An introduction to qualitative methods in health and health services research. *British Medical Journal*, 311, 42–45.

Pope, S. K., Smith, P. D., Wayne, J. B., & Kelleher, K. J. (1994). Gender differences in rural adolescent drinking patterns. *Journal of Adolescent Health*, 15, 359–365.

Porter, S., Fairweather, D., Drugge, J., Herve, H., Birt, A., & Boer, D. P. (2000). Profiles of psychopathy in incarcerated sexual offenders. *Criminal Justice and Behavior*, 27, 216–233.

Porterfield, A. (1946). *Youth in trouble*. Fort Worth, TX: Leo Potishman Foundation.

Powers, K. I., & Anglin, M. D. (1993). Cumulative versus stabilizing effects of methadone maintenance: A quasi-experimental study using longitudinal self-report data. *Evaluation Review*, 17, 243–270.

Poythress, N. G., Douglas, K. S., Falkenback, D., Cruise, K., Lee, Z., Murrie, D. C., et al. (2006). Internal consistency reliability of the self-report antisocial process screening device. *Assessment*, 13, 107–113.

Prager, K., Malin, H., Spiegler, D., Van Natta, P., & Placek, P. J. (1984 March/April). Smoking and drinking behavior before and during pregnancy of married mothers of live-born infants and stillborn infants. *Public Health Reports*, 99, 117–127.

Presser, S., & Traugott, M. (1992). Little white lies and social science models. *Public Opinion Quarterly*, 56, 77–86.

Princeton Religion Research Center. (1992). Church attendance constant. *Emerging Trends*, 14, 4–18.

Pyrooz, D. C., & Decker, S. H. (2011). Motives and methods for leaving the gang: Understanding the process of gang desistence. *Journal of Criminal Justice*, 39, 417–425.

Quinney, R. (1977). *Class, state, and crime*. New York: David McKay.

Quinsey, V. L., & Chaplin, T. C. (1988). Penile responses of child molesters and normal to description of encounters with children involving sex and violence. *Journal of Interpersonal Violence*, 3, 259–274.

Quinsey, V. L., Harris, G. T., Rice, M. E., & Lalumiere, M. L. (1993). Assessing treatment efficacy in outcome studies of sex offenders. *Journal of Interpersonal Violence*, 8, 512–523.

Quinsey, V. L., Rice, M. E., Harris, G. T., & Reid, K. S. (1993). Conceptual and measurement issues in the phylogenetic and ontogenetic development of sexual age preferences in males. In H. E. Barbaree, W. L. Marshall, & R. Laws (Eds.), *The juvenile sex offender* (pp. 143–163). New York: Guilford Press.

Raine, A. (1993). *The psychopathology of crime: Criminal behavior as a clinical disorder*. San Diego, CA: Academic Press.

Raine, A., & Dunkin, J. J. (1990). The genetic and psychophysiological basis of antisocial behavior: Implications for counseling and therapy. *Journal of Counseling and Development*, 68, 637–644.

Rantakallio, P., Koiranen, M., & Mottonen, J. (1992). Association of perinatal events, epilepsy, and central nervous system trauma with juvenile delinquency. *Archives of Disease in Childhood*, 67, 1459–1461.

Ratcliffe, S. G. (1994). The psychological and psychiatric consequences of sex chromosomal abnormalities in children based on population studies. In F. Poustka (Ed.), *Basic approaches to genetic and molecular biological developmental psychiatry* (pp. 99–122). Berlin, Germany: Quintessenz.

Redfield, R. (1930). *Tepotztlan: A Mexican village*. Chicago: University of Chicago Press, 1930.

Reese, S. D., Danielson, W. A., Shoemaker, P. J., Chang, T., & Hsu, H. (1986). Ethnicity of interviewer effects among Mexican-Americans and Anglos. *Public Opinion Quarterly*, 50, 563–572.

Reiss, A. J., Jr. (1971). *Police and the public*. New Haven, CT: Yale University Press.

Reiss, I. L. (1967). *The social context of premarital sexual permissiveness*. New York: Holt, Rinehart, and Winston.

Reitsma-Street, M., Offord, D. R., & Finch, T. (1985). Pairs of same-sexed siblings discordant for antisocial behavior. *British Journal of Psychiatry*, 146, 415–423.

Rekers, G. A., & Mead, S. (1979). Human sex differences in carrying behaviors and a replication and extension. *Perceptual and Motor Skills*, 48, 625–626.

Relethford, J. (1990). *The human species: An introduction to biological anthropology*. Mountain View, CA: Mayfield.

Renzema, M., & Mayo-Wilson, E. (2005). Can electronic monitoring reduce crime for moderate to high-risk offenders? *Journal of Experimental Criminology*, 1, 215–237.

Report of the American Psychiatric Association. (1992). Ethical principles of psychologists and code of conduct. *American Psychologist*, 47(12), 1597–1611.

Reynolds, M. O. (1998 August). Does punishment deter? *National Center for Policy Analysis. Policy Backgrounder*, 148.

Rice, B. (1978 June). The new truth machines. *Psychology Today*, 61–78.

Rice, B. (1980 October). The erratic life of "Scared Straight." *Psychology Today*, 28.

Richard, A. F. (1985). *Primates in nature*. New York: W. H. Freeman.

Richardson, J. T., Frankel, R. S., Rankin, W. L., & Gaustad, G. R. (1971). Computers in the social and behavioral sciences. *American Sociologist*, 6, 143–152.

Riecken, H. W., & Boruch, R. F. (1979). *Social experimentation*. Orlando, FL: Academic Press.

Robinson, M. (2005). *Justice blind: Ideals and realities of American criminal justice*. Upper Saddle River, NJ: Prentice Hall.

Robinson, W. S. (1950). Ecological correlations and the behavior of individuals. *American Sociological Review*, 15, 351–357.

Rockwood, T. H., Sangster, R. L., & Dillman, D. A. (1997). The effect of response categories on questionnaire answers: Context and mode effects. *Sociological Methods and Research*, 26, 118–140.

Rodgers, J. L., Billy, J. O. G., & Udry, J. R. (1982). The recession of behaviors: Inconsistent responses in adolescent sexuality data. *Social Science Research*, 11, 280–296.

Rodgers, J. L., & Rowe, D. C. (1990). Adolescent sexual activity and mildly deviant behavior. *Journal of Family Issues*, 11, 274–293.

Roese, N. J., & Jamieson, D. W. (1993). Twenty years of bogus pipeline research: A critical review and meta-analysis. *Psychological Bulletin*, 114, 363–375.

Rogelberg, S. G., & Luong, A. (1998). Nonresponse to mailed surveys: A review and guide. *Current Directions in Psychological Science*, 7, 60–65.

Rojas, A., & Kinder, B. (2007). Effects of completing sexual questionnaires in males and females with histories of childhood sexual abuse: Implications for institutional review boards. *Journal of Sex and Marital Therapy*, 33(3), 183–201.

Rokeach, M., & Ball-Rokeach, S. J. (1989). Stability and change in American value priorities. *American Psychologist*, 44, 775–784.

Rosen, A. (2018). Correlations, trends and potential biases among publicly accessible web-based student evaluations of teaching: A large-scale study of RateMyProfessors.com data. *Assessment and Evaluation in Higher Education*, 43, 31–44.

Rosenwaike, I. (1993). Ancestry in the United States census, 1980–1990. *Social Science Research*, 22, 383–390.

Rosett, H. L., & Weiner, L. (1984). *Alcohol and the fetus: A clinical perspective*. New York: Oxford University Press.

Ross, H. L. (1984). *Deterring the drinking driver: Legal policy and social control* (Revised and updated edition). Lexington, MA: D. C. Heath and Company.

Ross, H. L., McCleary, R., & Epperlein, T. (1982). Deterrence of drinking and driving in France: An evaluation of the law of July 12, 1978. *Law and Society Review*, 16, 345–374.

Ross, M. H. (1986). A cross-cultural theory of political conflict and violence. *Political Psychology*, 7, 427–469.

Rossi, P. H., & Freeman, H. E. (1989). *Evaluation: A systematic approach* (4th ed.). Newbury Park, CA: Sage.

Rossi, P. H., Wright, J. D., & Wright, S. R. (1978). The theory and practice of applied social research. *Evaluation Quarterly*, 2, 171–191.

Roszkowski, M. J., & Bean, A. G. (1990). Believe it or not! Longer questionnaires have lower response rates. *Journal of Business and Psychology*, 4, 495–509.

Rothman, J. (1980). Harnessing research to enhance practice: A research and development model. In D. Fanshel (Ed.), *The future of social work research* (pp. 75–90). Washington, DC: National Association of Social Workers.

Roubertoux, P. L., & Capron, C. (1990). Are intelligence differences hereditarily transmitted? *Cahiers de Psychologie Cognitive*, 10, 555–594.

Roubertoux, P. L., & Carlier, M. (1988). Differences between CBA/H and NZB mice on intermale aggression. *II. Maternal effects. Behavior Genetics*, 18, 175–184.

Rovira, R. F., Pons, I. F., Martinez, M. I. M., & Sanchez, R. R. (2002). Self-reported versus measured height, weight, and body mass index in Spanish Mediterranean teenagers: Effects of gender, age, and weight on perceptual measures of body image. *Annals of Nutrition and Metabolism*, 46, 68–72.

Rowe, D. C. (1990). As the twig is bent? The myth of child-rearing influences on personality development. *Journal of Counseling and Development*, 68, 606–611.

Rowe, D. C. (1994). *The limits of family influence: Genes, experience, and behavior*. New York: Guilford.

Rowney, D. K., & Graham, J. Q., Jr. (Eds.). (1969). *Quantitative history: Selected readings in the quantitative analysis of historical data*. Homewood, IL: Dorsey.

Rubin, D. H., Krasilnikoff, P. A., & Leventhal, J. M. (1988). Cigarette smoking and alcohol consumption during pregnancy by Danish women and their spouses—A potential source of fetal morbidity. *American Journal of Drug and Alcohol Abuse*, 14, 405–417.

Ruff, C. N., & Offord, D. R. (1971). Prenatal and perinatal complications in childhood schizophrenics and their siblings. *Journal of Nervous and Mental Disease*, 152, 324–331.

Ruse, M. (1987). Darwinism and determinism. *Zygon*, 22, 419–442.

Russell, B. (1945). *A history of western philosophy*. New York: Simon & Schuster.

Rust, K. F., & Johnson, E. J. (1992). Sampling and weighting in the national assessment. *Journal of Educational Statistics*, 17, 11–129.

Safer, D. J., & Krager, J. M. (1988). A survey of medication treatment for hyperactive/ inattentive students. *Journal of the American Medical Association*, 260, 2256–2258.

Sampson, R. J., & Laub, J. H. (2005). A life-course view of the development of crime. *Annals of the American Academy of Political and Social Science*, 602, 12–45.

Sampson, R. J., Raudenbush, S. W., & Fentin, E. (1997). Neighborhoods and violent crime: A multilevel study of collective efficacy. *Science*, 277, 918–924.

Sanchez, M. E. (1992). Effects of questionnaire design on the quality of survey data. *Public Opinion Quarterly*, 56, 206–217.

Sander, W. (1996). Catholic grade schools and academic achievement. *Journal of Human Resources*, 31, 540–548.

Sandler, J. C. (2007). Computer equivalency of the psychopathic personality inventory revised in a nonincarcerated population. *Criminal Justice and Behavior*, 34, 399–410.

Sanjek, R. (1990). *Fieldnotes*. Ithaca, NY: Cornell University Press.

Sapp, J. (1990). *Where the truth lies*. New York: Cambridge University Press.

Sattah, M. V., Supawitkul, S., Dondero, T. J., Kilmarx, P. H., Young, N. L., Mastro, T. D., et al. (2002). Prevalence of and risk factors for methamphetamine use in northern Thai youth: Results of an audio-computer-assisted self-interviewing survey with urine testing. *Addiction*, 97, 801–808.

Sattler, J. M. (1982). *Assessment of children's intelligence and special abilities* (2nd ed.). Boston: Allyn and Bacon.

Schaeffer, N. C. (1980). Evaluating race-of-interviewer effects in a national survey. *Sociological Methods and Research*, 8, 400–419.

Schlichting, P., Hoilund-Carlsen, P. F., & Quaade, F. (1981). Comparison of self-reported height and weight with controlled height and weight in women and men (with mathematical appendix by Lauritzen). *International Journal of Obesity*, 5, 67–76.

Schofield, R. S., & Coleman, D. (1986). Introduction. In D. Coleman & R. S. Schofield (Eds.), *The state of population theory: Forward from Malthus* (pp. 1–13). London: Basil Blackwell.

Schroder, J., De La Chapelle, A., Hakola, P., & Virkkunen, M. (1981). The frequency of XYY and XXY men among criminal offenders. *Acta Psychiatrica Scandinavica*, 63, 272–276.

Schuman, H., & Converse, J. M. (1971). Effects of black and white interviewers on black responses in 1968. *Public Opinion Quarterly*, 35, 44–68.

Schusky, E. L., & Culbert, T. P. (1987). *Introducing culture* (4th ed.). Englewood Cliffs, NJ: Prentice-Hall.

Schwartz, S. M., & Kemnitz, J. W. (1992). Age- and gender-related changes in body size, adiposity, and endocrine and metabolic parameters in free-ranging rhesus macaques. *American Journal of Physical Anthropology*, 89, 109–121.

Scott, J. E., & Schwalm, L. A. (1988a). Rape rates and the circulation rates of adult magazines. *Journal of Sex Research*, 24, 241–250.

Scott, J. E., & Schwalm, L. A. (1988b). Pornography and rape: An examination of adult theater rates and rape rates by state. In J. E. Scott & T. Hirschi (Eds.), *Controversial issues in crime and justice* (pp. 40–53). Beverly Hills, CA: Sage.

Scupin, R., & DeCorse, C. R. (1992). *Anthropology: A global perspective*. Englewood Cliffs, NJ: Prentice Hall.

Segal, N. L. (1990). The importance of twin studies for individual differences research. *Journal of Counseling and Development*, 68, 612–622.

Seligman, M. E. P. (1995). The effectiveness of psychotherapy: The consumer reports study. *American Psychologist*, 50, 965–974.

Senn, C. Y., Verberg, N., Desmarais, S., & Wood, E. (2000). Sampling the reluctant participant: A random-sample response-rate study of men and sexual coercion. *Journal of Applied Social Psychology*, 30, 96–105.

Sexton, M., & Hebel, J. R. (1984). A clinical trial of change in maternal smoking and its effect on birth weight. *Journal of the American Medical Association*, 251, 911–915.

Sharper, A. G. (1990). Alcohol and mortality: A review of prospective studies. *British Journal of Addiction*, 85, 837–847.

Shaver, J. P. (1992). What statistical significance testing is, and what it is not. *Journal of Experimental Education*, 61, 293–316.

Shearing, C. D. (1973). How to make theories untestable: A guide to theorists. *American Sociologist*, 8, 33–37.

Sheldon, E. B., & Parke, R. (1975). Social indicators. *Science*, 188, 693–699.

Sherry, J. L. (2001). The effects of violent video games on aggression: A meta-analysis. *Human Communication Research*, 27, 409–431.

Shiffman, S. (2000). Real-time self-report of momentary states in the natural environment: Computerized ecological momentary assessment. In A. A. Stone, J. S. Turkkan, C. A. Bachrach, J. B. Jobe, H. S. Kurtzman, & V. S. Cain (Eds.), *The science of self-report: Implications for research and practice (pp. 277–296)*. Mahwah, NJ: Lawrence Erlbaum.

Shively, M. G., Jones, C., & De Cecco, J. P. (1984). Research on sexual orientation: Definitions and methods. *Journal of Homosexuality*, 9, 127–136.

Short, J. F., Jr. (1997). *Poverty, ethnicity, and violent crime*. Boulder, CO: Westview.

Short, J. F., Jr., & Nye, F. I. (1957). Reported behavior as a criterion of deviant behavior. *Social Problems*, 5, 207–213.

Siemiatycki, J. A. (1979). Comparison of mail, telephone, and home interview strategies for household health surveys. *American Journal of Public Health*, 69(3), 238–245.

Sienko, M. J., & Plane, R. A. (1976). *Chemistry* (5th ed.). New York: McGraw-Hill.

Sigall, H., & Ostrove, N. (1975). Beautiful but dangerous: Effects of offender attractiveness and nature of the crime on juridic judgement. *Journal of Personality and Social Psychology*, 31, 410–414.

Silberner, J. (1982). Cheating in the labs. *Science Digest*, 90, 38–41.

Silva, R. R., Campbell, M., Golden, R. R., Small, A. M., Pataki, C. S., & Rosenberg, C. R. (1992). Side effects associated with lithium and placebo administration in aggressive children. *Psychopharmacology Bulletin*, 28, 319–326.

Silver, B. D., Anderson, B. A., & Abramson, P. R. (1986). Who overreports voting. *American Political Science Review*, 80, 613–624.

Simberloff, D. (1976). Species turnover and equilibrium island biogeography. *Science*, 194, 572–578.

Skinner, B. F. (1953). *Science and human behavior*. New York: Free Press.

Skinner, B. F. (1966). Operant behavior. In W. K. Honig (Ed.), *Operant behavior: Areas of research and application* (pp. 12–34). New York: Appleton-Century-Crofts.

Skog, O. (1992). The validity of self-reported drug use. *British Journal of Addiction*, 87, 539–548.

Skogan, W. G. (1976). *Sample surveys of the victims of crime*. Cambridge, MA: Ballinger.

Smeeding, T., & Gottschalk, P. (1996). *The international evidence on income distribution in modern economies: Where do we stand (vol. 2)*. Oxford, England: Oxford University Press.

Smith, D. I., & Burvill, P. W. (1986). Effect on traffic safety of lowering the drinking age in three Australian states. *Journal of Drug Issues*, 16, 183–198.

Smith, R. J. (1985). Scientific fraud probed at AAAS meeting. *Science*, 228, 1292–1293.

Snyderman, M., & Rothman, S. (1988). *The IQ controversy: The media and public policy*. New Brunswick, NJ: Transaction.

Sobel, M. E. (1992). The American occupational structure and structural equation modeling in sociology. *Contemporary Sociology*, 21, 662–666.

Social science triumphs in Congress after setback on American teenage study. (1991 September). *Footnotes*, 19(1), 12.

Sommer, B., & Sommer, R. (1991). *A practical guide to behavioral research*. New York: Oxford University Press.

Sorenson, S. B., Stein, J. A., Siegel, J. M., Golding, J. M., & Burnam, M. A. (1987). Prevalence of adult sexual assault: The Los Angeles Epidemiologic Catchment Area Study. *American Journal of Epidemiology*, 126, 1154–1164.

Spencer, B. A., & Taylor, G. S. (1988). Effects of facial attractiveness and gender on causal attributions of managerial performance. *Sex Roles*, 5/6, 273–285.

Spierenburg, P. (1994). Faces of violence: Homicide trends and cultural meanings. Amsterdam, 1431–1816. *Journal of Social History*, 27, 701–716.

Stacey, T. (2006). Electronic tagging of offenders: A global view. *International Review of Law, Computers, & Technology*, 20, 117–121.

Stack, S. (1987). Publicized executions and homicide, 1950–1980. *American Sociological Review*, 52, 532–540.

Stanistreet, D., Scott-Samuel, A., & Bellis, M. (1999). Income inequality and mortality in England. *Journal of Public Health Medicine*, 21, 205–207.

Stankiewicz, J., & Rosselli, F. (2008). Women as sex objects and victims in print advertisements. *Sex Roles*, 58(7/8), 579–589.

Stattin, H., Romelsjo, A., & Stenbacka, M. (1997). Personal resources as modifiers of the risk for future criminality. *British Journal of Criminology*, 37, 198–223.

Steenhuis, R. E., Bryden, M. P., Schwartz, M., & Lawson, S. (1990). Reliability of hand preference items and factors. *Journal of Clinical and Experimental Neuropsychology*, 12, 921–930.

Steffensmeier, D., Zhong, H., Ackerman, J., Schwartz, J., & Agha, S. (2006). Gender gap trends for violent crimes, 1980 to 2003: A UCR-NCVS comparison. *Feminist Criminology*, 1, 72–98.

Steiner, R. (1909/1965). *The education of the child*. London, England: Rudolf Steiner Press.

Stephan, F. J., & McCarthy, P. J. (1963). *Sampling opinions*. New York: Wiley.

Stevens, S. S. (1946). On the theory of scales of measurement. *Science*, 103, 677–680.

Stewart, A. L. (1982). The reliability and validity of self-reported weight and height. *Journal of Chronic Disease*, 35, 295–309.

Stewart, D. W., & Shamdasani, P. N. (1990). *Focus groups: Theory and practice*. Newbury Park, CA: Sage.

Stokes, J., III. (1974). "Purity" of science. *Science*, 185, 399.

Stone, A. A., & Shiffman, S. (1994). Ecological momentary assessment (EMA) in behavioral medicine. *Annals of Behavioral Medicine*, 16, 199–202.

Stone, L. (1983). Interpersonal violence in English society 1300–1980. *Past and Present*, 102, 23–33.

Stoney, C. M., Matthews, K. A., McDonald, R. H., & Johnson, C. A. (1998). Sex differences in lipid, lipoprotein, cardiovascular, and neuroendocrine responses to acute stress. *Psychopharmacology*, 25, 645–656.

Stroebe, W., & Diehl, M. (1991). You can't beat good experiments with correlational evidence: Mullen, Johnson, and Salas' meta-analytic misinterpretations. *Basic and Applied Social Psychology*, 12, 25–32.

Strunin, L., & Hingson, R. (1992). Alcohol, drugs, and adolescent sexual behavior. *International Journal of Addictions*, 27, 129–146.

Stuart, R. B., & Jacobson, B. (1979). Sex differences in obesity. In E. S. Gomberg & V. Franks (Eds.), *Gender and disordered behavior* (pp. 241–256). New York: Brunner/Mazel.

Stunkard, A. J., & Albaum, J. M. (1982). The accuracy of self-reported weights. *American Journal of Clinical Nutrition*, 34, 1593–1599.

Summerskill, J., & Darling, C. D. (1955). Sex differences in adjustment to college. *Journal of Educational Psychology*, 46, 355–361.

Sundin, J. (1992). Sinful sex: Legal prosecution of extramarital sex in preindustrial Sweden. *Social Science History*, 16, 99–128.

Sutherland, E. (1939). *Principles of criminology* (3rd ed.). Philadelphia: Lippincott.

Swanson, J. W. (1994). Mental disorder, substance abuse, and community violence: An epidemiological approach. In J. Monahan & H. J. Steadman (Eds.), *Violence and mental health* (pp. 101–136). Chicago, IL: University of Chicago Press.

Szatmari, P., Reitsma-Street, M., & Offord, D. R. (1986). Pregnancy and birth complications in antisocial adolescents and their siblings. *Canadian Journal of Psychiatry*, 31, 513–516.

Tambs, K., & Moum, T. (1993). How well can a few questionnaire items indicate anxiety and depression? *Acta Psychiatrica Scandinavica*, 87, 364–367.

Tambs, K., & Sundet, J. M. (1985). Heredity and environmental influence in educational attainment: The effect of genes and environmental factors on differences in educational attainment, intelligence, professional status, and need achievement estimated in a twin study. *Tidsskr. Samfunnsforsk*, 26, 437–456.

Tambs, K., Sundet, J. M., Magnus, P., & Berg, K. (1989). Genetic and environmental contributions to the covariance between occupation status, educational attainment, and IQ: A study of twins. *Behavior Genetics*, 19, 209–222.

Tappan, P. (1947). Who is the criminal? *American Sociological Review*, 12, 96–112.

Taylor, C. B., Hayward, C., King, R., Ehlers, A., Margraf, J., Maddock, R., et al. (1990). Cardiovascular and symptomatic reduction effects of alprazolam and imipramine in patients with panic disorder: Results of a double-blind placebo controlled trial. *Journal of Clinical Psychopharmacology*, 10, 112–118.

Taylor, K. W., & Frideres, J. (1972). Issues versus controversies: Substantive and statistical significance. *American Sociological Review, 37,* 464–472.

Teasdale, T. W., & Sorensen, T. I. A. (1983). Educational attainment and social class in adoptees: Genetic and environmental contributions. *Journal of Biosocial Science, 15,* 509–518.

Tehrani, J., & Mednick, S. (2000). Genetic factors and criminal behavior. *Federal Probation, 64,* 24–28.

Teplin, L. A., Abram, K. M., & McClelland, G. M. (1996). Prevalence of psychiatric disorders among incarcerated women: I. Pretrial jail detainees. *Archives of General Psychiatry, 53,* 505–512.

Terwogt, M. M., Hoeksma, J. B., & Koops, W. (1993). Common beliefs about the heredity of human characteristics. *British Journal of Psychology, 84,* 499–503.

The Sentencing Project (2007). Women in the criminal justice system: Briefing sheets. https://www.sentencingproject.org/wp-content/uploads/2016/01/Women-in-the-Criminal-Justice-System-Briefing-Sheets.pdf.

Thompson, J. W. (1962). Meaningful and unmeaningful rotation of factors. *Psychological Bulletin, 59,* 211–223.

Thompson, L. A., Detterman, D. K., & Plomin, R. (1991). Associations between cognitive abilities and scholastic achievement: Genetic overlap but environmental differences. *Psychological Science, 2,* 158–165.

Thorman, J., & Amb, T. (1974). The video tape presentation versus the live presentation: Better, worse, or the same? *The Journal, 1,* 24.

Thorman, J. H. (1975). Continuing education for adults utilizing videotape as an instructional component. *The Journal, 2,* 21.

Thornhill, R., & Palmer, C. (2000). *A natural history of rape: Biological bases of sexual coercion.* Cambridge, MA: MIT Press.

Thornton, A. (1977). Children and marital stability. *Journal of Marriage and the Family, 39,* 531–540.

Thornton, A., & Rodgers, W. L. (1987). The influence of individual and historical time on marital dissolution. *Demography, 24,* 1–22.

Thyer, B. A., & Geller, E. S. (1987). The "Buckle-up" dashboard sticker: An effective environmental intervention for safety belt promotion. *Environment and Behavior, 19,* 484–494.

Thyer, B. A., Geller, E. S., Williams, M., & Purcell, E. (1987). Community based "flashing" to increase safety belt use. *Journal of Experimental Education, 55,* 155–159.

Tittle, C. R., & Meier, R. F. (1990). Specifying the SES/delinquency relationship. *Criminology, 28,* 271–295.

Tittle, C. R., Villemez, W. J., & Smith, D. A. (1978). The myth of social class and criminality: Evidence of the relationship between social class and criminal behavior. *American Sociological Review, 49,* 398–411.

Todman, J., Crombie, I., & Elder, L. (1991). An individual difference test of the effect of vitamin supplementation on non-verbal IQ. *Personality and Individual Differences, 12,* 1333–1337.

Top, T. J. (1991). Sex bias in the evaluation of performance in the scientific, artistic, and literary professions: A review. *Sex Roles, 24,* 73–106.

Tourangeau, R., Smith, T. W., & Rasinski, K. A. (1997). Motivation to report sensitive behaviors on surveys: Evidence from a bogus pipeline experiment. *Journal of Applied Social Psychology, 27,* 209–222.

Traugott, M., & Katosh, J. P. (1981). The consequences of validated and self-reported voting measures. *Public Opinion Quarterly, 45,* 519–535.

Tsuang, M. T., Lyons, M. J., Eisen, S. A., Goldberg, J., True, W. R., Lin, N., et al. (1996). Genetic influences on DSM-III-R drug abuse and dependence: A study of 3372 twin pairs. *American Journal of Medical Genetics, 67*, 473–477.

Turabian, K. L. (1965). *A manual for writers of term papers, theses, and dissertations.* Chicago, IL: University of Chicago Press.

Turkheimer, E. (1991). Individual and group differences in adoption studies of IQ. *Psychological Bulletin, 110*, 392–405.

Turner, C. F., Ku, L., Rogers, S. M., Lindberg, L. D., Pleck, J. H., & Sonenstein, F. L. (1998). Adolescent sexual behavior, drug use, and violence: Increased reporting with computer survey technology. *Science, 280*, 867–882.

Turner, T. B., Bennett, V. L., & Hernandez, H. (1981). The beneficial side of moderate alcohol use. *Johns Hopkins Journal, 148*, 53–63.

Tyler, T. R. (2004). Enhancing police legitimacy. *Annals of the American Academy of Political and Social Science, 593*, 84–99.

Udry, J. R. (2003). The National Longitudinal Study of Adolescent Health. Paper presented at the annual meeting of the American Sociological Association, Atlanta, GA.

US Department of Commerce, Bureau of Census. (1984). *Current population reports, series P-60, no. 142. Money income of households, families and persons in the United States: 1982.* Washington, DC: U.S. Government Printing Office.

US Department of Health and Human Services (2019). *The Belmont report: Ethical principles and guidelines for the protection of human subjects of research.* https://www.hhs.gov/ohrp/regulations-and-policy/belmont-report/index.html.

US Department of Health and Human Services. (1984). *Vital statistics of the United States, 1979. Volume 3: Marriage and divorce.* Hyattsville, MD: US Government Printing Office.

van der Put, C. E., Lanctôt, N., De Ruiter, C., & Van Vugt, E. (2015). Child maltreatment among boy and girl probationers: Does type of maltreatment make a difference in offending behavior and psychosocial problems? *Child Abuse & Neglect, 46*, 142–151.

Van Griensven, F., Supawitkul, S., Kilmarx, P. H., Manopaiboon, C., Korattana, S., Mock, P., et al. (2001). Rapid assessment of sexual behavior, drug use, HIV, and sexually transmitted diseases in northern Thai youth using audio-computer-assisted self-interviewing and noninvasive specimen collection. *Pediatrics, 108*, E1–3.

Van Wyk, P. H., & Geist, C. S. (1984). Psychosocial development of heterosexual, bisexual, and homosexual behavior. *Archives of Sexual Behavior, 13*, 505–506.

Varki, A., & Gagneux, P. (2017). How different are humans and "Great Apes"? A matrix of comparative anthropogeny. In M. Tibayrenc and F. J. Ayala (Eds.), *On human nature: Biology, psychology, ethics, politics, and religion.* Elsevier (Academic Press).

Vasiliauskas, D., & Beconytė, G. (2016). Cartography of crime: Portrait of metropolitan Vilnius. *Journal of Maps, 12*(5), 1236–1241. doi: 10.1080/17445647.2015.1101404.

Vasquez, J., A. (1996). The causes of the second world war in Europe: A new scientific explanation. *International Political Science Review, 17*, 161–178.

Viney, D. W. (1986). William James on free will and determinism. *Journal of Mind and Behavior, 7*, 555–565.

Visher, C., & McFadden, K. (1991). *A comparison of urinalysis technologies for drug testing in criminal justice.* Washington, DC: US Department of Justice.

Vogel-Sprott, M. (1983). Response measures of social drinking: Research implications and applications. *Journal of Studies on Alcohol, 44*, 817–836.

Vreeland, A. D. (1981). *Evaluation of face-to-face: A juvenile aversion program.* Dallas, TX: University of Texas Health Science Center.

Wachter, K. W. (1988). Disturbed by meta-analysis? *Science, 241*, 1407–1408.

Waldman, I. D., DeFries, J. C., & Fulker, D. W. (1992). Quantitative genetic analysis of IQ development in young children: Multivariate multiple regression with orthogonal polynomials. *Behavior Genetics, 22*, 229–238.

Walker, G. (2003). *Crime, gender and social orders in early modern England.* Cambridge, England: Cambridge University Press.

Walker, S. (1999). *Police in America: An introduction* (3rd ed.). Boston: McGraw-Hill.

Wallerstein, J. S., & Wyle, C. (1947). Our law-abiding lawbreakers. *Probation, 25*, 107–112.

Wallis, C. (1983 February 28). Fraud in a Harvard lab. *Time*, 49.

Walsh, A. (2006). *Correctional assessment, casework, and counseling* (4th ed.). Lanham, MD: American Correctional Association.

Walsh, A. (2019). *Reinforcement sensitivity theory: A unifying framework for biosocial criminology.* New York: Routledge.

Walsh, A. & C. Jorgenson (2018). *Criminology: The essentials.* Thousand Oaks, CA: Sage.

Walsh, A., & Ellis, L. (2004). Ideology: Criminology's Achilles' heel? *Quarterly Journal of Ideology, 27*, 1–25.

Walsh, A., & Ellis, L. (2007). *Criminology: An interdisciplinary approach.* Thousand Oaks, CA: Sage.

Walters, G. D. (1991). Examining the relationship between airborne pollen levels and 911 calls for assistance. *International Journal of Offender Therapy and Comparative Criminology, 35*, 162–166.

Walton, K. A., Murray, L. J., Gallagher, A. M., Cran, G. W., Savage, M. J., & Boreham, C. (2000). Parental recall of birth weight: A good proxy for recorded birth weight? *European Journal of Epidemiology, 16*, 793–796.

Wang, M., & Mahoney, B. (1991). Scales and measurement revisited. *Health Values, 15*, 52–56.

Ward, N. (1995). Measuring variables and relationships. In K. Hoover & T. Donovan (Eds.), *The elements of social scientific thinking* (6th ed., pp. 91–133). New York: St. Martin's Press.

Warwick, D. P. (1975 February). Social scientists ought to stop lying. *Psychology Today*, 105–106.

Waters, H. F., & Wilson, C. H. (1979 April 23). Telling it like it is. *Newsweek*, 101.

Watts, D. P. (2004). Intercommunity coalition killing of an adult male chimpanzee at Ngogo, Kibale National Park, Uganda. *International Journal of Primatology, 25*, 507–521.

Webb, E. T., Campbell, D. T., Schwartz, R. D., Sechrest, L., & Grove, J. B. (1981). *Nonrestrictive measures in the social sciences* (2nd ed.). Boston, MA: Houghton Mifflin Company.

Weiner, C. (1975). Sex roles and crime in late Elizabethan Herefordshire. *Journal of Social History, 8*, 38–60.

Wells, L. E., & Rankin, J. (1991). Families and delinquency: A meta-analysis of the impact of broken homes. *Social Problems, 38*, 71–83.

Whalen, C. K., Henker, B., & Dotemoto, S. (1981). Teacher response to the methylphenidate (Ritalin) versus placebo status of hyperactive boys in the classroom. *Child Development, 52*, 1005–1014.

Whalen, C. K., Henker, B., Swanson, J. M., Granger, D., & Kliewer, W. (1987). Natural social behaviors in hyperactive children: Dose effects of methylphenidate. *Journal of Consulting and Clinical Psychology, 55*, 187–193.

Wheeler, M. (1976). *Lies, damn lies, and statistics: The manipulation of public opinion in America.* New York: Liveright.

Widom, C. S., & Maxfield, M. G. (2001 February). An update on the "Cycle of violence." *National Institute of Justice Research in Brief*, 1–8.

Wiebe, R. (2009). Reconciling psychopathy and low self-control. *Justice Quarterly*, 20, 297–336.

Wierson, M., & Forehand, R. (1995). Predicting recidivism in juvenile delinquents: The role of mental health diagnoses and the qualifications of conclusions by race. *Behavior Research Therapy*, 33, 63–67.

Wilcox, R. G., Hughes, J., & Roland, J. (1979). Verification of smoking history in patients after infarction using urinary nicotine and cotinine measurements. *British Medical Journal*, 6197, 1026–1028.

Wilkinson, R. G. (1989). Class mortality differentials, income distribution and trends in poverty, 1921–1981. *Journal of Social Policy*, 18, 307–335.

Wilkinson, R. G. (1997). Comment: Income inequality and social cohesion. *American Journal of Public Health*, 87, 1504–1506.

Williams, K., & Paulhus, D. (2004). Factor structure of the Self-Report Psychopathy Scale (SRP-II) in non-forensic samples. *Personality and Individual Differences*, 37, 765–778.

Williams, S., & McGee, R. (1994). Reading attainment and juvenile delinquency. *Journal of Child Psychology and Psychiatry*, 35, 441–459.

Williams, S. M. (1991). Handedness inventories: Edinburgh versus Annett. *Neuropsychology*, 5, 43–48.

Wilson, D. B., Mitchell, O., and Mackenzie, D. L. (2006). A systematic review of drug court effects on recidivism. *Journal of Experimental Criminology*, 2, 459–487.

Wilson, G. T. (1991 November 6). Who should police fraud in research. *Chronicle of Higher Education*, 38, B3.

Wilson, J. Q., & Herrnstein, R. J. (1985). *Crime and human nature*. New York: Simon and Schuster.

Wilson, J. R., Erwin, V. G., DeFries, J. C., Peterson, D. R., & Cole-Harding, S. (1984). Ethanol dependence in mice: Direct and correlated responses to ten generations of selective breeding. *Behavior Genetics*, 14, 235–256.

Wimer, R. E., & Wimer, C. C. (1985). Animal behavior genetics: A search for the biological foundations of behavior. *Annual Review of Psychology*, 36, 171–218.

Wing, R., Epstein, L., Ossip, D., & LaPorte, R. (1979). Reliability and validity of self-report and observer's estimates of relative weight. *Addictive Behaviors*, 4, 133–140.

Witte, A. D. (1980). Estimating the economic model of crime with individual data. *Quarterly Journal of Economics*, 94, 57–84.

Wittenberger, J. F. (1981). *Animal social behavior*. Boston, MA: Duxbury.

Wolf, J. G. (Ed.). (1989). *Gay priests*. New York: Harper & Row.

Wolff, N., Shi, J., & Bachman, R. (2008). Measuring victimization inside prisons: Questioning the questions. *Journal of Interpersonal Violence*, 23, 1343–1362.

Wolfgang, P., Figlio, R., & Sellin, T. (1972). *Delinquency in a birth cohort*. Chicago, IL: University of Chicago Press.

Wood, P. B., Gove, W. R., Wilson, J. A., & Cochran, J. K. (1997). Nonsocial reinforcement and habitual criminal conduct: An extension of learning theory. *Criminology*, 35, 335–366.

Wooldredge, J. D. (1998). Inmate lifestyles and opportunities for victimization. *Journal of Research in Crime and Delinquency*, 35, 480–502.

Wrangham, R. W. (1999). Evolution of coalitionary killing. *American Journal of Physical Anthropology*, 110, 1–30.

Wright, L. S. (1985). High school polydrug users and abusers. *Adolescence*, 20, 853–861.

Wuensch, K. L., Castellow, W. A., & Moore, C. H. (1991). Effects of defendant attractiveness and type of crime on juridic judgment. *Journal of Social Behavior and Personality*, 6, 713–724.

Wultz, B., Sagvolden, T., Moser, E. I., & Moser, M.-B. (1990). The spontaneously hypertensive rat as an animal model of attention-deficit hyperactivity disorder: Effects of methylphenidate on exploratory behavior. *Behavioral and Neural Biology*, 53, 88–102.

Wyatt, G. E. (1989). Reexamining factors predicting Afro-American and white American women's age at first coitus. *Archives of Sexual Behavior*, 18, 271–298.

Yammarino, F. J., Skinner, S. J., & Childers, T. L. (1991). Understanding mail survey response behavior: A meta-analysis. *Public Opinion Quarterly*, 55, 613–639.

Yarborough, J. C. (1979). *Evaluation of JOLT as a deterrence program*. Lansing: Michigan Department of Corrections.

Yoshitake, N., Okuda, M., Sasaki, S., Kunitsugu, I., & Hobara, T. (2012). Validity of self-reported body mass index of Japanese children and adolescents. *Pediatrics International*, 54, 397–401.

Young, D. J., & Fraser, B. J. (1990). Science achievement of girls in single-sex and coeducational schools. *Research in Science and Technology Education*, 8, 5–21.

Yu, J., & Cooper, H. (1983). A quantitative review of research design effects on response rates to questionnaires. *Journal of Marketing Research*, 20, 36–44.

Zeiner, P. (1999). Do the beneficial effects of extended methylphenidate treatment in boys with attention-deficit hyperactivity disorder dissipate rapidly during placebo treatment? *Nordic Journal of Psychiatry*, 53, 55–60.

Zillman, D., & Bryant, J. (1984). Effects of massive exposure to pornography. In N. M. Malamuth & E. Donnerstein (Eds.), *Pornography and sexual aggression* (pp. 115–148). New York: Academic Press.

Zillmann, D. (1984). *Connections between sex and aggression*. Hillsdale, NJ: Erlbaum.

Zuckerman, M. (1979). *Sensation seeking: Beyond the optimal level of arousal*. Hillsdale, NJ: Lawrence Erlbaum Associates.

Photo Credits

Index

A

ABAB design, 157, 308. *See also* reversal design
abstraction, 57–58
abstracts, 32–33, 293
Academic Search Premier, 33
accidental sampling, 95, 293
accuracy, 72–73
  correlation and, 71–72
  degrees, 80
  inaccurate data usefulness, 82
  measurement accuracy, 83
  precision, 80–81
  reliability, 73–74
ACJS (Academy of Criminal Justice Sciences), 293
  code of ethics, 46
adolescent-limited offenders, 8, 293
adoption studies, 178, 293
aesthetic appeal, 293
  theories and, 60
after-only experimental design, 154–155, 293
aggravated assault, 121, 293
aggregated units of analyses, 224, 293
  ecological fallacy, 225
All-Points-Anchored response option, 188–189, 293
alternative hypothesis, 64–66, 262, 308. *See also* research hypothesis
altruism, 61–62
analysis
  aggregated units of analyses, 224
  archival data, 226–229
  ecological fallacy, 225
  factor analysis, 81
  levels of analyses, 224, 302
review articles, meta-analysis, 230–232
  secondary, 226
  unit of analysis, 224

animal model, 62–63, 293–294
anonymity, 294
  dishonesty minimization, 109
  of research participants, 41
ANOVA (analysis of variance), 265–266, 293
anthropology, 5, 294
  biological, 5–6, 305
  criminal, 9–10
  cultural, 6, 297
  forensic, 6
  physical, 5–6, 305
APD (antisocial personality disorder), 140–141
applied research, 294
  diagnostic, 239
  epidemiological, 239
  evaluation/evaluative, 239
  feasibility, 239
approval for research, institutional, 45–47
archival data, 225–229, 294
Aristotle, 8
arithmetic average, 252, 294. *See also* average; mean
arson, 121
artifactual cultural variables, 24, 25, 294
artistic expression, 266
ASC (American Society of Criminology), 293
  code of ethics, 46
assault, aggravated assault, 293
atavistic traits, 4, 294
Atlas of World Cultures, 229–230, 294, 299
attitudinal self-report item, 294
attitudinal self-report items, 193
audio-CASI (audio-computer-assisted self-interview), 103, 294
augmenting effect, 294
  experimental factorial design and, 160
availability sampling, 95, 293